VINCENT TERESA TELLS ALL. . . .

"Sometimes you have to do things you don't like. Sometimes people who were real close to you have to be put to sleep. I went to so goddamn many funerals of guys who were like brothers to me, I can't count them."

"Crime families can vary in size. In the whole country, there is probably 6,500. Nothing gives the mob a bigger laugh than when some expert says the mob is nothing to worry about because there are only six thousand members. Hell, behind those six thousand you got a whole army."

"You wake up every morning thinking, 'Don't trust anyone except your immediate family.' Not even your best friends. You never know if anyone's going to take a shot at you from the house across the street."

"It can be fun. Take me, a guy with an eighth grade education. I've beat big businessmen, bankers, legitimate millionaires, guys with all kinds of education. It's a nice thrill."

My Life
in the Mafia

by Vincent Teresa

with Thomas C. Renner

A FAWCETT CREST BOOK

Fawcett Publications, Inc., Greenwich, Connecticut

To BLANCHE TERESA and to NANCY RENNER

Contents

My Life
in the Mafia

Foreword

I met Vincent Charles Teresa in a motel in Providence, Rhode Island, in September 1971. The location of the motel, even the name of the city, had been kept secret from me until the very last minute. I was escorted there by U.S. deputy marshals, with the greatest of caution, and as I talked with Teresa, six marshals guarded him at all times. They were heavily armed, for Vincent Teresa is precious to the government, and his life is in danger. He is the only high-ranking mob figure ever to turn informer against the Mafia, and the mob has offered five hundred thousand dollars to anyone who can find and kill him.

The interview was the first in a series of secret meetings at various government hideaways, during which Teresa recorded hundreds of thousands of words on tape. What unfolded during those long weeks of interviews and during many weeks of back-up research is the story of twenty-eight years in organized crime by a remarkable man whose whole life was the Mafia.

Vincent Teresa is no ordinary hoodlum. He is no Joseph Valachi, a low-level soldier in the mob. He is not a petulant Salvatore Bonanno, son of a crime boss, telling a disingenuous tale of service to crime for his father's sake. Teresa was a top Mafia thief, a mobster, and at times at brutal enforcer, and he dealt at the highest levels of organized crime. Had he not been caught, had he not been doublecrossed by those he worked with and trusted, he would still be a powerful and successful criminal.

Teresa, in three short years, has become the single most effective and important informer the U.S. government has ever obtained. His testimony has convinced juries from Florida to Massachusetts. He is responsible for the indictment or conviction of more than fifty organized crime figures, including the mob's biggest money-maker, Meyer Lansky. He has contributed intelligence of great value to dozens of law-enforcement agencies at both the federal and state levels. To the mob he has become their most dangerous adversary, and repeated attempts have been made on his life.

In the more than a year that has followed since our first meeting in Providence, Teresa and I have talked of crimes and criminal personalities, of mob discipline and assassinations, of victims who lost millions of dollars, of businessmen's greed, of every conceivable facet of society that falls prey to an opportunistic mob. There are few aspects of organized crime that Teresa has not dabbled in, and there are few high-ranking hoodlums that he did not personally know.

All the more remarkable, then, that Teresa turned informer, for to Teresa, the act of informing is a violation of a code that he has lived by since childhood. "Men of respect"—men of the Mafia—never, never talked, no matter what the provocation. There was a strong sense of loyalty among them. Differences were settled personally, sometimes violently, but never by breaking the code of silence. Inbred in them also was the greatest possible mistrust of law enforcement. They knew all too well how easily the police and courts could be twisted and corrupted. Money bought cops, politicians, and judges, and a member of the mob who was foolhardy enough to place his trust in them was merely ordering his own death.

Teresa talked, not out of any great moral concern for the welfare of society but because of the treachery of members of his own mob. As is revealed in this book, they made the mistake of stealing his money and menacing one of his children, and it was this that made him break the code, not the reduction of his twenty-year federal sentence to five years or the immunity from prosecution granted him by the U. S. District Court in the District of Columbia. Only concern for his family could have made Teresa talk.

What Teresa has revealed—about mob infiltration of business, about some of the highest-ranking crime figures in the nation, about crooked casinos and gamblers, fixed horse races, gang wars, Mafia discipline, and stock thefts—provides the most comprehensive inner look at organized crime to date. He has confessed to every kind of crime he participated in but one: murder. There, Teresa has no immunity and he knows it. He denies having been a "made" member of the Mafia, for to be made, one must first have murdered.

In the book that follows, Teresa makes no attempt to excuse his way of life and neither does this author. Teresa tells his story matter-of-factly, sometimes with emotion, sometimes with humor, but seldom with regret. He enjoyed his life of crime and the benefits he derived from it. Yet he possesses a warmth, a charm, and a brilliant mind. Despite the fact that he has only a ninth-grade education, had he turned his many talents to honest work he undoubtedly would have become a wealthy man legitimately. He possesses boundless energy and great imagination, and he displayed innovative genius in every project he tackled. He chose crime simply because it was his heritage—and an easy way to take what he desired. Teresa was a master at the art of taking. Not only was he the top moneymaker for the New England mob; he also trained scores of other mob figures in the art of swindles, and they, in turn, have stolen countless millions on their own. There is simply no way to estimate how much more would have been stolen had Teresa not been arrested and convicted.

Today, Teresa lives under a different lifestyle. Gone are the expensive clothes, the cars, the women, the jewels, the furs. Gone are the rich foods and the lavish houses that he and his family became accustomed to. The lifestyle of more than two decades has been swiftly reversed, much to Teresa's dismay. Under the Organized Crime Control Act of 1970 he can get $1,080 a month from the government for as long as he is a federal witness. By Teresa's standards, this is a "ham sandwich," a paltry income. He is anxious to break free of his dependence on the government.

Yet in the past three years, it has been boredom and not imagined penury that has become Teresa's greatest enemy. During his criminal career, he often worked eighteen-to-twenty-hour days. Today he is confined, not by prison bars, but by the threat of an unseen enemy that silently searches for him, waiting to strike when he makes the mistake that will enable it to kill him. Whether he hides with his family in a remote Michigan "safehouse" under the constant watch of deputy marshals, or in the suburbs of Virginia in a rented development home, he is unable to move about, unable to do anything but sit and try to pass the time. He lives in a kind of limbo, desperately missing his freedom but always aware of the ever-present danger of mob reprisal.

There are many behind the Teresa story, many who have contributed enormously toward turning Teresa into the nation's most effective mob informer. Among those who deserve special recognition are the FBI and particularly Agent John Kehoe, who convinced Teresa he should turn on the mob and who then stood by him and his family during their most difficult hours. Kehoe is today the director of public safety for the Massachusetts State Police. There is also Ted Harrington, director of the New England Federal Strike Force, who has daily listened to Teresa's problems, helped him where possible, and adeptly handled him in the courtroom. Special mention is due Senator John L. McClellan and the staff of his Senate Permanent Subcommittee on Investigations, particularly the investigator who worked most closely with Teresa, Philip R. Manuel. Not only have they helped develop the witness program and its supporting legislation, but they have stood guard over it, and they have cut through red tape when necessary to use witnesses such as Teresa in alerting the public to the cancer of organized crime. Much credit is due also to Reis Kash, the head of security protection for the U. S. Marshals Service, and to the many dedicated deputies, such as John Partington and Kenneth Renzi, who have daily risked their lives to protect Teresa and many other informers.

Without all of these people, there would be no book, no Teresa, no informers willing to point the finger of accusation at the mob and risk its swift and violent retribution.

Thomas C. Renner

1

The Informer

The federal penitentiary at Lewisburg, Pennsylvania, is a modern, well-run prison. Its buildings are enclosed with high stone walls on twenty-six acres near the Susquehanna River, and they confine as many as two thousand convicts. One of those convicts, in the summer of 1969, was a forty-year-old, 325-pound mobster named Vincent Charles Teresa.

Teresa was a high-ranking figure in the New England Mafia. He answered to only two men, the boss and underboss who directed crime across six states with the snap of a finger or the nod of a head. For them, he supervised the activities of scores of thieves, bookmakers, and swindlers. His own mob connections extended well beyond New England—to other U.S. crime families, to the Caribbean, and to Europe.

Teresa himself was one of the most proficient money-makers the mob had ever known. In a lifetime of crime he had stolen more than $10 million for himself—which he had spent on horses, women, and rich living; and he had stolen another $150 million for his bosses and confederates. In the Mafia, thieves of that order are held in special regard.

Teresa's grandfather was a Mafia don in Sicily who had come to the United States in 1895 and had become a noted figure in the early years of the mob in America. Teresa spent his boyhood among Mafia leaders, as their protégé in crime.

15

His whole background and culture, in fact, had been the Mafia. And so it was fitting that when he finally was caught and jailed, for an immense stock swindle, he was sent to Lewisburg's Mafia Row.

"As prisons go, I didn't find Lewisburg too bad. As a matter of fact, the mob calls it 'the country club.' Not that it's heaven. Anywhere else in Lewisburg, prisoners can come and go pretty much as they want, but not in G Block—maximum security . . . Mafia Row. The doors between Mafia Row and the other parts of the prison are always locked, and when you want to leave your cell, you have to stick your arm out the bars and wave it up and down until the hack [prison guard] in your area can see you. Then he'll open your cell and let you out.

"So the men on Mafia Row are under top security. But the good thing about it is that they run the place pretty much the way they want to. They work it so they have a pretty good life for themselves, all things considered, and they can give their protection to all the Italian prisoners and the people they know.

"When you arrive at Lewisburg, it doesn't take long to find out the power of Mafia Row. The first place you see it is in the prison barbershop. That's where you learn it pays to have friends on the inside. Mafia Row knows who's being brought into Lewisburg every day, because a notice with the names of all new prisoners is posted the day before. They check the list to see if there's anyone they know. If you're Italian or somebody who worked for the mob, they send a representative to the prison receiving station the day you arrive. They make sure that you get a decent haircut from the prison barbers and that you have enough cigarettes and get the right kind of clothes.

"When I arrived at the prison, I came with a suitcase filled with clothes, like I was going on a vacation. Everything except one suit was sent back home to my wife. But when I got to the barbershop, two mob guys were waiting for me, my old partner Danny Mondavano, and also Jerry Traina. They got me a nice haircut and then took me to the clothing room. Now, if you don't know anybody in the clothing room, you won't do too good, the clothes won't fit. But Danny and Jerry saw that I was taken care of right. I had all my clothes fitted as though I'd gone to a tailor shop in Manhattan. The prisoner who fitted me was a nice kid named Whitey, a former New York bank robber. Because I'm fat, he made the clothes look thinner at the bottom so my legs wouldn't look bowed. As an added touch, he put different-colored buttons on my uniforms. Most prisoners get plain black buttons, but I had pearl buttons on all my clothes. My shirts were special too. I hate long sleeves, and it's a prison rule that all prisoners have long sleeves. Whitey cut the sleeves off my shirts. Later on, when some of the hacks would ask where I got the short-sleeved shirts, I'd just tell them that they were issued to me that way.

"The homosexual problem at Lewisburg was terrible. I guess it's bad at any prison, but at Lewisburg it was really terrible. They overrun the place. When I was there, 25 to 30 percent of the prisoners were homosexuals, maybe more. From the moment a new prisoner walks through the prison's doors, the fags start watching for him. The first chance they get to see the new prisoners is in the mess hall. They look at the new prisoners as if they were mentally stripping a girl. What happens after that is horrible, especially if you're a young, clean-looking kid. Sooner or later they catch him alone in the showers, six or seven of them, and they whack him on the shower floor, they rape him up the rear end. That's one reason Mafia Row offers their protection to the incoming prisoners they know. It's up to you whether or not you want their protection, but anyone that doesn't take it is a fool.

"There were about four hundred Italians in Lewisburg when I was there, and they were a close-knit group. They had to be. The black population of the prison outnumbered us three to one. But the blacks treated us with respect. We almost never had trouble between the blacks and the Italians. It was a matter of mutual respect. The fags, though, were something else. But if they attacked a protected prisoner, there was no place they could hide. Sooner or later they'd be caught and get a shiv rammed into their gut.

"Now the Capo di Tutti Capi [boss of bosses] of Mafia Row is Lillo, Carmine Galente. Lillo was the underboss to Joe Bananas [Joseph Bonanno] until he was jailed on a narcotics rap. He was doing twenty years. He's a stone killer. I think he took care of at least eighty hits himself. He is about five-foot-three, bald-headed, and he walked around with a mean look on his face. Lillo was fifty-seven years old, but he didn't have an ounce of fat on his body. He was always playing handball and he was as trim and lean as any athlete you could name. While we were at Lewisburg together, he never had much to say that was good about anybody, and he talked to even fewer people. I was one exception; so was Jimmy Hoffa, the labor leader. There were a few others, but damned few.

"In or out of prison, Lillo is Mr. Big, and anyone who thinks different don't know what makes the mob tick. He ought to be out of jail soon, and if he is, the New York mobs are in for real trouble. He hated Vito Genovese while he was alive. To him, Genovese was a pimp, two-faced, a man you could never trust. But the man he hated most was Carlo Gambino. 'When I get out,' he used to say bitterly, 'I'll make Carlo Gambino shit in the middle of Times Square.' Why he felt that way, he never really explained, but he used to tremble with fury when he heard Gambino's name. Joe Colombo he considered to be a fool. I remember one night when we were talking he predicted that Colombo would get whacked out. 'Joe Colombo should have kept his mouth shut,' Lillo said. 'He's making too many waves [by leading the Italian Civil Rights League protest marches against the FBI]. He's gonna get hit in the head and the Gallo brothers are gonna do it and I don't blame them.' I never knew how right he was until June 1971, when Colombo was shot in New York.

"There was no doubt in my mind that Lillo planned to take over the New York mobs when he got out. He's got the en-forcers, an army of them, to make it stick. He's been off the street for years, but he's still got tremendous influence and re-spect. 'Vinnie,' he used to say, 'when you get out you got a place next to me in my mob. That Boston mob is no good. For a money-maker like you, they should have moved the world to protect you. With me you'll get the best.' I believed him, and if things had broken different I'd have joined him. Lillo was a real man and a terrific leader.

"Inside Lewisburg, Lillo was the boss. The warden ruled nothing—Lillo did. At the snap of his finger, he could have turned that prison into a battlefield. Instead, he was Mr. Law and Order. He ruled G Block with an iron fist, and there were 150 long-term prisoners there. Jimmy Hoffa was in that block, so was Louie [the Fox] Taglianetti. Vincent Rao, the consig-lieri of the old Thomas [Three-Finger Brown] Luchese mob [now known as the Carmine Tramunti crime family] was there, so was Tony Pro [Anthony Provenzano, a Genovese crime family captain and top executive of the International

Brotherhood of Teamsters], and a dozen others. It was a Who's Who of the mob, but I can't remember all the names now.

"On G Block everyone lived by Lillo's Law. His most important rules were no fights, no booze, no arguments. If he saw you arguing with someone, he'd come walking over, like a Little Caesar with that big cigar sticking out of his mouth. 'Okay,' he'd say, 'what's the problem? Let me hear your side,' he would say to one. Then he'd turn to the other. 'What's your story?' He'd stand there for a minute and think, then he'd snap: 'You're right, he's wrong.' That was the end of it. No one dared question his decision. I remember he stepped in between a couple of tough mob guys, one was named Angelo, while they were starting to get rough and he growled: 'We don't want any trouble in this block, understand? You want to rough it, go to the baseball field and do it . . . not here.'

"G block was considered the toughest block in the prison, but it was the best-run block of all. Nobody dared get out of line while Lillo was there. The result was we had hacks that were on the ball. They appreciated the fact that there was no trouble in the cell block and they showed that appreciation. For example, we were the first cell block in the prison to receive mail. When it came to go to supper, right on the dot at 4 P.M., the hacks would let us out so we'd be the first in the mess hall. Laundry night it was the same way. They would take care of our block first. They'd line us up one night a week and escort us to the laundry room. Once there, you'd take your dirty laundry and dump it in the bin for dirty clothes and then walk to your clean-clothes bin to pick up your washed stuff. Now, most of the prison would have to stand on line to do that. Not G Block . . . we'd go right through.

"When I got into G Block, Lillo knew all about me. He'd checked me out from A to Z. I wasn't in there a week before he knew exactly where I came from, what I was in for, who my associates were, how close I was to Henry Tameleo and Raymond Patriarca [New England mob bosses]. He knew everything. Then one day he started calling me 'Fats' and asked me to play cards. Lillo was terrible to play cards with. If you beat him you were a bum. If he beat you, you were still a bum. If you were his partner and you made a play he thought was a mistake, he'd tip the table over and scream at you: 'You gone crazy . . . don't you know how to play? Why don't you stay home?' I used to tell him: 'Lillo, I don't want to be your partner tonight. I can't stomach you when I'm your partner.' But he was a fair guy and he treated me with respect.

"I got to really like Lillo. I'm sorry we can't be friends any more because I became an informer."

On the seventeenth of December, 1969, the public address system at Lewisburg echoed through Mafia Row: "Vincent Teresa, prisoner 36132 . . . come to the control center. There is someone to see you in the office." For the prisoners, the announcement had an ominous ring, and as Teresa shuffled down the corridor past the other prisoners in the cell block, he could see the suspicion in their eyes, he could feel their gaze on his back, and the hairs at the base of his neck tingled strangely.

"As soon as I heard that speaker call me to the office, I knew it had to be a cop or a federal agent. Those are the only people who'd want to see a prisoner in the office. Anyone else would come to the visiting room. In prison, that's the one thing you don't want to do—be called to the office. Suddenly everyone in the prison is thinking. They're suspicious, they begin thinking you're a fink, no matter who you are. The first thing that enters their mind: Is this guy an informer . . . is he talking to the bulls?

"I told the cellblock hack I didn't want to go. He shook his head. 'You have to go to the office,' he said. 'Once you get there, when you see who it is, you can say you don't want to see him if you don't like who it is. If you don't go we'll have to put you in the hole. That's the way it is, Vinnie.'

"So I went. I was escorted to the office and when I looked in, two FBI agents were standing there. I looked at them. 'What can I do for you?' I asked.

" 'Your appeal was turned down,' one of them said.

" 'So what?' I said.

" 'Don't you mind?' the other asked. 'Maybe you'd like to talk to us. We understand that the boys aren't doing the right thing by you up in Boston. Your wife isn't getting any help . . . she's had to go to work.'

"I gave them a dirty look. I knew what they were trying to do. One of the agents was Robert Sheehan, who'd been on the detail that arrested me. 'Listen, Sheehan, no hard feelings,' I said, 'Let me do my time . . . I'll see you.' Then I turned around and walked out toward my cell.

"I knew they were right about my appeals. My attorney had told me they'd run the course in the federal courts. He'd managed to get the twenty-year sentence reduced to fifteen, and he predicted that eventually he'd get another five years knocked off. That meant I'd have ten years to do, If I was on my good behavior, I'd be out in three years. But there was a nagging feeling in the back of my skull as I left the agents— their words about the mob in Boston not doing the right thing. For months my wife had told me everything was fine. This was the first I knew she was in trouble.

"The next week was Christmas and she came for a visit, so I had a chance to talk to her, to get the truth out of her. I was steaming. I'd had this thing turning over in my mind for a week. 'Blanche, I want the truth,' I said. 'Have you been getting your money from Joe Black [Joseph Lamattina]?'

"Blanche looked upset. She's never lied to me since we've been married, but I knew she'd been keeping things back from me. How else would the FBI have known? She didn't look at me. She looked down at her hands, and they were fidgeting. 'Well, I   ' she stammered.

" 'The truth, Blanche, I want the truth,' I shouted.

" 'No, honey, I haven't heard from anyone,' she answered. 'They didn't even send a Christmas card . . . not a fifty-dollar bill.'

" 'Did you get in touch with Joe Black?' I asked.

"She nodded. 'He told me he's got his own troubles.'

"Then she told me the whole story. My three kids were sitting there listening. Just before I'd gone to jail, my oldest son, Wayne, had gotten into some trouble. He had a friend and they were at my house where they had had a bottle of beer. Then they went out driving. The other boy was driving the car. There were some really crummy cops in North Reading [Massachusetts] at that time. They wouldn't dare stop me, but they liked to pick on kids, particularly the son of a mobster. So they stopped the car, smelled beer on the kid's breath, and charged him with drunken driving. They took Wayne to the stationhouse with him. Wayne told the judge in court that his friend had had a bottle of beer, but wasn't drunk and that they hadn't been speeding. His friend took the stand, got rattled by the prosecutor, and admitted he'd had a few drinks before he reached our house. The next thing I knew they'd charged Wayne with perjury. Imagine, charging a seventeen-year-old kid with perjury on something like that!

"Blanche went to see Joe Black to get a lawyer. 'Don't worry about it,' he told her. 'When it gets time to go to court, I'll have a lawyer for him.' By this time I was in jail. Blanche bailed Wayne out. They'd set the bail at five thousand dollars for a kid who'd never been arrested. It was unheard of. When it came time for the court hearing on the perjury charge, no lawyer showed up. Another lawyer friend of ours was in the courtroom at the time, and he stepped in and got the case postponed. Joe Black was nowhere to be found. Then she found the lawyer Joe said he was sending.

" 'What happened?' she asked him. 'You were supposed to be here. Joe Black said you would defend Wayne.'

" 'I never heard a thing about it,' the lawyer answered. 'Joe Black didn't tell me to come.'

"Joe had thrown my son to the wolves, but that wasn't all he'd done, Blanche said. One night she received a call from Joe. He told her to meet him at the Fenway North, a motel, and he told her to come alone, without my sister. Blanche had always been careful when she'd see Joe. She always brought my sister along. That way he'd be afraid to try anything funny. For some reason, Blanche never trusted Joe. She was smarter than I was. At any rate, Blanche smelled a rat. She was right. It was a setup. Joe was planning to get rid of her.

"Then my kids piped in. They told me about something that had happened to my daughter Cindy. They said that Cindy and another girl were coming home from a school dance when a big black car pulled up in front of her. There were two men in the car and one of them pulled a gun out and told her to get into the car. Cindy and her friend screamed instead and ran. The car took off. Now they were trying to hurt me in any possible way. I knew the Boston mob hated me because I defied them, but I never dreamed they'd try to get at me through my family while I was in prison. It was against all the rules to go after a man's wife and kids, to try to kill them.

"I thought back, trying to figure out why and who was behind it. Then I remembered a time in Pittsfield where I'd had to go on trial for car theft and beat the case on a mistrial. I went to Larry Baiona [Ilario Zannino] and asked him to get in touch with Skiball [Francesco Scibelli], who had a lot of influence in that area. Baiona and Skiball were very tight and I thought Skiball could help. 'See what he can do about this case,' I said.

"Baiona nodded. 'Sure . . . don't worry about a thing, Vinnie.'

"A couple of days later I saw Skiball and he told me the same thing. When I got to court with my attorney, everything wasn't all right. The state was throwing the book at me, trying to nail me in any way possible. They don't want to talk about deals or pleas or anything. After I got the mistrial, I went back to see Baiona. 'You son-of-a-bitch,' I shouted. 'What were you trying to do, set me up?' I was hot under the collar, and I was embarrassing him in front of a group of people. Now at this time he was the second-highest-ranking mob member in Boston. My shouting at him, accusing him of being the rat he was, caused him to lose face. Later on I found out that he'd put out a contract to kill me. I didn't know it then. I learned it later.

"Now what the FBI agents had told me made sense. Everything began to fall into place. I realized for the first time that Joe Black, Baiona, and the rest of the mob had stolen everything I had—millions of dollars and were out to get me in any way they could. I was furious. I wanted to tear the bars off the prison. It was the most frustrating feeling I've ever had. Here I was, stuck behind the walls of a prison, Blanche needed help, and there wasn't a thing I could do about it.

"Then she told me how bad other things had gotten. She had taken a job at the Transcontinental Record Company for seventy-five dollars a week handling record orders. She refused to go on welfare. 'I'm not lazy . . . I'm not sick, thank God,' she said. 'I've got my health and I'm going to support our kids as best I can.'

"For Blanche I knew that would have to be pretty tough. She was forty years old. She hadn't worked for twenty years, and now she had to go out plugging to work every morning. I looked at her and thought about what she must have been going through. I thought to myself, 'What a woman . . . what a helluva woman I married.' It made me realize what a goddamned fool I'd been all those years. All the money I made, all the tramps I knew, none of it could hold a candle to that family of mine, and now I'd thrown that all away for twenty years in the can. Through all those years, from the old days when I was robbing banks, Blanche had stayed at home and watched the family. I wasn't home much . . . maybe I'd sneak home for supper one or two nights a week . . . but when I was home she took care of me like I was a king. My meals were always ready, my kids were always dressed right. The house was always neat as a pin. She worried a lot. She asked me not once, not twice, but a million times to get out of what I was doing. She never realized how deep in I really was because I kept a lot of things from her. I was trying to protect her in my own stupid way.

"Now I had a lot of regrets. I regretted all the time I'd stayed away from home, from Blanche and the kids. The only day of the week they could count on my being home was on Sunday, but even then the phone was ringing and there was business to do. God, there was never a king in Europe that got taken care of better than I did when I was home. Now that was all gone, and Blanche was scraping to make ends meet, and there was a danger she was going to lose our home in North Reading. Suddenly there were creditors popping up with bills I'd never run up—a lot of phoney liens on my house. It was the mob trying to stick it to me.

"That home in North Reading—I'd make a sucker named Al Grillo buy it for me. It was in his name, and the only smart thing I did before I went to jail was make him put the house in Blanche's name. He didn't want to. He said I'd already taken too much of his money. When he balked, I took a gun out of my pocket, put it against his head, and cocked the hammer back. 'Now sign the papers, Al,' I said, 'or I'll splatter your brains across the wall.' He signed. I'm glad I did that. If I hadn't, Blanche would have been thrown out on the street by Grillo and the mob.

"That Christmas visit at Lewisburg really upset me. Just before Blanche and the kids left, we had a family council. She told me that the FBI had been to see her to try and get me to talk, but she said she had refused to say anything to me. 'What do you want me to do?' I asked. 'I've never been an informer. I can't bring myself to do something like that. I was born and raised with these people. I just can't do it. My kids would never respect me again.'

" 'Vinnie,' she said, 'I don't know what we're going to do. I'm afraid.' There were tears in her eyes. I'd only seen that on rare occasions, once when she learned about Rosie, a woman I was running around with. I knew she was getting panicky, and she was afraid for the safety of our kids. 'We're going to lose the house,' she said. 'I'm worried about Wayne . . . he's getting mixed up with some bad kids.'

"I'll be honest, I felt crushed. All my life I'd been loyal to the mob. It never crossed my mind to be an informer, a pigeon for the cops. I'd rather die. But my family had always come first with me, and now the mob was trying to hurt them, stealing the bread from their mouths. The words came hard . . . harder than any words I've ever spoken. 'If I decide to talk, will any of you be against it?' I asked, looking at each one of my kids. I looked straight into their eyes. I wanted to see how each of them reacted. 'I want the whole truth from each of you. If just one of you is opposed, I'll do my time and that's the end of it.' They all shook their heads. They all stood by me. Whatever I decided, they said, they'd back me up, no matter what it was.

"It was about three weeks later, on January 16, 1970, that Sheehan and another agent showed up at the prison for the second time. 'Vinnie,' Sheehan said, 'things are very bad for your wife. The word's all over the street that you haven't any money . . . that you're broke.'

"I looked at him for a minute, a long minute. The words almost choked in my throat as I spoke. 'Listen, Sheehan, I'd like to talk to you . . . but not in here.' With that I turned and started to walk out. Sheehan nodded at me. He knew what I was getting at. A couple of days later the prison squawk box blared out my name again. This time I was ordered to the warden's office. 'Pack your clothes,' he said. 'You're being shipped out to Baltimore.'

" 'What for?' I asked. 'I've already got twenty years . . . how much more time can they give me?'

" 'Just pack your clothes,' he said.

"With all the calls from the office broadcast over the loudspeaker, there started to be some talk among the mob guys from the New York area. As I returned to my cell, one of them snapped: 'What are you doing, Teresa? Turning stoolie?'

"I gave him a look. 'Go check with the boys in the office,' I said. 'Ask them how much I'm talking.'

"Lillo came walking up and cut the talk off immediately. 'Don't bother with these punks,' he said. 'You don't have to explain what you're doing to crumbs like these.'

"So I was shipped to Townsend County Jail in Maryland. While I waited, Sheehan showed up with another agent, John Kehoe. Kehoe is now the Commissioner of Public Safety for the Massachusetts State Police, but at the time he was famous for monitoring the bug in Raymond Patriarca's office. 'Can we talk a bit, Vinnie?' Sheehan asked.

" 'Sure,' I answered. I wanted to see what they had to say, what they were going to offer. They put salt in the wound right from the start. They told me how my wife was being treated. They showed me a photograph of Joe Black in his new Cadillac. It was Joe Black this and Joe Black that. They knew I was going to lose my house. They knew I had had a ton of money out on the street and suddenly it was all gone.

" 'They haven't treated you right, Vinnie,' Kehoe said.

"I nodded. 'You're right,' I said. 'They didn't treat me right. They had no right to treat me this way.'

" 'Well, what are you going to do about it?' Kehoe said. 'Are you going to let them get away with it?'

" 'Look, what can you do for me?' I asked. 'What about my family?'

" 'We can't promise you anything,' Kehoe said, 'but we can tell you that your family will be protected. You'll be moved out of the jail to another place. There will be a deal made. You'll probably hit the street soon, but we can't promise you that.'

"I listened and then I began to talk. 'Here's what I'm going to do. I'm going to tell you a story. If you think it's worth anything. . . . Now you got to give me your word that anything I tell you isn't going to be used against me. . . .'

"Kehoe nodded. 'You've got our word on that.'

" 'Okay. If you think the story is worth anything,' I said, 'you let me know in a little while.' "

2

The Heritage

Vincent Teresa is third-generation Mafia. His grandfather Vincenti, he believes, was a Sicilian duke, a member of the House of Bourbon and the Two Sicilies, who, as a young man, had forfeited his rights as an aristocrat to join the Mafia. He had become a *pezzi da novanta*, a big shot among The Friends of Friends, leading bands of horse thieves, exacting tolls from the landed aristocracy. In a moment of anger, he had killed a man who had dared defy his demand for tribute. The *carabiniere* had come after him, and he had had time only to gather a small amount of clothing and money before escaping with his bride, Katerina, who formerly had been his chambermaid. Together they fled, as had other Mafioso before him, to a new life on the golden shores of America. Mafia friends arranged passage to North Africa aboard a fishing boat. In North Africa they were smuggled aboard a ship bound for Boston, Massachusetts.

They arrived in the summer of 1895. Don Teresa had been provided with a list of names and addresses of people he had been instructed to contact when he reached Boston. All were of the Honored Society. All had an obligation to aid him in his start in America. With their help he settled quietly in the Little Italy of Boston's West End. There he found little had changed from the Sicily he had known.

The Sicilians and southern Italians who had left densely packed slums in their mountain villages and port cities had recreated virtually the same conditions they had fled. They had brought with them their own types of food, their own methods of making wine, their own dress, and their own brand of Catholicism, a different sort from that of the Irish immigrants who had come to Boston before them and now were beginning to dominate its political and social structure. Instead of the stone-and-mud hovels of Sicily, the new immigrants lived ten and twelve to a room in ramshackled, smelly, wooden cold-water tenements. Rats and cockroaches slithered from every corner.

Some had come to Boston bearing a slip of paper with the name of the *padrone,* or work foreman, to whom they were assigned to labor as virtually indentured slaves. On their slips, their only document for admittance to the United States, immigration officials rubber-stamped "W.O.P." (Without Passports). To the immigrant Sicilian, the domineering, hardnosed Irish and the haughty, aristocratic Anglo-Saxons were the Saracens and Bourbons of a new society, people who plotted to exploit their ignorance and their poverty. They found work afforded those on the lowest rungs of society. Though they were often men of crafts, men of the land with talents for turning barren soil into gardens of plenty, they swept floors, dug ditches, hauled bricks, cleaned barns, swung sledge-hammers, and worked for wages often half those of their non-Italian counterparts. They were abused and cursed, called Dagos, Wops, and Guineas, pilloried and insulted in this new land of freedom.

There were some, however, who found independent employment, operating small barber shops and butcher shops, produce and fish markets. Among these more fortunate was Don Teresa. As a man of respect, a member of the Mafia, he was quickly established in the produce business. But his skill as a produce seller was minor compared to his talent as an organizer in Little Italy. Within a year, he had established his own small mob.

The success of Don Teresa's miniature Mafia "family" and those of its many counterparts was due largely to the clannishness of the Sicilians. They retained their ancestral mistrust of constituted authority and law. The only laws they knew and followed were those within their insular communities, rules laid down by the men of respect. Their differences were not to be adjudicated by alien judges with Irish brogues but by stocky men with long mustaches who sipped black coffee in small rooms and passed moral judgments often in matters that meant life or death to the participants. It was to such men that the Sicilians went to settle matters of honor, such as when a daughter was compromised. It was through such men that revenge was accomplished, that the bluecoats of the law were paid off and mollified in matters of crime within the community. It was also to such men that the immigrant paid his tribute. Such a man, despite his youth, was Don Vincent Teresa.

* * * *

"It wasn't long before grandpa got himself set up right. He organized his own little mob in the West End of Boston, and he took over a section of the community there. He ruled it like a feudal baron, with an iron fist, but my relatives told me he was fair when he held sitdowns to decide disputes.

"He wore the handle-bar mustache, like all the old Mustache Petes did then. It was a symbol of status to show that they were Mafioso, men of respect. Though he was taller than I am, they tell me I was a dead ringer for him and that he had the same hot head and quick temper I used to have. Most of all he knew how to make a fast buck. Maybe that was something I inherited from him, who knows?"

One of the methods Don Teresa used to accumulate his funds for high living was the protection racket. New to law enforcement at the time, it was old hat to the Sicilian who had for centuries paid tribute in one form or another to their oppressors. For Don Teresa, the produce business was a natural vehicle for protection. With his small gang of hoodlums and methods reminiscent of the later days of Chicago's Al Capone, Don Teresa began offering a type of insurance to the push-cart owners, open-air markets, and butcher shops of the West End. Those who were at first reluctant to buy his insurance, to pay for his protection against accidents, soon found that their fruit was stolen, their pushcarts overturned by roaming gangs of hoodlums, their meat ruined by foul-smelling substances. If the need for protection still eluded them, there were more violent accidents resulting in personal injuries.

To maintain his expanding fiefdom, Don Teresa was forced to fight his way through a series of small gang wars. He always came out on top. Gradually the small gangs merged, creating larger mobs with bigger, more profitable territories. Don Teresa was among the most powerful of the new bosses of these gangs.

As his power grew, so did his family. Altogether he sired three sons and four daughters. Cosmo Teresa, who was to become the father of Vincent (The Fat Man) Teresa, was the oldest son. Born in 1905, Cosmo Teresa eventually chose to ignore the Sicilian tradition of following in one's father's footsteps. During World War I, while his father engaged in a variety of rackets that included protection and black-marketeering, Cosmo studied in school and worked in the marketplace, seeking no favors or special jobs in the name of his feared father.

"My father hated his father's life and what it stood for and he would rarely talk about grandpa. Only Uncle Dominick, we called him Sandy, would talk to me about him. Even then it was kind of in whispers, like it was a forbidden subject to talk about. As a boy I only knew he was a big man in the rackets, but when I'd ask my father about it, he'd just turn me off, like I hadn't said anything to him."

Despite Cosmo Teresa's distaste for the life his father followed, he never for a moment failed to show the traditional respect to Don Teresa. When his first son was born, he named the child after him. And Don Teresa was treated with reverence in the Teresa household.

"My aunts told me that grandpa ruled with an iron fist when he was home. My father, my aunts, my mother, everyone would all stand aside when he came to dinner and wait for him to sit down and start eating before they would sit down at the table with him. They said that if you made the mistake of sitting down before he motioned you to, he would just stare at you with eyes that could chill you to ice.

"I remember one of the old Mustache Petes I got to know real well. He always held grandpa up as a man of courage, a real knock-around guy, and he'd give me hell if I suggested that what was done in his time was penny-ante compared to what we do now. He talked about the Prohibition days when he and grandpa used to go out to heist booze from warehouses. He said grandpa would get behind the wheel of a big, specially built truck and smash right through the warehouse doors with guns blazing to get at the liquor. In those days it took a lot of guts. Now we do things a lot different, with a lot more sophistication. We steal your money and most of the time you don't even know we're stealing it while we look you in the eye."

Don Teresa died before Vincent Charles Teresa was born on November 28, 1928. His death was neither violent nor glorious. There were no blazing guns, no bullet-riddled cars. Only a sudden pain in the chest. But until 1971, Teresa was never sure how his grandfather died. The family never talked about it, and those whom he knew in the mob never mentioned it.

"I never asked because there was a sort of mystery to it. I didn't want to show my ignorance with other mob people who knew it. I mean, how would it look to them if I said, 'How did my grandfather die?' I'd look like a fool. So I always thought he died in some sort of gang fight. It wasn't until recently that a relative told me he died of a heart attack."

Such tales of bravado, the whispered words of respect from relatives, the awe with which mob members spoke of Don Teresa, the secrecy surrounding his death—these stamped an indelible impression on the young mind of Vincent Teresa. But there were other things that influenced Teresa—and pointed him in the direction of a life of crime.

. . . .

The earliest years that Teresa can remember were when he was five and his family lived in Revere, a small community on the outskirts of Boston. To Teresa, Revere was the country, a place where the city folk went for vacations. Today, Revere is a bustling, suburban community of over forty thousand. Though it has changed in size, it hasn't, according to Teresa, changed in character from the days of his grandfather. "It's still in the bag. The mob has always owned some of the key cops and officials and it still does."

Teresa's fondest memories of childhood rest in those early days in Revere. He recalls with pride that the family lived in a cream-colored, wood frame house with a flat roof and an acre of land on a dead-end street, Eastern Avenue. The community was predominantly Italian; on Eastern Avenue there was just one Irish family.

"I lived there until I was nine. Life was happy there. We always had something doing. We'd play ball or hide and seek. There were always lots of kids around. In those days you never heard of narcotics or anything like that. We grew up enjoying everything around us. I remember we'd go hunting with beebee guns and slingshots for rabbits or squirrels or birds, but there was never any trouble. I even did O.K. in school there.

"My father, God rest his soul, even though he never made a lot of money, always took care of us. I had my own room. We had chickens and geese and ducks and everything else to chase after, play with, and watch grow.

"Dad wasn't a big man. He was maybe five-foot-five, barrel-chested like me. We resembled each other a lot. He was a real tough guy, I mean with his hands, but as honest as the day was long. He worked like an animal, that man. He drove trucks, he worked on public projects during the Depression, and then he worked with my uncle, Al Lizzo, my mother's brother-in-law, in the poultry business. I can still remember when they had a slaughter house down in the cellar of our house at one time. They used to kill the chickens and sell them to everybody in the neighborhood, all the Italians; they like fresh-killed chickens, you know. They'd drive up to Maine and buy the fresh, live chickens and bring them down to slaughter."

While Teresa's father was hard-working and honest, the two remaining sons of Don Teresa were not. Cosmo Teresa would hustle in the marketplace to get a job for all three, but when it came time to work, Giuseppe, also known as Mickey, and Dominick were elsewhere enjoying life while Cosmo was doing their work as well as his.

When Teresa was seven years old, Uncle Giuseppe had trouble in Boston. He'd already spent time in jail, and somehow he became embroiled in an argument with then Mayor James Michael Curley and punched him in a fight.

"Uncle Mickey was in real trouble. They were going to throw the key away on him. Dad took him into our house and hid him there while the cops were looking for him. Then he made some calls and one of them was to Joseph Palombo, the rackets boss of Gloucester. Dad and Palombo had grown up together on Pitts Street, in the West End of Boston, but Palombo had moved to Gloucester and taken control of all the fishing piers up there and he had all the gambling concessions.

"Dad got Palombo to straighten things out with Mayor Curley. There was only one hitch. Uncle Mickey would have to stay out of Boston for good. So dad and Palombo got Uncle Mickey a job in Gloucester, working on the fishing boats. It was the best thing that ever happened to him. He liked the boats and the work and he met a nice woman up there and they got married. He turned into a hard-working, honest guy until he died."

Cosmo Teresa was more than just a protector of his often shiftless brothers. He was a father of rare perception and devotion to family.

"Dad was always there if I needed anything. I can't blame any of the trouble I've been in on him or my mother. They did their best to keep me straight. He always said to me: 'Go to school, go to work, earn your own way.' I heard that from the minute I was old enough to remember anything. He never finished school himself. He was the oldest in the family and when grandpa died he was expected to take care of the family because he was the oldest man. But he wouldn't have anything to do with the rackets."

January 7, 1961, was and still is the blackest day in Teresa's memory. It was the day that his father died.

"When he died I thought I was going to jump in the grave after him. The whole world was crashing around me. He was tough but he was something special to me, something very special. He wasn't just a father, he was a friend. My father grew up with trouble around him. He understood. He knew what it was for a guy to get in trouble and how it could happen. When I went to him and said: 'Pa, I need two thousand dollars to pay a shylock,' it was just like going to a friend and saying, 'Hey, Louie, let me borrow two grand . . . I need it.'"

At his father's wake, Teresa noticed an assortment of high-echelon racketeers from cities throughout the nation. One of them was Joseph Zerilli, the crime boss of Detroit, a leading power of the national syndicate and a one-time member of the notorious Purple Mob that terrorized the Midwest during Prohibition days. The presence of such men at the funeral of his father, a man who hated the rackets and what they stood for, puzzled Teresa.

"I couldn't understand it. Why would guys like Zerilli and other big-time racketeers come to the funeral of my father? He'd avoided the mob like the plague. I remember we were sitting around a table having a cup of coffee in my mother's house and I wondered out loud why the big shots had come. That's when Zerilli put his hand on my shoulder and looked me in the eye and said: 'You don't understand, kid. Your father could have been on top of the pile, if he wanted to. He took this route himself. He could have had anything he wanted. He was the oldest of the Teresas. He could have taken over from his old man, but he didn't want any part of it. But we respected him and that's why we're all here.' That's when I realized my father was a big man in a different way. He could have gone to any big shot in the mob and had his say. He never did, except when I got in some trouble one time with the loansharks."

Dominick (Sandy) Teresa, the youngest of Don Teresa's three sons, was another sort altogether. He had chosen the road to the rackets as his father had. He liked the expensive suits, the flashy cars, the variety of easily attained women that money could buy, the diamond stickpins and jeweled pinky rings. He liked the fear and the respect his station in life engendered. He not only liked his life, he bragged about it, and his most avid listener was his impressionable nephew, Vincent.

"I loved my father. I remember how hard he'd work, how rough his hands were, and yet how gentle he could be. He was taking home maybe seventy or eighty bucks a week in the 1930s—that was good money in those days. But he was breaking his back to do it. His clothes were cheap and rumpled. I don't think he had an expensive suit to his name. But Uncle Sandy seemed to have everything. He was always flashing a big roll of bills, and it made dad as mad as hell. 'He's a bum,' he'd say. 'He's no good, that uncle of yours, he's got no respect for other people. You stay away from him.' I couldn't understand then how he could talk that way about his own brother."

It was at the funeral of one of his aunts during World War II that Teresa got a glimpse of what his father meant about his uncle's lack of respect. There was a large gathering of the family in the house for the wake, and then Uncle Sandy showed up.

"He was half in the bag, shooting his mouth off and flashing money around. Someone asked if he had any nylons—he was working black-market deals at the time—and he said he'd go out to the car and get all they wanted. While he's making a big show of it, my father is fuming. I can see his face flushing, and he's clenching his fists. He walks out to the car to say something to Uncle Sandy, and as he does Sandy dropped his cigarette. When he stooped to pick up the cigarette, a gun fell out of his holster to the ground. My father just picked him up by the lapels. I thought he was going to beat his head against the car. 'You bum, you lousy bum,' he shouts. 'Even at her wake you got to come here like this. You got no respect for anyone.' Then he dropped Sandy to the ground and stalked off."

While Teresa's father was strong-willed, his mother was soft, quiet, and generous. Her cooking constantly filled the home with odors of delight, and Teresa still uses her recipes to whip up Italian specialties for his family and guests.

"She made great Sicilian-style macaroni and stuffed artichokes, and she could do things with fish that were unbelievable. I'll never forget the Christmas holidays in those days. We'd all go over to my mother's uncle, the whole family. There would be maybe forty or fifty people there on Christmas Eve and they'd sleep on the floors and chairs and couches until the next day. They'd have live eels downstairs, and I can still remember my father going to the cellar and whacking their heads off while they squirmed in his hands, and then my mother would prepare them in the frying pan after he'd cut them up for her. When it came time to eat, you couldn't name the kinds of fish that we didn't have on the table the night before Christmas. There'd be eel, octopus, squid, baccala, bass, lobster, cod, and all kinds of sauces. The next day she'd be up early working most of the day with my aunts preparing turkey with incredible stuffing, and hams and roast beef. It was a time of joy like people today don't understand. People were just happy to be together. The feasting, the wines, the toasts, the laughter, the presents for everyone . . . oh, that was something to remember."

Teresa's mother not only provided good food and love and comfort in the home for her children but also the strength for her husband to resist the temptations of mob affluence constantly flaunted in his face by Uncle Sandy.

"I remember one night I was sitting on the stairway in the dark. They didn't know I was there and my father was saying that he was unhappy because he couldn't give her all she should have and that maybe he should have done what Uncle Sandy did. 'Charlie,' my mother said, 'I'm just as happy to see you bring home enough to put bread and water on the table than go with your brother Dominick. At least I know you're coming home every night.'"

Vincent Teresa was nine years old when his family moved

from their home in Revere to a house on Willard Avenue in the town of Medford, Massachusetts. It was a move that was to have a marked effect on Teresa's life.

Like Revere, Medford was suburban, a bedroom community for Boston. Its population was nearly double that of Revere, and its business community was growing. It was also a community sought out by mob members who wanted pleasant homes for their families while they plied their dirty business on the streets of Boston. One of those mobsters who turned to Medford was Uncle Sandy, who shared a home with a crippled sister and his aging mother.

"On Sundays my father used to bring me to grandma's, and I'd spend the day there with the family. Uncle Sandy would come in—and at that time I was about his size—and he'd say: 'Here, kid, come here.' He'd take me to his closet and say: 'Here's three suits for you. I want you to look right.' They were beautiful suits. He bought suits like they were candy. So there I was, going to school wearing three-hundred-buck suits, all silks, the finest cloths. Sometimes he'd ask me to give him a shine, and when I finished he'd hand me ten or fifteen bucks. To me, this looked like this was the answer. I'd think: 'I don't know what this guy's doing, but whatever it is, I want to do it.' Then he started taking me down to Pinetree Stables in Framingham."

Pinetree Stables was anything but a riding academy. There were no fox hunts or jumps, no high-society charity horse shows or aristocratic riders. Its rambling acres, expensive barns, and lushly appointed main house served a hidden purpose. Outwardly, it was a breeding farm for thoroughbred racing horses that carried its colors at race tracks throughout New England. Secretly, it served as a remote, heavily guarded sanctuary for national mob meetings, a sort of New England equivalent of Apalachin, New York, without the barbecue. Each Sunday, polished limousines would thread their way along the entrance road to the main house, which was hidden from the curious by acres of green fields, fencing, and tall trees. Flashily dressed hoodlums would step from the rear of their cars while bodyguards held the door. They would stop to watch the prancing stallions on the nearby training tracks and then saunter into the main house to meet with the celebrated owner of Pinetree, Massachusetts crime boss Joseph Lombardo.

The roster of criminal dignitaries would have dazzled the

government intelligence agent of today. But at the time there were no intelligence agents, no government understanding of the growing national crime syndicate. Japan had bombed Pearl Harbor, the Nazi juggernaut had swept across Europe, and America was mobilizing to fight its greatest world war. The machinations of criminals were of little interest to a government concerned with spies and sabotage. Even if the government had known of the meetings in Framingham, even if it had had the trained manpower at the time to watch such meetings, it is doubtful that officials would have understood their importance.

But to a thirteen-year-old boy whose heritage was steeped in the tradition of the Mafia, such congregations of criminals were more significant than the summit conferences of world leaders. Before his eyes paraded the hierarchy of organized crime, the bosses of the nation. They would pause to pat him on the head, shake his hand, or peel twenty-dollar bills off huge rolls of cash and give them to him for small services. From Louisiana came Carlos Marcello, known as "The Little Man," the acknowledged power of crime in the southwestern United States. From New York came Anthony (Fat Tony) Salerno, the numbers racket king of Harlem and the representative of Charles (Lucky) Luciano, the boss of all crime bosses. From Buffalo, the hub of the narcotics trade that extended across the Canadian border, came Stefano Magaddino, a member of the powerful "Commission" that ruled the nationwide syndicate. The New England contingent consisted of men who had helped reorganize the small local fiefdoms of the Sicilian Mafia dons into two cohesive crime families, one in Rhode Island and the other in Massachusetts. Among them were mob luminaries such as Frank (The Cheese Man) Cucchiara of Boston; Michael (Mickey the Wiseguy) Rocco of Boston; Philip Bruccola, later to rise and retire as the crime king of Massachusetts and today enjoying the fruits of his labor in his native Sicily. With them were Frank (Butsey) Morelli, the first crime boss of Rhode Island, and his current successor, Raymond Salvatore Loreda Patriarca. And there was Joseph Lombardo himself.

Lombardo looked more like a gentleman farmer than a racketeer whose name caused other mobsters to tremble. His clothes, generally light gray, were cut trimly. A small pearl-gray star sapphire flashing on the little finger of his left hand was his only concession to mob extravagance. Small in stature, less than five-foot-six, he wore glasses and walked with a rolling gait. Though he spoke in broken English, there was a polish to it, and he seldom raised his voice, even when angered. But behind the veneer of the country gentleman was the powerful crime king of New England.

Though he was never privy to the discussions or an observer of the card games that were played for high stakes in the main house, Teresa nevertheless had a privileged view of Lombardo as he exercised his power at Pinetree. For at Lombardo's side, almost invariably, was Uncle Sandy, Lombardo's faithful bodyguard and enforcer.

Uncle Sandy and Lombardo had become friends and comrades by accident in a Boston bar. As Teresa recalls it, the bar was located in Boston's West End and Lombardo, then a rising star in the Boston mob, was ordering the owner to buy the mob's liquor.

"It was during Prohibition days and a couple of wiseguys decided to jump Lombardo. Uncle Sandy said he was standing at the bar and when he saw them knock Lombardo to the floor he decided to jump in because he didn't like the odds that were stacked up against the little guy. He didn't, at the time, know who Lombardo was, just that he was a member of some mob. During the fight one of the attackers pulled a knife and cut Sandy's face, and for a while he had the nickname Scarface. Sandy and Lombardo won the fight, and Lombardo offered him a job as his bodyguard. The two men who made the mistake of jumping Lombardo were later killed. I don't know what their names were.

"But after that Sandy had it made. He worked as Lombardo's chauffeur and his enforcer. He was sent all over the country to Chicago, Los Angeles, Phoenix, you name it. His job was to pick up or deliver money to mob bookmaking operations that laid off their big bets with Lombardo. You see, Lombardo ran the layoff center for the New England area and a good part of the country. That is, when bets got too big in, say, Phoenix for the local mob to handle, they would bet their action with Lombardo because he could handle any size bet. At the end of the week, they would figure out who won and who lost, and Sandy would be sent out to settle accounts. He knew Al Capone and Marcello and dozens of top hoods all over the country during Prohibition days and later on because of Lombardo."

Tales of Lombardo's power often rang in Teresa's ears. Yet

while Teresa was impressed and influenced by the life he saw top mobsters living, there were other factors affecting his childhood and changing the character of the small, rough-and-tumble boy from Revere into a young Medford delinquent with big ideas.

Unlike Revere, Medford provided Teresa with few outlets for his youthful exuberance. There were no children his age in the area for him to play ball or hunt with. The only boys he knew were older, and they picked a local poolroom to congregate in.

"I had no one to hang around with. I'd stand in the street all alone and everyone was in the poolroom. I begged my father to sign a card that would let me in the pool hall. Finally he agreed. That's when I started gambling. I'd lose two bucks here and two bucks there, and that was a lot of money in those days for a twelve-year-old. I didn't have the money so I had to figure out ways to go out and get it. My mother used to give me a buck, sometimes two bucks a week, but what good is a buck when you're losing fifteen?"

So it was that at twelve Teresa joined two other boys in the burglary of a meat market on Harvard Street in Medford. All three were caught by police, and Teresa was paroled in the custody of his parents. "I remember my mother and father ranted and raved, but it didn't mean anything. I don't know why he didn't beat the hell out of me. He came close, but he didn't do it."

Six months later, Teresa found a part-time job at the Royal Tomato Company with the help of his father. Each day after school he would hop a ride on the trolley car—without paying—to get to the North End of Boston where his job was. It wasn't long before he began to notice that company officials left a lot of cash in a drawer. One day he stole a set of keys from an old Italian who worked in the plant. That night Teresa and one of the boys he'd been caught with in the earlier burglary used the keys to enter the company office.

"When we were through getting the cash from the drawer, we made it look like the place had been broken into by breaking a window of a rear door. Then we counted up our loot. There was fifteen hundred bucks, a helluva lot of money for a couple of kids. We didn't get caught. I think they suspected me but they never said anything. We spent a little of the money, hid some of it, and we paid off all our gambling debts."

The money didn't last long, however, and soon Teresa was using the family meat money to pay off his pool-hall debts. Each week, his mother would hand him twenty dollars for the meat from the market. Sometimes Teresa never got past the pool hall. There would follow beatings by his father, but the gambling bug had bitten Teresa and the temptations were too great to resist. Finally his mother stopped trusting him with money and went to the market herself.

School, meanwhile, had become another source of trouble for Teresa. In Revere, he had been a good student, and initially in Medford he did well. But his penchant for associating with older, tougher boys and the fever of gambling that consumed him followed him to school. Often he would sneak to the basement of the school to play in dice games. The games led to bigger and bigger debts, to more and more burglaries, and finally to a debt to a loanshark who later became Teresa's partner in bigger crimes, Robert (Bobby) Visconti.

"I remember in junior high school we used to shoot craps in the basement almost every day. There was this kid, Fat Louie, we used to call him Buckets, who had a hot hand in one of the games. I'd just been out on a burglary the night before and already I'm down forty bucks in the game. Now this little fat bastard is hauling in my forty bucks and he's betting forty on the next pass. I said I'd cover it and then I looked at him and said: 'Buckets, if you make this pass, I'm going to kick you right in the face.' He did and I kicked him right in the kisser.

"The shylocks were getting too much for me, though. I was getting in so deep I'd never get out. I owed Visconti alone three thousand bucks and I couldn't pay the money. That's when I found out the kind of respect my old man had with the mob. He found out the kind of trouble I was in and that I was about to get my head beaten in. He didn't say anything to me. He just paid a visit to Visconti and a couple of other shylocks. He told Visconti: 'If you bother my kid, I'll make a call and I'll have your legs busted in an hour.' Visconti later told me about it. But all my debts to the shys were canceled just by his visit."

When Teresa wasn't gambling or burglarizing stores, he was in constant trouble with his teachers, two in particular. One teacher ruled the corridors with an iron fist.

"His name was Mr. McGuiness. He was hell on wheels. As students walked from classes into the hallway, he'd stand there directing them to their next classes, stopping them from slipping out to do something else. I figured he was always picking on me. One day as I walked down the corridor I heard him holler: 'Hey, you, Vinnie.'

" 'What's the matter now?' I asked him.

" 'You're always in a hurry to get nowhere,' he said.

" 'I'm not in any hurry. I just wish I was going home,' I answered.

" 'Come here,' he snapped.

" 'What's the matter now? What have I done this time?' I said.

"Now I was in trouble and I knew it. I had a cigarette in my hand and I wasn't supposed to and I'm trying to duck it. He saw the cigarette and the next thing I knew he had whacked my hand. 'Take it easy,' I told him. But he gave me a shove. That's when I knocked him flat. I hit him three quick shots and he dropped to the floor. They suspended me for three weeks. I was fourteen then."

There was also a music teacher named Miss Espanola.

"I'll never forget her as long as I live. I was in the music room this day and I wasn't paying any attention. My mind was off a hundred miles away. I'm wondering how I'm going to pay off my gambling debts and the shylocks. Now she had a very nasty habit of coming by your desk and whacking you on the hands with a ruler when you weren't looking. So she spotted me daydreaming and, bam, she whacked me hard on the hand. 'Wait a minute,' I said, 'don't you do that to me.' The next thing I knew I felt a whack on the top of my head. She had a pocketbook she used to carry, about a foot long, filled with instruments and books and whistles and paper. I saw stars for a minute. Then—it was pure instinct—I jumped up and gave her a real hard shove. She fell to the floor.

"God rest his soul, my poor father was so ashamed of me. He had to come to the school and they had told him what I had done—pushed a woman! What a beating he gave me that day. He was shouting: 'Say you apologize! Tell Miss Espanola you apologize!' She was sitting there, so prim and smug, smiling while I was getting whacked around. 'Bullshit, you old bitch!' I shouted. 'You'll drop dead before I apologize to you!' I didn't apologize but I couldn't move for days because of the beating my father gave to me. The principal told me that when I finished ninth grade not to bother coming back to school. I didn't."

By the time Teresa had left school, he had committed more than a dozen burglaries and stolen more than five thousand dollars. He'd gambled it all away and was still in debt. Now he was out of school, and bigger crime beckoned. He was only sixteen, but he'd hobnobbed with the big men of crime and he wanted the rich life that Uncle Sandy seemed to lead. There was one hitch. He was too young to step up into the mob.

3

Apprentice Criminal

It wasn't out of any sense of patriotism that Teresa joined the U. S. Navy on November 29, 1945, the day after he became seventeen. The war was over. The Japanese had surrendered. Europe was occupied. The Mediterranean was an American lake. Teresa simply felt lost. There was nothing to do. The older boys he had grown up with, gambled with, burglarized with, were all in the service.

"There just wasn't a damned thing to do. I hated hanging around. I'd go to the pool hall and there was hardly anyone there I knew. I couldn't play craps in school. I'd been kicked out. Even if they had let me go back, and they wouldn't after the record I had there, I'd have had no interest. I figured if I kept hanging around I'd wind up in the can on some two-bit burglary. I figured, what the hell, join the Navy and see the world. My father agreed. He said it would make a man out of me. So I joined."

Before taking the step that would take him off Massachusetts streets for three years, Teresa had some goodbyes to say—to a girl. She was fifteen, pretty, with blue eyes, a soft voice, and a temperament to match. Her name was Blanche Rosselman. They had met when Teresa was very young, but it wasn't until he was a freshman and deeply in trouble that they became close.

"She was a gorgeous girl and, for some reason that I could never figure out, she liked me and stuck by me through the trouble I got into in school. My family was crazy about her. They thought the sun rose and set on her. Her family hated my guts. I was always what they called 'one of them I-talians.' They also knew about my reputation in school. Blanche's father was a plumber. He never said boo about anything. He was hen-pecked. Her mother was always criticizing me. She told Blanche not to go out with me."

Blanche saw Teresa as something special. He was lithe and handsome and he was tough, but with her he was gentle and considerate. Blanche enjoyed just being with him. She enjoyed the occasional visits to Pinetree Stables and meeting the people she was introduced to. She didn't want to know who they were or what they were. It was sufficient for her to know that they were important to Vinnie. That was all that mattered.

In December of 1945 Teresa left for Bainbridge, Maryland, and basic training. Boot camp was a snap. He was in good physical shape before he arrived, and the rigors of basic training didn't bother him. Only the discipline, the "Yes sirs," the "No sirs," the salutes, the carefully washed and pressed clothes, the long hours of marching and the loud-mouthed petty officers annoyed him.

"I didn't like being told to do this or that, clean pots and pans or mop up someone else's shit. I had a few scraps, nothing serious then, and I wound up on the short end of the stick on some details because of my attitude, but I finished boot training."

Teresa was assigned to be a cook aboard a destroyer that was sailing to the Mediterranean.

"I was always in trouble in the Navy. Every time we'd hit a port and I'd get a twenty-four-hour liberty, I wouldn't come back for two or three days. I'd be out boozing and running around with broads, raising hell and having a ball. I'd come back to the ship, they'd give me a summary court-martial and restrict me to the ship or put me in the brig for a few days. What's worse, they were always fining me. By the end of the month, when the eagle was supposed to shit, I'd look at the paylist and it would read: 'Teresa: zero.' I don't think I drew a dime in pay while I was overseas and that was for almost three years. I was always getting docked pay for a few lousy nights of fun onshore."

Not all of Teresa's excursions landed him in the ship's brig, however. In Istanbul, Turkey, Teresa found unexpected friendship in the middle of a fight.

"One night we hit this club—I don't remember the name of the place now—and we're having a drink with a couple of broads when we hear this commotion. We look around and there's three guys piling on this one guy and one of them has a knife. Now this guy on the bottom is giving a pretty good account of himself. He was built like a bull and the best-looking guy I'd ever seen. I hate to see odds like that so I looked at Smitty and he nodded. Both of us dove in to help this guy and we beat the hell out of the other three.

"Suddenly the place is filled with cops and I figure, oh, oh, here I go back to the brig. But this guy we'd helped pulls out his wallet and hands them a passport and the next thing I know they're apologizing to him and to us. That's when I found out we'd helped Turhan Bey, the movie actor. We became terrific friends after that. Everytime we'd come to Istanbul, we'd call him and he'd take us out on the town. There wasn't enough he could do for us. Broads, money, high-class places, parties, everything you could imagine. He was the most handsome guy I've ever met. I mean he was a sheik out of *The Arabian Nights*. For years after, he'd write to me—I've still got some of his letters—asking if he could be of some help to me. He was a helluva nice guy—down-to-earth, decent, always thinking of his friends. They don't come like that any more. At least the entertainers I met since then don't."

The Navy was providing Teresa with an opportunity to see the storybook cities of intrigue and romance—Tangiers, Nice, Naples, Athens, Casablanca, Gibraltar. But to properly enjoy the life such cities offered required money. Teresa's constant shortage of funds due to fines forced him to think of ways to pay for the high living he loved.

One of the first things Teresa had noticed as he hit various ports of call was the thriving black market that dealt in whatever American-made goods could be obtained from opportunistic servicemen. Most were content to deal in a few cartons of cigarettes or a pound of coffee. Some even sold guns they could steal. Teresa, however, noticed what he felt was a foolproof way to keep his friends and himself rolling in money at Navy expense. What was even more enticing about the scheme was that theft wasn't even involved.

"We had a regular routine when we would hit a port after a period of time at sea. The ship would anchor off the port, load up with new supplies, and those of us in the galley were told to empty out the hold and dump everything that was perishable overboard. That included butter and meat and eggs and even flour. We had to make room for the fresh goods. Now to me that was a crime. Here people in these ports were begging for food. They were selling their sisters, themselves, for scraps. You'd see them raid the garbage cans at military bases at night. And here we were, throwing food into the sea.

"I had a bright idea one day when we slipped into the port of Lerapetra, off the southern coast of Crete. I'd talked about it to a friend named Frank, and I could see the cash register bells ringing in his head as I talked. I told him I'd go ashore and see if I could make contact with someone in the black market who would buy the stuff we would have had to throw overboard anyway. There was nothing wrong with it; it wasn't as if we were stealing the stuff.

"So I floated around a couple of bars in Lerapetra and I talked to some bartenders. They moved me to a couple of black-market guys who operated in the area. We made a deal to sell them butter we were told to get rid of. We had sixteen or twenty cases of the stuff at the time. Each case weighed twenty-four pounds. We agreed to sell them the butter at a dollar a pound. All they had to do was haul it away and say they were dumping it at sea from their barge for us.

"Frank told the officers he had made an arrangement to have a couple of guys dump ship's garbage at sea for a sawbuck. The officers liked the idea. They wouldn't get criticized for littering the waters with garbage. They even put up the ten bucks to pay for hauling the garbage away.

"It was beautiful. We worked that scheme in ports from Tangiers to Naples, but we didn't just stick to selling butter. We'd sell them flour, hundred-pound bags of flour, that used to get a little bit wormy from the dampness in the hold. That was worth three bucks a bag. We'd sell them smoked hams—they'd get a little moldy from the dampness. Hell, that was nothing. We'd cut out the mold and sell the ham to the black-market guys at four bucks apiece. Frank would just tell the captain we had bad meat in the hold, and he would order us to get rid of it. We even dumped hindquarters of beef, and for that we'd make a good score, maybe three hundred bucks apiece."

When Teresa and Frank weren't selling ship's stores to black marketeers, they were running dice and card games. There were constant inspections by ship's officers to locate the gambling events they knew took place daily aboard ship, but the two wheeler-dealers figured out ways to keep games running, even while searches took place.

"They would check the hold, the bay, the decks, the men's sleeping quarters, the ammunition room, every place they could think of but one—the kitchen freezer. All the chief petty officers came to the freezer room game because that was where the big money moved. There we'd be, bundled up in heavy coats and gloves, sitting on cases of frozen butter, dealing cards all night. At least twice that I can remember officers had walked through the galley looking for the game but never spotted us in the freezer."

Most of the games, whether they were card games in the freezer or craps in the boiler room, were for high stakes. Teresa recalled dropping as much as four thousand dollars in one card game and winning more than eight thousand dollars in a dice game. The dice games, however, were often rigged by Smitty.

"We had a bunch of hillbillies from Tennessee on board who didn't know wrong dice from right dice. When we figured we had them set up, Smitty would switch the dice and we'd cut them to pieces. They never figured out what was going on."

Whether Teresa won or lost, the games provided him with the excitement he missed and filled his growing need to gamble. For the most part he won because of crooked dice. His pockets and his locker were filled with money. A night in port was a night of fancy living. Expensive women, high-priced nightclubs, the best in liquor and food at the finest restaurants—all this became routine. His friends were lavishly treated to all that Teresa enjoyed, and for many he was the most popular man on the ship. But inevitably, the hour would come to return to ship and Teresa would be dallying with a woman or a bottle and would fail to return on time.

"I knew every square inch of that brig better than anyone on the ship. The officers were pretty stupid. They never figured out how I got the loot to finance my portside visits and they continued to let me go ashore. They'd ask around, they'd check with their chief petty officers, but everyone would dummy up. They weren't about to kill the golden goose."

Trouble became Teresa's middle name. Finally, in Boston, the trouble became serious.

"When I was in the Navy, I was a bad drunk, a nasty drunk. I don't touch the stuff now, but then I was terrible. This one night I started drinking at Izzy Ort's bar in Boston and I got plastered. I don't know how it happened to this day, but I got in a fight with a Marine captain, beat the hell out of him, and wound up in the brig. The result was that I was given a general court-martial. That's like going to a federal court on a felony rap. They found me guilty and they sentenced me to sixty days on bread and water and a bad-conduct discharge. But for some reason they suspended the sentence and gave me a second chance."

Teresa learned nothing from the experience. He was sent back to the ship and ordered to stand extra duty guard detail at night. Cooks weren't supposed to stand guard duty, but Teresa was a special case. The Navy wanted to keep him out of mischief while he was in port. Trouble found him this time.

"This one particular night, I was standing guard on the ship and this lieutenant, who I didn't get along with anyway, came aboard the ship drunk. Man, was he loaded. Anyway, it's two in the morning, and in the dark I can't see who it is, so I shout: 'Advance and be recognized.' The next thing I know this guy is coming up the gangplank, cursing a blue streak. 'You guinea bastard, you Yankee fuck, get outta my way,' he yells. He gave me a shove and when he did that I hit him with the butt of the gun and knocked him down. Now you know who the Navy's going to believe. Not a bum like me. They believe this southern cracker who's an officer and gentleman by act of Congress even though he smells like the inside of a barrel of mash and is slobbering all over himself."

The incident wrote a rapid end to Teresa's career as a Navy cook. His earlier sentence was ordered carried out and he was shipped to the Brooklyn armed guard center.

"Now, it was illegal for them to give me sixty days in a row on bread and water according to Navy regulations. So they circumvented that. They put me on thirty days bread and water, let me out for a day, and then put me back in the cell on bread and water for another thirty days."

From Brooklyn, Teresa was shipped to Newport, Rhode Island, where he was issued a bad-conduct discharge on February 7, 1948. For many men, the disgrace of a bad-conduct discharge can have a psychological as well as economic effect. It strips a man of his honor for his time in service, it bars him of the privileges of a veteran. Instead of mustering-out pay and the benefits of the G.I. Bill of Rights, Teresa was given a suit of clothes and twenty dollars.

"I didn't cry too hard about that. I had fourteen grand in cold cash stuffed in my dufflebag, the dividends of an evil life at sea. That was more money than the entire crew of my ship saw in a month."

* * * *

The fourteen thousand dollars simmered in Teresa's pockets for about as long as white-hot coals could lay on a bed of tissue paper. Neither Blanche, who had been waiting for him to return from overseas, his father, nor his mother could persuade him to save a penny.

"Blanche was the type of woman who wanted nothing. She was happy if I just took her to a movie. Sometimes she would suggest I should be saving some of the money, but she didn't interfere. I wish she had. But at that time I wouldn't have listened to God, let alone her. I was hooked. Every day, it was out to the race track to bet on those damned bangtails. At night it was a card game or sometimes a nightclub. I think I know what it's like to be a junkie. I hated junkies—I still do—but I was as much an addict as they were. Christ, there were times I think I would have bet on which of two flies would take off first from a table."

Within nine months, life on the reckless merry-go-round of fun, laughter, and booze came to an abrupt halt. The party was over. Teresa was stone broke. To support himself he had to go to work. And there was Blanche. They were thinking, now, of marriage, but Teresa had no money. With the help of friends, he landed a job on the trucking platform of the H. B. Welch Trucking Company in Medford.

"It wasn't a bad job. It was hard work, but I didn't mind that then. The trouble was that it didn't make much money, and I needed money. Those ponies were calling all the time to me. I think I had a sure hunch on every race that was ever run in those days."

Two friends helped him out of his dilemma, Joseph (Joe Putsy) Puzzangara and James (Jimmy) Coyne. Both later became small-time hoods dealing on the fringes of the mob, but at the time they were merely former schoolmates, friends he could count on in criminal ventures. They had one other thing in common. They were, as Teresa puts it, "degenerate gamblers" who'd rather bet than eat.

"We used to use the time on trucking routes to spot places that looked like good targets for B&E's [break and entry]. I'd known Jimmy and Joe when we were kids in school, knocking over stores or whatever. All of us needed money. We were all suckers for the horses or card games."

They were also highly successful burglars. In a matter of months they had committed more than a dozen burglaries without so much as a whisper of trouble from police. They would hit stores when they could. And they ransacked private homes.

"We'd spot a home that looked like an easy touch. One of us would go up to the house and knock on the door. If someone answered, he'd just ask directions. If there was no answer, we'd go around to the rear, break in through a door, and clean out the bedrooms. Some of the jobs were only good for a few hundred bucks, but a couple were worth twenty to twenty-five grand. The job lasted about a year, and I made about forty grand doing these burglaries, but I blew it all on the horses."

On March 7, 1949, Teresa and Blanche were married. It was a turbulent time in the Bosselman home.

"Her mother was dead set against the marriage. She knew I was broke, she didn't like my reputation, and she didn't think Blanche should be marrying a Catholic, particularly an I-talian Catholic. Her father wasn't like that. He's a helluva nice guy even though he lets his wife make waves. He's the type of man who would never accept something he thought was hot. I used to bring him television sets and watches, later on, or suits or furs and he'd refuse them. 'Vinnie,' he'd say, 'no hard feel-

ings, but I'll go to a store if I need a watch or a television.'
They were both honest, hard-working people. But when it
came to Blanche and me getting married, they were against it.
In fact, they wouldn't even show up at the church rectory for
the marriage ceremony."

Marriage didn't change Teresa. Through his father, he got
a new job at the Atlas Paper Company, as a truck driver. And
because he'd had to borrow the money to get married in the
first place, Teresa turned to his father for temporary quarters
to live in with his new wife.

"My father was the second employee that Atlas ever had.
My mother's uncle was the first. The owners thought the sun
rose and set on my father, and when he asked them to give
me a job, they jumped at it. I didn't have any money, so dad
converted his house, a two-family house, into a three-family
home. I lived on the first floor. He and mom lived on the second floor, and after my kid sister got married, she lived on the
third floor. I remember I'd come home two or three in the
morning stone drunk. Blanche wouldn't wait up. She'd be in
bed, but my father would be at the door waiting to give me
hell. He thought Blanche was an angel and I was a bum for
not treating her right."

Although his salary at Atlas was adequate for most working men at the time—a hundred dollars a week—it was hardly
enough to meet the gambling demands of Teresa, and soon
opportunity knocked to make an illegal buck. Opportunity
came in the form of a corrupt clerk at Atlas.

"The clerk was the shipper in the place. My father was the
head receiver. One day he came to me. I had a route in the
Blue Hills, a Jewish section of Boston, delivering napkins, toilet paper, wax for floors, and wrapping paper for meats.

"He said: 'Vinnie, you have a stop at Joseph's Market. I
want you to throw on three extra rolls of blank paper. The
guy will give you fifteen dollars for each of them, and I'll split
with you—all right?' I agreed, then I found out he was doing
the same thing with a couple of other drivers. From then on
in it was a sleighride. After a while I was averaging four
hundred to five hundred bucks a week extra for myself, selling company products I heisted to mob guys I'd known since I
was a kid. I was making so much money on the truck, I hired
a guy off the street to help me unload thirty stops. I'd go like a
son-of-a-bitch to unload the truck and complete the route by
one in the afternoon. Then I'd head to the track. I'd give a

guy at the track a deuce to let me park the truck way down by the stables so nobody would see it. I'd take the canvas and block off the Atlas lettering and then I'd run to the betting windows and play whatever loot I'd made that day. Then one day I'm at the track betting like a nut and who do I bump into but the boss's son. He's a salesman with the company and he wasn't supposed to be there either. So he taps me on the shoulder and says: 'I won't say anything if you don't.' I said: 'Your secret's safe with me, kid.' "

Every day wasn't a loser for Teresa at the track. There were times that he won thousands of dollars. But in the end he lost more than he won, and despite his mounting thefts on the company routes he wound up in hock to a Medford loan-shark-bookmaker by the name of Robert Visconti.

"I knew Bobby since I was a kid. He was the local book-maker, the first bookie I'd ever known. He was also the local tough boy, but he wasn't a made man, a member of the mob. He was strictly a punk. He was the easiest guy in the world to get in hock to, to get money from, but what a hog he was when you owed him. He never did it to me, because he knew better, but I know of people he would call up at two or three in the morning and threaten their families, their wives and kids, because they were behind a few bucks in payments. And he didn't mind using pipes to break an arm or leg when he thought it was needed.

"I got started betting a hundred bucks with him when I was short. The next time it would be two hundred bucks. Then I'd tell him I had only twenty bucks but I'd like to bet a hundred. 'Go ahead,' he'd say. 'Bet for the hundred—you can owe it to me.' Before I knew it I was in so deep to him that the interest I had to pay him each week amounted to twelve hundred bucks alone. I would come home at night sometimes, sweating blood over how I was going to make the next payment—wondering what I was going to rob the next morning to meet the bill.

"I should have known better. You don't beat the horses no matter what anybody says. Some of the biggest racketeers in the country that I know play the ponies, and they lose a fortune. But once you've been bitten by the bug, you play. You're busy stealing with one hand and losing it with the other. It's stupid and you know it, but you don't care. That's the way it is with a gambler. There was one thing about me, though. I never bet the money Blanche and the kids had coming every week to run the house and set the table. I inherited that from my father. The house and the family were always taken care of first. Then the gambling."

The gravy train at Atlas lasted a year before the company realized it was being taken for a ride and that Teresa was the engineer. Customers who normally bought large quantities along Teresa's route now bought less and less, and there were known mob men who seemed to have large stocks of Atlas products that sold at unusually large discounts. Salesmen complained that their customers were getting large stocks of Atlas goods from someone else for less.

"My father suspected me of clipping, and he was upset. I'd made him lose face, but he didn't holler or tell me to get the hell out. He stuck by me. The company tried to fire me, but the Teamsters Union wouldn't let them. The union threatened to walk out if I was fired. Things got hot, though, so hot that the clerk, Mitchie-kovich, couldn't give me anything to sell. So suddenly I was down from making five hundred bucks a week to a hundred a week. Now the job don't seem so special any more. I'm breaking my back, lugging rolls and cartons of papers up three flights of stairs in the North End of Boston for a lousy hundred bucks a week. I was twenty-three. I figured there was easier ways to make money. So I quit."

4

The Mafia at Bay

The early 1950s were a period of turbulence, unsettled leadership, and occasional violence for the men of respect who had ruled New England's organized criminal elements peacefully since the gang wars of the 1930s. The turbulence began in February 1950, when President Truman's Attorney General, J. Howard McGrath, called a National Conference on Organized Crime at the behest of mayors and state attorneys general throughout the country. In May 1950, when Senator Estes Kefauver of Tennessee launched a seventeen-month investigation of organized crime throughout the nation, the mob went on the alert, carefully appraising the antimob campaign that was gathering steam. By late 1951, Kefauver had mobilized public opinion against the mob with televised public hearings in cities across the nation.

Teresa recalls that during his visits to Pinetree Stables in this period, more and more important mobsters began appearing for the monthly conferences with Joseph Lombardo. As each arrived at the entrance to the three-quarter-mile driveway, husky, imposing men checked each car and its occupants. Heavily armed enforcers could be seen at the private lake where horses bathed to strengthen their legs. The enforcers skulked around the tracks where horses galloped for coming racing events. They watched the employees' mahogany-lined quarters for signs of a stranger or a too-inquisitive employee. Their job was to prevent any possibility of infiltration by law-enforcement or Kefauver tipsters.

"There were guards all over the place. It was like an armed camp. My wife and I used to go there for picnics at Lombardo's invitation. At the time I didn't know that big decisions were being made, that changes were taking place at the top rungs of the mob. Once a month, on a Sunday, limousines from all over the country came in. It wasn't like the times I saw them as a kid. Now they came from Canada, with Lou Greco of Montreal [a leading trafficker in narcotics, gambling, and smuggling], and Anthony [Big Tuna] Accardo from Chicago [a member of that city's ruling mob council] —from all over. They weren't there to just play cards and split up the action. I found out later they were there meeting to figure out how to deal with the heat Kefauver was generating. I don't know what went on at the meetings, but a lot of changes took place during that time because of the meets."

Until 1950, New England had, for two decades, been ruled peacefully by a coalition of crime leaders, all Sicilian or Italian immigrants or descendants of immigrants. They had attained their positions of power by surviving the intergang wars that rocked the Boston area during the 1930s. Moving from their roles as rum runners and protection racket bosses, they had carefully cultivated public officials and corrupted policemen to establish a gambling empire that for its day was highly sophisticated and immensely profitable.

The top man among the coalition of bosses was Joseph Lombardo, an enigma to police and federal committee investigators. To the community of Framingham, Lombardo was a pillar of honesty, a wealthy, successful businessman who owned a highly regarded racing stable. Police records show that little was known about him during the 1950s and that nothing was known of Pinetree Stables and its role as a headquarters for high-level conclaves of the national mob.

But within the secret society, Lombardo was the power, the highest-ranking man of respect. He ruled quietly, but he ruled, and New England was his kingdom. He was a boss among bosses, but he was neither greedy nor dictatorial. He was a diplomat, a negotiator, a wily politician in a society of sharks.

"Lombardo was the Mr. Big of the mob. There was no doubt of what he was when you saw him with others. Everyone bowed down to him—treated him with respect. He ran a nationwide gambling layoff syndicate, and Kefauver never tabbed him for it. Whether you were a boss in Rhode Island or in Springfield or in a section of Boston, you went to Mr. Lombardo for a decision. If he said no, that was it—there were no further arguments."

None of the bosses around Lombardo were part of what would now be considered one crime family. Each had his own small gang of underlings, and when decisions were to be made affecting statewide, citywide, or multistate interests of criminal activity, they would sit in council with Lombardo either at Pinetree Stables or at an old Italian club in Boston. Chairman of the board at all meetings was Lombardo.

Lombardo himself took the lion's share of crime in Boston, the North and West Ends, where Teresa's grandfather had once been a dominant force. In Boston's South End was Anthony Santonello, another of the old-time Sicilian dons. He was to die during the Kefauver period, quietly, unrecognized as a crime leader.

Springfield, Massachusetts, was run by Salvatore (Big-Nose Sam) Cufari, an elder statesman with family relationships to prominent New York crime figures.

In Rhode Island, however, the situation was more complicated. For more than thirty years, the undisputed ruler had been Frank (Butsey) Morelli, one of five brothers who had moved to New England from Brooklyn during World War I. He had organized a terrorist gang that ran roughshod across Massachusetts, Connecticut, New Hampshire, and Rhode Island during and after World War I. But in 1947, Morelli's long career as a crime boss came to an end. He had cancer, although he didn't realize it, and he was drinking heavily. Mistakes were being made, rackets weren't operating efficiently, and mob members weren't being supervised properly. Lombardo had no choice. He replaced him with a favored Boston don and boss, Philip Bruccola (Buccola).

"Buccola was the boss of Boston's East End. He was an old greaseball who'd worked his way up in the mob through a string of battles. He had his own mob, but he did what Lombardo told him to—everybody did—and Lombardo wanted him to run things for Morelli. He put Butsey on the shelf—in retirement—but he ordered everyone to treat Butsey with the respect due a retired boss."

For Bruccola, the new assignment was a mistake. Crime

figures came to him with their problems. He was forced to direct operations in gambling and to strengthen mob interests in Rhode Island as well as in his section of Boston. The result was that he attracted the attention of police, federal investigators, and Kefauver. All zeroed in on him in the belief that he was the crime leader of New England. But in the background was the wily Lombardo, untouched by notoriety. For Bruccola, the heat became too much. Grand juries and Kefauver's investigators were haunting him. Subpoenas were issued, and he thought he could see jail ahead. His answer to the problem was to flee to his native Sicily. He remains there to this day, still collecting dividends from New England's mob for his loyalty.

For the retired Butsey Morelli, however, the one-time terror of Rhode Island, Lombardo's decision was a relief.

"Butsey was a tough stone killer, an old don who wouldn't give the right time of day to anybody he didn't like. When I first saw him as a kid at Pinetree, he was full of vitality, strong, dominant. When I got real close to him in later years, every breath was torture for him. Every living breath made him pray to die. It was a few years after the Kefauver thing. The doctors had taken the whole side of his jaw and face away. It was terrible to look at. They didn't really force Butsey out. He didn't want to stay at it. It was too much for him and he had an adopted kid, Buddy. That boy was his life, and he didn't want to embarrass him with the publicity the mob was drawing."

In later years, Teresa learned how far the retired crime boss was willing to go to protect his adopted son from the shame of Butsey's past life. Teresa's insight came from a discussion he and Morelli had about the famous Sacco-Vanzetti robbery-murder trial of 1920, a trial that generated a vast controversy over the justice of the verdict.

In 1920, Butsey and his gang were wheeling violently across New England. One of their specialties was rifling railroad freight cars filled with textiles and shoes. On a certain occasion their target was a load of shoes produced by the Slater and Morrill Shoe Company of South Braintree, Massachusetts. They were caught, and in December 1919 they were indicted for a similar crime. Then on April 15, 1920, a violent robbery took place in the street near the Slater and Morrill Shoe Company plant. Two men, paymaster Frederick A. Parmenter and guard Alessandro Berardelli, were killed in the $15,773 holdup. Although it was reported that four men had participated in the holdup, only two, Nicola Sacco, a shoe-maker, and Bartolomeo Vanzetti, a fish peddler, were arrest-ed. They were convicted and executed. Both Sacco and Van-zetti, described as Italian-born anarchists who advocated the overthrow of the government, were persecuted by police, prosecutors, and judges in a tide of superpatriotism. To the last moment before they were electrocuted, they maintained their innocence.

The controversy over the guilt or innocence of Sacco and Vanzetti continued to boil. Newspapers revived the case peri-odically. Authors and lawyers cited the case as a classic in the mishandling of justice.

"I remember, this was long after 1951, that the Boston *Globe* printed an article that said Butsey was behind the rob-bery-murder in the Sacco-Vanzetti case. Butsey sued. I asked him, 'What the hell are you suing them for? You can't beat a newspaper.' He said: 'They're implicating me in this Sacco-Vanzetti thing. What they said was true, but it's going to hurt my kid. I don't give a damn about myself. I'm ready to die anyway. But look what it's doing to my boy. He's a legitimate kid. He never knew what was going on before.'

"I looked at Butsey. I didn't know much about the case ex-cept what I'd heard. But he was upset because of what was happening to his boy, not what happened to Sacco and Van-zetti. 'We whacked them out, we killed those guys in the rob-bery,' Butsey said. 'These two greaseballs [Sacco and Vanzet-ti] took it on the chin. They got in our way so we just ran over them. Now after all these years some punch-drunk writer has got to start up the whole thing over again—ruin my repu-tation. I gotta sue even though I don't expect to win. I gotta sue for my kid's protection.' I said: 'Did you really do this?' He looked at me, right into my eyes, and said: 'Absolutely, Vinnie. These two suckers took it on the chin for us. That shows you how much justice there really is.'

"Butsey's dead now. I don't think he ever told the story to anyone else, except maybe a few close friends he had in the mob. The only thing I know for sure is that Butsey wasn't the kind of guy to tell tales. He didn't brag about anything —ever."

Of major concern to the councils of crime in the 1950s was Kefauver's attack on a key organization in the national gambling picture, the Continental Press of Chicago. The Continental Press was a mob-run wire service which, through both legitimate and illegal means, obtained information from race tracks on racing results and transmitted them to bookmakers across the country for a fee. Continental was part of the Chicago mob's operation, and it maintained a branch office at 84 State Street in Boston under the name, "The Daily Sports Digest." In early 1951, as Kefauver put the spotlight on Continental's nationwide operations and sordid history of mob violence, Continental did fold. This left New England bookmakers without a wire service, and so Lombardo and Bruccola set up their own independent service operated by Frank Ferrara and Angelo (Munge) Rossetti.

"Ferrara and Munge weren't made guys, but they were experts in the business. The idea behind it was instantaneous results from tracks in various parts of the country. They had men at these tracks with binoculars stationed in buildings overlooking race tracks, or with walkie-talkies inside the track talking to a guy outside the track in a car. They'd have an open phone to Munge in East Boston while the race was going on.

"I remember Munge used to sit in this big room, behind a table he had made special. It had the middle cut out. He used to sit in the middle in this swivel chair, him, Frankie, and another guy. They had fifteen phones on each side. As each phone would ring, Munge would tell the bookie wire room calling in on the other end: 'Okay, that race goes off at 2:02. I'm going to lay you off' [keep the phone open until the race begins]. The bookie wire room would be calling in, asking for a description on the race as it was being run, say at Gulf Stream in Florida. At post time, all thirty phones were open to bookmakers around New England waiting for the race. At 2:02, Munge would start getting the description direct from his man at the phone who was getting it right from the men at the track. Munge would say: 'Okay, they're off at Gulf Stream. The two horse is leading . . . it's the one horse at the top of the stretch . . . the one horse is the winner at 2:03.' That was it . . . bang . . . the result was flashed to the thirty bookie centers. They in turn flashed the results to hundreds of street bookies working for them. Each bookie paid fifteen bucks to the wire service for the result on each race. Munge might be handling two or three tracks that afternoon—eight or nine races to a track. It was a gold mine.

"It was also a great protection for the bookie. They couldn't get past-posted by some sharpie who had a guy at the track feeding him results by radio so he could make a bet at the last second when he knew who the winner was. You couldn't beat the time results of the wire service. When Munge said on the phone the race was off at 2:02, the bookie took no more bets, no matter who it was."

The Ferrara-Rossetti wire service operated in East Boston for years, often with the complicity of crooked policemen. Teresa recalled that police were paid to ignore the operation, but that as added insurance, the mob changed the location of the wire service every week or two. The locations are recorded in police records at times as being at the Colombian Club at 231 London Street, East Boston, a club organized for charitable purposes in 1947. Among its board of directors was Rossetti. On other occasions, police said Munge's home at 209 East London Street, East Boston, was used as a phone center.

The complicated telephone operations required the services of expert telephone men.

"The mob has the best telephone service in the country. They can send one of their electronics experts in and he'll put a phone in every room for you in ten minutes and hook it up to some other poor sucker's service. The guy will never know about it until he gets the bill. At one time, we had a phone that you could use to call anywhere in the world, and the outfit that wound up paying the tab was Hertz Rental Service. The boys cut into a cable at the airport in East Boston and hooked into the Hertz line. They had a guy I knew as Flungo. He was a genius with phones. They'd call him in to set up the service and overnight he'd have the whole location wired with phones. If you wanted open phones so you could talk to a dozen or four dozen people at once, he'd rig it up. The mob was getting fifteen bucks a race on each phone and the telephone company was picking up the tab. The phones, the wires, the cables they cut into were all telephone company equipment."

One of the customers of the mob wire service was a bookmaker in Providence, Rhode Island, known as Carlton

O'Brien. O'Brien was an ex-convict, a strong-arm man, and a suspect in armed robberies who ran several bookmaking locations in Rhode Island. As long as he bought the mob's wire service, he was permitted to operate. He had been an original customer of Continental and he continued his relationship with the Ferrara-Rossetti service. But Kefauver's investigations were proving costly for the mob. They required frequent new locations, often new equipment, and more personnel than were previously needed. Higher overhead meant higher prices to customers. O'Brien rebelled. He refused to pay. Instead, he began bootlegging a service of his own to bookmakers who were balking at the mob's demand for higher charges. To cope with O'Brien, Bruccola sent over a rapidly rising star of the mob, Raymond Salvatore Loreda Patriarca, to rectify the situation. O'Brien's bookies were held up, his betting parlors were wrecked, and his runners were viciously beaten and robbed. O'Brien remained defiant. It was a fatal decision. As he walked into his home early one morning in June 1952, a shotgun blast cut him down from ambush.

"O'Brien had to go. The wire service was one of the most profitable rackets the mob had going. They couldn't let a punk like him defy them. It could give other people ideas. So they whacked him out and everyone fell in line after that. There was no more trouble."

*   *   *

Lombardo was anxious to salvage the wire service, but he wasn't anxious to bring Kefauver's investigators bounding into his back yard. They might uncover the bookmaking and policy rackets that had been flourishing almost openly in the city of Boston, not to mention his large bookmaking interests in outlying areas and in other states. It made sense to Lombardo to do nothing to endanger that empire and his immensely profitable layoff center. Kefauver seemed to be concentrating on big bookmaking operations, getting at them by connecting them with the Continental Press.

"When Kefauver started the fuss, Boston's biggest city gambling operations were run either by Lombardo's men or by the Palladino brothers, Joe and Rocco. The Palladinos were independent, but they paid Lombardo for the privilege to operate.

"Anyhow, the heat turned on by Kefauver made Lombardo make a decision that was to make a punk I knew in Medford one of the biggest guys in the New England mob. Lombardo decided to close down all gambling in Boston, and he ordered the Palladinos to close down their city operations. That way when Kefauver's boys got to the city, they'd have nothing to lay on Lombardo. It was fantastic. You couldn't bet a number in Boston, no matter who you were. The order was out: No bookmaking, no numbers. That's when Jerry [Gennaro] Angiulo got his start in the big leagues."

Jerry Angiulo of Swampscott, Massachusetts, is today, at age fifty-three, the underboss of the New England crime family. He is the ruling boss of Boston and has been described by law-enforcement intelligence agents as the gambling czar of Massachusetts. He also has business interests that include real estate, golf courses, hospitals, restaurants, bowling alleys, finance companies, and other enterprises from Florida to Maine. His fortune is estimated at three hundred million dollars. But in 1951, Angiulo was nothing.

"I knew him when I was a kid in Medford. We never hit it off. I remember particularly his mother Jennie. She was an old doll, a real hustler who ran a place on Prince Street called Jennie's Dog House. She used to serve hot dogs and soda and candy and things like that. On the side, she was the hottest card player I ever knew. Every day after work, I'd go down to Jennie's and play gin rummy with her and she'd clean me out. What a gin player that old lady was. She must be in her late eighties now. Jerry would get mad as hell when he'd see us playing cards. She'd call me Sonny and he'd explode. 'Don't call him Sonny, his name is Vinnie,' he'd shout. She'd tell him to shut his mouth and holler some cuss words in Sicilian at him and keep playing cards and calling me Sonny while he fumed.

"At that time, Jerry wasn't in the mob. He was driving a truck and running pushcarts, picking up fruit around town with his seven brothers. Jerry was ten years older than I was and I used to hang around with his two youngest brothers, Smigsey and Frankie. When we were in school, the three of us used to play football on cement—not tag; tackle—on cement. When we weren't banged up and bleeding from football, we were out getting and giving lumps in gang fights on the street or moving dice in the school basement."

By 1951, Angiulo had moved to the fringes of the mob, working as a policy racket runner for Nicola Giso of Boston. Giso is a mob member and operates the Coliseum Restaurant in Boston, but in 1951, according to Teresa and police, he was one of Lombardo's top gambling operators and loansharks.

"Angiulo had a bright idea, and he went to Lombardo with it. He said: 'Mr. Lombardo, you don't want to take the numbers, the bets. Is it all right if I do?' Lombardo didn't care —he was making his bundle other places, so he told him: 'Look—you'll be taking a big chance. Things are bad here now. They're investigating everybody. But if you want to, go ahead. If you get caught, you're on your own—remember that. The organization's got nothing to do with you and you've got nothing to do with us.' Of course, that wasn't all true. Old Joe got a piece of the action, but what he meant was that all the responsibility was on Angiulo's shoulders if something went wrong.

"Angiulo went to his father and borrowed a couple of thousand bucks to set up his operation. He had a helluva scheme going for him, I'll give him that. He'd go to some old greaseball and say, 'You want to bet a number?' The guy would want to, naturally. Jerry would say: 'For every number you bet a buck on, I'm going to give you a quarter back.' What he did was make that old greaseball a bookmaker. In other words, this old guy would go out and get his brother's buck and bet his buck and collect fifty cents back. So he was getting two bucks' action for a buck fifty. So Jerry went to everybody that he knew and he told them the same thing. Everybody who was a bettor became a sort of amateur bookmaker. They could get 25 percent of all the dollar bets they could collect. They could make a pretty good living that way. Pretty soon, Jerry winds up tying up the whole city this way. Every kid on the street, every old greaseball, every old lady scratching for pennies, everybody bet with Angiulo for that lousy 25 percent. He got together with his brothers and the next thing you knew the money was rolling in. Kefauver never touched him and he became a millionaire."

Becoming a millionaire while handling gambling action can have its disadvantages when you are not a member of the mob. You lack mob protection, you lack friends to intervene in high places. Most of all you become a victim for every two-bit hoodlum with a mob connection that comes down the pike. Such was the fate of Angiulo.

"He owned a joint called the Monte Cristo. All the wiseguys, the mob members, like Maxie Baer [Anthony Cataldo, now a New England mob soldier and enforcer] and Larry

Baiona [Ilario Zannino, currently the second-highest-ranking member of the Boston branch of the mob] were going in and shaking the place down. They'd tell Jerry to give them two or three grand. At first, he'd give it to them, but when they came back for more he got a little hard-nosed and refused to put out. So they would beat the hell out of him and finally he'd give them the money. I even tried to take ten grand from him and he ran out the door to get away from me."

Angiulo could take the shakedowns no more. It was one thing to be a millionaire; it was another to be milked continually by every hood that decided he needed a touch to tide him over. Kefauver had gone. Lombardo had retired. Bruccola had succeeded Lombardo as a boss and then fled to Sicily. Into the vacuum had moved Raymond Patriarca, with the approval of the retired but still powerful Lombardo. Now the supreme commander of the underworld from Rhode Island to Maine, Patriarca was the man that Angiulo, in desperation, decided to turn to.

"One day, while Angiulo's sitting in the Monte Cristo, he gets a bright idea. He takes fifty grand in cash and puts it in an envelope and heads for Providence. He'd never met Raymond Patriarca in his life before, but he got in his car and drove straight to Raymond's cigarette vending company in Providence, the Coin-O-Matic. He goes inside and says to the guy in front: 'I'd like to see Mr. Patriarca.' The guy he meets says: 'Who are you?' Jerry answers: 'I'm Jerry Angiulo from Boston. I've got to see Mr. Patriarca on a private matter.' The guy looked at him, went back to talk to Patriarca, and then came back. He frisked Jerry from head to toe and then led him into Raymond's office in the back of the vending company.

"Patriarca said: 'What do you want?' Now when Raymond says that the way he does, he makes you shake in your boots, and Jerry was shaking. But he kept his cool. He said: 'I've been having a lot of trouble. I took over the numbers in Boston and I had an okay from J.L., you know, Mr. Lombardo.' Patriarca says: 'So what's that got to do with me?' Jerry looks at him. 'These guys keep coming in and shaking me down for money and I'm getting tired of it.' Now Patriarca just sort of smiles with that crooked smile of his and tells Jerry: 'If you don't like it, why don't you fight them?' Jerry answers: 'Well, I have an idea. Here's this envelope. I'll give you twice that much every year—at least that. Then we can work on a percentage. Please, just tell these people to leave me alone.' Raymond opened the envelope and found the fifty grand. He gave Jerry a long look. 'You're going to give me twice this much?' he asked. Jerry said: 'Guaranteed.' Raymond smiled. 'Okay kid, go back to Boston. I'll make a phone call.' He did. He called Baiona and some others and told them that he wanted the shakedowns to stop. 'Angiulo's with me now,' he told them. That's how Jerry became a made man. He went up the ladder of the mob with cash. He bought his way all the way to the top. It was a mistake, but that's what happened. He never handled a hit [murder], he never took any chances the way other made guys did. But Patriarca made him, and there was nothing anyone could do about it. If they tried to shake Angiulo down, they would be, in effect, shaking down Patriarca, and that was a sure way to get hit. Now you can't bet a number in the whole state of Massachusetts without it ending up in Angiulo's pocket, and half of that goes to Patriarca—whether he's in jail or not."

5

Early Swindles

Kefauver and the high-level machinations of the mob in New England were of little concern to Teresa. He was more concerned with meeting his mounting gambling debts. The more he bet, the more he lost and the deeper in debt he got to Robert Visconti, Medford's leading loanshark.

"I was in hock to Visconti for my shirt. My juice [interest payments] alone would run more than a thousand a week. I had to figure ways to pay it. Visconti wasn't pressing me. He knew better. But the juice kept adding up, multiplying. Finally, I went to work for Visconti. I hustled bets for him, I handled burglaries, I even collected debts for him, but I was always behind."

While Visconti didn't squeeze Teresa as he did his other loanshark victims—most likely because he feared the mob connections he knew Teresa's father had—he used Teresa to make money. Visconti saw in Teresa a rare talent. Teresa was a talker, a con artist. Visconti decided to turn Teresa's talent loose on the Columbus Associates Credit Union of Cambridge, Massachusetts.

The credit union was a small loan firm run by and for immigrant Italians of the area. The manager of Columbus Associates was Pasquale (Patsy) Varto, an engaging, naïve old-country Italian. Varto owned a laundry near the credit union office and unsuspectingly had become indirectly involved with Visconti and his clientele.

"Visconti had some guys on the hook in a grocery store next to the laundry. They couldn't make their payments and Bobby began to squeeze. He told them if they didn't get up the money, he'd have their legs broken. They were scared to death. Then he told them to borrow the money from Varto."

The Visconti debtors followed instructions and obtained loans from Varto. The ease with which they got the money, simply on their signatures, gave the scheming loanshark ideas.

"That's when Visconti sent me to the store and had the old greaseballs put me next to Varto. Visconti told me I could get myself out of hock with this guy. 'With that line you got, you'll wind up owning the joint,' he told me.

"Varto was a nice old guy, but he was a sucker for a story —any story. He ran this credit union for all the old greasers. They'd save all their money in this credit union. They didn't trust banks or anything that wasn't run by their own people. So they put their money into this credit union and it was supposed to use their money to make money through small loans of one or two grand.

"Now, Varto was a real greaser. He talked in broken English and he guarded the money like it was his own. But the way he ran the business, anyone could get a loan. All you needed was two signatures, yours and a cosigner. So I conned him into a one-grand loan right away and I paid the money to Visconti. Then I told Varto I could build his business, that I had friends who'd like to borrow from an honest man like him."

It was almost too easy. One loan followed another, and, while Teresa made some payments, the bill at Columbus Associates spiraled higher and higher. At the same time, Teresa's debt to Visconti dropped dramatically.

"I used to arrange tombstone loans with poor old Patsy, God bless him. I'd get a name off a tombstone in town and I'd walk into Patsy's office on the second floor. 'Patsy,' I'd say, 'I got this friend, Larry O'Donnell, who needs a loan. I'll cosign for him. He's as good as gold.' Patsy would give me the application form and I'd fill them out with phoney information. He never saw who he was giving the loan to. The next day I'd pick up the check, cash it, and pay off Visconti. At one time I must have had forty loans like that with Patsy. I even used the name of my three-year-old son, Wayne, to get a loan from Patsy."

Teresa, however, was still betting the wrong horses, and occasionally he'd have to borrow through one of the hoodlum friendships he'd made in the North End of Boston after he'd left the Navy.

"One of the kids I used to break into stores with when I was in school in Medford was a kid named Pat. I don't want to use his full name and embarrass him now. He's gone straight, runs a bar, and has a family. But in the old days he was a helluva gutsy kid. We heisted the tomato company together and we were busted in our first burglary of a Medford meat market. Pat came from the North End of Boston before he moved to Medford, and he introduced me to a lot of his friends, guys that I was to move with later in the mob."

One such friend was Salvatore Cesario, currently a well-known enforcer, loanshark, and sometimes bodyguard for New England mob underboss Jerry Angiulo. Cesario operated in the North End, picking up bets, muscling loanshark victims for higher-ranking mob figures. Occasionally, Teresa would borrow money from Cesario who, unlike Teresa, didn't squander his money on horses.

"I owed Cesario a grand—I'd bet some bad horses again—and I'd promised to pay him before Thanksgiving. I'd made an arrangement with Varto to borrow the grand, but I hadn't picked up the money yet. Now here it was Thanksgiving morning, and I haven't got the money for Sal. I figured that the next day I'd be in town seeing this animal Cesario and it would be embarrassing not to have his money. Sal wasn't pressing for it, but he was unreliable. He was an animal, particularly when you owed him money.

"It was dinnertime and old Patsy was just sitting down to his turkey when I called. 'Vinchenza, what you want now?' he asked. 'Patsy,' I said, 'I gotta have the money you promised me.' There was a silence on the phone for a minute. 'Tomorrow, Vinchenza, tomorrow. I eat my turkey now.'

"Now, old Patsy was a sucker for a hard tale, so I began working on him. He had planned to be away from work for the whole Thanksgiving weekend and he didn't want to have any part of me. But he listened and when I get going I can sell the moon, believe me.

" 'Patsy,' I said, 'you sitting down eating turkey now?'

" 'Atsa right,' he answered.

" 'You know where I am? I'm in a phone booth outside my house. I can't go into my house because they're waiting for me.'

" 'Whosa waiting for you, Vinchenza?' he asked.

" 'There's this guy there, seven feet tall, who's going to break my legs unless I get up the money,' I answered. 'I'm coming over your house—now.'

"Before he could say another word I was on my way over to his house. I parked outside. Now, he's trying to eat his turkey with his family and relatives and I'm outside blowing the horn. Finally, he came out, got in my car, and I drove him to his office twelve miles away. I wouldn't leave. I made him write the check out for two grand, instead of the one grand he had promised me. I needed the extra grand for myself. The things I did to that poor man. I drove him crazy.

" 'Vinchenza,' he said at the office one day, 'the day I meeta you, I shoulda cutta my hand offa here.' He pointed to his right wrist, and drew a line across it. 'No, no, Patsy,' I said, 'then you couldn't sign checks.' He looked at me. 'Specially, thisa hand,' he said. 'The one thata signa the check. I should cutta the hand off. You maka my life miserable.' "

Just how miserable Teresa made his life, Varto never really knew. Swindling him with tombstone loans—some sixty-five thousand dollars' worth—wasn't the only method the enterprising Teresa used to part Varto from the credit union's money. During one particularly lean period, Teresa planned and arranged a robbery. Again Teresa called on contacts he'd made in the North End of Boston. One was Albert (Al Judd) Georgio, a compulsive gambler who became a premier burglar and bank robber. The other was Chris Mustone, a low-echelon thief and armed bandit. Both were to participate with Teresa in later years in a wide variety of crimes. On this occasion, all were in need of a quick score to pay for their gambling escapades, and Varto was the target.

"I knew Patsy would be in his office on the second floor, and I knew there was usually about fifteen or twenty grand in his safe. So I drew up a plan for Al and Chris. I told them I couldn't go with them because Patsy would recognize me right away. I told them to put stockings over their heads and hold him up. That's what they did. They went to the second floor and put a gun to Patsy's head. The poor old guy was trembling. He was scared to death. He opened the safe and they cleaned it out. There was fifteen grand in cash and a bunch of checks. We burned the checks and split up the fifteen grand. Patsy never figured out I was involved. This will be the first he knows about it."

Varto tried, and failed, to collect some of the thousands of dollars that Teresa swindled out of him. He took Teresa to court, but Teresa won on legal technicalities. Varto had to admit shoddy loan practices. He had never seen, talked to, or investigated the persons he approved loan applications for. He couldn't find them or identify them. It was impossible. They all lay dead in a cemetery.

Varto taught Teresa one lesson. The young hoodlum was now convinced he could make a sucker out of any man with his line. He had the patience and the ability to size up his victim, to find his weaknesses before bleeding him to death. The art of the con was to become a Teresa tool that would bring millions of dollars pouring in. But in 1956, Teresa was still young and violent. There was little sophistication to his methods. He was still a penny-ante hoodlum, a compulsive gambler. His friends were street men—burglars, gunmen, bookies, small-time loansharks—not the mob elite.

Teresa decided he needed a cover for his operations. "Suckers are made, not born. You got to have money, an operational front, to draw in the sheep." The front Teresa chose was the Broadway Ice Cream Bar in Somerville, Massachusetts.

"The ice cream bar was sort of a branch office for Visconti.

I had to do something to make a buck. Wayne, my first son, was a year old and Blanche was beginning to wonder what I did besides gamble to make the money I was bringing home to her every week. The store was the answer. It was a perfect front. You couldn't get more respectable than run an ice cream bar. I could handle numbers for Visconti and I could move stolen property from the back room. Everyone's looking for bargains, you know. So the fathers, the mothers, even the grandparents of the kids who'd come in for ice cream or a hamburger or hot dog would bet numbers with me or buy things they couldn't afford that I could sell them at bargain prices. The cops never bothered me; Visconti took care of that. He had most of the cops there in his pocket. I didn't even have much overhead. I had a couple of teen-agers working for me, but every time payday would come we'd go in the back room and I'd knock them dead in a card game. They'd wind up owing me their next week's salary."

The opportunity for quick riches came in the form of a man named Frank Metrano, owner of Metrano's Sun Oil Company of Somerville. Metrano had delivered oil to the previous store owner. Now he was delivering oil to Teresa.

"One day, I'm having some coffee in the place and Metrano hands me a bill for twenty-six bucks. I give him the money and I guess I looked like hell. I'd been out the night before, playing cards, and my head was splitting. I'm holding both sides of my head, hoping the hammers will stop pounding.

" 'What's the matter, you got problems?' he asked. Now I need this guy's questions like I need the hammers pounding in my skull. Who the hell wants to talk to this bum? He was dirty, oil all over him. He looked like he'd crawled out of an oil barrel. 'You got money problems?' he asked. 'Who hasn't?' I grumbled. 'I could let you borrow a thousand, if you need it,' he says.

"Now this starts to clear my head and I'm wondering what's this guy Metrano up to. Is he a loanshark on the side? 'At what rates?' I asked him. 'No rates,' he said. 'You're a customer of mine. I loan money to a lot of my customers.' My eyes opened up like saucers. Where did I find this angel from? 'Yeah,' I said. 'I could use a G-note.' So he gave me the grand and I told him I'd pay it back within a week.

"My mind was running on all cylinders, now. The headache was suddenly gone. I had me a beauty. All I had to do was cultivate him, carefully."

Street knowledge had long since convinced Teresa that every man was looking for something for nothing, for a quick way to make a dollar that Uncle Sam wouldn't know about. The trick was to convince the prospective sucker that he could get away with cheating the tax men. Teresa put the thousand dollars into his pocket. A week later, he took it out of that pocket, added fifty dollars to it, and gave the money to Metrano.

" 'Here,' I said, 'this is for doing me a favor.' His eyes lit up like neon lights. 'Geez,' he said, '5 percent for a week. That's great.' From that point on he was mine. I'd borrow more and more money from him, increasing the amount I'd borrow each time, and pass him some interest money every few weeks. But I'd keep the principal, the original amount I'd borrowed. All he was getting was a few bucks' interest. He thought he was doing great."

Teresa cultivated the oil dealer for a variety of schemes. One of them had been used by street men and corner hustlers for years and is used in most major cities. Throughout the country, the mob has shady jewelers who will put together watches that look expensive but have cheap works that break down after a short time.

"The mob can provide any kind of watch you want. Omegas, for example. They sell for three hundred bucks or more on the legitimate market. The mob makes them for seven bucks. They make up the outside casement so that it's an exact duplicate of the Omega, down to the little gold horseshoe and the twenty-four-karat engraving on the back. We call them gaffs in the mob or one-lungers. The mob's jewelers can make any kind of watch you want. They'll put Mickey Mouse on the face if you want it. Anyone who goes to a big city has bumped into the creeps on the street who sidle up to you and whisper: 'Want to buy a hot Omega?' Now the sucker knows the Omega starts at three hundred bucks, and when the hustler says he can have it for fifty, he jumps at it. The most it can cost the hustler is eighteen bucks, and that's for a real beauty.

"For Metrano, I had cheaper one-lungers—Bulovas and Swiss watches. I'd pay two bucks apiece for them and he'd pay ten bucks, thinking he'd bought hot watches at a real bargain. Oh, he was a beauty. You could see the dollar signs in his eyes when I offered him a deal."

Soon Teresa had led Metrano into a variety of other bad

deals, including a nonexistent load of electric frying pans for eight thousand dollars. "He gave me the eight thousand. The next day I told him the whole load had been hijacked on the way to town. He believed it."

Teresa used a similar line to inveigle Metrano to invest in a trailerload of what he said was high-priced stolen gin. Each case, he told Metrano, was worth forty dollars, but they could buy it for twelve dollars a case. Together, they could make more than fifty thousand dollars on an investment of twelve thousand dollars. Teresa produced two thousand dollars that he said he was going to invest as his share. Naturally, most of the profits were to go to Metrano.

"I told him I needed ten grand, but he wasn't buying that day. He said he didn't have it, that he was just mailing in his income-tax check and had only about four grand left in the bank. He showed me a check made out to the Internal Revenue Service for eighty-two hundred bucks. So here I am, looking at this check. I know he's got money in the bank for this —he isn't going to write a bum check to the government.

" 'Listen,' I said. 'Here's what we do. You give me a check for ten grand—' He protested. 'But it's no good,' he said. 'Give me the check for the ten grand,' I said. 'I'll go to these people and tell them to give me the load and to hold the check. They'll go for it. They're friends of mine.' Bang, I've got him—I can see it. He writes out the check for ten grand. I excuse myself for a minute to get a pack of cigarettes. I run around to the candy store and call his bank. Sure enough, there's more than enough to cover the ten grand. So I go back and tell him I have to go to these people to cover the liquor deal. I close the ice cream bar and make a bee-line for the bank, where I cash the check. A week or two later the tax boys come down ready to bust him because his check to them bounced. He almost went out of his mind. He called me everything under the sun. Naturally, there wasn't any liquor."

Metrano tried every means he could think of to force Teresa to pay back the money he'd swindled—more than seventy-five thousand dollars in less than a year.

When Metrano was unable to get satisfaction, he decided to take his problems to friends he had acquired that had influence with the mob. One of those friends was Sal Cesario.

"Sal came down as sort of a joke. He tried to get me to give him ten grand of the seventy-five I'd taken from Metrano. He said he'd tell Metrano he was even. Now Sal and I are friends, and I know he's trying to con me. He wanted to pocket the ten grand himself and tell Metrano to get lost. I shook my head. I told him I wasn't giving him anything. 'Metrano's a sucker,' I told him. 'He was a sucker when I found him, he's a sucker now, and I don't pay suckers back, and that's the end of it.' Sal just laughed and took off. Metrano didn't try sending any of the boys around again.

"The trouble with Metrano, like a lot of suckers I have dealt with, is that he always wanted to be a wiseguy himself. He liked to be with racketeers. You can't imagine how many guys are like that. To them it's like being out with a celebrity. They like to go out and eat with you and when you walk into a restaurant, be by your side when the head waiter comes out and says, 'Over here, Mr. Teresa,' and takes you to the best seat in the house because you slipped him twenty bucks. They'll do anything to stay on the right side of you. There's a kind of excitement to it all for them. But most of all they've got larceny themselves. They want to make a fast buck, and that's how they get caught. That's how Metrano got swindled. He was a sucker for the promise of a fast buck. What's he going to do—complain to the cops that he gave Teresa money to buy a load of stolen goods? He's got no one to blame but himself and his own greed."

6

Cashing Checks and Robbing Banks

Although Teresa had stolen more than a quarter of a million dollars since his discharge from the Navy, the police had not charged him with one single major crime. He had run numbers, loansharked, swindled, burglarized homes and stores, sold stolen merchandise, planned a robbery and committed grand larceny at a trucking company, yet his police record showed no criminal complaints. As far as Teresa could see, crime paid.

"I knew that the only way I could live in the style I liked was by being a thief. It was easier than working for a living. The money rolled in. Sometimes it went out faster than I could steal it, but I liked the life. I liked the excitement. There was kind of a thrill to everything I did. The cops weren't as smart as they are today. In fact, most of the ones I knew always had their hand out for something, so I didn't worry about them. It's hard to explain, but there was a feeling of power being on the street with men that were always hustling, outfiguring the straights. It seemed that everyone I knew or grew up with was a thief of one kind or another. We were all living pretty good, spending high, dressing fine, hitting all the good spots. It was a helluva life."

In 1957, Teresa, fresh from his conquest of Metrano, came up with a new scheme. It had all the appearances of a sure-fire way to make easy money. All that was needed were some smart partners. Teresa settled on cutting in his old friend Al Judd and three other men he had met in Boston's North End: Herbert Serino, Robert Daddieco, and Edward (Whimpy) Bennett.

"Whimpy Bennett had a contact, an old-time printer that was a real artist in making duplicates of checks. All you had to do was show him a check from companies like the Metropolitan Coal Company or the John Hancock Insurance Company and he'd have copies ready for you in twenty-four hours. He could also make copies of state drivers' licenses, which we needed for identification in cashing the checks.

"The scheme was simple, really. We had the old printer make up batches of checks of various companies. In the trunk of our car we had telephone books from all over the state. We needed the phone books to select the names we wanted to use on drivers' licenses. The names we picked had to be from the area we were going to hit. We also had a check-writing machine and a typewriter in the car trunk. Every day, we'd take this stuff and head for a different section of the state and whack out that section with bum checks. Sometimes we hit supermarkets and department stores, but most of the time we went for banks.

"What we would do was split up in teams. One of us would go to a bank and cash a legitimate money order to start off with to see what the operation inside the bank was. If it looked easy, that is, if it looked like the bank manager didn't ask too many questions about checks, we'd send in different members of the team in cold turkey with paychecks of $120 to $150 each to cash. If, when we tried to cash the money order, the teller needed an okay from the manager and he wanted to see identification, we used a different technique. We'd send in a guy dressed in work clothes with the money order. He'd be sent by the teller to the manager, who would write his okay on the money order. But instead of cashing it right away, our man would come back outside the bank and bring the money order to the car. There we'd trace the bank manager's signature or initials on the phoney checks we wanted to cash. Then we'd wait for the manager to go out to lunch, and, while he was out, five of us would hit the bank with the phoney checks and cash them. We took the Charlotte Bank in East Boston for over three grand that way and scores of other banks and stores throughout the state and Connecticut. But our best score was on Wall Street in New York."

New York is worldly and wise to the ways of criminal dodges, but it wasn't prepared for the machinations of Teresa and Serino. In less than two weeks they had cleaned tellers' cages out of more than twenty thousand dollars without so much as a hint of trouble from the police.

"Our first target was the First National Bank on Wall Street. They're all very correct in there, but they were suckers for a line. Before we tapped them, we went to another bank with twenty bucks and got a legitimate money order. Then I headed straight for the First National Bank.

"The first place I head for was the teller's window. The girl there was kind of pretty. I handed her the money order and asked her to cash it for me. 'Have you any identification?' she asked. I told her I didn't, knowing exactly what her next step would be. 'You'll have to see the manager,' she said, pointing to a guy sitting behind a desk. That was the gimmick. I wanted her to send me to the manager and see me talking to him.

"I walked over to the manager. 'Would you mind giving me an okay to cash this?' I asked. He asked for identification, and I pulled out my driver's license and some other papers. He looked it over, smiled, and initialed the money order. Now, I'd been with him for a few minutes and the teller had seen me talking to him. I knew she'd know I had an okay from him. I made sure she was busy and I walked over to another teller's window. I pulled out a ten-dollar bill and asked her to give me some change. This was to have the manager see me at the teller's window and think I was cashing the money order he'd okayed. Meanwhile, I've got the money order in my pocket.

"After getting my change, I walked out of the bank and took the money order back to the hotel where Herbie and I were staying. We took a piece of glass and put it on top of the lamp shade. On top of that I put the money order and on top of the money order I put a phoney check made out for four grand to a phoney name. On that check, we traced the bank manager's initials and a phoney license identification number. On a second check we printed exactly the same name and the same amount, only we left out the bank manager's initials and the license number.

"Now Herbie, he was a good-looking guy, he would dye his hair and get dressed up. He looked more like a Wall Street broker than a Wall Street broker. He'd head for the bank with the two checks and walk up to the teller's window. He pulled out the check with no okay on it and asked her to cash it. Naturally, she would send him to see the manager. While he walked over to the manager, he'd slip the check in his pocket. Then he'd sit down with the manager while the teller was watching and ask him about bank charges in taking out an automobile loan. This would give him time, in case anybody was watching, to have someone see the bank manager writing on something while Herbie was sitting at his desk.

"Herbie would stay about ten minutes with him, thank him for the information, and then walk toward the teller's cage. Now he would reach into his other pocket and pull out the check with the traced bank manager's initials on it. He'd walk straight to the teller's cage and hand the girl the check. She'd see the manager's initials and think she'd seen the manager initial the check herself. She'd count out the money, hand it to Herbie, and off he went. We worked this scheme at four or five locations of that bank and picked up more than twenty grand before we decided we'd better move our operation back to Massachusetts."

In Massachusetts, however, things were getting hot. Banks were complaining about the ease with which criminals were obtaining and using forged licenses as identification for cashing checks. To thwart the check-cashing thieves, the state adopted a new form of driver's license.

"The state kept changing the type of license to screw us up and break our operation. They succeeded. We were stuck. We needed licenses real bad, and nobody on the street could supply them. You couldn't even buy counterfeits. There just weren't any around. So I got this bright idea one day while I was with Al Judd.

"'Al,' I said, 'let's go up to the registry where they make the licenses.'

"'For what?' he asked.

"'I'm going to go in there,' I said. 'I'm going to take my jacket off, roll up my sleeves, and act like I work in the joint. I'm going to see if I can cop a box of new licenses.'

"Al figured I was crazy, but I walked into the registry. The first girl I saw I said: 'Gee, I'm new in here. My boss sent me to get a box of licenses for the registry room. Would you tell me what floor they're on?' The girl didn't bat an eyelash. 'You'll find them on the second floor in back of the registrar's office,' she said.

"That's where I headed. I walked in the office with a pencil on my ear, whistling, like I own the place. A real busy beaver. I spotted a guy sitting at a desk and I noticed his name on a name plate. I remember the first name like it was yesterday. Eddie. I walked to the desk and leaned down. 'Hey, Eddie,' I said, 'John sent me up to get a box of licenses. Where do you keep them?' He didn't even look up, let alone ask me who John was. 'Over there in the corner,' he answered. So I walked over, picked up a box with a thousand licenses in it, and, still whistling, I walked by the desk. 'See ya, Ed, thanks a lot,' I said, and walked out of the joint. I'd never seen the guy before in my life and he'd never seen me, but I walked out of the building on Nashua Street in Boston with a box of a thousand drivers' licenses. We had a rubber stamp with the state seal made up, a real good forgery, and we had a field day. It was a helluva score. I got fifty bucks apiece for the licenses, the ones we didn't use for check cashing. Everyone wanted them. They were like gold. Young broads who wanted to go in bars and drink bought them. Guys who had lost their licenses driving jumped at them, and mob guys who needed different identifications out of state ate them up."

The bubble of success finally burst on July 3, 1958, but not before the enterprising check cashers had taken banks and department stores from Massachusetts to New York for more than five hundred thousand dollars, not to mention fifty thousand dollars for licenses.

"Thomas McBrady ratted on me. McBrady was a partner of mine in the Broadway Ice Cream Bar. He'd been put in the place by Bobby Visconti, who he owed a ton of money to. I guess Visconti figured McBrady would watch me and I'd watch McBrady and with both of us watching no one would chisel Visconti on his take. Anyhow, McBrady got caught passing some of the checks we had. We'd taken him along a few times when we hit an area, but the bastard went out on his own and got caught cashing checks. Rather than go to jail, he blew the whistle on me. The cops had been trying to nail me for years, but couldn't until he chirped like a canary. When I got my hands on him later, I beat the hell out of him. I'd have killed him, but Tommy was a helluva hustler.

"When the cops picked me up, I figured I had no way out but to plead guilty. On July 5, 1958, I was sentenced to eighteen months in jail on seven charges of larceny by check in Lynn and East Boston. The judge gave me a lecture and a suspended sentence and put me on probation for two years. Hell, everybody gets caught sometime. I'll do two years' probation for a half million bucks any day in the week."

The check-cashing scheme was dead for the time being, but banks still held a fascination for Teresa. They were full of the cash he needed for the gambling excursions that were becoming continually costlier. An afternoon at the track for Teresa could cost as much as twenty thousand dollars. And by nightfall, he was busy sweating out the fall of the cards in a high-stakes poker or blackjack game. He became desperate for money, and in his desperation he turned to a more violent form of criminal activity.

It was Teresa's friend, Judd, who provided the opportunity. Judd was closely allied with a group of armed bandits that included two of Teresa's friends, Chris Mustone and Robert Daddieco. Three others included Thomas Richards, John (Red) Kelley, and Billy Aggie Agostino (George W. Agistoteleis). Banks, and later armored cars, were their specialty.

"The boss of the holdup team was Billy Aggie. Billy was small, about five-foot-seven. He was the shrewdest man in the robbery business. There was no one like him—no one. He had the patience of a saint. He'd watch an operation for months before he'd make a move. He'd invest money in makeup kits so that when you staged the holdup you could walk up barefaced ten minutes later and no one would recognize you. He'd put a scar on one side of your face, make your eye look like it was cockeyed, add a mustache. Christ, your own mother wouldn't recognize you when he got through.

"I got involved with them in four bank robberies. We hit banks in Cambridge, Brighton, Coolidge Corners, and Brookline [all in Massachusetts]. Each of the jobs were planned by Billy. He made them so easy. He was really a genius at it. He timed everything out. Precision was a must. He looked for spotlights, crossroads, anything that might interfere with a getaway, any place where a police car might be hidden. He'd get up early and watch the guards come in. He knew when the armored cars would come and go and how many guards they had. He put a lot of effort into knowing just who would be where in each bank and what time we could expect to make the biggest killing. Naturally, he got a bigger share than the rest of us. If one of us made four grand, he made ten grand, but it was worth it to the rest of us. Every now and then an accident would happen, one of those things you don't plan on.

It was one of those accidents that made me figure the risks weren't worth the money.

"We were robbing the Brookline Bank and Trust Company in Brookline at the time. I was running toward the bank when Al Judd dropped his gun as he jumped out of the car. Bang!! The gun explodes and the bullet misses my head by inches and ricochets off the wall. That's when I quit. That was the last bank robbery I got involved in. I figured I got to be crazy. I got forty-three hundred bucks as my share and almost had my head blown off. It wasn't worth it. The biggest score I ever got was sixty-three hundred bucks as my end, and I lost that in a card game in one night. You figure you got Uncle Sugar [the FBI] looking for you—and there's always the chance that some innocent slob gets hurt. To me bank robbery was a stupid move. But not to Billy Aggie."

While Teresa pursued different criminal ventures, Aggie and the others continued in the field of armed holdups, one of which won international headlines in 1962.

"Let me tell you a story about Aggie and Red Kelley. Now this is the real story about the Plymouth Mail Robbery. To everyone, the great mastermind behind the job was Kelley. Not that he was innocent. He handled the job all right, but he wasn't the guy who planned it. I know, because I knew Billy and others that were involved, including Kelley."

The Plymouth Mail Robbery took place on August 14, 1962, on Route 3 in Plymouth, Massachusetts. It was one of the most carefully executed, daring holdups ever staged. A red, white, and blue mail truck was en route to Boston. About 8 P.M. a man dressed in a policeman's uniform appeared on the road and waved the mail truck to a halt. Several gunmen jumped from two cars parked at the roadside and forced the guards inside the truck to open it up. Tied with tape, the guards watched helplessly as the gunmen unloaded mail sacks at several locations, transferring $1,500,000 in cash to waiting cars.

"Billy set up the Plymouth job. Red Kelley worked for him at the time. So did Tommy Richards and Pro [Maurice] Lerner and a few others I don't remember. All of them were the best thieves in the state at the time. But when Billy talked, they all listened and followed his orders to the T. They knew when he planned a job there wasn't a detail left out.

"Now to plan a job the way Billy did cost money. Billy

used to get that money from Jerry Angiulo, the bum that's the boss of the Boston branch of the mob now. He'd need six or seven grand for makeup kits, special equipment, shotguns, and special clothing for a real big job. So before the Plymouth job, he went to Jerry and got the money. Naturally, he told Jerry what he was planning. He told Jerry because Jerry always fenced the money from Billy's jobs. That's why it was so tough for the feds to ever nail these guys.

"Most bank robbers and stickup men get caught because they have to split up the money from a job they do and spend it. They don't have connections the way Billy did, so they spend it. When they spend it they leave a trail for the FBI to track down. When you heist a bank or an armored car, the bank or the security men have a list of numbers of some of the federal reserve notes. When the money is stolen, they notify the FBI, give them the numbers of the bills, and the FBI puts out a hot list to its offices as well as banks throughout the country. That way, when a bill drops with a number that's on the list, the FBI gets called and starts tracking down who spent it. Eventually the trail leads to a member of the holdup gang.

"Billy was smart. When his group would take a bank or an armored car, they didn't split up the money and go out and spend it. Billy would just take the whole haul to Angiulo and fence it. If the money was real hot, Angiulo would give him sixty cents on the dollar. If it wasn't considered too hot, he'd give him eighty cents on the dollar. Angiulo could find out how hot the money was through contacts he had in banks and in the Boston city police, who would get notices on the hot list that the FBI put out.

"Now, Angiulo had millions of bucks coming in from his numbers operation. He could afford to pay out sixty grand on a hundred-grand score and bury the hundred grand in a vault somewhere until the heat cooled off. In ten years he'll use it. He didn't need it right away. It's as simple as that. With Angiulo, he doesn't ship money all over the world to get rid of it. He just goes and buries it. Eventually, it's going to be good. He invests a lot. He owns a lot of property. He had a golf course with Patriarca, he had a hospital in Boston where the bookies used to operate. He owns hotels and motels in Florida, a bowling alley at Cape Kennedy where they fire all those space shots from. He's got a million ways to unload the money at the right time and in the right place, and he's got the smartest lawyers in the world working for him. That's why the Internal Revenue Service hasn't nailed him. They've tried, but he beat them.

"Anyway, Billy borrowed about eight grand from Angiulo for planning the Plymouth job. What that man went through to get the timing down was unbelievable. He dressed up in women's clothing and went down to Hyannis in a convertible and followed that mail truck from place to place. He had a different disguise for each day. Every day for two months he detailed the routine of the mail truck and its drivers until he had everything down pat. He knew where every light, every stop sign, every crossroad, every police car was.

"Then a week before the job was to take place, Billy had a heart attack and he was taken to the hospital. He called up Red Kelley and told him he was sorry but he was sick. He said that the doctor said he'd be all right in a couple of weeks. He told Red to put things off. Red agreed.

"Red had all the detailed planning that Billy had put in at his fingertips. So he called the boys together and they pulled the job off. They got a million five from the job and Kelley, who was close to Angiulo himself, fenced the money to Angiulo. Kelley got eighty cents on the dollar from Jerry. The reason Jerry gave them such a high percentage was that most of the money couldn't be traced. It had come out of all little joints, nightclubs and stores along Cape Cod. There might have been a few federal reserve notes that could be traced, but 99 percent of it was clean money. To Angiulo, it was like having blocks of gold in Fort Knox. He couldn't lose. He made a quick three hundred grand for himself without moving from his office.

"Billy was sore as hell when he got out of the hospital. He went straight to Kelley and demanded his share of the loot. Kelley denied he or the boys had anything to do with the heist.

"Billy knew Kelley was lying. There was a real beef about the whole thing. Billy went to Angiulo and complained. He'd borrowed the money from Angiulo to plan the job and now he was out of it and he still owed eight grand to Angiulo. Jerry sent for Kelley. There was a big sitdown [meeting] on the whole thing. Richards and Agostino disappeared after that and were believed murdered and dumped by members of the Plymouth mail robbery. They never found Richards' body. Lerner, he's in jail for planning the shotgun murders of Rudolph Marfeo and Anthony Melei with Kelley. That's another whole story I'll come to later. And Kelley, he went on, after Aggie, to become one of the biggest and best holdup men in the country. I'll give him this though, he never took credit for planning the Plymouth Mail Robbery. He's still got to be tried for a $582,000 holdup of a Brink's armored truck in Boston's North Station in 1968. He also held up an armored truck of the Skelly Detective Agency in Fall River [Massachusetts], where they got $177,000. Now the mob wants to kill Kelley—he's become an informer for the feds. Because of him, lots of people are behind bars. The mob tried to use me to get up $250,000 bail to get Kelley out of jail so they could hit him. It didn't work. The feds guard him like he was made out of gold —just like they take care of me and my family."

7

Other Stickups

When Teresa decided holding up banks was too risky an occupation to follow, it didn't mean that he had ruled out all forms of robbery. Robberies, under special conditions, could be highly profitable, particularly if there were no federal agents to worry about or marked money that required fencing.

In the city of Boston, as in most major cities throughout the nation, floating dice and card games are popular, though illegal, pastimes. They attract doctors, lawyers, politicians, judges, and businessmen, who flock to the moving games in search of excitement. Most of these games are controlled by mob representatives, who take a percentage of each pot. The percentage pays house expenses for police protection, chauffeured limousine service to and from the games, and rental of the game's location. Some of the games operate honestly, but others are rigged; the mob slips in "mechanics" (card and dice experts who can manipulate the game) to work on players targeted by the mob as suckers. And, as an added profit-making device, the mob provides its own friendly loanshark to lend money to losers on the spot at high interest rates.

"There were some independent games in the city, but most were run or protected by some wise guy. You don't just set up a game in the North or East End of Boston without having some kind of protection. For the most part, the protection that they are supposed to provide is phoney. It's just a way to cut a percentage off the top of every game. The only really protected dice game around in those days was the Big Apple. It was protected by Jerry Angiulo. The players would just go to a designated restaurant and a car would pick them up and take them to the location set up for that particular week. That was a game nobody fooled around with, cops or heist men."

In the dead of one night Teresa got a call from Robert Daddieco.

"I was pretty crazy in those days. This was back in 1959. I'd try anything for a quick buck. Daddieco called me. He and Chris Mustone, Al Judd, and Herbie Serino were going to stick up a card game. They wanted me to join them. I figured why not? I'd lost my share of dough at some of those games. This was a chance to get some of that loot back. At the last minute, Judd and Serino didn't show and Mustone brought Daddieco's cousin, Bingy, along as a replacement. Later on, Bingy died in an arson contract. He got trapped while torching a place with some other mob guys. He was burned to a crisp. It took the cops two weeks to identify him.

"Now, the games in town floated from location to location each week, and it wasn't too hard for a street man to find out where the action was. Daddieco knew where a game was being held, and he said it was a perfect setup for a heist. None of us asked or cared if the game was protected. We just wanted to get at the money. So we hit the game like "Gangbusters." We scooped all the money off the table and then we made everyone in the joint strip down to their bare asses. It was kind of funny. All of them standing there shivering while we're rifling their pockets for any money they had stashed. We got a few thousand bucks and when we left we took their clothes with us. That way they couldn't follow us.

"We found that was a pretty good technique. Naturally we wore stocking masks to distort our faces. We hit about a dozen games in about three months—no trouble at all. At least two of the games were worth about twenty-five grand each."

While Teresa and his friends didn't have police or federal agents looking for them, there were other people attempting to identify the holdup team. One of them was Michael (Mike the Wiseguy) Rocco, a powerful and influential Boston mobster.

"Mike the Wiseguy was one of the old Mafioso who worked for Joe Lombardo down at Pinetree Stables. He was a big numbers man and loanshark and he controlled some of the dice and card games we had been holding up. On paper, he had a legitimate job. He was a public relations man for a Ford agency in Boston and he worked at Whitehall Liquor, the big booze distributing outfit owned by Joe Linsey, the big Boston millionaire."

Joseph Linsey, today seventy-three, is one of Boston's most controversial citizens. He portrays himself as a benevolent philanthropist, a successful businessman, the president of Whitehall Company, Ltd., of Allston, Massachusetts, and an investor in real estate. He also describes himself as a friend or associate of such personages as Israel's David Ben-Gurion, the late President John F. Kennedy, and President Harry S Truman. Yet Linsey has been the target of various federal and state investigations. His name was mentioned over FBI electronic bugs on the office of crime boss Raymond Patriarca. A onetime bootlegger, he has been linked to such criminal luminaries as Meyer Lansky, the financial wizard of organized crime, Patriarca, Rocco, and other hoodlums. Linsey has admitted knowing mob figures but has denied any criminal activity since he was convicted of bootlegging in 1927.

"I've known Joe Linsey for years. I never did any business with him because he was with other people. The truth is that he and Mike the Wiseguy knew each other from the bootlegging days. Linsey was a bootlegger with most of the mob guys and he took a fall for bootlegging. But when Prohibition ended, Linsey became the front man for the New England mob. He was close to Joe Lombardo, Phil Buccola, Tony Santonello, Raymond Patriarca, Henry Tameleo—all those guys. What he does is invest their money in things like race tracks, hotels, liquor companies, real estate. There's nothing really illegal in that, but Linsey's been with the mob for years no matter what he says. I remember Patriarca saying he had invested $150,000 with Linsey in a race track. There was another time when some guys were going to hold up Linsey at his home. Patriarca heard about it and he warned them to stay away or they'd get hit in the head. 'Linsey's with me,' he told them.

"Linsey is kind of the Meyer Lansky of New England. He takes care of the boys' money. That's why Rocco was with him—to make sure everyone got an honest count and no one shook Linsey down. They wanted him because he had a lot of influence with politicians, and he helped the mob when some of their people got in trouble. I never got involved in the politics end of it, so I can't say from my own knowledge what he did in that area."

At the time, Teresa was unconcerned about Rocco's affiliation with Linsey, Patriarca, or anyone else. He was concerned about rumors that Rocco's strong-arm men were looking for him.

"One of the two-bit loansharks that Mike the Wiseguy had working for him was a guy named Guido, the guy I mentioned whose restaurant was taken over by Lombardo. I'd borrowed about two grand from Guido and I'd paid most of it back. I think I owed him about four hundred bucks at this time, including the juice.

"One day this Guido sees my Uncle Sandy and he says to him: 'You know, if I bump into your nephew, I'm going to hit him on the head with a two-by-four to get my money.' Uncle Sandy comes to me and tells me about what he said and I explained to him that I'd paid this guy most of his money back and he had no beef coming. Sandy tells me not to worry about Guido. He says when I have the four hundred bucks, to pay him back, and that's the end of it.

"Now, I'm hanging around with Daddieco at this time and I tell him what my uncle said. Daddieco was crazier than me, crazier than most of the hoods around at the time. He says to me: 'We can't let this guy talk this way about you and get away with it. Let's go down and straighten him out.' I figured he had a good idea. So we found out that Guido hung out at the Cozy Corner, a bar on Salem Street in Boston. I got a .38 revolver and Bobby grabbed a sawed-off shotgun and we went down to the Cozy Corner. I blew the horn.

" 'Is Guido in there?' I hollered. Guido sticks his head out the door and makes a dirty remark. I think he called me a son-of-a-bitch or something like that. As he did, Daddieco jumped from the driver's side of the car and pointed the shotgun at him.

" 'Get on your knees,' Bobby shouts.

" 'What did you say?' Guido asks.

" 'I said get on your knees, you lousy greaseball,' Bobby answers.

"I get out of the car and walk toward Guido, who's dropping to his knees, shaking as he looks at the two barrels of Daddieco's shotgun. There's also a whole lot of guys standing around near Guido. 'I understand you're going to break my head with a two-by-four,' I said to Guido, waving the revolver in his face. He's really sweating now. I walked up right next to the bum, and, bam, I whacked him across the head with the gun. There's blood all over his kisser now. 'You want to tell me what you're going to do in front of everybody here?' I asked him. 'I ever hear another word of this, I'm going to come in and shoot you—not through the heart, through the brains. I'm going to blow your brains out.' All this time Daddieco's standing there, waving the shotgun, saying: 'I hope somebody moves. I sure hope somebody moves.' Nobody did."

As far as Teresa was concerned, the incident was closed. Guido, nursing an aching head and a healthy fear, had other ideas, and those ideas resulted in a call to Teresa from his Uncle Sandy.

"Uncle Sandy was having a fit. 'What's the matter with you?' he said. 'Have you gone crazy? You know, that guy is with Mike the Wiseguy. You gave him stitches in the head. You threatened to kill him in broad daylight in front of witnesses. What, have you gone out of your mind?' "

Uncle Sandy warned him that one of Rocco's strong-arm men, Joseph (Little Bozo) Cortese, was looking for him. Cortese, a violent man, was one of Rocco's principal operators of dice games in Boston.

"Uncle Sandy told me to stay out of sight until he got things straightened out. But I didn't listen. One night, Little Bozo catches up with me in a bowling alley in Medford. Now, he's a little runt, a weasel, and I was about 220 pounds and as tough as steel. I was pretty crazy. I'd have ripped Christ off the cross in those days.

"This little weasel walks up to me and says: 'You're in a whole lot of trouble.' I looked at him. 'Who the hell are you to tell me I'm in a lot of trouble?' I said, 'I'll split your head open like it was a melon.' He gets defensive right away. 'Wait a minute—take it easy. I'm with Mike the Wiseguy. He wants to see you.' So I said: 'Well, I respect Mike. I'll go and see Mike myself. He didn't have to send anyone like you after me.'

"So I called Daddieco and we drove over to this restaurant where Mike the Wiseguy had his headquarters. Daddieco stays outside and I walk in. Now all the headcrushers are there. Maxie Baer [Anthony Cataldo] and Lou Grieco start telling me I'm in trouble for holding up their card games and for beating up Guido. It looks like I'm really in for it because Mike the Wiseguy is raving at me too. All of a sudden Daddieco yells in the door, 'Hey, youse greascballs! If Vinnie don't get out of there in five minutes, I'm going to shoot the first guy that comes out that door with a shotgun. If you think I'm kidding, look out the door.' Oh boy, I figure. Here I go, out in a pine box.

"Maxie Baer right away blows his cool. Who the hell is this punk to be threatening him? So he storms for the door and looks out. 'Baro-o-o-m . . .' Daddieco lets go a shot. He splatters the whole wall. Maxie Baer dives for the floor shouting. 'That crazy bastard is really out there with a gun.' There's a real ruckus now. I have to tell Mike the Wiseguy that Daddieco don't know what's involved and that I'll calm him down. That's what I do. I tell him not to do anything else foolish. Then Mike the Wiseguy grabs me. 'I should put you in a box right now for what you've done.'

"Mike the Wiseguy decides to let me sweat for a while. Then he picks up a phone and calls my Uncle Sandy. Sandy tells him I was a little crazy in the head and that I had had a lot of problems raising my family. That carries some weight. Then he calls Joe Lombardo. Now Lombardo was Mike's boss. He'd retired by then but he was still the *consigliere*, the adviser for the whole mob. When he spoke, they all listened. When he said something should be this way, that's the way it was. There were no arguments. Mike asks him about me and Lombardo tells him that I'm a good hustler and that I'll pay the money I owed Guido. He also tells Mike that Guido was out of line threatening to bust my head open. Without Lombardo and Sandy I'd have been buried right then and there.

" 'Let me tell you something, kid,' Mike said to me. 'Don't you hit any more poker games or any more dice games. The next time you end up in a box no matter who goes to bat for you.' I never held up another game from that time on. I saw the light."

8

The Underboss

The experience with Mike the Wiseguy Rocco taught Teresa two important lessons. First, there was no room in the underworld jungle for nonaligned, free-wheeling hoodlums. Their survival rate was poor. Second, to prosper in a career of crime, a man needed powerful friends. And indeed it was the associations of childhood, the hours spent among high Mafia members at Pinetree Stables, that were to spell the difference between success and failure, between an ordinary street thief and the upper echelons of crime for Teresa.

In the years that Teresa had spent on his own, living high on nerve and brains and a glib tongue, the structure of organized crime in New England had changed dramatically. The small, local, factionalized mobs were dead. In their place had grown an octopus whose body was New England and whose tentacles reached from Florida to Maine. The leader of this crime family was Raymond Patriarca, and under him were a cadre of men who had pledged fealty and their lives to the secret society. They numbered more than one hundred, but their control extended to more than five thousand underworld figures and had influence in the highest levels of politics, even in governors' mansions and the halls of Congress. Patriarca was the supreme leader, but the man who made the operation work and who was to affect the future of Teresa profoundly was Enrico Henry (The Referee) Tameleo.

"I'd met Henry when I was a kid at Pinetree Stables. He was with Butsey Morelli then, and Butsey had taken a liking to me. So did Henry. Occasionally, when I'd heist some diamonds or furs in a burglary, I'd contact Butsey and he'd get Henry to fence my stuff. After a while I was just going to Henry whenever he came to Massachusetts from Rhode Island. He got to know me over the years, and he trusted me. He said he saw real potential in me and he took me under his wing after my trouble with Mike the Wiseguy."

Tameleo was something special in the New England mob. Born in Providence in 1901, he had developed as a mobster first under the tutelage of Morelli and then for a time in the rackets of New York. At the age of seventeen he was arrested for theft of an automobile. From that point on, he progressed rapidly into such crimes as larceny, procuring for prostitution, assault with intent to rob, and carrying a concealed weapon. These, however, were only the crimes the police had been able to charge him with. They were hardly representative of his talents. He had murdered, robbed, directed slayings, handled stolen goods, operated loanshark rackets, set up fraudulent diamond rackets, swindled businessmen, and gambled.

"When Butsey was replaced as a boss, Tameleo could have had the job if he wanted it. But it wasn't what Henry liked. When you hold the seat, when you're the boss, that's it. You're sitting on the throne. You don't go anywhere, you don't do anything but give orders. Henry wasn't like that. He'd been Butsey's No. 2 man, and he'd moved around. He couldn't live in an ivory tower, be an untouchable. He liked being out on the street, dealing with the wiseguys, setting up and moving rackets. But when you're a boss, you're a king sitting on a throne, and all your advisers do the business for you.

"Henry was about five-foot-ten and weighed about 175 pounds. He had a bald head with white hair all around the side. He always dressed conservative, but he had a strange thing about what he wore. He always wore white stockings and suspenders. If you didn't know him and you saw him for the first time in some office, you'd swear he was a banker with his glasses, his soft speech, and his ways. He was the softest-spoken man I've ever known, but he could chill you to your grave with his tone and those hard brown eyes of his when he thought you'd done something wrong. And he could be vicious at the drop of a hat. He could be smiling at you and all the while he was figuring out how he was going to cut you up in little pieces. I can't even count the number of men who went to their graves because of Henry. He was a man you had to be careful with.

"Beneath that businessman exterior and that vicious nature was a real swinger. He wasn't flashy about it, but he loved the nightlife, the young girls, the cabarets, the good food, and the high living. You can't do that if you're a boss. You got to be prim and proper. Not Henry. He liked living. That man could put away more booze than you could count. I've never seen anything like him. He'd start drinking at eleven in the morning and by three the next morning he was still pouring it down, and, if you talked to him, you'd swear he'd never had a drop to drink.

"He was also a spender. He gambled worse than I did. That man blew millions. I remember during the football season, he'd have bets on every pro and college football team in the country going. There would be twenty or thirty grand riding each weekend. He'd win and lose that kind of money without even thinking about it. When he cabareted, he spent money like it was water. The waiters used to knock over customers just to get to serve him and the people he was with. When he left a tip, it almost came to the cost of the whole damn bill. But if he owed you a dime and he said he was going to pay you the next Tuesday, he'd drive through a driving blizzard to pay you on time. But God help the man who owed him a dime and didn't pay on time. He'd whack a man out in a second if he didn't keep his word.

"I don't think Henry ever slept more than three hours at a time. I'd leave him at four in the morning in a motel in Boston and by 7:30 A.M. he was on the phone telling me to hurry up and pick him up. He was a human dynamo, that man.

"Henry's best thing was diplomacy. That's what he was an ace at. He thought that negotiations, compromise, maneuvers were the best way to make a deal work. I don't mean he wasn't willing to fight when he had to. If he thought murder was the best way out, he'd use that. But he preferred to use reason and peaceful means to get his way when it was possible. I remember once he said: 'We're not in politics, but we have to be; it's the only way we can survive. Politics is today's method of power.' And he used politics to get the things Patriarca wanted. He could reach out to a governor's office or a police precinct or a city council or a state legislature, even a congressman to get the things the mob needed. Like when they wanted the parole for Ralphie Chong [Ralph Lamattina] when he was in the can for mail fraud, Henry had people reaching out to the Massachusetts State parole board and the state legislature to get Ralphie Chong out. Or when Patriarca wanted to broaden his race track interests, Henry arranged for a state legislator to introduce a bill. The bill didn't pass, but that didn't mean anything. Patriarca kept making money in tracks anyhow.

"Henry had tremendous power. Patriarca couldn't have survived as long as he did without him. He depended on Henry in everything. At the snap of his finger, a guy lived or died. He could order gang wars to start or stop. But his biggest asset was his power over Patriarca. I don't know how he did it, but he could always cool Patriarca down when he lost his temper and was ready to make a foolish move. Henry was always calm, always quiet in the face of real trouble. I learned an awful lot from that man."

•   ·   •

In the Borough of Brooklyn, New York City, gang wars are a recurring phenomenon. The war that was to concern Teresa most occurred in 1961. For more than a year Joseph (The Old Man) Profaci, the olive oil king, had been contesting with a group of young turks in his organization headed by three brothers: Joseph (Crazy Joe), Lawrence, and Albert (Kid Blast) Gallo. The contest was over the territory of a policy racketeer known as Frank (Frankie Shots) Abbatemarco. In November 1959, Abbatemarco had been killed on the orders of Profaci by Joseph (Joe Jelly) Giorelli, the premier assassin of the Gallo gang. Abbatemarco's death was ordered for his failure to pay fifty thousand dollars in "taxes" levied by Profaci, who exacted tribute from all rackets in Brooklyn. Profaci had promised to turn the territory over to the Gallos if they killed Abbatemarco, but he welched on his word.

Anger over the injustice of Profaci's action simmered within Gallo ranks until December 1960. It was then that the Gallos planned the overthrow of the aging Mafia don. Their plot finally crystallized in February 1961, when, in a well-planned raid that stretched from East Islip, Long Island, to Brooklyn, four of Profaci's top leaders were kidnapped. Profaci himself was a target, but he accidentally eluded the Gallos' net when he checked into a Miami Beach hospital. Caught by the Gallos, however, were Joseph (The Fat Man) Magliocco, Profacci's underboss and brother-in-law; Salvatore (Sally the Sheik) Mussachio, a *caporegime* (captain); Frank Profaci, the boss's brother, and John Scimone, a bodyguard of Profaci.

The Gallos' insurrection took Profaci by surprise. He tried negotiations and failed. Finally, in desperation, the old crime leader appealed to the Commission, the ruling body of the nationwide Cosa Nostra. The Commission was composed of twelve ruling bosses of crime families across the country, including Raymond Patriarca. Profaci served on the Commission, but, in this instance, he was not permitted to give any opinion other than as an injured party. The Commission ordered the Gallos to free the prisoners. In return, the Gallos could present their case to the Commission. The Gallos agreed.

The Commission listened to both sides. Profaci contended that Abbatemarco had been killed not because he failed to pay tribute but because he had plotted Profaci's death. Furthermore, he said, he had never promised the Gallos anything. The Gallos, on the other hand, insisted that they had done Profaci's bidding under the promise of operating the numbers territory and that Profaci had gone back on his word. After the Commission listened, it ordered both sides to sit down with an emissary, who would be sent from another crime family to negotiate a settlement fair to both sides.

"Patriarca called a meeting on the New England mob's advisory council to decide who would be sent to Brooklyn. Now, the advisory council is something special in our area. I don't know if other mobs have the same operation. In those days, the council was made up of old Mafia dons, the Mustache Petes who made the mob of New England during the 1920s and 1930s. Joe Lombardo was a member, so was Mike the Wiseguy Rocco. There was also Joe Anselmo, we called him Joe Burns, from Arlington [Massachusetts], and Don Peppino [Joseph Modica]. There was also Peppino's cousin, Nene [Nazzarene Turrussa].

"These were all the old dons that bought Boston. They were the ones who went around shooting cops and buying politicians and judges in the old days. They got the town in the bag, and it's been in the bag ever since. They were the ones who made the connections with the police departments. They'd had connections in the district attorney's office for thirty or forty years. They made the mob. Then the new young punks like Jerry Angiulo put them down just because they got old. If it wasn't for them there wouldn't be a mob in Boston. Do you think you could move into a city like that and open up a racket now? They got in while everybody was still dumb. They were the ones who drove the big bootleg trucks through barriers and had running battles at sea with the Coast Guard. They made millions of dollars to start the new punks off with. All these new punks came from poverty. They'd never have got their start without the old greaseballs bankrolling them.

"Raymond had respect for them. So did Henry Tameleo. So while the old greaseballs didn't do much except stand around corners, Patriarca and Henry made sure they still had their slices of action, whether it was loansharking or gambling, working for them. But when there was a big policy decision to make, they were called in to meet. Patriarca knew that they knew all the ins and outs of mob thinking across the nation. They'd dealt with all the dons who ran things in other cities, like Profaci. That's why he turned to them when the Commission handed him the Gallo potato.

"A meeting was called in the back room of a Boston restaurant owned by one of the council members—I can't remember the name of the restaurant now. Outside, waiting, was Tameleo, who they told to wait for their decision. After a few hours, he was called in and they told him what they thought should be done and they told him to go to Brooklyn to negotiate the settlement they had agreed on. I drove Henry to Brooklyn for the meeting. His job was to arrive at a peaceful settlement of the dispute. This was in the spring of 1961, March or April, I think. It was right after the Gallos had released the hostages.

"We drove to this restaurant in Brooklyn. It was late at night and I didn't notice the name, but I remember thinking I was in on something big. We went to the back room of the place and I sat at a table with a couple of Brooklyn wiseguys. Henry sat at another table with the Gallos and with Frank Profaci and a couple of other people. They spent hours ironing things out. When we left, Henry told me: 'It's all straightened out. I don't blame either one of you. They were stepping on each other's toes. This way, one now has a section and the others have a section. Let's see if they keep it. If they don't, let them kill each other. We did our part.' They didn't keep the peace. Old Joe Profaci double-crossed everyone. He got Carmine Persico and his guns to start a war with the Gallos and try to wipe them out. I remember Henry saying when he heard that there was an attempt to kill Larry Gallo [August 14, 1961]: 'See, they don't keep their word. Let them kill each other.' "

Tameleo's role in trying to settle the Gallo-Profaci dispute earned him the title of The Referee. His diplomacy in Brooklyn, the satisfaction that both sides had expressed over his handling of the dispute, had won him respect throughout the Cosa Nostra.

9

The Don

For Teresa, Providence, Rhode Island, was a far cry from the lavish world of Pinetree Stables. In place of rolling, green pastures were the noisy, open-air markets of Atwell Avenue, their vendors loudly hawking their wares to rotund women chattering excitedly over the prices of tomatoes and eggplants. Instead of trim, muscular hoodlums standing guard at the white-picketed entrance to the farm, gnarled old men with undersized fedoras watched suspiciously from their chairs propped against the walls of darkened social clubs, ready to make hand signals when a stranger approached. Here, high on Federal Hill overlooking the state capitol, organized crime flourished amid the secrecy and the clannishness of the Italian-American tenement district.

"Atwell Avenue was an armed camp. It was impossible to move through that area without being spotted and reported. We had a spotter system that was faster than an electronic eye. The minute a stranger moved into the area, the word was flashed to the boys at the National Cigarette Service Company. That was a vending outfit that Raymond Patriarca owned and set up in a two-story, wood-frame building at 168 Atwell Avenue. Across the street was another Patriarca company, the Nu-Brite Cleaners. Nearby, in another building on the second floor, we had an old man who used to sit in the window all day long watching for strange cars. There was a gas station next to the vending company that had spotters. Christ, there were spotters everywhere, in restaurants, bakeries, vegetable markets, you name it.

"As you entered the National Cigarette office, men stopped you at the door if you hadn't been recognized by the old men. Inside, there were pinball machines and jukeboxes all around. You had to sort of thread your way past them to a repair station where mechanics worked on the machines. Behind the repair section was a twelve-by-twelve-foot room with an overhead door that you had to pull up to enter. That was the Office, the headquarters of the New England mob, where Raymond ruled like a king on a throne.

"We didn't call it the Mafia or Cosa Nostra. The last time I heard the term Mafia used was when I was a boy. I never heard Cosa Nostra used. There were Mafioso, but they were the old dons who came here from Sicily to organize the mobs in New England. Joe Valachi, the guy who blew the whistle on the mob on television, talked about *caporegimes* and *soldati* in New York, about Cosa Nostra or 'Our Thing.' We never used those terms. There were made men, wiseguys, who were members of the Office. Some of the made guys had more clout than others, and they were called bosses. Patriarca was the top boss, the *padrone*. The No. 2 man, the underboss, was Tameleo. We called him The Referee. Jerry Angiulo was the No. 3 man, the boss of Boston, and under him was Larry Baiona [Ilario Zannino]. We used different titles, but the setup was pretty much as Valachi described it. We never called the Office a crime family, but then other places didn't either. In Buffalo, they call the mob the Arm, and in Chicago it was the Outfit. But whatever you called it, it was a secret society with made members and bosses and associates.

"The associates were guys who worked for the made men and the bosses to make money, but weren't accepted in the Office as members. First of all, to be a member you had to be an Italian. There were no other nationalities. We worked with Jews and Portuguese and blacks, anyone to make money, but they could never be made members because they weren't Italian. Over everyone was the Commission, a ruling council of bosses from different areas who made decisions on rules and policy involving mobs across the country. They didn't interfere in local affairs unless it was something like the Gallo-Profaci war, and even then they only gave advice. One thing we never talked about in the Office was the Commission. We all knew about it, but it was something you never talked about.

"Valachi talked about the blood-and-fire ritual in joining the Cosa Nostra. That may have happened in the old days, but I never heard of it happening in New England. To be a member of the Office, you had to have a sponsor, a top guy who recommended you for membership. But before you were picked you had to have your notches for the organization, you had to have proved yourself by killing a guy you were ordered to hit. The only guy I know that was an exception in New England was Angiulo who, as I said, bought his way in. When a guy was made, the members of the Office, like Tameleo and Patriarca, sat down with you and your sponsor. At that meeting they explained the rules of membership, and No. 1 on the list was complete silence forever. You were never to talk about the Office or its members or anything they did to anyone, not even your own family.

"Silence is what protects the Office. Each man is a wall protecting the next guy higher up. Let's say you want to do business with Tameleo. You can't do business with him. You got to do business with someone down the line who does business with him or a guy between. We figured every man is a wall. When you come to me, I'm a wall and I stop. Let's say I did business with you, and after that I did business with Tameleo. You would never know it. You could turn me in to the law, but the law would never nail Tameleo because I don't talk about what I did with him. If you go to Tameleo, you could go no farther than him—you couldn't get the *padrone*. Tameleo's been on death row for years for a murder, but he's never said a word to put Patriarca on the spot.

"That's the way the wall or buffer or insulation, whatever you want to call it, is supposed to work. Sometimes it don't. Sometimes people make mistakes and deal direct with lowerechelon guys, and that's how they get in trouble. Or sometimes the mob don't live up to its obligations and a guy like myself opens up.

"When you're made by the Office, they own you, body and soul. They more or less own you as long as you're on the street working for them anyway, but at least you have a chance to refuse to do something if you're not made. When Henry Tameleo took me under his wing and started to train me, he schooled me in the rules of the Office, because someday he wanted to sponsor me as a member. I never wanted to go that far. I wanted to work for him and make money, but I didn't want to join as a member, and I never did. Henry said: 'Always remember this: The Office comes first above your family and everything. You think of the Office first and then your family.'

"That means that if the Office told you your kid was out of line, go whack him in the head—if you don't, they whack you and him out. That's how a lot of mob hits are set up. They use a man's relative, his best friend, to set him up. He trusts them —he shouldn't—but he does. So the bosses tell the relative or friend, bring so-and-so here and then get out of the way. The assassins will be there waiting to take care of everything. Sometimes, they make you do the job yourself. That was the one rule I couldn't live by, and I told Henry. 'My family comes first and then the Office, Henry,' I said. He told me it was a decision I didn't have to make yet because I wasn't ready yet to even be considered.

"In later years, when Raymond wanted me to join, I talked my way out of it. Henry couldn't understand until I explained it to him. 'It's the way I feel—I'd rather be just the way I am. I still do all my business with you and Raymond because we're partners together in certain things, but I'd rather be on my own,' I told him. He respected me for taking my position, but you got to understand that it isn't easy to say 'No' when they say they want you. They can whack you out for refusing. One day after I talked to Tameleo, I bumped into Raymond. 'I understand you had a talk with Henry,' he said. 'Any particular reason—is something or someone bothering you?' he asked. I said: 'No, Raymond, you know I'm a loner, a gypsy. I like to jump from here to there. I may decide I want to go to Florida—spend the winter there. I don't want to have to explain it to anybody. The way things stand right now, you and I are partners. As long as I hold my end of the deals up, you got no beefs. But if I have to become a member of this little party of yours, I might not be able to go to Florida tomorrow —I might not be able to do anything tomorrow. You might tell me you want me to go stand on a street corner for a month and I got to do it. I got to show you that respect. The way it is now, anything within reason, I can refuse.' He said: 'You know, I can see your point. I respect you for it. That's the way we'll let it stand—for now.' "

There were other rules that Teresa learned were important. One of the rules concerned respect. Even the police observed that a telltale sign of power within organized crime was the measure of respect paid by some members of organized crime to other members. Lower echelons often held doors, got up from their seats, bowed and scraped when high-ranking dons came into a room. That respect extended not only to the higher ranks, but to retired Mafioso as well.

"If you are called by one of the dons or the bosses, you go and see what they want no matter what else you are doing. You answer them respectfully. You never yell or swear at them, no matter what they say to you. Henry demanded that respect. I got fresh one time, not really fresh, but I lost my temper. I had this kid working for me, Peter Martinelli, and we were partners in a loanshark business. I was operating the business for Henry and Raymond at the time. I didn't know it then, but this Martinelli kid was a pimp, and he was pimping his wife out. He'd been married three times, and three times he turned them into hookers. I mean, how the hell do I know what he's doing with his wife? Somehow or other, the word went back to Henry that I had a pimp working for me. Now, there's a hard-and-fast rule in the Office that you don't deal with pimps. They are *cornuto,* the lowest form of life, the vilest thing in Sicilian. That's how the Office felt about pimps. If they would sell their own wives, live off their bodies, how could you trust them? Anyhow, one night I'm down at a nightclub in Revere and in walks Henry. He sat down at a table and called me over. There were three or four guys sitting at the table with him at the time.

" 'What's the matter with you?' he asked. 'Are you crazy?'

"I said, 'What have I done wrong?'

" 'Have you got a pimp working for you?' he asked.

" 'Who are you talking about?' I said.

" 'Peter Martinelli.'

"I told him I didn't know anything about it. He was in a bad mood anyway. It was on a Monday and he'd taken a bath in the football pools the day before. He was taking it out on me, reading me up and down, in front of the others. Finally, I just couldn't take it any more. I'd had a bad day myself. I said: 'Hey, shut up for five minutes, you old bastard.' Oh man, everybody at the table got up. They were afraid like death now. They figured there's going to be some trouble. I said: 'Shut your mouth—let me explain to you—'

"Henry's face was as dark as the sky before a storm. Those brown eyes of his were as cold as steel. 'Do you know who you're talking to?' he said. At that point I didn't care. I'd completely lost my temper. He walked up to me, nose to nose, while the others were scattering. 'Take a good look,' he said. 'This is your Uncle Henry. Now just shut up and sit down.' I sat down. You know, he cooled me right down; otherwise I might have completely blown my top, slapped him in the mouth, and wound up on a slab myself."

No less stringent was the Office rule against dealing in narcotics of any kind. While pimps were considered untrustworthy, those who dealt in narcotics were considered dangerous to the safety of the organization in another way. They attracted public attention and the white-hot heat of an aroused law enforcement. The penalty for a mob member dealing in narcotics was violent and final.

"There was nothing worse than dealing in narcotics as far as Patriarca was concerned. It was a rule that preceded him. None of the old Mafioso ever fooled around with it. For that reason, Patriarca always hated Vito Genovese and never trusted Joe Bonanno. They both dealt in junk. So did their mobs. 'Never trust them,' he told me. 'Never trust that New Jersey or New York crew. They fool around with junk. Don't you ever get involved with any of them that handles that stuff—understand?' I understood. There was a kind of finality the way he said it. It impressed me.

"Ralphie Chong [Ralph Lamattina] tried dealing in junk one time with Ronnie [the Pig] Cassesso. Cassesso's on death row now in a murder case with Tameleo. He's a made guy like Ralphie Chong is. Raymond found out, and he called Ralphie Chong into the Office. He told him point blank, 'You're out of business or you're dead.' As far as Ralphie was concerned, there were no buts about it. He knew Patriarca meant it. The only reason he was given a warning was because he was a made guy. Waddy David, a Boston numbers operator who worked for Larry Baiona, wasn't so lucky. Raymond found out Waddy was dealing in junk and was drawing a lot of heat. He gave a contract out to hit Waddy. They found Waddy's body [on August 21, 1965]. He was shot three times at the base of the neck. There was another guy, a black, who worked for Abe Sarkus. Abe is a mob bookmaker too. This black guy was fooling around with junk. Whimpy [Edward] Bennett took care of him. He cut his throat.

"The rule was made for a reason. First of all, they don't need narcotics to make money in New England. There's so much money to be made in gambling, bookmaking, loansharking, legitimate business, and stocks. No one in the New England mob ever starved, whether they were made guys or working for the organization. Patriarca wasn't like Genovese or old Joe Profaci. He made sure his men got well paid. Junk only draws heat. There's more been written about junk than any other crime there is. The more that's written, the more that people get disturbed and the more people get up in arms. That guy in the newspaper office with a typewriter can murder you. Dealing in junk gives him an excuse to stir everyone up.

"The last thing you want in the mob is publicity. If you catch a bookie taking a number, everybody laughs about it: What are they bothering that poor guy for? they ask. The people figure everybody gambles. But when the cops catch a guy selling narcotics, the first thing they say in New England is 'Skin him alive,' 'He's no good,' 'Throw him in the can.' Then everyone's in the soup. Raymond didn't want that nonsense.

"I got in trouble with Henry one time because I even thought about helping a guy that was handling junk. The guy's name was Kid Goomey, I don't remember his right name now. Goomey had just got out of jail on an eight-year rap for dealing junk, and he was desperate. He came to me to borrow some money. I wouldn't give him the money. 'Goomey,' I said, 'you're a desperate man, and I don't like to deal with desperate men.' Goomey said he had connections in New York who would provide him with junk if he could come up with the money. I went to Henry to tell him the story and find out if I should lend the kid any money. I started off the conversation wrong. I said: 'Listen, Kid Goomey came to me. He's got a shot to handle some junk.' I didn't get another word out. Jesus, you'd thought I was insulting his mother. 'Don't ever talk to me about that—don't even mention it,' he screamed. It was the first time I'd ever heard Henry raise his voice like that. That was it. I had to tell Goomey to get the hell out of town or he'd get hit.

"There was another rule you had to live by. It wasn't a rule you were told when you were made, it was one that Henry taught me meant survival. He said always remember the mob was filled with treachery. 'It's something you have to learn to live with,' he said. 'Never trust anyone, no matter who it is. There is always someone who'd like to get up a little higher by stepping on you. I don't care how good you are, you make enemies.' He was right. I was a pretty well-liked guy on the street, but I knew that didn't mean a thing. Maybe one day one of those guys you think is a friend is going to brood about why he's where he is and why you're where you are and decide to get you.

"What the hell is a bullet? You're a dead man. Any sucker can pull a trigger—it don't take a superman to do that and you don't have to have courage to do it. Just close your eyes and point—it goes off by itself. This is what you worry about. But you school yourself this way. You school yourself on the streets. No. 1, be a diplomat all the time, be able to stay on both sides of the fence at the same time. You have to have guts, you need intelligence, and you have to be shrewd. You have to have knowledge of the way everybody else you're dealing with thinks. Learn who to trust to a point and who not to trust, but don't really trust anyone to start off with. Most of all never trust cops, and for sure never trust a local or a state cop. Don't ever put your trust in them because you can't. If he's taking from you, he's taking from somebody else too. He'll sell you to someone else.

"When you're on the street, it's like going to college. You learn something new every day. The only thing is you don't get a diploma. Graduation is staying alive. Every morning you graduate when you wake up. The biggest thing in mob life is being able to wake up in the morning. That's like hitting the number—it's the big score. Any damn fool can make money. I don't care if he's an idiot. He can work washing dishes and earn money. But being able to wake up in the morning is the hard thing when you got five thousand animals who may be looking to whack you out for any number of reasons. This is why you got to be careful every waking moment. Henry drilled that into me day after day. I never forgot. That's why I'm still alive today. For that I'll always thank him."

*   *   *

The man who ruled the Office, Raymond Patriarca, has been described by law-enforcement experts as the most destructive force in the history of the New England underworld. Born on St. Patrick's Day, 1908, to hard-working immigrant parents in Worcester, Massachusetts, he moved with his family to Providence while a child. His father, Eleuterio, ran a liquor store there. For the first seventeen years of his life, Patriarca stayed out of the law's hands. But in 1925 his father died, and within months Patriarca was arrested and convicted —for violating Prohibition laws in Connecticut. In the thirteen years that followed, Patriarca acquired a record that included failing to stop for a policeman, breaking and entering, masterminding a jailbreak in which a guard and a prison trusty were killed, and white slavery.

More important, he acquired the cunning of a fox. Between 1930 and 1938, he eluded the law and labored as a made member of the Joseph Lombardo organization. It wasn't until 1938, however, that his importance to the secret society of New England crime became apparent. Sentenced to a three-to-five-year term for armed robbery and possessing a gun and burglar tools in a jewelry store heist, Patriarca served just eighty-four days before winning a pardon under circumstances that sparked a scandal reaching the Massachusetts governor's mansion. In a three-year investigation that followed his release, it was found that the petition filed for Patriarca's pardon was fraudulent to begin with. Of the three clergymen who reportedly signed it, one was nonexistent and two denied having anything to do with it. The man who drafted the petition and guided it past government officials was Governor Charles Hurley's right-hand man, Executive Councilor Daniel H. Coakley. In 1941, Coakley was impeached and barred from ever holding public office by the state legislature, the first act of its kind against a Massachusetts public official in more than a century. That was the Patriarca known to law enforcement. That was history. The Patriarca known to Teresa was different.

"I first met Raymond at Pinetree. He was a cold and vicious man even then. But he was a brain, a genius at organization and at moving men. He stands about five-foot-six and is on the slim side, but not skinny. He has always dressed very conservative and like Tameleo, he always wore white socks. He smoked cheap nickel cigars or guinea stogies. His face was like a hawk, and craggy, with the coldest brown eyes I've ever seen on a man. He could bore a hole right through you with a look. He always combed his hair straight back. For a man with a ton of money, he dressed in the cheapest clothes of any mob guy I know. But he wore two rings, one with five diamonds that he wore on the right hand, and a big diamond ring that he wore on the left. Before he went to jail, he had a very bad case of sugar diabetes. But the thing I remember most about him was his temper. He had a temper like a rattlesnake. When he lost control, it was like a storm boiling over. He'd bite down on that cigar of his, then watch out—sparks would fly. I can remember many a time when he blew his top. There was one time in particular that my life hung in the balance with his temper.

"I got a tip from Barney Villani, a little weasel who used to sneak around corners, picking up tidbits for the wiseguys. Barney was from Medford, and he came to me and said he had a good score for me in Worcester. He figured that if I made the score, he would make a quick buck and at the same time stay in my favor.

"'There's this house down in Worcester, Vinnie,' Barney said. 'The guy that owns it is Andy the Fruit Man. The other night Tony Talia [a small-time hoodlum] and me had a chance to buy some liquor—we needed fifteen grand. Now, Talia knows this guy Andy, and he called him at ten-thirty at night and told him what we needed and this guy says, "come pick it up." We went down to this house and he was upstairs maybe fifteen minutes and he came down with the money. We paid him back two days later. The thing is, this guy's got a lot of money buried upstairs.'

"I looked at the weasel and I thought to myself, this guy might be trying to set me up. So I grabbed him by the shirt and I squeezed him real hard. 'How good do you know this guy?' I asked.

"Barney squirmed. 'Honest, Vinnie, I don't know him at all, but Talia says he's a nobody.'

" 'You're sure he's not connected?' I asked. Now, if a guy's connected—that is, he's got friends in the Office—you don't do him harm. That's why I asked Barney.

" 'Guaranteed he's not connected,' Barney answered. 'No one knows him.'

"So Joe Putsy [Puzzangara], he's another thief I knew when I was a kid, and myself take a trip to Worcester and we looked the place over. Sure enough, just like Barney said, every Friday and Saturday night this guy Andy and his wife go out for supper and a movie. They leave at seven-thirty and come home by twelve-thirty. I had never seen the bum before in my life, so I figure everything's okay. Finally, one Saturday night, Joe and I bust into this house and we go right upstairs to the bedroom and we punch holes in the wall, look in all the closets, we toss the joint upside down. Nothing. We are half out of our heads for two hours trying to find something, but we can't find anything. All the time I'm thinking, wait till I get my hands on Villani, I'll wring his neck.

"Finally, I'm on my hands and knees on the wooden floor and I pick up the rug, and sure enough I find a little crack. We get the crowbar and we pull up the floor and, bang, we find forty grand. There was a gun there, watches, and some cameos and jewels, and we scoop the whole thing and scoot.

"Now, about four days later, I found out that Barney had been given a beating by the mob. I didn't know the reason until I get a call from Tameleo. 'Go to a pay phone and call me back,' he said. So I went to the phone and I called him. 'Did you go out to a house and B&E [break and enter] it a couple of days ago?' he asked.

" 'Yeah,' I said, 'I'm not going to lie to you.'

" 'You better get down here, fast,' Henry said. 'Raymond wants to see you—and don't try to hide.'

"I knew there was nothing to do but go to Providence. I couldn't figure out what the hell I'd done wrong. I called Joe Putsy and asked him to come with me. He was scared to death and wouldn't come. So I went there myself. I'm responsible to these people, and if they call, I go. I get to Raymond's office and there he is, walking back and forth, puffing that cigar like a steam engine. He's white in the face as he looks at me. 'You big fuckin' guinea—did you rob this guy?' he shouts.

"I'm scared to death now but I know better than to let him see that. 'Yeah,' I answered. 'What's the matter, did I do something wrong?'

" 'Wrong—wrong?' he shouts. Now the steam is coming out of his ears. 'That's my cousin's house—my *first* cousin's house.' He's raving like a maniac now. 'He wants the money back, he wants the watches, the cameos—'

"I looked at him. I figure once I score, I'm not going to give any money back, I don't give a shit who tells me or who it belongs to. 'I haven't got any money,' I said. 'I blew it.' Then I told him the whole story, about the tip from Villani, about how I'd asked if this Andy was connected and how I'd been told he wasn't.

" 'If you're lying, Vinnie,' Raymond said, 'you're in trouble —you go out of here in a box.'

"Now I'm scared, and that's no lie, because my life is hanging on the word of that weasel, Villani, but Raymond checks and finds out what I told him was true. Now here's the kick in the ass.

" 'You know, you think you're such a smart guy,' Raymond says.

"I said: 'What do you mean?'

" 'You found the trap, huh? You took forty grand,' he said. 'That shows how stupid you are. There was another trap underneath that one with over two hundred grand in cash. That forty grand was bait for suckers like you.' This guy had a quarter of a million in his house and I had got only forty grand and nearly lost my life to boot."

•   •   •

Patriarca's temper wasn't the only thing that impressed Teresa about the *padrone*. He learned quickly that no matter what deal Patriarca was involved with, he never lost a dime. Others might lose their shirt, but if Patriarca had an investment, his money was as safe as if it were in Fort Knox. Anyone who dared not to protect the *padrone*'s money faced swift and often violent retribution—even old Mafia dons.

"No matter what went on in New England, Raymond got a piece of the action. He always had a piece of the profits, but he never had a piece of the losses. That's the type of boss he was. I remember one time I had bought a load of heisted cigarettes from Walter Bennett, Whimpy's brother. I gave him twenty-two grand in front for the load, money I'd got from Tameleo and Patriarca. Two days after I paid Walter, he was knocked off on Patriarca's orders. He never told me what was going to happen. Now, we had the load stashed in a garage in Revere, and some nosy woman sees people going in and out of there, bringing out cigarettes. She called the FBI and they got the whole load. They didn't arrest anyone, but they got the cigarettes. You think Raymond wanted to know anything? He just wanted his twenty-two grand back. He's a partner in profits only—not losses. I paid him his money back.

"Raymond not only wanted a share of profits, but anyone who fooled around with his money was a candidate for a hit. There was one incident I remember vividly with an old Mafioso, a guy we called Don Peppino whose real name was Joe Modica. Peppino was a member of the advisory council, and he was well respected. He was pretty active, even for an old guy, but he had a son who was a real bum, a kid named Vincent who was a lawyer.

"Don Peppino had set up a company with a financier named George Kattar. They called it the American Finance Company. To set it up, they got money from Raymond and Tamelo and Angiulo about three hundred grand all told. Kattar wanted in because he liked being next to wiseguys, so he fronted it and put a lot of his own money into it, about two hundred grand. For some reason, Kattar was scared to death of Don Peppino, I think because he was an old Mafioso. Anyhow, one of the people in the company was Peppino's son. The kid was mixed up with women and gambling, and one day Patriarca said he *spent* two hundred grand of the company's money.

"One day I got a call from Don Peppino and I went to see him. 'Vinchenza,' he said, 'they wanta me to kill my kid.' He's crying, this tough old guy who got his spurs in the old days, was crying. 'I no can do it. I don't know why he donea this thing . . . he don't needa the money . . . he'sa crazy gambling, running around with thesa girls. He never coma home to his wife. But I no can killa my kid. I donna have the money, but I getta the money. They insist ona it . . . they say I gotta killa my kid. I gotta go to New York to see people. I knowa I losa face, but I can'ta help it. . . .'

"It was pathetic, but I tried to quiet him down. Then I got a call from Raymond. He was furious. 'Get that old man down here, quick,' he shouted. So I got ahold of Don Peppino and I told him: 'The *padrone*—he wants to see you in Rhode Island.'

"So I picked him up and drove him down like I always did. It was a big, big beef. I'll never forget it. Peppino walks in the office, and I stayed in the repair room, but I can see Raymond puffing that cigar, chewing the end. I've never seen him so mad. All of a sudden I hear Peppino. He slams his fist on the table. 'I demanda respect,' he shouts to Raymond.

"Raymond was shaking with anger. I can see that face twisted with fury. 'Respect? You demand *what* respect?' Raymond shouts back. 'Don't you come in this joint giving me respect when your kid robbed my eyes out blind. I don't want to hear none of that shit. How much respect did you show us when you wouldn't whack out that kid of yours?'

"The old man starts to weep now. 'Pleasa, Raymond, no tella me to killa my kid . . . I can't do it. Raymond . . . pleasa!' Raymond told him to get the hell out of the office, and I had to drive the old man back. He was like a baby. They didn't kill him or his kid, but only because Tameleo talked Raymond out of it. 'Whatever deals he's got,' he told Tameleo, 'he's your piece of business from now on. I don't want to ever see him here again.'

"That was the end of Peppino as an important mob member. He came up with the money, though. He went to Kattar and he scared the hell out of him, and Kattar raised the money for him. After that Peppino was on the shelf. He got an envelope every week and he had a small loanshark and numbers operation, but he couldn't sit with the council, and whenever he called and said he wanted to talk to Raymond he was told to forget about it—call Tameleo. That was the way Raymond was. He was a man you didn't fool around with—not for a minute."

10

Defying a Crime Boss

It wasn't long before Henry Tameleo realized that he had acquired a gold mine when he draped his protection around the young thief and let it be known in the organized underworld that he was Teresa's "patron saint." Teresa proved his value quickly with the help of an old acquaintance, Joseph (Little Beans) Palladino, the son of a well-known Boston bookmaker. Short and stocky, with an eye for a fast deal, Palladino was an ideal partner for Teresa at that stage of his climb.

"One day Joey came to me with an idea. He wanted to go into the bust-out business. He said he had a Jewish guy, we called him Billy, who was a genius at setting up a bust-out. Now, bust-outs are big business in New England. The mob makes millions off them every year, and it's hard as hell for the law to get a handle on it. Everyone has his own technique, but the way we worked it was to first get a guy to front for us who had a good credit rating and no criminal record. That's not as hard as you might think. People are greedy, especially businessmen, and if they see a way to make a fast buck, they'll grab at it. Once we had a front man, we'd put a few thousand bucks in a bank under a corporate name and lease a store or a large building. We'd always start the operation in the springtime. We'd start to buy toys or appliances a little at a time from a manufacturer and pay, say, half the bill. Then we'd go to another company and buy some goods. This way we built up a credit line. We would do it slow, buying a little from this company and a little from that, but always keeping up our payments even if we had to store most of the stuff in a back room. A few months before Christmastime, we'd send out large orders for toys or appliances to maybe thirty or forty manufacturers who we now had credit with. Maybe we'd get three or four grand worth from each company. At the same time, we'd insure the store and its contents. Now, when the toys and other stuff come in at that time of the year, the manufacturers aren't expecting any money from us until after January because of the Christmas rush and the confusion over sales. We'd sell as much as we could before the Christmas rush and then we'd hire a torch artist, a good arsonist. But before he torched the place, we'd move all the toys and appliances out the back door and sell them to a fence. All we left in the place were some broken toys and crates or some refrigerators and stoves we took from a junk pile. Then when the place burned down, we'd collect the insurance and declare bankruptcy.

"The first place we worked the bust-out in was a place called Auction City at Davis Square in Somerville [Massachusetts]. We used a cousin of Ralph Lamattina as a front for the place. At the same time, Joey and I set up a small store in Medford. When we were ready to bust the two places out, we called in Billy [Pilgrim] Tomasino. Now, Billy was an artist when it came to handling an arson. When he burned a building down, believe me, you could put what was left of the place in a teacup. He would get a fire so hot that it would melt the steel girders and everything else. I don't know what he used—he had some special stuff that he'd never tell anyone about. He charged five grand for a job, and when he was through the insurance company had to pay off because there was no way they could prove an arson. I remember Billy handled one place, Joseph's Department Store on Washington Street in Boston. It was a five-story building located just four hundred yards from the Boston fire station. By the time the Fire Department got to the fire, the place was in a teacup. They didn't find a thing.

"The Auction City job brought us about three hundred grand in insurance payoffs and money we got from selling the toys we'd taken out of the place before the fire. We sold the toys through a fence we had in Revere—Arthur's Farm. It wasn't really a farm. It was a roadside stand where the mob used to and still does push stolen goods. Everyone bought stuff from the place—cops, politicians, mob guys, everyone. The cops let it operate because Revere was in the bag.

"Tameleo made about sixty grand off the Auction City deal. I always cut him in for a slice of anything I did, and he'd cut Raymond Patriarca in. In around two years' time, Joey and me and some of his relatives handled about six big bust-outs. We took manufacturers and insurance companies for more than five million bucks. Out of each deal, Henry Tameleo got a slice, sometimes as much as a hundred grand. That was the way you did things when you worked for connected people. They got a piece of whatever you did, whatever money you made. You got their protection and a guarantee of no interference by other mob guys who might want to muscle in. Joey finally got arrested for arson on one of the bust-outs. I made forty-five grand in that deal, but I wasn't arrested. The charges against Joey were later dismissed for lack of evidence, and the insurance company had to pay off. The place was called Magee's on Revere Beach Parkway in Everett [Massachusetts].

"In 1960, I spotted an ad in the classified section of the Boston *Globe*. It looked like it could make a good bust-out. The asking price was fifty-five grand. Joe and I went to take a look at the place. It was a ramshackle building with a few acres of land around it located on Route 3A near Whitehorse Beach in Manomet, right in the heart of the Cape Cod resort area. We chiseled the owner down to forty-three grand and we got a mortgage in the name of Pat Troisi, a guy I'd known as a kid who agreed to front for us. We had a real setup.

"The whole idea behind buying and fixing this place up was to burn it down and bust it out. We had put about twelve grand into it and we insured it for over 130 grand. We made Troisi the manager and paid him about five hundred bucks a week. The plan was to burn the place down on Labor Day when the season ended. We'd made a good profit on it during the season, selling stolen booze through the bar and using it to fence hot goods to bargain hunters. One thing went wrong. We called it Chez Joey's, and I think Palladino fell in love with the idea of having a nightclub named after him. It was his baby, his nightclub, and suddenly he didn't want to bust it out.

"When Labor Day came, I decided, Joey or no Joey, I was going to burn the place down. So I got ahold of Tomasino and he gave me some of the juice he used to burn the place down. I went down to the club with the stuff one night and starting spreading it all over. I started lighting the fires and a couple of them are just getting started when who pulls up but Joey. He's almost in tears. 'Don't do it, Vinnie—please don't do it,' he yelled. The next thing I know he's running around like a madman with water and sand putting out fires as fast as I'm lighting them. Finally, I gave up. I was on probation at the time in the check-cashing arrest, and I figured I'd better get the hell out of the area before some cop spotted me and arrested me for arson."

While the bust-out had literally busted out due to Palladino's interference, Chez Joey's had potential as a base for other criminal activities.

"The nightclub was making money, but it was strictly a grind, and who needs a grind when there's easy money to be made? One day while I was sitting in the office of Chez Joey's, I noticed a lot of activity in a supermarket that was located across the street. During the summer, this place was doing one hell of a business. So I decided to take a look at the operation. I walked into the place and looked around. There weren't any bugs or burglar alarms. Then I noticed the place had a small office with a small safe. It looked like a good setup for a B&E [break and entry]. I had nothing else to do, so I kept my eye on the supermarket from Chez Joey's. I noticed that the store manager didn't go to the bank much. He'd go on Monday, Wednesday, and Friday mornings to pick up change, but he didn't go Friday night or Saturday night to drop off the weekend receipts. It was obvious they kept the money in that crackerbox safe they had.

"One Sunday night in July I called Bobby Daddieco, and the two of us hit this place. We broke in through the front door. The people who ran the market lived upstairs, but they didn't hear a sound, although I'll never know why. We went to the office, rolled the safe right out the front door, and dumped it in the back of a stationwagon we used at Chez Joey's. When we got the safe to Revere and busted it open there was fourteen grand in cash.

"A month later, I walked back into the supermarket to buy some food and looked around and there in the office was another safe almost identical to the one we'd taken. Not only that, nothing had been done to bug the place. It was unbelievable. The owner hadn't made a change. So I watched the place for a week from Chez Joey's and, sure enough, they hadn't even changed their banking routine. This time I decided to do the job myself. About two Sundays later, just before Labor Day, I broke into the place and moved the safe out myself. There was seventeen grand in it this time.

"It's funny about the way people fail to safeguard their property, to take the easy precautions that can save them money. If that supermarket had switched its banking routine or put an alarm in the place, I wouldn't have touched it.

"Almost the same thing happened to me two years later on Boylston Street in Boston. I'd spotted a fur store that looked like an easy score so I contacted Jimmy Coyne, who I knew as a kid, Joe Puzzangara, and a couple of others and we hit the place the night of the assassination of John F. Kennedy, in November 1963. We took more than three hundred grand worth of furs. I took them to Tameleo and he paid us sixty grand. He made a bundle on that deal. They were top furs. It's almost impossible to trace a fur. All you have to do is take the lining out and put a new lining in for a hundred bucks and you can sell the coat new in any store. Tameleo had a contact in New York where he unloaded furs by the ton. Anyhow, about three weeks later, we were driving down Boylston Street again and the same fur store was all stocked up again. So we went down the back alley again, broke in, and pulled out another load of furs, worth 175 grand. Tameleo gave us forty grand for that load. The owner of the fur store went bankrupt. He couldn't survive the losses. But it was his own fault. There wasn't a burglar alarm in the place both times we hit, and everything was out in the open, just asking to be stolen.

"That whole Boylston Street area was a gold mine to us. We hit dress stores, clothing stores, you name it, time and time again and they wouldn't change their internal security. In a couple of months we must have taken that area for better than a million bucks, and not one of us got busted for it. We all made out. I blew almost everything I made at the tracks. But the biggest score went to Tameleo. He made a fortune off the stuff I turned over to him."

.   .   .

Chez Joey's had, in Palladino's estimation, a great future. It was in the heart of the resort area of Cape Cod, where thousands of tourists flocked to soak up the summer sun. With the crowds was a shortage of motel and hotel space. Surveying the acreage they owned around Chez Joey's, Palladino began thinking of expansion, of using the nightclub as the heart of a complex that would include a large restaurant, a motel. Palladino was convinced that not only would such a complex draw tourists and make money legitimately, but it would draw in hundreds of suckers who could be bled dry in the dice and poker games, the loanshark racket, and the stolen property operation that he and Teresa had already set up. Palladino, however, lacked two things: the necessary funds for such an elaborate expansion and Teresa's support.

"Joey kept talking, talking—build, expand, it's a gold mine. I wasn't interested. It was a grind. I could make a bigger score in one night than that damned club could make in six months. But after a while he had me half believing that the club had potential. Then along came this shrewdie, a customer from New Jersey called Bernie. He got cozy with Joey and invited both of us to a cocktail party he was throwing at the Mayflower Hotel for some friends. He wanted us to supply the band and a couple hundred lobsters for the night—for a healthy price, of course. So we went along. It was a helluva blast. Two nights after the party he came back to the club.

" 'You guys ever think of building a motel around here?' he asked. Joey's eyes lit up like they were neon lights. He figured he had a sucker for his dream.

" 'We've thought about it,' I said, 'but we haven't got the financing for it.'

" 'Tell you what I'll do,' he said. 'If you own it, I can put up the whole motel complex and it won't cost you a quarter. You supply the land, I'll handle everything else. Then you make payments to me on what I spent.'

"Now his plan sounded terrific. We had a twenty-grand mortgage on the place. He said he had a company from Michigan that put up prefabricated motels—from rugs to silverware for the restaurant, from pillows to furniture for the motel. Then he threw in the kicker. He wanted ten grand as good faith. 'As soon as the building is halfway finished, I'll give you your ten grand back,' he said. I should have smelled a rat then, but with Joey hustling me to go along I agreed to the deal and we gave Bernie ten grand."

Construction on the motel complex was scheduled to begin

in the early fall of 1962. The weeks stretched into months, and nothing happened. Twice Teresa called Bernie and twice he was told that construction would begin within three weeks. After that when he called, Bernie was always out on business. Finally, Teresa could take no more.

"I called Joey and told him we'd been suckered. 'I don't want the motel now, Joey, all I want is our money back,' I told him. Joey said to call Bernie one more time. I did.

" 'Look,' Bernie said, 'don't worry about it. If you don't like the deal, you can have your money back and your expenses, but don't bother me. I'm a busy man.' Now, that was the worst thing he could have said to me. So I called a friend of mine from Maine. His first name was John, but I can't remember his last. The two of us hopped a plane and headed straight for Bernie's home. A maid came to the door.

" 'I'd like to see Bernie,' I told her.

" 'He's busy now,' she answered.

" 'Just tell him Big Vinnie's here and I want to see him—now,' I said.

"I heard her talk to him and then Bernie said: 'Tell him I'm not in.' That did it. I shoved the door open, pushed the maid aside, and barged in.

" 'What is this bullshit!' I shouted. 'I want my money!'

"Bernie just stood there smiling. He pulled a package from his pocket and waved it in my face. 'I have your money right here—but you're not getting a quarter,' he said. Then he added: 'Can't you understand? You've been suckered.'

"Now, this Bernie stands about six-foot-three. His wife and kids are in the room, so I asked them if they'd mind stepping outside so I could talk to Bernie in private. John goes with them. Once they're outside, I hit this guy a ton. I broke his nose and closed one of his eyes and he hit the floor like he was a piece of lead. There was blood all over the furniture. I opened his coat, took out my ten grand, and then pulled another six hundred bucks from his wallet to cover my expenses.

" 'Kid,' he mumbles, 'you're in a lot of trouble. I'm with Joe Paterno.' Now, Joe Paterno is one of the bosses in New Jersey, a *caporegime*, as Valachi would say, with the Carlo Gambino family, and he's got things locked up in parts of Newark. He was a tough guy to tangle with and he was out of my league at the time.

" 'You never told me that before,' I told Bernie. 'It don't matter now. If you was with Joe Paterno, you had no right pulling a swindle on a connected guy like me.' He tried getting up again, and I slugged him. This time I knocked him out.

"When I got back to Boston, I headed straight for the Cape and gave Joey his share of the money back. I couldn't have been there fifteen minutes before the phone rang. It was Sal Cesario, Jerry Angiulo's muscleman. 'Jerry wants to see you,' he said. 'You're in a lot of trouble.' I asked what was the matter. 'You knocked some guy around in Jersey. He's a big moneyman with Paterno.' I tried to explain to him what had happened, but Sal didn't want to hear it. 'Don't tell me, tell Jerry. He's steaming. You better get to town right away.' "

Teresa was well aware of what a meeting with Angiulo would mean. There would be a kangaroo court, and Angiulo would pass sentence without listening to any appeals. Angiulo, he knew, hated him, particularly since he had become a confidant and protégé of Tameleo. Every day that Teresa operated, every dime that he stole, caused Angiulo to lose stature in the eyes of the hoodlums he controlled in Boston. Teresa was from Boston, yet he gave Angiulo no share of his criminal proceeds, he took no orders from Angiulo, he answered only to Tameleo and, on occasion, Patriarca himself. It was a slap to his prestige as boss of Boston that Angiulo found hard to bear. Now, Teresa realized, Angiulo had the excuse he needed to eliminate Teresa, the thorn. Paterno had called Angiulo and demanded that Teresa be hit.

"I knew there would be no reasoning with Jerry. I figured now was the time to find out if lining up with Tameleo was going to pay some dividends—help me out of this jam. It was 2 A.M. but I called Tameleo and I told him the whole story. 'Look, kid,' he told me, 'your name's in the hat for what you did. New Jersey wants to whack you out and Jerry's got the contract. Don't run. Go to a motel and wait until morning. We'll talk this thing out with Raymond then.' So I called Blanche and told her I wouldn't be home that night and I checked into a motel and waited. The next morning I went to Providence and picked Tameleo up and we drove to Lancaster Avenue, where Raymond had bought a house. He was sitting down having some breakfast when we walked in.

" 'Vinnie,' he said, 'I don't think I can help you this time. You really broke the rules this time.'

" 'Wait a minute,' I said. I was sweating blood now. Without Raymond, I was dead. 'Don't you even want to hear my side of the story?' He nodded, and I told him the whole story from beginning to end. I told him I didn't know this guy Bernie was with Paterno until after I whacked him and took my money back. Then I added: 'No. 1: If this guy was with Joe Paterno, he had an obligation to check out first with you.' I hit the right note with that argument: Now *his* man had been suckered. *He'd* been made a fool of. Bernie hadn't checked with Raymond's people before he tried anything.

" 'You're right,' Raymond said. 'They had no right taking that money until they found out who they were swindling.' He took me to an outside pay phone so I could hear, and he called Angiulo. 'Jerry,' he said, 'you get that guy in Jersey on the phone and you tell him that if they harm one hair of this kid's head, there's going to be a war like they never seen. You tell them that guy is lucky he's still alive. He opens his mouth once more, I'll send Vinnie down to shoot him.' Jerry started to argue. I could see Raymond's face get chalky white like it does when he gets mad. He kind of growled into the phone. 'Do it now, Jerry,' he snapped. 'You call me back at the office when you've done it.'

"So Jerry did what he was told and Paterno shook Bernie up and down to find out the true story. Bernie had lied to Paterno. He'd said that I'd been told he was with Paterno before I slugged him, which was a lie. If I had done those things, it would have meant that I had no respect for Paterno, that I was spitting in his face. Paterno had to put me in the bag. When he found out what really happened, they gave Bernie a terrible beating. After that, Paterno and I got to be pretty good friends.

"Angiulo's attitude was typical. Instead of defending his own, he jumped the gun. He had it in for me because he didn't like my doing business with Tameleo and Patriarca. I was from Boston, but he had no control over me, and it burned him. Raymond once said: 'Vinnie, if you had half a brain, you would have went with Jerry. He'd have made you a czar. The money you made—he'd have given you four cities of your own to run. You're the kind of guy he wants.' It would never have worked, and I told Raymond. 'Jerry wants yes-men. I could never be that,' I said. Raymond just smiled."

* * *

Chez Joey's offered Teresa a home base for loansharking, gambling, and local thefts, but he hated being stuck to one location. And so when one of Tameleo's tipsters, Michael (Mickey) Napolitano of Portland, Maine, called with a location of a good score, Teresa was quick to jump at the opportunity.

"Mickey had a good setup in Maine. He'd come up with a few that had made all of us some money. Naturally he got a cut. Portland had become a regular hunting ground for a few of us, including Al Judd, Chris Mustone, and Donny Anderson. Donny was a top stickup guy who worked a lot with Billy Aggie [Agistotelcis].

"We'd go out as a team and hold up places in the outskirts of Portland, Bangor, and Lewiston. We'd knock on the door of the target and when someone answered, we'd hold them up, tie them, and take their money. If no one answered, we'd go in and ransack the place. One of the people we held up was an old greaseball woman who was a shylock in Portland. We took her for forty grand in cash. Then we hit a house owned by some people who owned a bakery. They had a fantastic coin collection. It was worth about two hundred grand. We unloaded it with a Rhode Island fence we knew as Jerry the Jew, through Tameleo. We came out of that deal with more than sixty grand and Henry got at least as much, but it was a hairy one. Chris and I went to the house and were greeted by a big growling German shepherd that wanted to tear our throats out. Chris slugged him on the head with a crowbar and killed him on the spot. We had a helluva time lugging those coins out. They must have weighed 150 pounds. Mickey had tipped us on that deal too, but the biggest deal Mickey came up with was when he made that call in early April 1963. The score was a big estate at Falmouth Forside [Maine]. It was the home of Mrs. Byron Miller. Her husband used to be the president of the Woolworth Company.

"Mickey's information was that the place was protected only by an old caretaker. He said that in the cellar was a big score of jade. That was all he knew, that and that the jade was in a big vault. So on April 5, 1963, Al, Tony, Chris, Donny, and me headed for this estate. It was really something. We grabbed the caretaker, knocked him out, and tied him up. Then we busted into the house and went into the cellar. Inside of that were seven boxes of Ming Dynasty jade. It was worth a million, two hundred thousand bucks. What a headache that jade turned out to be.

"After the hit, we brought the jade back to Boston. We had

a Chinaman from San Francisco come in and look at it. Then there was another guy from Chicago. We even had a mob attorney dickering with the insurance company to buy it back, because it was insured for eight hundred grand and if they didn't get the jade back in ninety days they'd have to pay off. We wanted three hundred grand. Finally, I called in Tameleo. At first he offered me thirty grand, and I said no dice. Then he brought George Kattar, the financier who ran the American Finance Company and other outfits for Patriarca, Tameleo, and Angiulo. I told Tameleo that for him, I'd accept just a hundred grand. He and Kattar said they'd let me know. Then one day—it was sometime in July—I spotted the FBI nosing around. They were watching my house. Two or three different cars kept going by, and I checked their cars out through a source I had at one of the police departments and found out they were FBI cars."

What Teresa didn't know was that the FBI was aware of the most intimate details of the theft through a secret and illegal electronic bug that had somehow been planted in the Providence cigarette company office of Henry Tameleo and Raymond Patriarca in 1962. For more than a year the FBI had recorded the conversations of the crime boss and his underboss. The recordings were to continue for three years—until 1965, when the FBI was forced to make public the fact that it had illegally bugged the mob's conversations not only in Rhode Island but in more than a hundred mob business offices across the nation.

On July 31, 1963, the electronic ear recorded a conversation that Tameleo had with Patriarca in the Office. It reported that Tameleo and an unnamed man had gone to Teresa's home in Somerville to inspect the jade. An FBI analysis of the conversation reported further: "Tameleo is of the opinion that if ———— will purchase the jade for seventeen thousand dollars, he will hold it for a week and tell the thieves he has an offer of twelve thousand dollars. He believes the thieves will take the offer and he could pocket the difference of five thousand dollars plus whatever small amount they give him for selling the jade." The bug reported further that eight to ten pieces of the jade could be sold immediately, but that the remainder would have to be buried for at least two years before it could be sold to collectors. Tameleo was further reported as saying he would get an additional twenty-six hundred dollars from the thieves because his contact, Mickey, had fingered the theft.

The figures quoted in the FBI transcript were later to surprise Teresa when he read them in a story in the Boston *Globe*. "I told Henry to make whatever he could on the deal, but we were talking a hundred grand, not seventeen grand, with Kattar. Maybe Henry was holding out on Patriarca. Anyhow, the whole deal fell through."

Once Teresa had spotted the FBI, he knew he had to unload the jade or wind up in jail. On August 1, 1963, FBI agents knocked at his door and asked if they could search his home. Teresa refused. He was surprised when the agents simply walked away. They had no search warrant. What Teresa didn't know was that the FBI could not obtain a search warrant because they had learned of the jade theft and its whereabouts illegally, through the electronic bug. They had to flush Teresa and the jade out of the house, and the knock on the door was a ruse to make him panic. Teresa fell for the ruse, but he didn't panic.

"When the agents walked away from the house without producing a search warrant, I couldn't figure it out. I figured they were headed for the court to get a warrant. Of course, I didn't know about the bug. I figured someone had tipped them off, but I couldn't figure out who. I knew I had to move fast. Up to the time they knocked on the door, I'd been putting the jade in my car, a box at a time whenever I saw one of the cars go by the house. Once the car was loaded, I waited for the agents' car to pass the house again, and, when it did, I took off. I didn't want them to bust me in the house with all my family there.

"I headed for Boston, and sure enough, I see another car following me. I was able to shake the tail in traffic and I stopped at a pay phone and I called Uncle Sandy. 'Sandy,' I said, 'meet me over in front of my father's grave at the cemetery. Do it right away.' It was getting dark, and I used the dark to my advantage. I shook the tail in traffic and pulled into the Holy Cross Cemetery in Malden [Massachusetts]. There was Uncle Sandy, parked right near my father's grave. I took the jade out and dumped the stuff into his car in a hurry. Now it was pitch black out and I told him what had happened. I said: 'Now, you go ahead. Make sure no one's following you. I'll take them on a wild goose chase. You dump the stuff someplace. Get it out of your car in case we get busted.'

"I took off out of the cemetery, and in minutes I had the tail back. Then they pulled me over, rousted me, and took me to the FBI headquarters. Meanwhile, although I didn't know it at the time, Uncle Sandy had picked up a tail, shaken it, and dumped the jade in an abandoned taxicab in a Boston parking lot. Then the FBI grabbed him.

"I hadn't been in the FBI's headquarters ten minutes when I saw them come in with Uncle Sandy. When they tried to question him, all he would give them was his name and address and ask for a lawyer. We were there for six or seven hours. I didn't know Uncle Sandy had dumped the stuff. I figured they'd caught him with it because they kept showing me pieces of the jade and asking me about it. I just clammed up. They had to let us go. If either of us had said a word they might have had a case.

"I thought someone had blown the whistle on us. I'd thought that all these years, until I read a story in the Boston *Globe* in 1971 about how the FBI had learned of the jade theft. Now I understand why the FBI didn't arrest or charge us with stealing that jade. They couldn't make a case with an illegal bug. They might have made a case if they'd caught us with the jade during that tail. I bet the agents that blew that one got sent to Siberia by J. Edgar Hoover. Imagine knowing where the stuff was, following us with it, knowing everything about the theft and the negotiations, and not coming up with an arrest. What a goof."

What Teresa didn't realize was that the FBI had successfully recovered the jade and at the same time protected the secrecy of the electronic bug that was providing the FBI with intelligence on mob activities. That bug was worth its weight in gold. The agents, in fact, had done their job exactly as planned.

11

Entertainers and the Mob

In the operation of a crime family, there is an orderly chain of command that must be observed. Associate members may talk to soldiers, soldiers seek rulings from captains, captains talk to *consiglieres* (advisers) or the underboss, and only the underboss talks to the crime leader. Those who deviate, those who deliberately break the chain of command and show a lack of respect for their superiors, are dealt with severely—often fatally. Such is the discipline of a crime family. But in Boston in 1963, something new and irregular had occurred. A thirty-four-year-old thief by the name of Vincent Teresa had bypassed the authority of Gennaro Angiulo, the boss of Boston, and successfully sought the protection of Angiulo's superiors, Henry Tameleo and Raymond Patriarca.

In the eyes of his underlings, Angiulo had lost face in the Bernie affair. He had been unable to carry out his decision to kill Teresa at the request of New Jersey crime figures. The turn of events was not lost on rank-and-file Boston mobsters, who had previously answered only to Angiulo or his right arm, Ilario (Larry Baiona) Zannino. Suddenly a young thief few had heard of had emerged with unprecedented power and prestige. Teresa wasn't even a made member of the secret society, yet he literally had the power of a boss as the deputy of the second most powerful criminal in New England: Tameleo. Although Teresa was required to respect the rank of Angiulo, he was answerable only to Tameleo and Patriarca. To the underworld, Teresa now represented a balance of power, a court of appeals from Angiulo's arbitrary decisions. They could now seek out Teresa for help, for financial backing in criminal enterprises and, in effect, reach for the protection of the hitherto unapproachable Tameleo.

One of the first to approach Teresa was thirty-four-year-old Richard Castucci, the owner of the Ebbtide, a Revere Beach Parkway, Massachusetts nightclub. Castucci had operated on the fringes of the mob for years. His uncle, Arthur Ventola, owner of Arthur's Farm in Revere, was one of the state's most notorious receivers of stolen goods. Castucci himself had a criminal record that included convictions for forgery as a juvenile, illegal sale of liquor, assault, promoting gambling, and larceny. How he had managed, with his wife, Edith, to obtain a license to operate the Ebbtide was no mystery to law-enforcement officials; obviously he had friends in the state liquor licensing agency.

In 1963, Castucci had run afoul of a vicious young hoodlum who was to attain notoriety in later years as New England's most terrifying paid assassin. The hoodlum was Joseph (The Animal) Barboza, a Portuguese enforcer with a violent temper.

"Richie Castucci came to me about Barboza. Barboza used to hang around in the Ebbtide, Richie's nightclub, and one night he got nasty and gave a terrible beating to Richie, Art, and Junior [Nicholas] Ventola. Richie said Barboza had promised to return the next night and kill everybody. He and his uncles were scared to death.

" 'Can you talk to him, Vinnie?' Castucci asked me.

" 'Why don't you go to Angiulo?' I asked him.

" 'Angiulo never does anything but talk,' he told me. 'He won't give me any protection. He can't control this animal.'

"I told Castucci that the only guy who could help was Tameleo. 'I'm not going to talk to Barboza on my own,' I said. 'He's crazy.'

"I knew Barboza, not too good, but I knew him by reputation. He had a vile temper. He'd kill you as soon as look at you, and there was no one who could control him. He didn't even work for the mob at the time. He was a wild-eyed independent with a small gang of thugs who worked with him, loansharking and shaking people down. It was a wonder that no one from the Boston branch of the mob had hit him yet, probably because Angiulo was scared to death of the guy. Barboza was the type who wouldn't have hesitated at going after Angiulo himself.

"I left Castucci, called Tameleo, and made an arrangement to meet him in Rhode Island. I picked him up and explained the situation to him.

" 'Henry,' I said, 'this looks like a good spot for you to step in and pick up an envelope. Castucci's making money—he's carrying a lot of cash. He'll do anything to get this Barboza off his back.'

"Henry liked the idea. He told me to drive him to Revere, where we met with Castucci and Arthur Ventola. Henry told them it would cost them if he provided protection for them from Barboza. Richie jumped at the suggestion. He said he'd pay us a grand a month and we'd get a piece of the profits of the Ebbtide if we could keep Barboza and animals like him in line. When we left the place, Henry sent me to East Boston to see Barboza. I found him in a bar.

" 'Henry Tameleo wants to see you,' I told him.

"He looked at me for a minute. He's got a crude-looking face, a head like a caveman. He looks as cruel as he is. He's only about five foot tall, but he's powerful. He was once a prize fighter. He'd gone to jail for armed robbery and then led a jail revolt and escaped. And he acted like he was a caveman. That's why everyone was scared of him. 'What does Mr. Tameleo want?' he answered.

" 'What does he want?' I said. 'He wants to see you. You want to come, fine. You don't want to come, you don't have to, but he'll send someone else to see you.'

"He smiled for the first time. 'No, I'll come,' he said. 'I've always wanted to meet Mr. Tameleo.'

"So we headed back to Revere. We were to meet Henry at 3 P.M. at the Ebbtide. Henry played him like he was a violin. He told Barboza in a diplomatic way that from now on he had to be a nice boy. If he was a nice boy, he'd get some work and make some money with the mob. If he wasn't a nice boy, he'd end up on a slab. Barboza knew where the power lay. He was in awe of Henry anyway. And he had dreams of becoming a made member—which he could never become, because he wasn't Italian.

"Barboza agreed not to bother anyone at the Ebbtide. It wasn't long after that that the word went out that the Ebbtide was a protected club. It was the best thing that ever happened to Castucci. From that point on he made nothing but money, hand over fist. All the wiseguys from New England came to the place and spent their money, and the people who liked to be near wiseguys flooded the place."

The ease with which Tameleo and Teresa had moved in on the Ebbtide gave both men ideas. They saw in Barboza an opportunity to use the fear he generated to collect money in what amounted to an old-fashioned protection racket. Barboza and his men would take all the risks. Tameleo and Teresa would reap the dividends. Nightclubs appeared to be the best target, since many of the owners operated on the fringes of the underworld themselves.

"We had a talk with Barboza. We told him that if he followed orders he could pick up a good monthly envelope for protecting nightclubs and get some backing for his loanshark business at the same time. Barboza wanted in so bad he could taste it, and he teamed up with Romeo Martin, a small-time thief and enforcer, and Ronnie [the Pig] Cassesso, who's now doing time for a murder and who became a made man. The deal we worked out was that Barboza would get 25 percent of the take from each club. Henry, Patriarca, and I also got 25 percent each.

"We sent Barboza and his animals to more than twenty nightclubs. One was the Living Room, a club on Stuart Street in Boston. Another was Alfonso's Lonely Hearts Club in Revere. All of the places were swinging joints that weren't owned by mob members. Some were owned by fringe guys, like the Living Room, which was owned by Pete [Skinny Pete] Fiumara, or the Four Corners, a nightspot owned by bookmaker Abe Sarkis. Barboza and his men would go into these places and tear the joints apart. They'd bust up a few people, break the furniture, smash the bar, and storm out. These people would come running to us to complain about Barboza, to ask for protection. We never went to them. They knew about what happened at the Ebbtide, how we protected it. We told each one of them that it would cost a grand a month to have our protection. It wasn't long before we had twenty clubs paying a grand a month to keep Barboza in line. We kept collecting that twenty grand a month until Barboza went to jail in 1966 and started blabbing to the law.

"Barboza wasn't easy to control. He respected Henry and me—I think he was afraid of Henry—but he'd do crazy things. In the time I knew him, he handled more than twenty-three murders, most of them on his own—I mean, they weren't ordered by the Office. Romeo Martin is a typical example of what I mean. This was in 1965, in July. I'd been out all day with Castucci and Romeo playing golf. Romeo was planning to leave for Florida the next day with his wife. He'd just gotten married and was going to Florida for sort of a honeymoon. After we'd played golf, I told Romeo to come over to the Ebbtide for a steak dinner and a couple of drinks. While we're talking, he said that he and Barboza, after busting up a club, had had an argument. He said he'd shaken the owner down for more money than he was supposed to and had held out on Barboza. Barboza had found out and threatened to kill him.

"I told Romeo not to worry about it, that Barboza would cool off. After all, they were supposed to be close friends. Romeo headed for home. He left his clubs with me and said he'd pick them up that night after we'd had dinner. My son Wayne still has his clubs. That night he met me at the Ebbtide and we had the dinner and a few drinks. There wasn't any trouble. Romeo said he had to leave and that he'd get the golf clubs from my car.

" 'I'm going home, Vinnie,' he said. 'I'll get my bag and I'll come back and have one more drink with you. Then I'm going to get my wife and we'll take off.' Those were the last words I ever heard out of Romeo. When he went outside, Barboza and Cassesso were waiting for him. They grabbed him, took him someplace, and pumped five slugs into him before dumping his body.

"When the cops found him, Tameleo blew his top at me. 'You knew they were mad,' he said. 'Why didn't you get ahold of Joe and stop it?'

"I shook my head. 'I didn't know they were going to knock the guy off,' I said. 'They were just having an argument at the worst. Christ, Henry, they were supposed to be friends. Who knows this animal is going to kill him?' That's how treacherous Barboza was. The slightest thing, the slightest word and he'd want to kill you.

* * *

"Nightclubs are big business for mob guys. They pick them because they like to cabaret, themselves. It gives them a place to meet, rather than, say, on a street corner. A nightclub is a great place to do business. If I hang around a club and you come in and buy me a drink, there's nothing really suspicious about your meeting me in there, not with dozens of other people all around. If you want me, you know where to find me and still get some entertainment to boot. It's also a place to go where you'll find women, loads of women, and you get a chance to be in the limelight.

"There's one thing everyone should understand about mob members. Most of them like to be in the limelight. They like to get all dressed up and go into a fancy place with a broad on their arm and show off. Ninety percent of all mob guys come from poverty. They grew up with holes in their pants, no shoes on their feet. They had rats in their room and they had to fight for a scrap of bread to eat. Now they made it. They got money, five-hundred-buck silk suits, hundred-buck shoes, ten-grand cars, and a roll of bills big enough to choke a horse. It doesn't do any good to just look at it. They want everyone to know they've made it. They like it when they walk into a club and the headwaiter comes to them and says: 'Sit down, Mr. Teresa, here's your private table.' I liked it, and I didn't grow up with holes in my pants. Most of the mob guys are big spenders and tippers, but once in a while you'll find one with short arms—like Carlo Mastrototaro."

Carlo Mastrototaro is the boss of Worcester, Massachusetts, and is considered the fourth most powerful boss in the current New England hierarchy of crime.

"Carlo is about five-foot-seven. He has jet-black dyed hair that he combs straight back. He moved into Tameleo's spot after Henry was sent to death row. He's always impeccably dressed. He's a multimillionaire, but if you were to open the trunk of his car at any time, you'd find rolls of twenty-five-cent slugs that he used in telephone booths to save money on phone calls. He has beautiful clothes, but he never went to a store to buy them—he buys from boosters [small-time street thieves]. He'd check into the best New York hotels under a phoney name so he could beat the tab—I'm not exaggerating. He'd check into a hotel under the name of Mr. Brown, with a small bag. Most of the time the bag, which was stolen, was empty. He'd stay two or three days, leave the bag in the room, and never pay the bill, and he'd run up some big tabs.

"But as cheap as he was, he was as honest as they come in the mob when you dealt with him. If you had a cent and a half coming from him, it didn't make a bit of difference if you didn't show up to collect for six months. When you got there, the money was there waiting for you. He never tried to beat anybody in the mob. If you made a deal to split fifty-fifty with him on an operation, he wouldn't try to tell you expenses were higher than expected. It was: 'Here's your 50 percent, here's my 50 percent.' But in a nightclub he was a tightwad. If he spent a hundred bucks for an evening, the waiter was lucky to get a ten-buck tip.

"Carlo was the exception to the rule. Most mob guys are generous to a fault when they hand out tips. They'll give waiters 25 or 30 percent of the total tab. Henry Tameleo was worse. He'd give as much as 50 percent. When he walked into a club, the waiters were busy throwing customers out of a booth to find him a seat.

"Now, not every club recognizes a mob guy, at least not right away. But most of these clubs operate on a thin line. A mob guy finds out they're in financial trouble, and pretty soon he makes an offer to lend the owner some money. Before the club owner realizes it, he's in hock up to his eyes and suddenly he's got a silent new partner. There are thousands of clubs all over the country that operate with mob guys as silent partners. Once that happens, the word gets around fast who owns what. Some of the biggest clubs and restaurants in Boston and Revere were owned by the mob. Take the Mayfair, a really plush nightclub that used to operate in Boston. That was owned by Larry Baiona and Rocco and Joe Beans Palladino, Sr. Giro's was owned by Joe Lombardo. Then there was The Frolics that Chickie Spar [Anthony Dellarusso] owned in Revere, and the Basin Street South that Ralphie Chong [Ralph Lamattina] and I took over in 1968 in Boston.

"When a mob guy owns a club, it's a guaranteed success— you can go to sleep on that. They draw business and broads and entertainers like flies. It's bound to make money. Don't ask me why, but people seem to want to come to a mob place. Maybe it's the excitement of mingling with mobsters. Maybe it's something else. Outside of the general public, the mob guys generate business themselves because they do other business in the club. Take the Ebbtide. It was a gold mine. I operated my loanshark business there. I set up hijacks, bought stolen goods, arranged for stolen stock deals and other deals. So did Henry and Richie Castucci. When I was there at my table, maybe forty or fifty guys would come in with their dates to see me. A guy would come to my table, sit down, have a few drinks. Maybe we'd talk fifteen or twenty minutes. Then he'd go to his own table and buy drinks and dinner for himself and his girl. He'd also pay for the drinks at my table. Now, this would go on from seven at night till two or three in the morning. So the club had a guaranteed, steady flow of customers. After a guy met with me for business, it was rare for him to get out of the club without running up a tab of, say, a hundred bucks. You multiply that by forty and you're doing four grand a night business just from people coming to see me. Others would come to see Tameleo, Castucci, and Art Ventola, and still others would just come because the Ebbtide was a swinging place to be. That's the way most mob night-spots operate. That's why they always make money.

"A lot of people came because the girls flocked to places like the Ebbtide. The girls were usually waitresses, secretaries, or clerks looking for a night of fun. They loved to be near mob people. I guess it was the thrill of danger and violence and doing something they knew was wrong. They were all young. Any girl over twenty-three was an old maid. Most of them were eighteen or nineteen years old, and they'd do anything we wanted them to. They'd draw the men like flies, the middle-aged men in their fifties who were lucky to get to their wives once in six months. Now they'd come to the club for a good time, and the first thing they ran into was some eighteen- or nineteen-year-old dressed in tight pants, wiggling her tail around, rubbing up against him. Man, he doesn't want to know anything after that. He's a setup, a target for a score. We'd get him up tight with one of those young chicks, and before you knew it, Mr. Middle Age was willing to do anything to bed that broad. We'd get him laid and take him upstairs and knock him out in a card game.

"The Ebbtide was a rock 'n' roll place. There had to be ten girls to every guy in the place, and all the girls were just dying to be recognized. They liked to walk into a place and have some mob guy say, 'Hi, Barbara,' as though they were somebody. They didn't care what you asked them to do as long as you were a mob guy who gave them a little recognition. If we wanted them to go to bed with a guy—to blow out his pipes—they'd do it without question. They couldn't care less. They didn't get money. They didn't ask for it. All they wanted was recognition. Every now and then, when one of them did you a favor, you'd give them a gift. Maybe, I'd have a load of stolen dresses upstairs. 'What size you wear, Julie?' I'd ask. Maybe she said Size 8 or 10. 'Go upstairs—tell Richie I said to give you a couple of dresses and slacks.' That was a big thing for her. Or if some creep was bothering one of them, they would come walking over and say: 'Vinnie, that guy is bothering me.' So I'd walk over to the clown and tell him: 'Julie's a friend of mine. You go off and mind your business or get out of here.' Now Julie felt very important. It was all a bunch of bullshit—all con. I couldn't have cared less if that guy killed Julie or whoever. But by keeping on the right side of her, by using a little diplomacy, I could call on her to take care of some sucker I was setting up for a score.

"Girls weren't the only people who went nutty over mob guys. Entertainers are worse. They want to be around mob people because they know the mob controls the better places. So they come in, they get cozy with you to get on your right side, and then they ask your help in getting them a spot at a place like the Mayfair or the Copacabana in New York. It was good for our business to have them. We paid them the union scales, and for the top names we paid top dollar. But a lot of them were gamblers, and they'd end up losing what they had coming in salary. Like Fats Domino. He was a helluva entertainer. He'd play at the Ebbtide maybe three times a year at twelve grand a week, and he'd end up owing us money. I remember one night he ended up not only owing us his salary, but we took his diamond cufflinks as well. We'd take him upstairs and knock him out of the box in a rigged dice game. He never knew what happened. We did the same with Lou Monte at the Chez Joey's. I think we paid him eleven grand a week. He'd wind up losing it in a crap game. I felt sorry for him. His kid had an incurable disease and he went all over the world to try to find a cure for him. Lou was a nice guy.

"Some of the entertainers used us. That used to boil me. They'd use us, move up to the top, and then ignore you. Like Jerry Vale. Jerry began playing The Frolics, a club owned by Chickie Spar. It became a regular appearance. He was great. Jerry knew all of us. We packed the place for him. But when he got well known and he was working places like the Copacabana in New York or the Ed Sullivan television show, he didn't remember anybody. I bumped into him one night at the Copa in New York City. He ignored me as though he didn't know me. I pulled him aside. I said: 'I don't want to embarrass you, now . . . but do I embarrass you by saying "Hello"?' If he'd said anything, I'd have given him a whack in the mouth. All he said was that my face slipped his mind. How could my face slip his mind? He'd seen it every day for months. That's the way it is with some of the entertainers. They use us to get started, then they shy away from us when they make it, they wipe their hands clean.

"Dean Martin was different. He came to the Mayfair at the recommendation of some of his friends from Ohio. He was just getting started, but he was a barrel of laughs whenever you saw him and he never forgot a face, never forgot to say 'Hello' to you no matter where you were. He's just a nice guy and a helluva entertainer, and everybody liked him for it.

"Jimmy Roselli was like that. He was a friend of Leo Santaniello, a made guy from Springfield who's got a record for everything from larceny and manslaughter to making book and extortion. Roselli himself had been in the can for bookmaking. Anyhow, he had friends in the Boston mob. They sent him to the Copacabana in Boston. It later became the Mayfair. At that time it was owned by Joe Beans and Rocco Palladino. Later, Larry Baiona had a piece. Roselli was a nice guy with a terrific voice. I never could understand why he didn't make it big as a singer. Maybe he didn't have the looks or the personality onstage, but he was always friendly. I remember one time later on I held a big anniversary party in 1968 for my wife's parents at my house. Santaniello brought Roselli over, and Roselli sang with the band in the back yard —all the old Italian songs the greaseballs loved to hear. He didn't want a dime. He just mingled in and enjoyed himself.

"The only guy the Boston mob couldn't stand was Frank Sinatra. Let me tell you a story about him. This was before he made the big time again with that picture, *From Here to Eternity*. He was begging for spots to sing at, at the time. The Palladinos let him do his stuff at the Copa in Boston, and they paid him a good buck for it. He did all right, not sensational, but all right. Then he went to Joe Beans and asked if he could borrow some money. He told Joe that he could deduct what he borrowed the next time he came in to play the club. He said he'd be back to play the club in about a month after the movie came out. Joe was glad to help out. Then the picture came out, and it was a smash hit, Sinatra paid Joe back what he owed him, but he never came back to play the club like he promised, because he and Joe had a falling out.

"Sinatra has a helluva lot of talent, but he's got no class. He picks his spots to be a tough guy with people. I've been in his company in Florida two or three times, and I don't like the man. It's my personal opinion, and I'm entitled to it. He was close to Sam Giancana, the boss of Chicago. Sinatra's always talking about the mob guys he knows. Who gives a damn, especially if you're a mob guy yourself? He's very boisterous, loud, but I know mob guys who idolize him, like Butch [Frank] Miceli. He used to stick close to Sinatra like glue, and he carried a phone book around with Sinatra's private number on every page.

"Now Sinatra's a big man. Don't get me wrong, he's earned his reputation as an entertainer. He's a real showman onstage. But he's got a lot of mob friends as well as friends in all walks of life. I don't begrudge him a thing, and one thing, he doesn't forget his friends, either. But I get a big kick out of these phoney politicians that gravitate around him like flies. Look at Spiro Agnew, or before they knew better, President John F. Kennedy and his brother Bobby. They used him to help them raise money. Then they turn around and say they're great fighters against corruption. They criticize other people for being with mob guys. They're hypocrites. They don't criticize Sinatra for the people he knows.

"I'll give that to Sinatra. You'll never hear him badmouth Sam Giancana or someone else, although they're mob guys. The only thing I don't like is the way he treated Joe Beans Palladino. He should have played Joe's club after he made it big.

12

Piranha, Inc.

Teresa's power as Tameleo's right arm was soon extended to the heart of Boston, Angiulo's exclusive domain, through a finance-company operation.

"We began with the old American Finance Company on Hanover Street in Boston, the one that Don Peppino's son spent the money from. That outfit had been set up to lend money to mob people. If you had had a Triple-A credit rating but weren't a friend of the mob, you couldn't have got a nickel's worth of loans. American Finance loaned money to mob people so that they'd have records to show busybody tax people who wondered where their money came from.

"The front for American was George T. Kattar. He's a multi-millionaire real estate speculator who has land interests in areas from Canada to Sicily. The guy is a genius, but he's got one fault: He loves being around mob guys. He got his start with Don Peppino when the old Mafioso was the boss of the Lowell-Lawrence area of Massachusetts. Kattar used to hustle numbers and horses for Don Peppino. He was a real street operator, rough-and-tumble, born and raised in the tough life of the streets. But he made most of his money legitimately. He got his big start in a Syrian restaurant in Lawrence, wound up taking it over, and then, through some smart manipulations, took over a finance company called Community Loan, Inc. He parlayed that into motels, real estate, trucking companies, resorts, and finance companies all over New England. But even though he was rich on his own, he had a thing about dealing with mob guys. He was in awe of Don Peppino, a real-life, old-country Mafioso.

"One day, Kattar went to Don Peppino and told him he wanted to open up a finance company in Boston that would deal with mob people. That's how they formed American Finance. Don Peppino and Kattar went to Patriarca, got permission to set it up, and then started lending money out to mob guys. Kattar put up two hundred grand, and Patriarca, Tameleo, and Angiulo put up another three hundred grand to finance the operation.

"The mob thought they were using Kattar, but the truth of the matter is that Kattar was using the mob. He made ten times what the mob made through this operation. He had half a dozen other finance companies, and the word went that you paid Kattar on time or you had problems with the mob. He was shrewd that way, always thinking. Kattar had friends in high places outside the mob. He had law-enforcement friends in Maine, and he could get anything he wanted there. In New Hampshire, he and the State Commissioner of Public Safety, Robert Rhodes, were close friends. Rhodes sold some real estate for Kattar one time. I met him at Kattar's home. So Kattar had it both ways. He had the mob helping him on one end, and politicians on the other. Money talks, and he knew how to make it shout with the right people.

"American folded after Don Peppino's son stole the money from it, but they kept the finance license and created two new companies. The first was called Pan American, which, like American, loaned mainly to the mob, to finance their loan-shark rackets or hijacks or whatever. Pan American started with three hundred grand put up by Kattar and the mob. George put his brother, Pete, in as president, and George himself was treasurer, although he never kept an office at Pan American. Tameleo and Patriarca sent me in to supervise, to watch their money and to act as a collection agent for Kattar when he had a tough time collecting some loans.

"After Pan American got started, Pete Kattar raised 175 grand on his own to set up Piranha, Inc. Piranha was designed to milk small people outside the mob with high-interest loans that then were legal under state laws—as high as 20 percent. For getting Patriarca's permission to operate in Boston, where Angiulo was boss, Kattar had to pay six hundred bucks a week to Tameleo, who picked up an envelope every week. I got a salary of 250 bucks, which was meant to give me a legitimate income for the tax boys to look at. Don Peppino got two hundred bucks a week at Tameleo's insistence. Don Peppino was on a shelf after the fight with Patriarca and he owed his life to Tameleo, but Tameleo knew that the old guy had a hex on Kattar and that Kattar wouldn't dare chisel while Don Peppino was around. I was at Piranha, too, to keep an eye on everybody and to prevent Angiulo or any of his crowd from shaking down the Kattars while they were operating in Boston.

"Piranha, Inc., was given its name by Pete Kattar. Like his brother, he was a nut about the mob. He used to read dozens of crime magazines and tales about the mob. He was Lebanese, but he dreamed of being a made man in the mob. He used to dress up like Bat Masterson, the television character, complete with derby and cane, and he loved to pack a gun. He came to me one day about setting up Piranha. 'Let's name this company Piranha, like the man-eating fish,' he said. 'We want to be known as a real tough outfit.'

"After he set up the company he bought two live piranhas from a friend in Lawrence. He paid a hundred bucks each for them. Now, that's a lot of money for two lousy fish, but he bought them and put them in a huge tank near a couch in his office. He called them Gladys and Pete.

"Don Peppino was in charge of the fish. That was his biggest job in the office. He'd come in every morning early, sit down, and just draw pictures at his desk. I'd go into his office now and then to brighten his life with a little gin rummy. At about 10 A.M., he'd come out, get the goldfish that the secretary bought each day for Gladys and Pete, and go into Kattar's office to feed the piranhas. It was a regular ritual. I used to laugh like hell watching him.

" 'Herea Pete . . . herea Pete . . . coma ova for your breakfast now,' he'd say. One day he stuck his finger in the tank too far and the fish bit him. 'You sonabitch, Pete,' he shouted. 'You gotta no respect. Soma day I putta you in the frying pan and eatta you up.'

"We used to use the piranhas to scare some of the people who owed us money. We'd tell them we'd stick their arms in the tanks with the fish if they didn't pay on time. Then we'd throw in a few goldfish or a piece of meat, and they'd watch shaking as those fish chewed up everything in sight. On one occasion, we stuck one guy's hand in the tank: Anthony Talia of East Boston. Talia owed us a lot of money. He was a compulsive gambler and liar. He'd come to make a hundred-buck payment and wind up borrowing three hundred bucks more. We'd give him a slap in the face and once in a while Joe Barboza would beat the hell out of him. But he kept lying and paying late. One day we got fed up with his stories and we stuck his hand in the tank. Those crazy little fish were chewing the hell out of his fingers before we pulled his hand out.

"The story about the piranhas and Talia went through the street people like wildfire. We never had trouble collecting bills for a long time after that. And then one weekend, it was a holiday weekend, we forgot to feed the fish, and Pete ate Gladys. It was a Tuesday when we came in, and there was nothing left of Gladys but bones. He was a vicious little bastard, that Pete. And then one day someone killed Pete—stuck a pencil through him. It probably was Pete Kattar. He probably had a girl in his office, told her he was stabbing Al Capone, and stuck the pencil in poor Pete.

"Kattar used to get high in the office every now and then and shoot holes in the garbage pails with his gun. The next morning, Don Peppino would come storming into my office and ask: 'Vinchenza—you shoota up the joint?' I'd look at him real serious and speak in broken English. 'Me, Don Peppino —I no doa thingsa like that.' Don Peppino would frown at me. 'How coma you speka the broken English . . . you borna over here . . . you maka fun of me . . . you showa no respect.'

"Don Peppino was about five-foot-four, a real old Mustache Pete who'd come from the same small Sicilian mountain town of Monreale that my grandfather was born in. He's in his late seventies and he's still got all his own teeth, his full head of steel-gray hair, there's not an ounce of fat on him, and he's eaten a plate of macaroni every day of his life. In one form or another, he's the funniest man I ever met in my life. But years ago he was one of the toughest Mafioso in Massachusetts. In the old days, he was an enforcer, and he used to ride with my grandfather during Prohibition. They'd go crashing through walls with a truck to get at some booze. I teased him one day about it. I said I heard my grandfather was a bum. He blew his top. 'Donta you ever talka thata way abouta your grandfather,' he said. 'You never be the mana thata he was.' I told him I was only kidding. 'Don't you kidda thata way witha me . . . I no lika that stuff.'' He meant it. He could be very tough, very brutal when he had to be. He wasn't afraid of anyone, not even Patriarca.

"One day he had an argument with Barboza. Now, remember Barboza was a stone killer with a terrible temper. He was in the office and he'd said something that made Don Peppino mad. Don Peppino whirled around on him and snapped: 'Hey . . . you . . . an-i-mal . . . you nigger. You don'ta foola with me . . . youa punk. I throw you outta the goddamn window as big as you are. You showa respect whena you coma in here.' Barboza was stunned. He just looked at Don Peppino and said meekly: 'Yes Joe, whatever you say, Joe.' Then he walked out. Barboza wanted no trouble with Don Peppino. He knew the old don could turn an army loose on him if he got too smart.

"Respect was the one thing Don Peppino was always harping about. All the old Mafioso demanded that. It was part of their life. He demanded and got respect from Tameleo and Patriarca even after he got in trouble. In turn, he showed them respect. Respect means everything in the world to him, even from his dog, a little schnauzer called Buster. Every time I'd go to Don Peppino's house on Doonan Street in Medford, the dog used to jump up and bark. Don Peppino would get mad. He'd say: 'Buster . . . sitta down Buster, be gooda boy otherwise I'ma gonna blowa your brains out.' Buster would keep jumping and barking. 'You gotta no respect, Buster,' he'd shout. Then he'd look at me and talk about the dog. 'Vinchenza,' he'd say. 'Looka this dog. He's a jumpa here . . . he's a jumpa there . . . he'sa no do whata I tella him.' Then he'd wag his finger at Buster and shout: 'Soma day, Buster . . . I'ma gonna killa you, you son-of-a-bitch . . . I blowa your brains out.' One day I came back to the house, and sure enough, Buster was gone. I said, 'Don Peppino . . . what happened to Buster?' He said: 'I gotta rid of him . . . he hadda no respect.' Then he patted a new dog he'd gotten. He said to the dog, 'Sitta down.' The dog sat down. 'See?' he said. 'Thatsa nice dog . . . he gotta the respect.'

"Old and funny as he was, Don Peppino was as shrewd as they came, and he took care of his family no matter what they did. He owned his own little compound in Medford. He bought each of his two sons a house and his daughter a house, all on Doonan Street. Each house was worth at least eighty grand. His own house was worth a hundred grand. Every week he'd shop for the whole compound. He and Josephine, his wife, lived alone in their twelve-room house. Every room had a color television set. But Don Peppino and Josephine could always be found rocking in beach chairs in the kitchen, watching a cowboy show on a black-and-white portable.

"Don Peppino also had a deep fear of the Internal Revenue Service. He was always afraid that tax agents would catch him on back taxes and deport him. Because of that fear he used to drive around in an old 1952 Chrysler. I used to tell him to get rid of the old bomb. He'd look at me. 'Mr. Biga Shot,' he'd say. 'You thinka I'ma bigga shot lika you. You gotta the Cadillac . . . you gotta the yachit witha your bigga captain witha the hatta on. Soma day you goa to jail cause you bigga shot. I lika be nicca and quiet. I no wanta the Internal Revenue to picka me up and deporta me.' That was Don Peppino. He was a tough old nut, but everyone respected him and he handled a lot of assignments for the mob. I always liked that old guy. I really did.

"George Kattar and I got along pretty good in the finance company operation but I don't think he ever really trusted me. He figured I was pocketing money from the operation. I did, sometimes, but never money that was due Tameleo or Patriarca. There were times that I'd figure out how to make a few extra grand when I needed it from some of George's clients. One of those times happened in 1964, just before we closed the place up.

"George used to send me out to make collections for him. I'd get five hundred bucks, a grand, sometimes two grand for collections, depending on how big they were. Tameleo gave me the okay to handle George's problems because the mob was getting a cut of some of his operations. I'd go, apply a little persuasive muscle, and the clients would pay their debts. They got the message I was with the mob and representing Kattar, and they'd pay up without trouble. I never had to beat anyone up. All I did was shake them down with threats.

"One guy that owed Kattar a bundle, seventy-five grand, was a character named Willie, a salvage operator from Sayreville, New Jersey. George came to me and said: 'This guy isn't paying. He sent me a couple of bad checks. Why don't you go talk to him and see what you can do?'

"The next day I hopped a plane to New Jersey. George sent

along an Arab kid we called Black Sam to make sure that I didn't run off with all his loot. He was always worried about me because he knew how I gambled at the track. When we arrived in New Jersey, I hired a car and drove to this big salvage company that this Willie owned. I introduced myself. Now this Willie is a big, husky guy, real rugged, but not a bad guy.

" 'What are you going to do about this money you owe?' I asked.

"Willie was very upset. Particularly because I slapped him in the mouth. 'Mr. Teresa,' he said, 'I can't help it. Business has slacked off. I'm sorry I sent the bum checks.' Then he told me he had a bundle of money tied up in a racquet and country club on Long Island. He showed me pictures of it. It was a beautiful place, all white, with big tennis courts and swimming pools and a plush interior. It had an exclusive membership that included socialites and politicians and businessmen.

" 'I own this club,' he said, 'but I've got a partner. I want to sell it, but he doesn't. I'm a little scared of him.'

" 'Who is this guy?' I said.

" 'John Franzese,' he said. 'They call him Sonny. He's supposed to be a wiseguy with the Brooklyn mob.'

"Franzese didn't mean a thing to me then. I'd never heard of him, and to me he was nothing but some punk muscle from Long Island. What the hell did I know? I'd never been to Long Island. I didn't know he was supposed to be a *capo* in the Joe Colombo family—a real hard-nut killer with a stable of guns from Brooklyn to Montauk Point.

" 'Look,' Willie said. 'You get this guy off my back. I got a chance to sell this place for some serious money. You handle him—he forced me into signing some papers—and I'll sell it, pay George right off, and cut you in for a piece of the action.'

"This sounded great to me. I figured I'd go to Long Island, get ahold of this Franzese, beat him over the head with a bat, and make myself a good piece of change. So I agreed. But I made Willie give me thirty grand. I told him twenty-five grand was for Kattar and five grand was for me, for my time. I'd take the five grand to keep Kattar off his back until he sold the club and I straightened this Franzese out. So I headed back to Rhode Island for a talk with Tameleo. I explained the whole deal to him. It sounded terrific until I told him who Willie was partners with.

" 'Who is this half-assed wiseguy you're talking about?' Tameleo said.

" 'He's some clown named Sonny Franzese,' I answered.

"I thought Tameleo was going to drop dead on the spot. 'Franzese!' he said. 'You crazy guinea. You go after that guy, you'll look like Swiss cheese in ten minutes. He's one of the biggest hitmen on the East Coast. You'll have a war on your hands you go after him.'

"I said: 'I never heard of him.'

"Tameleo looked at me, shaking his head. 'Well, he never heard of you . . . so you're even. Now, you go see Franzese and tell him what this Willie wanted to do. You tell him a straight story. He's one of us, so you have to tell him the truth.' That's what I did. I made an appointment to meet Franzese, and told him the whole story at the Copacabana over dinner and drinks. I explained what happened, that I'd made a mistake. Sonny thanked me, and after that we became good friends. But poor Willie. What a beating he got from Sonny's boys from Brooklyn for trying to pull out of a deal and for owing Kattar all that money.

"The whole Pan American-Piranha deal folded a short time later because of Pete Kattar. Like I said before, he was sort of a nut. He was lending money to everyone and his brother, cabbies who couldn't begin to pay what he lent them, and the operation was starting to lose money.

"I was mad because money was going out and nothing was coming in for Tameleo and Patriarca. Kattar kept accusing me of making collections and pocketing the money. Then one day he sent this junkie, a pill popper named Paul Christie, over to see me and shake me down at the Ebbtide with a gun. Christie wasn't a bad kid, a little crazy because of the pills, but not a bad kid. He told me what Kattar wanted him to do—to shake me up with a gun.

"I talked to him calmly, took the gun from him, and told him to go back to Pete. 'Tell Pete that when I see him, I'm going to throw him off the top floor of the building. Tell him that. He's a dead man.' Then I called Tameleo and told him what happened. He blew his top. He wanted to kill Christie, but I talked him out of that. Then he called Pete and told him he had one day to close up the two companies and get out of Boston or he'd be dead. That night George Kattar came down to the Ebbtide to try and straighten things out. He was very upset. Henry was there, but he wasn't listening to Kattar.

" 'You tell that brother of yours he's lucky to be alive,' Henry said. 'If he isn't out of business by tomorrow, I'll send a couple of animals after him to finish him off.'

"That was the end of Pan American and Piranha, Inc."

13

Hijackers and 10 Percenters

In the back alleys of Boston, everybody has a sure-fire, get-rich-quick scheme. They're hatched in smoke-filled bars and in mob-owned nightclubs, over cups of espresso in darkened social clubs, and in the back rooms of dirty-book stores. They rarely get beyond the talking stage, and those that do generally fail. A few, a very few, result in enormous profits for organized crime.

To Teresa's table at the Ebbtide came an endless parade of petty thieves and loanshark debtors bubbling with ideas designed to free them of their mounting debts. Teresa often smiled as the earnest schemes unfolded. But unlike many mob people who brushed aside the ideas of small-time thieves, Teresa listened carefully. Listening cost him nothing, and, on occasion, an idea or a "hot tip" or an inadvertent disclosure was converted into action and cash.

"One night this guy comes to see me at the Ebbtide. He's in deep to the loansharks, and he's paying off his debts by setting up thefts where he worked, the Gillette Safety Razor Company warehouse in Boston. Now, it isn't known to a lot of straight people, but razor blades are a big mob racket. They make millions for us. We steal them by the thousands and sell them to drugstores, supermarkets, and other outlets across the country. No one asks questions when you're selling them by the case at a big discount. The store owners don't want to know. They just want to make a quick buck like everyone else. I think that's one reason why it's almost impossible to kill the mob. They grow and thrive because they use the greed of the average guy, the businessman in particular. Everyone's looking to save and make a buck that the government doesn't know about. Razor blades was just one of hundreds of stolen goods we peddled to so-called legitimate businessmen.

"This guy working inside Gillette, we called him a '10 percenter' because we gave him 10 percent of whatever he helped us steal and marked that much off his loanshark bill. Every week, and sometimes more than once a week, this guy would set aside ten or twelve cases of razor blades for us to pick up with a truck. We'd just drive up to the platform, load up the truck as though we were picking up an order, and drive off. Now, each case contained thousands of razor blades. They came ten blades to a package, and each package sold in the drugstores and supermarkets for about $1.95 a package. On a package of razor blades, those stores might be making thirty or forty cents at most. We'd sell them that same package for fifty cents, so they could make $1.40 on each package if they wanted to. We had a regular list of drugstores that would take all the blades we could come up with as fast as we could get them.

"One night the 10 percenter came to me at the Ebbtide and said he wouldn't be able to set up any heists for a while. When I asked why not, he said that Gillette was switching from one type of blade to another, and that it would be a few weeks before large enough stocks of the new blades would be available so that heists could be arranged without anyone noticing what was going on. I asked the guy what happened to the stocks of old blades they had in the warehouse. He said they had been shipped to a salvage outfit in Boston Harbor to be dumped at sea from a barge. At least two truckloads of blades had been sent to this salvage company.

"I figured Gillette should have its head examined for throwing away merchandise like that. I mean, I had a ready market for those loads. So I got the name of the outfit, and the next day I went to see the owner. He had the blades all loaded on the barge and ready to go. 'What are you going to do with all the blades?' I asked. He shrugged. 'We've been paid to dump them at sea,' he answered. After a little discussion over the situation, we agreed on a deal. I guaranteed him that Gillette would never know what happened. He'd get paid by Gillette for dumping them, and we'd pay him a half a cent a blade. There were millions of blades. We sold the blades for 2½ cents each. My share alone came to twenty grand on the two truckloads, and at least three other guys were involved and got almost as much out of it as I did. We packaged the blades in new boxes and shipped them to Philadelphia, where we unloaded them through Jack Mace. He's New York City's biggest fence. There isn't anything he can't sell for you, from diamonds and furs to securities and razor blades. The guy is incredible. He's worth millions, and mobs from all over the country use him to unload stolen goods.

"The razor-blade operation was a helluva good score, and we would never have pulled it off if that kid hadn't owed me money and come in to tell me what was happening at Gillette. That company must have taken a real bath in Philadelphia. Their salesmen must have gone crazy trying to figure out why all the stores had so many of the old blades in stock to sell at discounts when the new blades hit the market.

"We had a similar operation going at the Polaroid Camera Company when it was located on Atlantic Avenue in Boston. We had a black man working at the warehouse who was in hock to us up to his eyeteeth. He paid up his bills by setting up whole skids filled with Polaroid film on a warehouse platform. Now, each skid—it's called a skidrow—contains a hundred cases of film. The skid is used because it can be picked up with a blade truck and carried to a truck that's used to transport the film all over the country. One skid alone is worth fifty grand or more, now. It contained sixteen thousand or seventeen thousand small packages of film, and each one of those sold for three bucks in the stores. We could sell skid loads for twenty-five to thirty grand all day to fences.

"The film was the hottest product the mob could lay its hands on. Like razor blades, there's no way to trace film, and there were businessmen standing in line waiting to buy our loads at half price or less. The company knew they were being taken. Security at Atlantic Avenue was terrible. We'd just drive up with a blade truck, lift off a skid, and put it in one of our trucks and drive off without anyone saying a word. Finally, Polaroid moved to a new location, on Route 128. Security was murder there, and we couldn't pick up skid loads the way we had before. So we turned to a new method. We had our 10 percenter tell us when a truckload of film was moving out of the plant and what route it was taking. Then we'd hijack the truck on the highway and take the stuff down to Arthur's Farm in Revere. Each truckload would have at least three skids of film on it. In twenty-four hours, Arthur's Farm would have shelves filled with film selling at a discount. We used Arthur's to unload a lot of our razor blades too.

"Hijacking is big business for the mob. Most of the hijack loads, whether it's cigarettes, liquor, furs, appliances, or food, are shipped by the mob to discount stores they own or have connections with. That's why it's almost impossible to trace down a hijacked load. The stuff has a ready market waiting for it, and in a matter of hours it's distributed.

"Sometimes your hijacks get fouled up. I remember one morning—it was seven in the morning—when a guy called Fat Mike came to my house banging on my door. He and Bobby Cardillo had spotted a load of liquor, and the driver was gone. So I shook the sleep from my head, threw some cold water on my face, climbed into my clothes, and went with Fat Mike. Now it's broad daylight. We're on Highland Avenue in Somerville, and there is this big red trailer truck sitting on the roadside. I can see a cop standing on the corner, directing traffic. So I put a cap on my head, dangled a cigarette in my mouth, nodded to the cop, and climbed into the cab to start the truck. Fat Mike jumped in the cab with me. I waved at the cop as I threw the truck into gear and drove off.

"Ahead of me, Bobby Cardillo was driving a car. He was leading me to a warehouse in Everett where we could unload the truck. So I followed Bobby through the 8 A.M. traffic. All I could think of was that the driver would come out of his house and miss this load, spring the alarm, and have every cop in Massachusetts looking for me while I'm tied up in rush-hour traffic. Finally, we arrived at the warehouse. I backed the truck in and we broke the rear-door seal to get at the load. When I looked in, I wanted to die. I wanted to kill Fat Mike and Cardillo right on the spot. We didn't have a load of liquor. We had a load of bread. We just left the bread there.

"That wasn't the only time things went wrong on a hijack.

Cardillo and me hijacked a load of liquor we had set up through a 10 percenter. He was a driver, a black man. He said he had a load of high-class booze from Canada on his truck that he was supposed to deliver down South. He said he'd park the truck at a particular street corner and while he went in to eat, we were to roll off with the truck. Now, a load like this is worth fifty-five to sixty grand. We paid him his 10 percent and everything came off without a hitch until we opened the rear door of the truck at a warehouse we had rented in Pembroke [Massachusetts]. It was all good Canadian liquor, all right. It looked like a helluva score until we noticed the tax stamps on the bottles. They were all Virginia tax stamps. That meant we couldn't sell it in the bottles in Massachusetts. We had a helluva time unloading the stuff. We had to sell it five, ten bottles at a time to different bars and nightclubs that poured the stuff into empty bottles with the right tax stamps on it. We made only thirty-five grand on the deal.

"Hijacking is big business wherever you go in the country. In New England, though, we almost never used guns. It's too dangerous. People can get hurt. We concentrate on the 10 percenters. Most of the drivers and a lot of the warehousemen are gamblers. They lose their salaries at mob card and dice games, and the games are usually rigged. They get in a hole, and they start borrowing from the loansharks. Then you have them. They can never get even, never pay off all they owe, because the juice mounts up. That's when you start the squeeze. They have a choice. Broken legs or arms, a threat against the family, or provide us with information on truckloads of goods they're hauling. We promise to protect them from arrest. We arrange for them to park the truck at a certain spot and steal the load while the driver is eating, or we arrange to stop him on the highway, tie him up, and leave him in the empty truck when we've finished unloading it. When the cops find him, he gives them a phoney story about being held up and describes three or four guys dressed in stocking masks or something like that so he can't describe faces. The technique is used all over the country, not just New England. Most so-called hijacks with guns never happened that way. It was all set up before by the mob.

"The mob itself almost never handles the actual hijack. Only in my early days as a young thief did I get involved. When I was operating out of the Ebbtide, I never handled such things direct. No mob guy does. I'd get a tip from one of my 10 percenters or a loanshark I was providing money to and then I'd call in some fringe punks who I knew were reliable and usually owed me money. I'd give them all the particulars, and they'd make arrangements with the 10 percenter. He'd set up the heist, and the fringe guys would pay him his share. Naturally, the 10 percenter would give the money that he owed to me or some other loanshark. Sometimes, it would amount to all he had coming from the deal. Then the truck would be heisted and the guys I'd sent out to handle the score would bring the merchandise to me to unload. They'd get their cut, but I'd get the lion's share. Naturally, Tameleo and Patriarca got a piece of whatever I made.

"Cigarettes were a popular item. They still are. They'll always be a hot product as long as the states keep raising the ante on cigarette taxes. I could get rid of a truckload of cigarettes in a matter of hours. I'd give the thieves seventy-five cents a carton and double my money selling it to fences or discount stores in Boston and Revere and Providence. The discount store owners were greedier than the mob. They'd buy all you could get them, no questions asked, whether it was liquor, men's and women's clothing, furs, television sets, appliances, or shoes. I could have sold ten trailerloads of goods a day if I'd had them available, particularly around the Christmas holidays. These so-called honest businessmen would just put the goods on the counter and sell them at discounts to shoppers who came in looking for what they thought was a legitimate deal.

"One of my best outlets for really fine goods like furs, coats, and high-class clothing and diamonds was a Providence fence known as Alfredo [The Blind Pig] Rossi. He was a bald-headed man, about five-foot-five, on the heavy side, and blind as a bat—legally blind. He idolized Tameleo and Patriarca and they protected him. Everyone in the mob was ordered to deal squarely with him or else. He was an amazing character. He sold his hot clothes from the cellar of his home in Providence. When you went into the cellar there were racks of clothes and furs and coats the length of the house. Each one had a price tag on it. A 250-buck suit might sell for sixty-five bucks; a full-length mink coat worth three grand would go for eight hundred bucks; mink jackets sold for two hundred bucks, and stoles went for seventy-five bucks. Now, you'd think a blind guy like this could be taken advantage of by people who were buying his stuff. Not on your life. You'd bring a suit, a coat, or a sweater to him, he'd feel it and tell you exactly what price was on the tag. When a mob guy would bring him a hot coat to sell, he'd feel it, blow on the fur a little bit, and tell you to the penny what it was worth. With diamonds, of course, it was different. He couldn't tell the color, so you had to tell him about that. If you lied, Tameleo would have had you whacked out in a minute. But you'd hand Alfredo the diamond, he'd hold it for a second, and tell you within a point how many karats it weighed. But the thing that bugged me the most about him was the way he could tell the difference between the denominations of bills. I still don't understand how he did it. If I handed him a ten-buck bill and said it was a twenty, he'd say: 'Come on, Vinnie, don't kid around . . . this is a ten-buck bill.' All the time he was feeling the edges, where the numbers were. It was uncanny. His place was known everywhere. Cops, judges, politicians and just plain Joes would come in to buy stuff. They knew he handled only high-class merchandise, and no one asked questions.

"Alfredo's was my best outlet for quality goods, but for appliances and television sets and other stuff, we had another place where we could unload stuff by the truckload. We'd sell color television consoles, fifty, a hundred at a time for 120 to 150 bucks each. Portable sets went for about seventy-five bucks, and black-and-white sets brought about thirty bucks. The place was that roadside stand I mentioned earlier: Arthur's Farm."

14

Athletes, Corrupt Cops—
and the Mob

Arthur's Farm was a ramshackle roadside stand located in the thriving, suburban community of Revere, Massachusetts. Owned and operated by convicted fence Arthur Ventola and his brother, Nicholas (Junior) Ventola, it has served as a beehive of mob activity and a protected center for mob conferences as well as a dumping ground for stolen goods. For more than two decades it has survived raids by state police and federal agents, yet rarely has it been bothered by police of Revere. There was a reason.

"Revere was the mob's town. It probably still is. Nothing seems to really change in New England, only the faces. Years ago, Revere was owned lock, stock, and barrel by a Jewish guy known as Lou Fox. He was known to the public as a big real estate speculator and a multimillionaire philanthropist. Fox was really the Meyer Lansky of Massachusetts. He was very close to Lansky and to Joe Linsey. They were all bootleggers together in the old days. For fifteen years up to 1962, he had that town tied up in knots. Nobody could make book or loanshark or run any racket in Revere without first coming to Lou Fox for permission. The city was his to do with as he wanted. If you didn't have permission to operate, you got a visit from the cops or from some local muscle. His bag man was Flungo [Salvatore De Angelis], and if you were a mob guy and wanted to operate in Revere, you got ahold of

Flungo. We had a right to operate there, but as a courtesy you went through Lou Fox. You couldn't go in there and say, 'Well, he's a Jew, to hell with him.' You went through him and Flungo. You had to pay Flungo so much a month or so much a week. The fee was usually a couple of hundred a month, according to how many phones for betting you had. If you had five phones to pick up bets with, it could cost as high as a grand a month. In return for that money, you had a guarantee of police protection. It was an absolute guarantee. If the feds or state or other cops got nosy, you got a call about what they were up to from the Revere cops. Fox had the whole town in the bag. All the key cops and officials were on his pad. There was one rule you had to live by, though. You couldn't pull any jobs—robberies, burglaries, things like that —in Revere. That was the deal. The cops could show a good record fighting crime in the streets. Meanwhile, the mob was stealing the streets. More loansharks, mob nightclubs, fence operations, and meetings went on in Revere than any other community I know of.

"Fox wasn't a member of Patriarca's mob, but he was sort of a partner. He cut Patriarca in on the profits, and Patriarca guaranteed that no mob guy would try to muscle in on Lou. I remember a couple of Jewish hoods tried to muscle in on Fox. One of them was supposed to be connected with Lou Grieco, who was a made member of the Patriarca mob. Fox got the word back to Patriarca, and it wasn't long before both of these Jews were killed. One of them was dumped on Grieco's lawn as a message.

"Fox was really a nice guy. He was medium in height, always well dressed, and always a gentleman. He had an office on Shirley Avenue in Revere where he ran an insurance company. His right arm was a man named Marsie [Morris] Lynch. He took care of things when Lou was out of town. It was because of Lou and Marsie that the mob had complete protection all over town. Then both of them died, and Patriarca took over.

"The place that drew the most attention was Arthur's Farm. It wasn't really a farm. It was a vegetable stand that sold everything from tomatoes to television sets retail. It was the general hangout of the mob. Henry Tameleo, Patriarca, me, Maxie Baer [Anthony Catoldo], a whole raft of the mob members used to hang out in the place. It was a tumble-down old food stand, but everything you could imagine was sold there. For Christ sakes, Arthur used to do a grand to two grand in business a day there and then plead poverty when he'd get busted! A lot of the cops not only from Revere but from other towns and Boston used to come in and do their shopping. I'll bet most of the cops in a hundred-square-mile area got their television sets from Arthur's Farm, and every one of them were hot.

"In 1967, Arthur's Farm made *Life* magazine. They made a big fuss out of the fact that Babe Parilli, the quarterback of the Boston Patriots, used to come to the place. In fact, in one of *Life*'s pictures, I was seated in a chair at the place. But Parilli wasn't the only football player who came to the farm. Half the team and the coaches came there. They came to buy things at the place. *Life* said that Parilli and other guys were giving us information on games and that we were using that information to make a killing by betting the point spreads. That was a bum rap. Parilli and Gino Cappelletti, the Patriots' kicker, and the other guys never gave us a dime's worth of inside information. They were there buying things for their families. Sure the place was a betting center. You could bet on horses, games, or numbers with the Ventolas or me or others, but the players got a bum rap. Sometimes, in passing, they might sit down and have a cigarette with us, and Tameleo or I might ask how the game looked Sunday. Parilli would say: 'We look pretty good . . . we're playing solid.' But that's it. That's nothing to go out and bet your shirt on. None of them ever once said they would go in the bag to change the point spread and, I'll be honest, no one ever asked them to. They were just nice guys, and we liked seeing them from time to time.

"The same thing with Bob Cousy, the basketball coach. He runs the Cincinnati Royals now, but then he was the star of the Boston Celtics basketball team. *Life* made a big deal out of the fact that Cousy was a friend of Frankie Skiball [Francesco Scibelli]. Now, Skiball was a member of the Vito Genovese crime family then, and he worked for Big-Nose Sam Cufari, the boss of Springfield. Skiball ran a bookmaking business, and he was a great handicapper; that is, he figured out the odds and point spread of games with terrific accuracy. He had a partner called Andrew Pradella, and because they were so good at figuring the odds, they were known in the mob as the Scholar Group.

"Now, I'll admit that inside information can be a big help in figuring out the odds on a game. But Cousy had grown up with these people. He was one of the greatest stars the game of basketball ever had, but just because he was a star, he didn't forget his friends. He used to see and talk to Skiball and Cufari, but he never did a thing wrong. You can go to sleep on it that Cousy never shaved a point in his life for the mob. He wasn't that kind of guy. I won't say he didn't talk about basketball teams and their chances in particular games. He admitted that to *Life*. But he never did a thing illegal and I'd have known about it if he did.

"The reason Cousy got in trouble was because of Gilbert Lee Beckley. Beckley was busted by the FBI in January 1966, and they found some of his records. He was a big layoff man. The mob from all over the country used to lay off some of their action on sports with him. He could handle as much as three hundred grand a day in action. Anyhow, those records had Skiball's name and Cousy's name scribbled on them. The FBI put two and two together, thought they had four, but really had zero. Cousy wasn't feeding the mob with anything on the Celtics. Hell, the Celtics were beating everything in sight. They won six national championships and they hardly ever lost a damn game. Cousy's only trouble was he kept bad friends.

"Beckley was something else. He became a pigeon for the FBI and fed them information on how football games were supposed to be bagged by the mob in different parts of the country. He and other mob guys got inside information on player injuries, and sometimes they had players willing to make mistakes in games for the right price. That way they could bet the right way with other books across the country or raise or lower the point spread with regular bettors they were handling. But Beckley was in trouble with the mob, in particular Patriarca. That's why Beckley's no longer around. They never found his body, but the truth is that the mob had Beckley hit a few years ago. Beckley played games with the mob in his layoff operation.

"The way a layoff office works is this. If you're a bookmaker and you get a sudden flood of bets that you figure you can't pay off on if things go wrong, you phone part of your action to someone who can. That someone is a layoff. The layoff guarantees to cover your bets, and they pick up the marbles when things go right or pay off when things go wrong. But Beckley wasn't paying the guys when they were hitting. Patriarca warned him about it. He owed 190 grand to Joey Napolitano and Patriarca for some action they'd laid off with him, but when they came around to collect, he didn't have the money. When he was winning, he was right there to collect his money, though. Anyhow, Patriarca told him he was in serious trouble if he didn't come up with the money. He didn't, and the mob suspected he was tipping off the feds and would really blow the lid off if he went to jail. So they just whacked him out.

"The biggest protector we had in Revere was the former deputy chief of police, a guy named Philip Gallo. He'd been in the bag with Fox and later he was paid off by Lynch when he took over. After Lynch died, Gallo got his pay from Maxie Baer and Arthur Ventola, but he had a scheme to branch out, to take over the city with the mob's help. At this time, Tameleo used to come to Arthur's Farm once in a while, so Gallo figured he'd approach him with the idea. He made an appointment with Tameleo to talk alone, and they picked a parking lot in Revere. I found out later the meeting was watched by the FBI. He told Henry that he wanted to take control of the city and leave his job with the police. He told Henry that he could guarantee a wide-open town for the mob. What he wanted was more money and the mob's backing to run the town.

"Henry wasn't having any. He told Gallo that his job was to just keep tipping the mob on what the FBI and other agencies were doing and to protect the gambling and loanshark and nightclub operations in town. He told Gallo that the only way he could leave his job with the cops was to either get too old to work or to die. Gallo died a few years later. But while he was around he was a helluva valuable piece of merchandise to the mob. I've seen him come to Arthur's Farm many a time and whisper in Arthur's ear that the FBI was taking pictures in the parking lot or a raid was planned on the farm or cops were picking up license plates at this location or that. He tipped us on dozens of raids."

There were many Reveres in New England. Crooked cops were the mainstay of the New England mob. They made it all possible—the estimated seven hundred million dollars annually that flowed into the mob's treasury through loanshark, gambling, hijacking, and business infiltration rackets. Not all the policemen in Massachusetts, Rhode Island, and neighboring New England states were bought and paid for by the minions of organized crime, but there were many.

The buying of police protection had begun in the early days of the Mafia in Boston and Providence, when men like Teresa's grandfather reached America's shores from their native Sicily. In Sicily, police were not to be trusted, they were to be bought, and Sicilians who didn't pay quickly paid a different price to the men of law and order: They were beaten, tortured, and sometimes killed. The Mafia immigrants saw no reason why things should be different in America. Police turned their heads for a price.

"In the city of Boston I dealt with a couple of cops myself, but as far as the over-all protection for the Office and its members, that was always in Jerry Angiulo's hands. He had the connections, he took care of the payoffs. No one knew who they were, not even Tameleo or Patriarca, and that's the truth. We never asked. Angiulo at one time said he could control 300 of Boston's 360-odd detectives. I don't know if that's the truth or not, but we all operated pretty free in Boston. In Providence, Patriarca had half the city on his payroll. The cops used to drive by his office and wave to him as he sat in the chair outside sunning himself.

"At Christmastime, you'd see dozens of cops come to the Office to get their presents and their envelopes. I didn't know who they were. I didn't care. They were mostly plainclothesmen. They'd go into the back room empty-handed and come out with packages and cash. It was the same in Revere, and Somerville, and Springfield, and Boston. I've been in Larry Baiona's [Zannino] bar—the Bat Cove, they called it—the day before Christmas, and you'd see scores of cops coming in. Larry would go to the back room with them, dig in his pockets, give them some bottles of liquor to go with the cash, and out they'd go. I remember Larry telling me that at Christmastime he'd go for no less than five grand and sometimes it topped ten grand if things were particularly hot. Now, that's just for the flunkies. That's not the high-priced cops, who could move people around who were giving us problems, or the people that were paid by dozens of other wiseguys for special work.

"I had one special guy who was on my own pad. I'm not going to name him. He's off the force now and has a job with a big business as a security chief. But at the time he was on what we called Boston's bank squad. I'll call him Chuck. I started doing business with him in 1960. At this time, I was doing a lot of break and entries with Joe Puzzangara. We'd just done a few jobs, and this cop Chuck had a warrant for my arrest. He told a friend of his, a clerk of the courts who was close to Fred Sarno of Revere—Sarno was a hustler for the mob. This cop asked the court clerk about me, and the clerk asked Sarno. Sarno asked the clerk was there anything I could do to straighten out the warrant that the cop had. The clerk told Sarno: 'Chuck is all right. You can do business with him.' Sarno tipped me off and arranged for me to meet with the cop. I paid him five hundred bucks. 'Don't worry about a thing,' he told me. 'From now on you call me up when you have problems. You give me your home number, I'll give you mine. I'll call you if there are any problems.'

"After that meeting there were no problems large or small that Chuck didn't tip me to. Every time he made a call, he got an envelope. Sometimes it was a couple of hundred bucks, other times it was a grand. But he was valuable. He was worth every dime I spent. There was one time that a one-grand payoff saved me a lot of headaches. This was right after I'd burglarized the fur store on Boylston Street the second time and grabbed 160 grand worth of furs. Chuck called me on the phone and told me to meet him in Boston. When I met him there was another detective with him—I'll call him Bill; he's still on the force as far as I know. Chuck showed me a search warrant that Bill had. 'They think you got a load of stolen goods in your house,' Chuck said. 'Bill here is supposed to search the place, but he'll listen to reason.'

" 'What's it going to cost, Chuck?' I asked.

" 'It's a G-note, Vinnie,' he said. 'Bill has to report back on this warrant. For a G-note we'll say we searched your house and found nothing.'

"That was a big relief to me. I had 160 grand in furs in the cellar. They'd have had me cold. Bill got his grand, and Chuck made a lot more with me and a lot of other mob guys. He'd tell me the areas to stay away from when I was breaking into places. He'd tell me when the cops had locations staked out. He told me about streets, like Stuart Street and Boylston Street, where the patrols were carrying shots of me to catch me in the act on a B&E. He squashed a lot of beefs with the police for my friends and for me.

"There was one typical case that involved Sarno. He and I had a bank swindle going at the First National Bank of Boston. Sarno had a connection with some woman in the bank, and through her we were putting in phoney names to get bank loans. We were using the bank's money to loanshark on the streets. Now, Sarno was supposed to pay the bank loans back when the monthly payments came due, but instead he was gambling heavy at the tracks. One night Chuck called up and said the bank was putting a lot of heat on the department to solve the case. He said that for twenty-five hundred bucks he could straighten things out. He did. I don't know how he did it. We had taken that bank for more than fifty grand, but he got the heat off and we never paid another dime to the bank.

"I had a few other cops I paid off, but not regular like Chuck. There was a lieutenant in Revere. He's still on the force. He used to like to make trips to Florida, but he didn't like the idea of paying. One time, he and his wife and another couple wanted to spend a week in Miami. They called a partner of mine then, Bobby Cardillo, a real sharp hustler, a compulsive thief. He couldn't walk into a department store without stealing something as he walked through it. It might be perfume or a television set, but it had to be something. I remember one time he liked a furniture set he saw in the show window of White's Department Store in Boston. Now, this was in broad daylight. So he and a friend put on some work clothes, backed a truck up to the door, walked inside to the window display and began hauling the stuff out. A clerk asked what he was doing, and he told him that he'd been told to move the stuff for a new bedroom set that was coming in. In twenty minutes he'd cleaned out the window. Nobody asked him a thing. The bedroom set wound up in the master bedroom of his house.

"When this lieutenant called Cardillo, there wasn't any question we'd take care of him. This lieutenant used to tip us off whenever he learned that there was a raid being planned on one of our gambling locations or when he noticed federal agents nosing around the area. He even helped Cardillo cheat an insurance company. Cardillo's house had been burglarized one day, but nothing was really missing. Cardillo talked to the lieutenant, and they made out a big list of things that were supposed to be stolen. When the insurance company checked, the lieutenant verified the articles had been stolen. Cardillo gave him a piece of the pie.

"Anyhow, when this lieutenant and his wife wanted to go to Florida for a week, we sent him to the Thunderbird Motel in Miami. 'When you get there,' Cardillo told him, 'we'll check you in. You just sign a phoney name when you regis-

ter.' That's what this lieutenant did and so did his friends.
They signed for booze, entertainment, food, you name it.
They stayed for two weeks instead of one and then, under our
direction, they slipped out of the motel without paying the
tab. They beat the place for more than eighteen hundred
bucks. I mean, that takes brass. A cop, his wife, and his
friends beating a motel on a bill. He laughed about it. 'If the
chief could only see me now,' he said. This lieutenant didn't
get a steady envelope from the mob, but every time he gave
us a tip he got five hundred bucks or a grand. You can bet
he's still collecting.

"There were so many cops on the mob's pad, it's really
hard to remember them all. Corruption was a way of life in
places like Boston and Revere and Springfield and Somerville.
There were other cops in Maine, New Hampshire, and Rhode
Island, too, but I didn't deal with them. When we found a cop
we couldn't deal with, who was giving us a hard time, a call
was made to Patriarca. He'd get ahold of Angiulo, and Angiulo would get to one of the high-ranking officers he had on the
pad. It wouldn't be long before the cop was transferred to another location where he couldn't do us any damage.

"Sometimes the cops were real bad. I mean, they had less
scruples than some wiseguys. For example, it was a cop that
was responsible for the murder of Whimpy Bennett. Whimpy
was a moneymaker for the mob. He wasn't a member, but he
had his own little gang and he made a lot of money for Patriarca. He was in gambling and loansharking, and he handled
jewelry thefts and bond robberies long before I got involved
with securities. He and his brothers were all independents, but
to operate without problems, they kicked in a share to Patriarca. Whimpy had a lot of respect from mob members.
Then Whimpy got nailed by police with fifty-seven grand that
had come from a Brink's holdup. He went to jail in the case,
but all of a sudden a lot of guys who were involved in the robbery got nailed too. And there were other guys in other rackets suddenly getting nailed. It didn't figure. Then Whimpy got
out of the can on a short trip and started operating, and no
one seemed to bother him.

"Whimpy and I had been pretty good friends over the
years. We'd done a lot of business together. He'd given me a
lot of action, pushing hijack deals and other stuff my way. I
was seen with him quite often. Then one day in early 1966 I
got a call from Tameleo. 'Meet me,' he said. So I drove the

car to Providence and we met in my car in a parking lot.

" 'Stay away from Whimpy,' Tameleo said. 'He's a stool pigeon.'

"I couldn't believe it. I stared at Tameleo and couldn't believe it. 'How do you know this?' I asked. 'I've known this guy for years. I don't believe it. We've done a lot of things together over the years, and nothing ever went wrong.'

"Henry just looked at me. I guess he was a little pissed off that I should question his word. 'Listen to me,' he snapped. 'This is Uncle Henry talking to you now. We're talking in this car. Nobody knows this. Whimpy's gonna get whacked out. He's a stoolie. We got the information straight from our man on the Boston Police Department.'

"I just shook my head. I couldn't believe it. Tameleo said Whimpy had been a stoolie for years, that a lot of guys had hit the can because of him, but I'd never seen him do a thing wrong when we were operating together. 'How the hell did he operate, do all the things he did, then?' I asked.

"Henry's face was frozen. 'That's how he got away with all the things he's done. The cops gave him a license to steal to find out what was going on, who else was involved. He's hurt a lot of people, and the cop that told us proved it.'

" 'All I can say is Whimpy never turned me in,' I said.

" 'He liked you—that's why he didn't turn you in,' Henry said. 'Now stay away. He's going to be put to sleep. If you are with him, you go too. Remember that.'

"Tameleo's warning was clear as a bell. I didn't go near Whimpy. Then in November 1967, Whimpy disappeared. Steve [The Rifleman] Flemmi and Frank Salemmi handled the job. They're a couple of assassins for Patriarca. Both of them are missing, either whacked out or in hiding. They're wanted in a murder case, for killing Whimpy's brother, Billy. They hit Whimpy and dumped him in lye in a construction site that's now part of Route 93. After the mob hit Whimpy, they had to hit his three brothers. Walter ran a nightclub in Boston, and when Whimpy disappeared, Walter began talking about hitting Patriarca. He disappeared, too, without a trace. They found Billy in the Dorchester section of Boston on December 23, 1967. They indicted Daddieco, Salemmi, a kid named Peter Poulos, and another kid named Richie Grasso for the murder. Grasso was talking, so he was hit about six days after Billy Bennett got his. They found Poulos' body later on in the desert in Nevada. After that they whacked out the two other Bennett brothers. That's six guys that died all because a cop on the take fingered one man for the mob.

"Recently I tried to tell a top aide of the new commissioner of police in Boston about some of this. There were a couple of FBI agents and a federal prosecutor with me when I met this aide. I guess he's an honest guy, but he don't believe any of his cops are crooked. He didn't want to know. He just shoved a piece of paper in front of me to sign that would have made me liable to indictment. I said 'No, thanks' and walked out of the room with the federal marshals. I was trying to help the guy and he was looking to indict me for what I was trying to tell him. So he'll have to live with what he's got. Angiulo must have laughed himself silly when he heard about that.

"People have got to understand that there are lots of Reveres, lots of Bostons in this country. Don't think for a minute there aren't. The cops are reached because they aren't paid enough and they see the politicians taking and the judges throwing out cases they've worked long hours on. It don't take long for a cop to get the message. Everyone's making money and he isn't, so he just joins the parade."

15

Fixing Horse Races

"Every bettor who sets foot inside a race track and expects to win is a sucker. I was the biggest sucker of them all. I used to be at the track so much that my legs used to ache from the cement—every day, every meet. I'd bet as much as two and three grand a race, every race, when the money was rolling in. Sometimes, I'd come out winning a few thousand, but most of the time I'd come out a loser—five or six grand, and on a real bad day, it would be as much as twenty grand.

"There was hardly a race track in New England where the mob didn't put the fix in at one time or another. New England had—it still does—more banana races each year than any section of the world. I should know. I helped fix enough races. From the time I was a kid, I knew races in New England were fixed by the mob. Yet I kept going to the track and betting my shirt and so did all the big mob guys except Raymond Patriarca. He thought we were all stupid, and he was right. But that didn't stop Henry Tameleo, or Joe Lombardo, or any of the other wiseguys from slipping into the track when the security people weren't looking and betting their shirt, usually on races they knew were fixed. The trouble was you never knew how many fixes were in. That's how bad things had got in New England. In one race, there might be three different fixes for three different horses by three different wiseguys. Everybody was trying. One might have bought a jockey, another might have juiced a horse and bought the spit box [urine sample of the winning horse], you never really knew for sure. Yet we all came back, day after day, like the rest of the suckers.

"Look at Lombardo, the old New England crime boss. Who could have been smarter than Joe? He owned a stable of thoroughbreds. He fixed races himself all over New England. He had so much money from bookmaking he couldn't bury it all, let alone spend it. Yet every day of his life until he died he was at the race track. Rain, snow, heat, nothing mattered to him. He wouldn't even go to the clubhouse and relax. He'd stay in the grandstand on that hard cement and bet every race like a sucker. Or take Mike the Wiseguy Rocco. He owned a piece of Suffolk Downs in East Boston. He knew the races were so crooked you couldn't get them into the ground with a corkscrew, but he was there betting every day, losing a bundle. My partner later on, Joe Black [Joseph Lamattina], was just as bad. We'd whack up a big score on stocks or some dice game. Here—here's your fifty grand, here's mine. At least I'd bury some, give some to my wife to run the house with. Not Joe. He'd head for the track like a reindeer and at night he'd be at the dog track. And if there was baseball or basketball or football games, he was out betting on them. All of us—we were all degenerate gamblers, but the worst thing was we'd bet our bundles at the crookedest tracks in the world.

"A lot of the mob guys were banned from some of the tracks. In a way, that was pretty funny. I mean, Patriarca had a piece of Berkshire Downs, Rocco had his hooks into Suffolk Downs, and other mob guys like Joe Modica or Doc Sagansky [a Boston bookmaker] had interests in other tracks. And here you had track cops paid by mob fronts barring mob guys. It was all a farce—all for show. I remember one of my friends, Danny Mondavano, was with me one day at the track, and the track cops came up to us while we were sitting in the clubhouse. They told Danny he'd have to leave. He'd been accused of being in a murder, and he was a known bookmaker. I started to yell: 'Why don't you throw me out? Bar me. What is it, a bargain for me to lose fifteen or twenty grand every day? Throw me out of here, for Chrissakes!' They wouldn't listen. They just escorted Danny off the track. I could never get barred from the tracks. I never knew why, either. I had as good a criminal record as any of them.

"My first score in a bagged race was in the early 1950s when I was hanging around Pinetree Stables with my Uncle Dominick. He took me to Suffolk Downs with him one day and told me there was a sure thing running in the seventh race. 'If I come out and give you the high sign,' he said, 'go bet till your eyes fall out.' I looked at him and nodded and, as he walked away, I looked at the racing form. The horse he had was a stiff, a real pig from Canada. I remember thinking Uncle Dominick and Joe Lombardo were out of their minds. Anyhow, the time for the seventh race came up. I looked up at the tote board and the horse was listed at 20-1 odds. I thought to myself, I'm not going to bet this nag. Three minutes before the race was due to go off, out comes my banty-legged uncle carrying a bag in his hand. 'Go get No. 9 and bet till your hands go numb,' he whispered and headed for the hundred-buck window. I go to the fifty-buck window. I still don't believe him, but I bet about five hundred bucks anyway. When I left the window, there was a minute to go. I looked up at the tote board. In two minutes, the odds had dropped from 20-1 to 4-1. That's how much the Lombardos bet on the race. They made a fortune. The horse won by a country mile. I picked up over two grand and shook my head all the way home. I couldn't believe it.

"It wasn't long before I found out why guys like Lombardo

bet till their socks fell off. No matter what race track you went to, the mob had a guy who could put the race in the bag for you. At Suffolk Downs they had Fat Al Samenza. He was the bag man for the spit box. It used to cost five hundred bucks to buy the spit box. When you bought the spit box, you were really buying the switch of the urine sample from the one you knew had traces of drugs in it to a clean sample. What you would do was hit the horse you wanted to win with stimulants in the neck and, if you thought it was necessary, buy a little extra protection from some jockeys to ride interference for the horse you wanted to win. If the horse won, you switched the urine sample.

"While Samenza handled things for us at Suffolk Downs, the biggest fixer the mob had in New England was Joe Blondy Simonelli. He's a made guy who's been with the mob for decades. Blondy handled all the Rhode Island tracks, Narragansett, Lincoln Downs, as well as tracks in New Hampshire and Massachusetts. He had a long record of convictions and arrests for things like forgery, possessing lottery tickets, and having a pistol, but he was the field representative for the New England Horsemen's Benevolent Protective Association. That's the union for the horse owners. He was once barred from Rhode Island tracks, but Patriarca arranged to pay off the right people, and the Rhode Island State Racing Commission reinstated Blondy in 1961.

"Blondy's technique was usually to bag the jockeys, but he could get the spit boxes or do whatever you wanted to do illegally at the tracks. He could squeeze horse owners to enter certain races and to drop out of others so that a horse the mob wanted, outclassed all the others in a special race. He could arrange to have horses scratched at the last minute. But he did his best work bagging the jockeys. He'd get a jock to one of the mob nightclubs, fix him up with a broad, and get him laid. The kid would come back two or three times and be hot to trot. Sometimes, Blondy'd arrange for the jock to get knocked out in a rigged crap game so he was in hock up to his neck. Then he'd proposition him. 'Listen, you're riding a horse tomorrow in the fifth race,' he'd say. 'We want you to take a dive. We'll bet two hundred bucks on this other horse for you.' Now the jock had a choice. He could refuse and then get blackballed for hanging out with mob guys, or he could get a few ribs broken for not paying off his debts. He usually got the message fast and played ball. I can remember

Blondy coming to see Uncle Dominick back at Pinetree Stables and being told who Joe Lombardo wanted to win, who Lombardo wanted to ride a certain horse, when he wanted the spit box bought, and what jocks he wanted paid off. Blondy took care of everything for Lombardo. He's made a bundle for the mob over the last thirty years."

Fixing races was a complicated process. It required paying off exercise boys and stable hands to leave areas where horses were to be drugged. It meant reaching the right jockeys and cultivating the right owners. It meant dealing with the right people to obtain the most effective drugs. It also meant warning New England bookmakers working for the Office about bagged races—so they would not get hurt by heavy betting—while at the same time keeping out-of-state bookies in the dark about what was going on. The mob was not above cheating its own elsewhere in the country if it could get away with it. One of the biggest chiselers was Henry Tameleo.

"When races were fixed our bookies couldn't get hurt. We'd list a banana horse on the sheet that went out to all our bookmakers and he'd then refuse to take any action on that horse from anyone in the city. I think we had the best bookie protection setup in the country. We'd have lists of banana races from all over the country that our bookies would refuse to take bets on. Sometimes it was because the race was fixed. Other times it was because the horse looked too good on paper—it couldn't lose. Every time we had a banana race going in New England, Tameleo was on the phone calling layoff centers with bets in Chicago, New Orleans, Florida, and New York. They'd take the bets and they'd get burnt. Tameleo was hurting other mobs, but he didn't give a damn. He said they were doing the same thing to us, but our information about their activities was better than theirs about us. We got burned less in other parts of the country than most mobs.

"A lot of times things went wrong when we'd try and set up a banana race. You know, in order to junk up a horse, he's got to be a sound horse to begin with. He's got to be able to win on his own. All you're doing with junk, a stimulant, is to give him a little boost. In other words, you're giving the horse an extra thirty-five or forty feet. You got to make him feel better than he's ever felt in his life. Then you buy the spit box and you tell your jock what it's all about. Sometimes you take in some other jocks to help out, but usually you try not to, because jocks are all touts. The first thing they do is call up their sucker friends all over the country with tips, and the horse you might want to pay ten bucks winds up paying only four bucks on two bet. This is the major reason that you keep as few people involved in the fix as possible. You tell your jock: 'This horse has the stuff in him. Make sure you get him out front fast.' You tell him that because you don't want him to get in trouble on the rail or get boxed in by other horses. A juiced horse is no guarantee you'll win, but if he gets on the rail or boxed in he'll do crazy things to keep sprinting, and then you lose your edge and your money.

"Now, a lot of mob guys own horses that run at these tracks. Joe Little Beans Palladino had horses, so did Richie Castucci, Jerry Angiulo, and Lombardo. I had a few myself. Usually, we all owned them through fronts who got a piece of the action from us for allowing us to use their names. Most of us couldn't own them in our own names because we had criminal records, and the tracks and racing associations barred us from ownership. I remember one friend of mine, a bookmaker by the name of Johnny Grasso, owned several horses. One of them was a cripple. I can't remember its name, but it had real bad legs. At any rate, Herbie Serino, Al Judd, and me decided one day we were going to juice this horse up for a race at Suffolk Downs. Grasso didn't know about it.

"We knew this horse would open up on the tote board as at least a 20-1 shot. But to get this horse moving, we figured he'd need a barrelful of stimulants. So we went to a drugstore in East Boston where I had connections and we bought a full bottle of heart-shaped Benzedrine pills—the real strong ones. Herbie got a big, big carrot. We took the carrot, carved little holes in it, and stuck forty or fifty of the pills in the carrot. The next day we went to the stable area, and there was an exercise boy near the horse's stall. I gave the kid a sawbuck [ten dollars] to go buy a cup of coffee and when he disappeared we went to the horse. I grabbed the horse by a piece of flesh under his mouth, forced his mouth open, and Herbie jammed the carrot in and then we closed it. Just to make sure, we took a bucket of water and while two of us held his ears, we made him take a long drink. Then we walked across the barn area and watched.

"Christ, a half hour later he was kicking the barn down. His eyes were glassy and he was shaking his head and flexing his legs like he was a young colt. I bet a grand to win on the horse, and when I dropped the bet, the board showed the horse as a 60-1 shot. We didn't tell anyone what we'd done, not the jockey, not Grasso. Then the announcer shouted: 'They're off.' The horse at first got stuck in the gate a little bit, but that don't really mean anything—most horses on junk get stuck in the gate because they're so screwed up in the head they don't hear the bell or anything else. Suddenly that horse took off like a bat out of hell. The jock on top didn't know what was happening. He must have got scared. He knew he was riding a cripple, but the damned thing was acting like he was Citation. So he took the horse on the rail to try and calm him down. The horse got boxed in, but he was so juiced up and excited that he started bumping into other horses. He even tried to jump over one of them.

"To make a long story short, even if he'd won, it wouldn't have done us any good. He'd have been disqualified. As it was, he ran third and was disqualified from third to fourth for bumping the other horses. Poor Grasso was standing there in front of me in the stands watching and shaking his head. He was talking to his wife, Marie: 'What the hell is wrong with that horse?' he said. 'What's he gone crazy, for Chrissakes?' Two days later, the horse died of a heart attack. Grasso never figured out what happened.

"If we'd been smart, we'd have talked to the jock, but then Grasso would have known and we'd have been in a lot of trouble for doing something like that without letting him in on it. Jocks are the ones that can screw up the best-laid plans. When those little monkeys get up on top of a horse, forget about it—they can make Citation look like a workhorse. You can handicap all day, juice up any horse you can name, but the jock can ruin everything for you. Like the time with a horse I had called Bravad.

"Bravad was a horse I owned under my wife's uncle's name, a guy called Ralph Champy. He died in 1970. He was a wonderful person. He'd bought this horse for me under his name and we'd raced him a few times, but we hadn't done anything sensational with him. One day I decided to buy the spit box for half a grand from a guy I had at Suffolk Downs. Just before the race, I jabbed this horse with some juice to perk him up, and I hit his ankles with Novocain so he wouldn't feel anything. And just to make sure he felt like a real spring chicken when he got out on the track, I hit him with a cow kicker in the ass. The cow kicker is an electric wire. You put one end in the wall socket, and the other open end of the wire you jam against the horse's ass. It wakes him right up.

"Now, Bravad was running in the second race at Suffolk Downs, and I told the jockey what was up and what to do. Then I headed for the stands. In the first race, I got lucky and picked the first winner. That gave me a leg up on the daily doubles, and I had Bravad in the second race for the doubles and everything else you can imagine. All told, I would have won no less than fifty grand if he came in first. I'm looking out at the track through binoculars. Here comes Bravad. His eyes were as big as saucers . . . he's flipping his tail and prancing like a two-year-old colt. The bell rings, and they're off. Bravad got stuck in the gate for a moment, but by the time they came to the top of the stretch, he was leading by ten lengths.

"Now the jock looks back, and he sees no one is near him. He starts just hand-riding the horse—no whip or anything. He fell asleep on the horse, the son-of-a-bitch. He wasn't paying any attention to the field. All of a sudden, the announcer says: 'and here comes so and so'—whatever the hell the other horse was named. 'He's flying on the outside . . . he's caught Bravad.' They hit the wire neck-and-neck and this other horse beats Bravad by an inch in a photo finish. I was shell-shocked. I sat there and looked and looked and I watched. I sat there watching as they brought the horses in and I looked at this jockey and at Bravad as he prances like he'd just won the Kentucky Derby. All the while I'm boiling. I couldn't take it any more, and I excused myself from the people I was with and went down to the stable area.

"There they were. They're walking this nag around in a circle, cooling him off, and he's whinnying and looking at me, proud as hell of himself. There I am, the big shot. I've just blown fifty grand, and I'm standing there talking to this stupid horse. 'Why . . . why did you do this to me, you son-of-a-bitch?' I said. 'Why?' He just looks at me, and I'm standing there like a jerk waiting for him to answer. You understand, I'm so upset I'm talking to a horse and expecting answers yet. I turned to the jockey—I was ready to eat him alive right then and there but I didn't—and I said: 'Put him back in the stable over there.' So he did and I'm looking at that horse and he's looking at me. All of a sudden, I just went black. I couldn't see anything. My temper blew and I reached back and threw a right-hand punch to his nose. Pow—right on the soft part of his nose. Blood squirts from his nose, and his legs start wobbling. I almost put him out for the count. I stood there shouting: 'You son-of-a-bitch—' The jockey and a trainer held me. I think I would have killed him. He never won after that either. I was so mad that day that I left my car at the track. I couldn't drive home.

"That night the jock came to the Ebbtide to see me. 'Vinnie —' he started to say. I looked at him. My fists were white I was squeezing them so tight. 'Don't come near the table, Alf,' I said. 'Don't even open your mouth. Come near the table and I'll break a chair over your head.' The kid was trembling now. 'Do yourself a favor,' I said. 'Get out of here and don't come back because, if you ever come near me, I'm going to split your head wide open.' The jock took off like he was shot out of a cannon. But that's what I mean about jockeys. They can screw you up—they can foul up the best sure thing in the world.

"To junk horses we had two sources for the drugs we wanted. For stimulants we went to a guy named Dr. Charles E. Reilly of Charlestown. Doc Reilly was a regular physician, but he was also a gambler. All the mob guys would get their juice from him. They made a few big scores with him when he was junking dogs at the dog races, but then he got caught. I'm a fool as a gambler, but I'm not an idiot. I wouldn't go near dog races. They're all fixed. At least with a horse you get a little shake for your money.

"Doc Reilly would give you any kind of dope or medicine you wanted, as long as you gave him the name of the horse you were juicing. That's all he wanted. There was no charge for the stuff. Just give him the name. He supplied not only the juice, but the needles as well. He'd say: 'Now Vinnie, don't forget to call me with the horse's name.' And I did. He'd give me a stimulant solution that would give speed to the slowest nag alive. When we'd bag the horse we wanted to, we'd spread the word that another horse was going to win. Everyone would run to the bookies and bet, say, the sixth horse, while we had the seventh horse in the bag. Everyone made a killing that way except the suckers. The bookies had a field day and the guys that were part of the fix, like Doc Reilly and Tameleo, made a bundle.

"We didn't always use stimulants in a race. Sometimes we'd use depressants. I remember one race in particular: the Constitution Handicap on June 3, 1968. Tameleo, Bobby Cardillo, Chris Mustone, and me were all involved in that one. But this time we decided to use a depressant. The best stuff in the world for slowing a horse down came from Roy Patton in New York. He was a trainer and a horse tout, and he'd been barred from the races because of the things he did. He had some stuff that would have slowed War Admiral down to a walk. When horses were hit with his stuff, they'd act like they were walking on eggs. You had to be careful, though. If you gave them too much—particularly if it was a stallion—their joints would fall out and they'd run like they had three hind legs. It was terrible. That's how Rocco Palladino and Butch Rossi killed a horse. Rossi is a made guy who worked with Tameleo and handled a lot of loansharking and bookmaking for the mob. He was a sneaky bastard. He'd cheat his mother for a buck. He used to chisel Tameleo, but Tameleo never figured it out. He liked Rossi because Rossi used to provide him with young girls. That was one of Tameleo's biggest faults. He was a sex degenerate. He liked to go down on young girls. Rossi even gave him his own girl for a night to keep Tameleo happy. But while he was pimping for Tameleo, he was stealing him blind. He was supposed to cut in Tameleo, who he called 'Da-Da,' for a piece of his action. He might have made fifteen grand for one month, but he'd tell Tameleo he had a bad month and only made a few thousand bucks. If he owed Tameleo a thousand bucks, he'd chisel it down to 975 bucks. I'd hear him call Tameleo 'Da-Da,' and my skin would crawl. I remember one time when I thought Butch was a friend that I found out he was cutting in on my business. I called him up and told him I was going to shoot him. He ran to Tameleo and Patriarca and they told me I shouldn't tell Butch things like that—Butch was a good kid, they said. Finally, I told Butch one day: 'Don't ever cross me again. Forget about Henry and Raymond—I'll put a hole through your head so big you'll be able to drive a limousine through it.' He got the message. After that, he'd cross the street to avoid me, and he never came to my house again.

"Anyhow, Rossi and Palladino had this horse that was so slow he couldn't save his ass, but he was insured for ten grand. They decided to collect the insurance. They tried everything to get rid of him. They tried to give the horse pneumonia by packing ice around him. They filled his stall with wet straw and made him lie in it when he was all sweated up.

They even gave the poor animal rotten food to poison him, but the son-of-a-bitch wouldn't die. Finally, they went to Patton and got the depressant. Now, this depressant couldn't be found in the horse after he'd been hit with it unless you got to the horse while he was still hot and checked samples of his sweat. If you waited, you couldn't find a trace. So they jazzed the horse with an overdose, and it finally just laid down and died. They collected the ten grand.

"That was the stuff we decided to use at the Constitution Handicap. But instead of juicing the horse we wanted to win, we juiced the five other horses in the race with depressant. There were six really good horses: Dependability—the favorite, Sandover, Sister Carol, Its Blitz, and Slapstick, and the horse we wanted to win, Flauntless Light. It looked like the best bet to pay us a good price. We got the depressant and got ahold of a couple of stable boys. Cardillo, Mustone, and I paid them twenty bucks each to take a walk and then we whacked every one of the horses with the juice except Flauntless Light. When the race came, Flauntless Light won by seven lengths and paid $12.30 to win. The other horses looked like they were going to fall asleep before they reached the finish line. There was a big stink over the race, but the only horse checked for urine samples was Flauntless Light. I made twenty-three grand on the race. Cardillo made forty grand, and Tameleo must have made a hundred grand or more. He bet with every bookie in the country and cleaned up.

"It's really a crying shame what goes on at New England tracks, but they aren't the only ones. I don't care where you go—whether it's the trots at Yonkers Raceway in New York or the flats at Hazel Park in Detroit or a track in Louisiana—the mob can reach the horse it wants to. Banana races are run every day. Hazel Park was owned by Tony Zerilli and half the Detroit mob. If you think that track was on the square, you've got to be out of your mind. In Louisiana, old Carlos Marcello had everything locked up for fixes. And in New York, half the Colombo mob was making fortunes on twin doubles or in track fixes. Not only that, but I'll bet there's a thousand wiseguys in the country that own horses under different names. Everybody in the mob knows what's going on. So do a lot of the politicians, but they're getting their cut, and they don't say a word. We had a state legislator who helped us get racing dates changed at mob-owned tracks so they wouldn't be competing with each other.

"The only guy getting taken is the poor sucker who comes to the track every day to plunk down his two bucks each race. Maybe he goes just for the enjoyment—for a day in the sun with the crowds. Maybe he's a compulsive gambler. But whatever the reason he goes, he's getting taken not only at the track, but at his local bookmakers. The bookies know when banana races are being run, and they make a fortune off them. They take all the bets they can get on the horses that can't win, and the horse that's fixed to win can't be bet. How the hell can they lose? And if they're not taking suckers with bets, they're taking them in other ways.

"When Tameleo got his start as a jewel hustler, he used to work the race tracks in Florida. He worked with a fence we called Mike Ross. They would pull a switch. They'd show a sucker a real beautiful stone that might be worth five grand and tell the sucker he could get it for fifteen hundred bucks. They would give it to the sucker, take him to a legitimate jewelers, and let him get it appraised. Then they'd take the ring back and hold it until the sucker came back with the fifteen hundred. When he gave him the money, they'd hand him a gaff—a duplicate made of glass or of something else.

"There were dozens of rackets being worked by mob guys at the tracks. I know that in New York, mob guys would buy up twin double tickets from bettors who wanted to avoid the tax men, and then they used stand-ins to collect on the winners. There were even shakedown rackets to provide protection for those guys buying up the tickets. And when the mob isn't doing things like that, it's corrupting jockeys and trainers and track officials and then using them for other illegal rackets. If you have a jockey compromised with a broad and he's married, or if you have him in hock from a fixed crap or card game, you got a sucker that will move things like stolen securities or other hot goods for you if you want to squeeze him.

"New England is just now starting to smarten up about what's going on. There's been indictments in Rhode Island and in Massachusetts for race fixing, but that isn't going to clear it up unless they come up with better controls to stop mob guys from buying into tracks and horses and figure out ways to isolate the horses before races."

16

The Irish Gang War

Long before the Mafia reached the ghettos of Boston, Irish immigrants had come to the city and established their own brand of organized crime: tough, violent gangs that ruled South Boston and the harbor piers with armies of killers and leg-breakers. Like their political counterparts, the Irish gangsters were undisciplined rogues who constantly fought among themselves.

The factionalism of the "Irish Mafia" was quickly recognized by the old Sicilian dons when they first landed in Boston. Instead of challenging the authority of Irish gangs, the Mafioso quietly built disciplined criminal organizations within Italian tenement districts. But with the advent of Prohibition, the Mafia groups of New England moved to expand their horizons, to reach beyond the Italian ghetto and build their fortunes on the widespread craving for illegal liquor. Vastly outnumbered by their Irish rivals, the old Mafioso used traditional, devious Sicilian diplomacy to lure what was then the most powerful Irish mob, the Gustin gang, into a peace meeting in Boston's North End, the Mafia's base of power. The swaggering Irish hoodlums turned out for the meeting, confident that they could dominate the nodding little dons in the long coats and big hats. But the Mafia's method of mediation was with guns and, from ambush, they eliminated important members of the Gustin mob. The move was to change the face of crime in New England. From that point on, the Irish never ruled Boston with the absolute power they once commanded.

Raymond Patriarca, when he became boss of New England, realized that the old animosity between the Mafia and the Irish was unproductive. There were huge fortunes to be made, he reasoned, if he could eliminate the traditional ethnic rivalries. Using his skills at diplomacy, he slowly convinced the Irish gangs that there was more money to be made through mutual cooperation than in factional rivalries. Under the Patriarca formula for criminal success, each group could maintain its territories, its spheres of influence. But in major criminal activities, the groups would combine forces, using the resources of the national Cosa Nostra to move their illicit goods. Patriarca wasn't pro-Irish; he was simply pro-money, and he welded similar alliances with Jewish, Greek, Syrian, Lebanese, Portuguese, and old-line Yankee criminals. All paid tribute or did business through Patriarca's organization and, in return, received services that boosted their income and protected their territories from invasion.

On Labor Day of 1961, the glue that held these groups together dissolved in a violent dispute between the two most powerful factions of the "Irish Mafia," Bernard McLaughlin's Charlestown mob and James (Buddy) McLean's Winter Hill mob. The cause was an "affair of honor," a woman.

"It was such a stupid thing. It started with a kid named Alexander Petricone, we called him Andy, and George McLaughlin, a big, dumb Irishman who was always getting drunk and throwing his weight around. Andy was a quiet guy, a friend of McLean's. Anyhow, both of them were at Salisbury, a seaside resort north of Boston. Andy was with a girl and another friend, and George started getting fresh with the girl. He was drunk. Andy told him to buzz off, but George wouldn't listen. One word led to another, there was some shoving, and Andy and his friend beat the hell out of McLaughlin.

"A few days later, George and his brother, Punchy [Edward McLaughlin], came down Broadway, Somerville, looking for Andy. Now, this was McLean's territory at the time. George told McLean that he wanted Andy. 'We're going to hurt this kid for what he done to me,' he told McLean. McLean told George he was out of line. 'You were drunk,' he said. 'You shouldn't have done what you did.' George wasn't listening. Neither was Punchy, who was just as crazy as George. Punchy was a legbreaker for the longshoreman's union. His right hand had been cut off and his upper left ear was missing, and he used to show everyone the tattoos he had. One was an eagle with outspread wings on his chest. He had a woman smoking a cigarette on his left arm, and beneath that was a sailboat with three birds flying around. Punchy was a cuckoo and as hardheaded as they come. But so was McLean. He told the McLaughlins to get the hell out of his territory or they wouldn't be able to walk out. They left, but they didn't forget.

"About a week or so later, McLean went to get in his car. He noticed something was wrong. It wouldn't start. He had a mechanic look it over and he found a package of dynamite strapped and wired to the motor. The McLaughlins had wired the car with dynamite. McLean couldn't let that pass. On October 31, 1961, in broad daylight—it was about 2 P.M.—he caught Bernie McLaughlin walking near the elevated trains of City Square, Charlestown. Buddy walked up behind him and let go with a .45-caliber automatic, killing Bernie. McLean had to take off to Florida to let things cool. There was a witness to the shooting, a small-time punk called Ox [Robert] Joynt, and a woman. The woman was put in protective custody, but McLean's boys got to her family and threatened to kill them. She changed her story. Ox was something else. McLean arranged to have him disappear. They found his skull five years later at the Wellington Circle shopping plaza in Medford behind the J. M. Fields Department Store. Some barber went outside to shake an apron and found the skull in the field. They never found the rest of Ox's body.

"That was the beginning of the war. They say forty-eight died, but there were a lot more. They just haven't found all the bodies yet. But all the killings weren't just because of the war. A lot of people settled a few old scores, and the papers and cops thought they were part of the gang war. And there were some innocent people killed, people who had nothing to do with the mob.

"Everybody started taking sides. McLean had his own mob, but he had some friends that worked on the fringes with the Office, like Joe Barboza, Steve [The Rifleman] Flemmi, and his brother, Vinnie the Butcher. Vinnie got that nickname because he got his kicks out of cutting his victims up. Others teamed up with the McLaughlins, like Connie and Steve

Hughes, two animals who killed just for the hell of it. Before long, bodies were dropping everywhere and, like I said, some of them were innocent victims.

"I remember one in particular. It was November 15, 1965, and Barboza was searching for a member of the McLaughlin mob named Ray DiStasio. He worked as a bartender at the Mickey Mouse Club in Revere Beach. Barboza went into the club and caught DiStasio cold. The trouble was, a poor slob named John B. O'Neill, who had a bunch of kids, walked in to get a pack of cigarettes. Barboza killed them both because he didn't want any witnesses. DiStasio got two in the back of the head and O'Neill got three. It was a shame. I mean, this O'Neill was a family man—he had nothing to do with the mob. Barboza should have waited. That's why he was so dangerous. He was unpredictable. When he tasted blood, everyone in his way got it.

"Then there was one by Vinnie the Butcher. He killed a guy called Francis Regis Benjamin. Benjamin was a holdup artist who was also a friend of some of the McLaughlin mob. Anyhow, Vinnie and Benjamin got into an argument at Walter's Lounge. The Butcher got ahold of a gun—it was a cop's gun—and shot Benjamin. He took the body out to a housing project in South Boston, cut the head off, and cut up the rest of the body. The police found the body on May 4, 1964, but the killing took place a couple of days before.

"Stupid hits like that caused a lot of trouble. The bodies were dropping all over the place, and the public was starting to raise hell. The newspapers had big headlines every day, and the heat was on the cops to do something. What the hell could they do? They shook everyone down. I don't know how many times I was stopped and frisked for a gun. But I never carried one with me. It was always hidden in my car where I could get to it fast or in the Ebbtide in case somebody decided to try something there.

"Patriarca didn't really care what was happening for the first few years. The Irish were busy knocking each other off, and some old scores were being settled. He did like McLean, though; we all did. We'd done a lot of business with him. He used to sell me tons of cigarettes and other hijacked stuff, and he was a reasonable guy to do business with. You could talk to him, and he showed respect to Patriarca and Henry Tameleo. They liked him, but they wouldn't interfere in the gang war—at least for a while.

"I think that was one of Patriarca's biggest mistakes. Later he said he'd declare martial law if the killing didn't stop, but he should have done that earlier. He figured the more they knock each other off, the more he could take over and completely control. What he should have realized was that gang wars, no matter who they involve, only bring trouble. But for him and for some other members of the Office, the war was a method of fattening the pot and cleaning up some old grudges.

"One of the first scores Patriarca decided to settle was with a guy named Paul Colicci. He was an ex-boxer who was once very close to Patriarca. Colicci was a bad apple, a mean, miserable man. He had been in the can for a deal that involved Patriarca, and, while he was in jail, he kept sending nasty notes and letters to Patriarca. I remember some of the letters would say: 'Hey, boss, if you don't help, when I get out there's going to be trouble . . . you better take care of me.' He'd complain about not getting money, or Patriarca not moving the right politicians to get him a parole. Then when he did get out, he threatened Patriarca and called him a fag. Now you just don't get away with something like that. Patriarca would have lost face if he hadn't had this guy taken care of.

"It was in July 1964 that they got him. Colicci and a small-time thief named Vincent Bisesi were hustling color television sets and air conditioners in beach areas like Revere. They had a gimmick. They would go door-to-door and show suckers a brand-new color television or an air conditioner and offer them a special deal, a real bargain price. They'd plug in the set to demonstrate how good it worked. When the sucker would fork over the dough, they'd give him a brand-new set in a box. There was only one thing wrong. The sets in the box had no guts in them—they didn't work.

"At the time, they were staying in a motel in Quincy [Massachusetts]. The Office found out where Colicci was operating and Patriarca sent two of his best assassins after him. Bisesi was unlucky enough to be around when they arrived. They whacked both of them in the head and dumped them in the trunk of a car, which they left in a parking lot. The cops found them on July 23, 1964, because someone complained about the stink from their rotting bodies.

"Colicci wasn't the only one to get whacked for violating the Office rules. There was a kid named Robert Palladino. He was no relation to Joe or Rocco Palladino. He was just a street thief who'd done time for robbery and burglary. One night he and another thief named Tony Sasso burglarized a house and stole some mink coats. The coats belonged to the girlfriend of Mike the Wiseguy Rocco, and Palladino sold them to Ralphie Chong [Ralph Lamattina]. When Ralphie Chong found out what had happened, he sent two guys to take out Palladino and Sasso. I'm not sure who the assassins were, but they gave this kid Palladino a terrible beating before they shot him and dumped his body in the North End of Boston. Sasso's body was never found. I think he's part of the Wellington Shopping Center too. That happened in November 1965.

"Hits like these were considered to be part of the Irish war by the public. But they had nothing to do with the war. They were just matters of discipline. That's one thing about gang wars. A lot of people who have nothing to do with the fight get hit. It's a good time to settle old scores. I don't care where the war takes place, that's usually what happens. Mob guys use the headlines to settle debts.

"Sometimes, not often, the debts are personal, although they involve mob guys. Like the murder of Joseph Francione. He was gunned down in an apartment on South Avenue, Revere. His death caused me a lot of grief personally. Francione was a partner of Joe Puzzangara—Joe Putsy, I called him. I've told you about Putsy before. We grew up together, and he was a real character.

"Now, Francione and Joe Putsy were working a deal with a kid named Johnny Bullets. Bullets had stolen a load of furs and turned them over to Francione to sell through Tameleo. But instead of selling them to Tameleo, Joe Putsy takes them to New York, unloads them through Jack Mace, and he and Francione pocket the money. Bullets was furious, but he couldn't handle the two of them. But he was a friend of Joe Barboza. He told Barboza what the two had done to him, and Barboza went looking for them.

"Barboza found Francione in his apartment. At the time, I was across the street, trying to collect some money that Tony Talia owed me—Talia's the guy whose hand got pushed in the piranha tank. When Barboza got to Francione's apartment, Francione was talking on the phone with Joe Putsy. Francione told Putsy: 'Wait a minute . . . I hear someone knocking at my door.' He left the phone and walked to the door. Then

Putsy heard Francione cry out: 'No—don't do it! Don't do it—' There were three shots that followed. The cops found Francione shot through the back of the head, lying face down on the kitchen floor.

"I got picked up and grilled for hours by detectives who thought I had something to do with the hit. I just had the bad luck of being in the wrong neighborhood at the wrong time. That Talia was nothing but trouble for me. I should have whacked him out years ago. Putsy, after hearing what happened on the phone, headed straight for a police station and turned himself in to the police on some rap. When I tried to bail him out, I was told by a detective friend of mine that Putsy wanted to stay in jail. 'He's afraid Barboza's going to whack him out,' the detective said. He was right. Barboza was going to kill him. Putsy survived after I had a talk with Barboza.

"Another hit that was personal was the murder of William Fergnani. He was a businessman from Tyngsborough [Massachusetts]. In October, 1964, he'd been kidnapped by Al Judd [Albert Giorgio], Chris Mustone, and Danny St. Angelo, another holdup artist. They stuck him in the trunk of a car, kept him there for a day, and shook him down for some money. Then they released him. Fergnani went straight to the police and identified the three of them from mug shots. The cops arrested the three of them, and Judd was sent back to prison for parole violation. Mustone got out on fifty-grand bail and I found out later that two car thieves, one named Chuck and another called Mike, were hired to hit Fergnani. They got close to Fergnani because one of them, Chuck, dressed up like a woman. Fergnani was killed on May 20, 1965.

*   *   *

"The trouble with gang wars is they cost money. Everyone involved in a war and people on the fringes of the war lose. When you're hitting the mattress—holing up in apartments and houses—you can't run your bookmaking and numbers rackets, you can't case hijacks or robberies or move crap games. You are under cover most of the time when you're not whacking people out. If you don't keep out of sight, you're liable to get hit. You have to remember that in a gang war you can't trust anyone. You don't know if they've flipped sides, you can't be sure someone isn't out to settle an old score you've forgotten about. It's a heavy time. Now, the Irish war was hurting McLaughlin more than anybody else. All of his rackets had drained dry in South Boston. So he did the only thing he could do to pay for his fighting: He began shaking down bookmakers and nightclubs all over Boston. He didn't care who he and his men shook down. He was desperate. When you shake down bookmakers in Boston, you hurt only one person: Jerry Angiulo. The first person Jerry ran to for help was Patriarca. That's when I got directly involved in the Irish war. It all started with a phone call from Tameleo.

" 'Get ahold of these people: McLean and McLaughlin,' Tameleo said. 'Tell them I want to see them. Tell them to come to the Ebbtide and to come clean [without guns]. I want to see if I can iron this thing out for once and for all.'

"If anyone could settle the war it was Tameleo. He was respected by both sides. They all knew he was fair in negotiations and he wouldn't favor one side or the other. All Tameleo was interested in was bringing the war to a close. Patriarca had said if the killing didn't stop, he'd declare martial law. That's what the meeting was called for. There was too much blood being shed, too many headlines, and too much heat on everyone by the law. Everyone was suffering. In one week, Angiulo lost twenty-one grand on his numbers business, and that was incredible. Revenues from all the rackets were down because the cops were everywhere, making life miserable for all of us. So I went to McLean in Somerville. He was sensible when I talked to him. He wanted the war to end, and he said he was willing to abide by any decision Tameleo made. Then I went to see George McLaughlin in Charlestown. He and Punchy were a bit porky about the whole thing, but they said they'd come to the meeting. It was set for a Tuesday in the Ebbtide in early January 1965.

"Sure enough, comes Tuesday, McLean and a couple of his boys come in one door of the Ebbtide and the McLaughlin brothers come in another door. They're all carrying paper bags with them. Tameleo looked at the bags. 'What have you got in the bags?' he asked McLaughlin.

" 'We got our guns . . . we're not going to come in here unarmed with *them*,' he said, pointing to McLean. 'We're not crazy.'

"Now, this meant that Tameleo's word wasn't good enough for him. Tameleo blew his top. 'You bring guns to a peace meeting?' he shouted. 'Get out of here . . . all of you get out. Go kill each other.'

"Tameleo stormed out of the place. He was furious. He went back to Providence and told Patriarca what happened. He said McLean was willing to listen to a peaceful settlement, but McLaughlin wanted to fight. That's when Patriarca declared war on McLaughlin. He ordered the entire McLaughlin mob wiped out. Understand, there was no formal announcement. He just quietly told his assassins to team up with McLean and hit anyone they could find on the McLaughlin side.

"One of the first to go was a guy named Edward Teddy Deegan. Deegan was with the McLaughlin group. He and two of his friends, Harold Hannon and Wilfred Delaney, had been holding up some of Angiulo's bookmakers, and it was costing the Office a lot of money. They were all warned. They were called in in the summer of 1964 and told to pay back the money they'd stolen. Hannon and Delaney laughed.

"Hannon and Delaney got it first, in August 1964. They'd broken into the house of Carmen Puopolo, an Everett bookie, held a gun to his head, and robbed him blind. Deegan was with them. Hannon died hard. They strangled him with a Chinese knot made from thermal underwear and dumped him between some pier pilings at Logan Airport outside of Boston. They found Delaney the same day. He'd been beaten unconscious and dumped into the harbor, where he drowned. Both of them were tough stickup men. Deegan laid low for a while, but then he started holding up more bookmakers. On March 12, 1965, Barboza hit him on orders from Pete Limone, Angiulo's right arm.

"Deegan was suckered beautifully. Roy French, another thief who is now on death row for the murder of Deegan, convinced him he could make a big score if he went on a burglary of the Lincoln National Bank with Barboza, Ronnie Cassesso, and Lou Grieco. Now, Deegan didn't know that Patriarca had declared war on the McLaughlins, and he thought that they had forgiven him for the bookie holdups. He was stupid. The night of Deegan's hit, he didn't suspect a thing. They broke into the bank and when they came out, Barboza, Cassesso and Grieco turned their guns on him and killed him in an alley next to the bank. There was one bad thing about that hit. Two guys went to jail for murder that had nothing to do with setting it up: Tameleo and Joe the Horse Salvucci, a half-ass wiseguy. Tameleo didn't authorize the hit. Barboza said Tameleo did, but that wasn't true, according to Tameleo. Tameleo said he found out about it the next morning when he read it in a newspaper. I don't know if he was telling the truth, but I guess in a way it's justice. Tameleo set up a lot of other people and got away with it. The guy I really feel sorry for is Joe the Horse. He wasn't a bad guy, and he was just a flunky. What Barboza did wasn't right.

"After that, Barboza became the top gun for the McLeans and the Office. He handled more hits than any one guy during the war. On October 20, 1965, he and Chico [Joseph] Amico caught Punchy McLaughlin alone at the Spring Street Metropolitan Transit Authority turn-around in West Roxbury. Punchy had been shot twice before during the war, in November 1964 and in August 1965, but he'd survived both. He didn't survive this one. Barboza cut him down for good.

"Ten days later the guy we all liked, Buddy McLean, got caught in front of Pal Joey's Lounge on Broadway, Somerville. McLean was with two guns at the time, Tony Blue [Anthony D'Agostino] and Americo Sacramone. They'd just come out of Pal Joey's and were getting into their car when Steve Hughes, one of the toughest killers around, let go with an automatic shotgun. Hughes had been standing in the shadows of the Capitol Theater with the gun. He hit all three of them with three shots. McLean was killed, but the other two were wounded. They wound up back in jail for parole violations. There was one thing about Hughes. If he'd survived the war, he'd have ended up on top of the pile in the Irish mobs. He was smart and as tough as iron. But when he got McLean, it hurt everyone. McLean was a real moneymaker."

Hughes and his brother, Cornelius, were inseparable. Both had long criminal records that were amost identical. In their own way, they were as deadly as Barboza. Stockily built, with brown hair and hazel eyes, the brothers had dreams of seizing control of the Irish mobs and challenging the authority of the Office. If for no other reason, both men had to be killed. They were too dangerous to be allowed to live. The first to be caught by the Patriarca assassins was Connie Hughes, on May 25, 1966.

"Connie was in his car on the Northeast Expressway in Revere when Benny Zinna, a street hustler and sometime assassin, caught up with him. He shot him with a high-powered rifle.

"A few months later—it was on the July 4 weekend—I had a close call. I'd just left New York and I was driving my wife's new car, a candy apple red 1966 Ford convertible. Blanche and the kids were at Cape Cod, and I stopped at Arthur's Farm before I headed for my home in Medford to pack a few things and continue on to the Cape. After batting the breeze for a few minutes with Art Ventola, I climbed into the car and started driving along Eastern Avenue toward Medford. It was a quiet afternoon and I was sort of cruising along, in no big hurry, looking out the window. There wasn't too much traffic on the road. All of a sudden, I saw a car in my rear-view mirror. It seemed to go fast for a minute and then go slow. It was a big, black Oldsmobile, and I remember thinking: 'What the hell is this behind me?'

"It took a few minutes, but the car got in close enough so I could see two guys in the front seat and one guy in the back with sunglasses on. Now, this car is going fast and slow, then fast, almost fast enough to hit me, then drops back a hundred yards or so. I kept watching in the rear-view mirror, and I was sweating. I figured I was in trouble, and there was nowhere to go. If I stop I get hit in the head. If I keep going, I get hit. I was looking for an escape exit, but there was nothing around. Suddenly, I see the front end of this Olds lift up. The driver must have just jammed his foot on the accelerator. I heard a squeal of tires and I see he's starting to pull up alongside of me and there's a guy sticking his arm out the window with a biscuit [gun] in his hand. I figured, well . . . I'm going to get hit now. The only thing I could think of was to slam on my brakes just as they got near the rear of my car and started to pass. Just as I did, the guy let go two shots. They must have been doing eighty miles an hour as they passed. They missed. My car ended up on the sidewalk, and I crouched low on the seat. Sweat was pouring off me. When they went by I recognized the guy in the rear seat with sunglasses. It was Steve Hughes. I don't know who was firing the gun.

"The first thing I did after they passed was to get to a phone and call Tameleo. He told me to lay low at the Cape. I figure that Hughes and his boys must have had Arthur's Farm staked out, spotted me, and then followed. There was nothing personal in it. They just wanted to hurt the Office and let Patriarca know he didn't scare them. I guess it was Steve's way of paying Patriarca back for his brother. I think he'd have hit Patriarca if he could have got close enough to him. He was probably waiting to hit Tameleo at Arthur's Farm, and I turned out to be the next-best thing to go after."

Hughes' effectiveness as an assassin for the McLaughlins had a telling effect on the Office. Revenue dropped sharply because members were ordered to lie low. Those who did venture onto the streets were dogged by the police, who were anxious to prevent further bloodshed and to lock up hoods on any excuse they could find. With cops tailing them wherever they went, the mobsters couldn't do their normal business.

"Tameleo wanted Hughes stopped at any cost. He figured with Hughes out of the way and McLaughlin in jail, the whole thing could be brought under control. Hughes had been hanging around with a friend of Tameleo, a fence-loanshark-abortionist who'd made a ton of money for the mob, a guy by the name of Sammy Lindenbaum. Sammy had been paying Don Peppino for the right to operate in the Lynn-Lawrence area. He got involved with Hughes in some gambling action, and they'd become friends. Hughes did some enforcement work for him. Tameleo didn't like it, and he warned Sammy. 'Stay away from that guy,' Tameleo told him. 'He's going to get in a whole lot of trouble and you don't want to be with him when he does.' Sammy didn't listen. He was with Hughes on September 23, 1966, as they drove along Route 114 in Middleton [Massachusetts], near the Three Pines Restaurant. I don't know how, but Barboza and Chico Amico knew that Hughes and Lindenbaum were heading for Lawrence to take over some numbers and lottery action. They caught up with them in a car, and Barboza let go with a high-powered rifle that had armor-piercing shells. When Joe aimed a gun at you, whether it was from a moving car or whether he was stationary, he didn't miss. He was a master with a gun. He dropped Hughes and Lindenbaum right in their seats.

"Five minutes after the hit took place, I was at Arthur's Farm with Tameleo, Butch Rossi, and Bobby Cardillo. Henry got a call on the phone, and all I heard him say was: 'Go ahead.' He turned around to us and sent us to Lindenbaum's laundromat to search for whatever cash and valuables we could find. Cardillo and I hit the laundromat, and we found three envelopes filled with diamonds and about forty grand in cash. When we got back to Tameleo, we found out someone else had been sent to Lindenbaum's home on Revere Parkway and that he'd come up with eighty grand in cash buried behind a radiator. Later we took over his loanshark business: Tameleo, Patriarca and Don Peppino. I got a piece of it for supervising the collections.

"That was the end of the gang war. One other guy was hit five days later, John W. Jackson, but it had nothing to do with the war. He was a two-bit thief, but he'd made the mistake of being a witness to the murder of a woman, Barbara Sylvester, in November 1964.

"The war was costly. It had a bad effect on a lot of the Office business, and it led to a lot of trouble a short time later. It should never have happened. If Patriarca had been smart, if he'd done what he'd done before, he'd have imported the mob's assassination squads in the beginning and saved a lot of bodies from dropping.

"One funny thing is what happened to Andy Petricone, the kid whose girl friend caused George McLaughlin to get out of line, which touched off the whole Irish gang war. Today Andy's an actor. And what movie did I see him playing in? He played in *The Godfather*."

17

Assassination Squads

At 10:10 A.M. on October 25, 1957, a short, squat Sicilian hustled his way through the lobby of Manhattan's Park-Sheraton Hotel and entered the barbershop. He nodded to barber Joseph Bocchini and slipped into his chair for a shave.

Outside on Seventh Avenue, obscured by the milling crowds, two men stepped from a sedan and strode briskly behind a casually dressed workman who was walking toward the hotel. A man nodded at the doorway as the workman went in, followed by the two strangers. The workman paused briefly in front of the barbershop, pointed a newspaper at Bocchini's chair, and disappeared into the hotel.

The two men reached beneath the collars of their coats to pull handkerchiefs tied around their necks up over their noses. Drawing guns from their coat pockets, they walked into the barbershop toward the unsuspecting figure relaxing in Bocchini's chair. At ten-twenty, the quiet barbershop erupted in screams and shouts as shots echoed through the room. The man in the chair dove for the floor, but eleven bullets ripped into his body. Then one of the gunmen stood over the bleeding man and applied the *coup de grâce*, a bullet to the back of the head. Lying in a pool of blood before eleven startled witnesses who could never identify the assassins was Albert (The Executioner) Anastasia, the vicious chief of Murder,

Inc., and the boss of what is now known as the Carlo Gambino crime family.

Anastasia was a victim of his own specialty. For a quarter century, he had coldly arranged the murders of hundreds of victims with no more emotion than if he were ordering a plate of spaghetti. Fear was his weapon and the source of his power. It was also his downfall. For it was the fear of his cunning and wolflike savagery that prompted five crime bosses of Cosa Nostra to plan Anastasia's murder. Anastasia was too dangerous and uncontrollable to let live.

The murder of a crime boss involves secrecy of the highest order. It involves promises, compromises, deals, and trust among the plotters, whose lives depend on the loyalty of their coconspirators. The mastermind of this conspiracy was New Jersey boss Vito Genovese, whose life Anastasia had threatened. Genovese arranged communication among the bosses through his trusted aide and underboss, Anthony (Tony Bender) Strollo. In later years, Strollo was to fall from grace and become a victim of Genovese's cunning himself. He was murdered by his closest aide, Thomas (Tommy Ryan) Eboli, and dumped in a south Jersey lake. His body was never found.

Murders of such high order also require an inside man, a person close to the victim whom the victim trusts and confides in. Such a man was Carlo Gambino, Anastasia's own underboss and closest confidant. Gambino's role was to arrange for the absence of Anastasia's ever-present bodyguard, Michael (Trigger Mike) Coppola, during the assassination. He was also assigned to win the approval for the murder from the boss of another crime family, his daughter's father-in-law, Thomas (Three-Finger Brown) Luchese. Gambino, an ambitious man who preferred a modest demeanor to the flamboyant violence of his boss, Anastasia, was amply rewarded for his treachery. He was confirmed as the new boss of the Anastasia crime family a month later at the famous Apalachin, New York, barbecue attended by more than sixty crime figures.

Though the conspiracy was put together by Tony Strollo, acting for Genovese, the actual planning of the murder fell to a gang of young toughs headed by Lawrence and Joey Gallo. The Gallo brothers have often been depicted as clownish, rather harmless fellows, as Mafiosi go. On the contrary, there was nothing harmless about the Gallos. They headed the assassination squad for the Brooklyn mob, and it is believed that during their careers they were responsible for five hundred or more deaths across the nation. (Lawrence Gallo died of cancer in 1968, and Joey Gallo was killed in April 1972, after the unsuccessful attempt to assassinate crime leader Joseph Colombo; Gallo was gunned down in Umberto's Clam House in New York's Little Italy by two men he knew and had trained as gunmen.) Indeed, the Gallos had handled many murder assignments for Anastasia himself and were close to Anastasia, the Gallos having grown up with the Anastasia family.

But the Gallos had become even closer to Carmine (The Doctor) Lombardozzi, a favored Anastasia soldier who was a key man in the conspiracy against Anastasia and who, like Carlo Gambino, was to be elevated for his role in it. The Gallos had frequently worked for Lombardozzi as enforcers in his vast loanshark rackets. Lombardozzi knew first-hand about their resourcefulness as killers.

The Gallos were daring but not foolhardy. They understood the danger of an attack on Anastasia. They knew that the men assigned to pull the trigger would have to be men whom Anastasia would not recognize, and so they ruled themselves out and all of their regular companions as well. They decided to ask Raymond Patriarca for the use of Jackie (Mad Dog) Nazarian, an expert in murder, as the leader of the assassination team. And they chose one of their own hangers-on, a little-known but vicious enforcer they called "The Syrian," to be the backup gunman on the hit. The Gallos themselves would be present at the scene of the hit, though well hidden, keeping track of Anastasia and making sure everything went smoothly.

"The contract to hit Anastasia involved a lot of people. They were people he trusted, people he didn't suspect. They were also people who were afraid he wanted to take over the whole mob, become the boss of bosses.

"People I worked with in the Office told me Tony Strollo approached Raymond Patriarca for the gunman they needed. The New York boys wanted a gunman that Anastasia wouldn't know as well as a guy that wasn't afraid to hit him. Most of New York's hit men were scared to death of Anastasia. Strollo phoned Patriarca, who talked with the other bosses involved. Then Strollo sent the Gallos to Providence for a meeting with Patriarca. Patriarca assigned Nick Bianco to act as the liaison between Nazarian and the Gallos. Bianco came from Brooklyn and he knew what Anastasia looked like. He was also close to the Gallos. He was a punk at the time, but now he's a captain, a boss with the Colombo crime family.

"The idea of importing gunmen from other mobs isn't new. Anastasia used to send out assassins all over the country to handle hits for other mobs. Today, every mob has its own assassination squads made up of men who get a regular weekly salary just to be ready for the day a hit is needed. The members of the squad are hand-picked by a boss. Their talents always include three things. They are experts with a variety of guns and other weapons. They are cool under pressure. They also have no emotion.

"I remember there was one guy I heard about who worked for Anastasia's old Murder, Inc., who is typical of what I mean. They called him Ice Pick Barney. His technique was as cold and as calculating as they come. He and other men assigned on a hit would force their victim into a men's room. Then Ice Pick Barney would pull out his ice pick and, while the others held the guy, he'd put the ice pick through the guy's eardrum into his brain. The pick left a tiny hole and would cause very little bleeding. They'd wipe away the blood that trickled from the ear, but the bleeding in the brain would cause the guy to die. When a doctor examined him, he'd rule the guy died from a cerebral hemorrhage. They're a special breed, the assassins. They aren't like the average made guy. Every made guy, every member of the mob, has to make his notch: kill someone on assignment. For some it's tougher than for others. But for a rare few, it's a well-paid profession. They handle killings as though they were selling insurance.

"In New England, the Office had its own assassination squad. There was an average of a dozen solid guys who Patriarca could count on to go to the wall for him. They got good pay—a regular salary from the Office. Joe Barboza, while he worked for Patriarca during the Irish gang war, got nine hundred bucks a week just to be available for hits. Others, like Rudy [Rudolph] Sciarra, got a grand a week or more. That was their salary, but they had the right to pick up more money loansharking or counterfeiting or whatever they wanted to do as long as it didn't interfere with their main job of killing.

"Sciarra is a good example of what I'm talking about. He is a short guy, built rugged, with a rough face and light curly hair. He's a stone killer, but in other ways he's a nice guy.

Sciarra was big in the credit-card racket. He had a guy with a machine who could print counterfeits of American Express cards. You couldn't tell the difference from the real cards. Everyone in the New England mob used Sciarra's cards. He sold them for a hundred bucks apiece to mob-connected people, but I got them for fifteen bucks apiece because I was working for Henry Tameleo. I used the cards in cabarets, men's stores, hotels, and motels and to transport stolen cars to Florida and California. I thought nothing about running up a two-grand tab at the Fontainebleau in Miami when I was entertaining a group at a Frank Sinatra show. The head waiter knew what was going on. He didn't care. I'd give him 150 to two hundred bucks in tips. Sciarra's cards were like gold. Other guys in the mob, like Bobby Cardillo, bought airline tickets by the bucketful and sold them to suckers at discounts. American Express took a terrible beating on the cards until they caught up with Sciarra's operation because of an informer. ey never did find the printing press, but they found a list of the numbers that Sciarra's man had put on the cards, and they turned the heat on across the country. A lot of people got arrested as a result, but American Express lost a million bucks on the deal.

"When Sciarra wasn't hustling cards or shylocking, he was out on hits. One of the jobs he had to handle was Nazarian, the guy who hit Anastasia. Now, sometimes being a professional hitman means that if you handle a job like the Anastasia hit, you become a big man in the mob. That's what happened to Nazarian. He became a big man—too big. He was a miniature Anastasia. He threatened to kill anyone who stood in his way. Patriarca became afraid of him. Everybody on the street was afraid of him. Nazarian was a savage. That's why they called him Mad Dog. He once strangled a witness [Edward Hannan] slow with baling wire and dropped him on the city dump so everybody would know he was garbage—because the guy had decided to testify about seeing Nazarian kill George [Tiger] Balletto at the Bella Napoli Cafe in Providence. There were twenty-two witnesses to the Balletto killing, but only this one guy decided to talk. Nazarian could have killed him quick, but that wasn't the way he did things. He twisted that wire real slow, tortured the poor slob because he enjoyed it.

"But Nazarian wasn't happy just being Patriarca's top gun. Nazarian was making a fortune, but that wasn't enough. He figured he should be a boss. He bragged about killing Anastasia. Then he threatened Patriarca. Patriarca did what he had to do. He assigned Sciarra and Lou [The Fox] Taglianetti—he was Patriarca's boss of gambling in Rhode Island—to get Nazarian. Let me tell you, that took a lot of guts. Nazarian was a whiz with a gun. He could smell a bad deal a mile away. But he never suspected Taglianetti. He was a boss, the last guy he'd think would go out on a hit. That's why it worked so beautiful. That's why most mob hits work so good. The guy never expects to get it from the people who kill him. So on January 13, 1962, they hit Nazarian as he left a crap game in Providence. He was hit by five slugs before he hit the street, but even as he was dying he tried to choke Taglianetti.

"Assassination squads have a lot of different roles. They keep discipline in the mob where they work. They handle local hits when they're needed, and they protect the boss when he's in danger. They're also sent out to do other jobs for other mobs. There's no charge for the service—it's a favor from one boss to another. That's where Patriarca made his mistake during the Irish war. He didn't use the assassination squads from other mobs to whack out the people who were causing all the trouble. He hired guys that weren't made members, like Barboza, to do the dirty work. You can't trust people from the outside. They don't live by the same rules that made people do. Barboza didn't. He killed for the hell of it whenever he lost his temper. He became as hot as a pistol to the mob. What Patriarca should've done was import hit men from other mobs to come in and clean the troublemakers out right from the start.

"Our assassins had done the same thing for other mobs. They were used in the Gallo-Profaci gang war in the 1960s to whack some people. I know they were sent to New Orleans to handle a job for Carlos Marcello, the boss down in Louisiana. I don't know who the target was, but I know they had a contract down there. I remember one case where our assassins—I don't know which ones were used—were sent to whack out a guy called John [Futto] Biello in Miami.

"Biello was a captain in the Genovese mob. I remember Tameleo telling me that Biello had been a friend of Joe Bonanno's and that Bananas had told Biello that he was going to take over the New York mobs by whacking out some of the bosses. Biello was a treacherous bastard. He was one of those who tipped off the bosses about what Bonanno was planning to do. Then, when the mob kidnapped Bonanno and held him while the old dons decided what to do with him, Biello was one of those who voted to have Bonanno whacked out. Bonanno never forgave Biello for his treachery.

"That was a Joe Bananas philosophy: Never forget. Tameleo told me one day how Bonanno advised him to put people who rubbed him wrong, to sleep. 'Don't let the guy know how you feel,' Bonnano told him. 'Just keep patting him on the shoulder. Every time you see him, notice what a nice day it is. Pat him on the back. Tell him he looks good today. Sooner or later this guy will find a hole in his back when your time is right. Be patient. Never let anyone know you're laying for a guy because that guy will turn around and lay for you. Always be a diplomat. Make the guy think you're his friend until the right time comes, the right setup, and then you make your move like a tiger.'

"That was what Bonanno did with Biello. He never let him know there were any hard feelings. Then it happened. It was in March 1967, and I was in Florida with Cardillo and some other people. A friend of mine called Fungi, phoned me one day. We'd known each other for years and were good friends. Fungi was one of Bonanno's lieutenants. 'You want to go out with me?' Fungi asked. 'I got to go pick up the boss at the airport. Joe B. is coming in.'

"I didn't ask questions. What the hell did I know? So I went. Bonanno came in on an American Airlines flight from Arizona. I'd met him twice before, and he looked good. He got in the back seat of Fungi's car and we drove to the Dream Bar in Miami, a place that was owned by Pasquale [Patsy] Erra [a Genovese soldier]. About a half hour later, Patsy came in and walked over to our table. Joe Bonanno got up, and the two of them walked over to the corner table, had a couple of drinks together, and talked in each other's ear. Then Bonanno came back and told Fungi to take him to the airport so he could catch an 11 P.M. flight back to Arizona.

"It was either the next day or two days later [March 18, 1967] when I read in the paper that they had found Biello's body with four bullets in it in a car left in a municipal parking lot at Seventy-first Street and Bonita Drive, Miami Beach. The car was a rental obtained under a phoney name. Now, Biello was a big man. He had interests in a record company, and he was the hidden owner of the old Peppermint Lounge in New York and another in Miami that made a bundle out of the twist craze. He was a millionaire with a lot of influence, but he was still a walking dead man as far as Bonanno was concerned. Bonanno had a lot of friends in the mob, even though he was put on a shelf and kicked out of the rackets in New York. He still runs things in Arizona and Colorado and some other places. Don't think for a minute he doesn't. Bonanno's still a big man, but he doesn't sit with the bosses any more.

"After I read the paper, I bumped into Fungi again and he told me that the reason Bonanno had come to Miami was to arrange to have Biello put to sleep. I said: 'Look, Fungi, I don't want to hear about it.' I left and went back to Rhode Island. I had an obligation to tell Patriarca what happened right away. Particularly since I'd been with Bonanno. I told Patriarca: 'Fungi told me that Joe B. put the X on this guy—he gave him the kiss of death.' Patriarca looked at me a moment, then he said: 'Yeah, well, forget about it, Vinnie. Things will iron themselves out.'

"I didn't understand what he meant until later. I found out that it was Patriarca's assassins who were sent to Florida to handle the job. Patsy Erra set it up because he was a guy that Biello trusted. That shows you what I mean. In the mob you can't trust anyone. Bonanno was as treacherous as any guy there ever was in the mob. He was always looking to get ahead by stepping on somebody else. His son, Bill [Salvatore Bonanno], was different. I met him twice, once in Florida, the other time in New Jersey. He was a punk kid living off his old man's reputation. Fungi never had a good word to say about the kid; nobody did. He said Bill couldn't put both his feet into one shoe of the old man. No one in the mob had any respect for him.

"Probably the best assassination squad in operation was the one in New Jersey under Joe Paterno [Gambino family captain]. Frank [Butch] Miceli was in charge of that one with Frank [The Bear] Basto. They went anywhere on a hit. One of the jobs they handled was Willie Marfeo. That was a job that Patriarca did go out of town to have handled.

"Marfeo was a bookmaker, an independent who worked on Federal Hill in Providence. He and his brothers started running an illegal dice game on the Hill, and they weren't kicking in to Patriarca or Tameleo. Now, Patriarca was paying for police protection for that, and here this Marfeo was running games in competition with Patriarca's boys and at the same time getting the benefits of Patriarca's protection. Patriarca told Tameleo: 'Go down and tell these clowns we want a cut. Either they give us a piece or they're out of business.'

"So Tameleo went to see Marfeo, who was a wise punk. Marfeo said he'd pay, but a week went by and nothing was kicked in. Tameleo went back. 'Look, Willie, this is your last warning,' he said. 'Either we get a piece, you knock the game off, or you're in a whole lot of trouble.'

"Marfeo just smiled at Tameleo. Then he slapped Tameleo in the mouth. 'Get out of here, old man,' he said. 'Go tell Raymond to go shit in his hat. We're not giving you nothing.'

"Tameleo was trembling with fury, but he kept his cool. His voice was soft, but as cold as steel. 'Mister,' he said, 'go pay your insurance. You're a dead man.' He walked out. When he came back and told Patriarca about what happened, Patriarca went wild. He was so mad he was almost crying.

" 'Why didn't you shoot him right then?' Patriarca shouted.

" 'I didn't have a gun,' Tameleo answered. That's when Patriarca decided to import some outside hit men in. He knew Marfeo would be looking for one of Patriarca's men and would be careful. Marfeo wouldn't be expecting an import.

"Before you call in outside guns to handle a job for you, you got to have the whole hit planned to a T for them. You provide the guns, the cars, the best location for a hit, and the escape route. Patriarca and Tameleo took care of everything. Then a contact was made with Joe Paterno, and Miceli showed up at the Office for a conference. A few days later [July 13, 1966], Willie Marfeo was eating some pizza with friends in a place called the Korner Kitchen Restaurant in Providence. A guy he'd never seen before walked in, made everyone in the restaurant lie down on the floor, and pushed Marfeo into the phone booth. He closed the door and then he let go with four slugs that went through Marfeo's head and chest, killing him. That was in broad daylight. The guy escaped in the morning crowd, and nobody saw anything. Nobody ever saw anything if they knew what was good for them in Providence.

"That wasn't the end of the problem. Two years later, Marfeo's brother, Rudy, started threatening Patriarca. He was going to get even for his brother's death. This time Patriarca didn't go to New Jersey to handle the job. He used his own assassination squad, Sciarra and Pro [Maurice] Lerner. Lerner was something special. He had worked with Red

[John] Kelley and me and Billy Aggie Agostino on bank jobs, and later he worked with Kelley on some of the big armored car robberies. He was a college kid who'd played some professional baseball. You'd never in a million years have pegged him for being a hit man. But he was. He was the deadliest assassin ever to come out of New England. I remember one time he had to kill a guy who'd been screwing the mob. He knew the guy would answer the door when he knocked. For ten minutes before he knocked, Pro practiced a swing with a baseball bat so he would groove his swing to exactly the right angle. When he knocked and the guy opened the door, Pro hit him with one swing and smashed his face in, killing him on the spot.

"Patriarca needed someone to plan the job because Rudy Marfeo was very careful. It seemed like he was always protected and never followed a particular routine. Pro suggested Red Kelley, and Patriarca bought it. When it came to smarts, nobody could beat Kelley. He planned a job like he was putting a Swiss watch together. He used to set up armored-car jobs like ducks in a shooting gallery. He's got the patience of a saint. Kelley studied Marfeo for weeks. Marfeo didn't know him, and Kelley had a way of blending into the crowd so you'd never know he was there. He found out there was one time every day when Marfeo visited a particular grocery store. The next thing he did was plan a route from a golf course to the grocery store. Timing was everything in this job, and he timed everything on the route over and over and over again. He knew exactly how long it would take to reach the store and how much time they would have to get Marfeo when they arrived. He even figured how long it would take to drive in traffic on the escape route. He ran practice runs until everyone was sick of them. Then he went to New York and got a sawed-off shotgun and a carbine and some Halloween masks. He even got special Double-O buckshot shells because they're best for killing at a short distance. On the day of the hit, he waited with a couple of friends at a golf course for the guys who were to handle the job. So no one would notice them, Kelley and his friends were dressed in golf caps, and Kelley bounced golf balls in the parking lot. Then he met with Lerner, John Rossi, and Robert Fairbrothers, who were to handle the actual hit. They caught Marfeo and a friend of his, Anthony Melei, cold at the grocery store and gunned them down at the exact moment Kelley said they should.

"I think Patriarca should have used Miceli's crew on that one. Lerner was a great hit man, but if he'd have used Miceli, they wouldn't have needed Kelley to plan the job. Miceli would have worked it out himself rather than have an outsider, a guy who wasn't made, plan a job. Later on, Kelley fingered Patriarca in a murder trial.

"Miceli and Basto had a fantastic operation going. Their squad had ten men in it and they got a regular five hundred bucks a week, but that was only a fraction of what they made. They had the best counterfeit business going in the country. There wasn't anything Miceli and his gang couldn't provide. They printed phoney postage stamps, passports, drivers' licenses, stock certificates, and cash like it was confetti. New Jersey is the biggest center of counterfeiting in the country. Not only that, but in New Jersey you could buy just about any kind of gun you wanted from Miceli's group: machine guns, hand grenades, mines. I think he could have supplied you with a tank if you needed it. In fact, that's how I got in trouble another time with Jerry Angiulo: handling some of Miceli's counterfeits.

"It was in 1963. I had a chance to buy queer twenty-buck bills from Miceli for ten cents on the dollar. I took a couple of samples back to show Patriarca and Tameleo. We met in a hotel in Rhode Island, and I went into the men's room with Tameleo and showed him the queers. They were beauties. I told him I could move over a million bucks' worth overnight and sell them for twenty cents on the dollar.

" 'Look, kid,' Tameleo said, 'we don't want any part of it, but you got our okay. Just do one thing. Make sure none of these flood any of our card or crap games, and stay away from the race tracks. Don't you pass them!' No problem. All I was going to do was sell them to a contact. In three days, I unloaded five hundred grand in queers in the Boston area and made myself a quick fifty-grand profit. The next thing I know I get a call from Sal Cesario, Angiulo's strong-arm, to come to Jay's Lounge for a sitdown. So I went to the bar and I saw Smigsy, Jerry's brother. I asked him what Jerry wanted to see me about. He said he didn't know, but told me to go downstairs to the cellar.

"Now, the cellar of this place is really something: wall-to-wall carpeting, a private apartment for Angiulo, and in one main room where you entered there was a table about twenty feet long with all kinds of chairs around it. Joe Russo, another of Angiulo's musclemen, to!d me to sit at one end of the table. I waited about fifteen minutes and out comes Angiulo. I remember it like it was yesterday. He had gray silk pants on, black patent-leather slippers, a black velvet smoking jacket, with an ascot and a cigarette with a holder. He looked like George Raft, the actor, in a gangster movie. So he walked up to the other end of the table, looked down at me, and said: 'Oh, so you're the kid.'

" 'I'm the kid?' I said. 'Geez, Jerry, you've known me for years. What do you mean, I'm the kid?'

" 'Don't you lie,' he snapped. 'You brought in some queer twenties into the city.'

" 'I'm not lying to you,' I said. 'Sure I did. Why?'

"Now he's talking like he's in an old Al Capone movie. 'You may not walk out of this joint alive tonight,' he said.

" 'Whoa . . . take it easy, Jerry,' I answered.

" 'Now you shut up,' he shouts. Suddenly he's wild, loud, raving like a lunatic. 'You're in a lot of trouble . . . you may end up in a box. Your money has flooded all the crap games and race tracks and we got a lot of beefs from the law and everybody else.'

" 'Wait a minute,' I said. 'I got an okay from Raymond and Henry to bring the stuff in.' By now there's a dozen guys in the room. I don't have a chance, and I know it.

" 'From who?' he shouts. 'I'm the boss here.'

" 'I got it from Raymond and Henry,' I said. 'Here—here's Raymond's phone number. Call him.'

"So he sends one of his brothers out to call Patriarca, and about twenty minutes later he returns and whispers something in Jerry's ear. Angiulo turns to me and shouts: 'GET OUTTA HERE. Don't come back, and keep outta my sight.' He didn't mention it, but Patriarca told him I had the okay. I don't know how the stuff hit the games and tracks. The people I dealt with were told to move the money in other places.

"A creature of habits on the street is a complete fool. It can only lead to disaster for him eventually. A man who takes the same road home every night, goes to the same nightclub at the same time every night or the same restaurant, or leaves his office at the same time each day, is a perfect mark for assassins. That's one thing very few mob guys learn. Change your routine every day. Never do the same thing twice in a row. You'd think they'd learn, but they don't. There's always one habit, one routine they follow, and that's what can nail them.

"There are other things that help assassinations to come off so good in the mob. The favorite technique in setting up a guy for a hit is through the use of guys you do business with regularly. They might call you up and ask you to meet them at a particular location to look at a trailerload of hijacked goods they have for sale. They might ask you to meet them at a nightclub or at a house. When you get there—wham, bam, you're dead.

"Joe Palladino tried to set me up one night. We'd had a few beefs at Chez Joey's, our nightclub on Cape Cod, but I didn't think it was anything serious. I was home in Medford that night, one of the few nights I got to be with the family. I was lucky to see Blanche in the morning before I went to work. I used to be on the street eighteen to twenty hours a day, seven days a week. It was a helluva way to live with a family, but that's what happens in the mob. For a hustler, a moneymaker, there's almost no time for home life. At any rate, it was 2 A.M., and there was a knock at the door. Blanche and I were in bed at the time. I said to Blanche: 'There's something wrong. I've had this feeling following me all night.' It was that sixth sense of mine working again. Like extrasensory perception. I could sense danger. Many times I knew something was going to happen. I just felt it—and things would happen. This was one of those times.

"I went to the door, and it was Joey Palladino. 'Vinnie, I got a couple of broads down at the club,' he said. 'I'd like you to come down. We'll have a real ball.' Now, I just knew he was lying, even though he'd come up with broads at the last minute before. I agreed to go. I went back to the room and got dressed, telling Blanche there were some problems at the club that I had to take care of. But before I went, I got a gun from the dresser drawer. I don't normally carry a gun, but this time I had a bad feeling. As we drove to the club, I asked Joey why he decided to come at this hour. 'They're terrific broads, Vinnie,' Joey said. 'I thought you'd enjoy it.' When we got there I saw Bobby Daddieco standing near the bar, stone drunk. Bobby and I had had a beef over something minor, and I'd forgotten about it. But when I walked into the place, Bobby pulled a gun out and pointed it at me. He was planning to shoot me. I fingered the gun in my pocket. It was pointed straight at his gut, but I tried diplomacy first. Daddieco and I had always been close, so I started reasoning with him. I found out Joey had been working on him all night, convincing him that I was out to kill him and the only way to handle me was to kill me first.

" 'Joey tells me you think you're a real big shot,' Daddieco said. 'You're supposed to be smarter than I am, a big wheel with Providence.'

"I told Daddieco what a punk Palladino was. We talked for un hour. Palladino hadn't realized how close Daddieco and I were. We ended up beating the hell out of Joey for trying to set me up for a hit. But if I hadn't had my wits about me, if I hadn't sensed danger, I'd have been set up by a guy who was supposed to be a friend and killed by another so-called friend.

"Friends are only one of dozens of ways mob assassins use to set you up. Many times it's a guy's girlfriend. She may not be willing, but they'll make her do it. They'll threaten her life, or her kids, or her parents. Then she'll call the boyfriend and tell him to meet her at a restaurant or a motel or her apartment at a certain time. The assassins will just lie in wait in the dark, whack the guy over the head, carry him to a car, and take him someplace where they'll whack him out.

"Sometimes you have some nuts in the mob who think up some weird ways to kill a guy. Take Nicola Giso, an old made guy from Boston who used to be close to Joe Lombardo. Giso had lost respect in the mob in the early 1960s when he'd taken a hundred grand of Lombardo's money and blown it with Ralphie Chong in New York. The old dons of the mob had a round-table on whether or not they'd let him live. They agreed to, but he had to pay every nickel back with interest. Because of that, Giso tried everything to stay in the good graces of Tameleo and Patriarca. He was in Providence one day at Patriarca's office when a talk came up about what to do about Angie DeMarco, a two-bit hood who was going around Boston calling Patriarca a fag and threatening a lot of mob people.

"DeMarco was an animal, a part-time hit man crazy enough to make a try on Patriarca himself. Patriarca and Tameleo decided DeMarco had to be hit, and Giso piped up that he had a good way to do the job. He and DeMarco were pretty close, and he said he could get him to meet him in a restaurant for coffee. 'I'll sit down with him,' Giso said, 'and when he isn't looking, I'll put some poison in his coffee. He's too tough to get any other way.' Tameleo called Giso a stupid son-of-a-bitch. He said if Giso ever tried anything like that he'd have him killed. Later on Tameleo had two of the assassination squad catch DeMarco. They left him on the city dump in Everett [Massachusetts].

"Now, if it's a guy on the lam from the mob, there are other things used to help the assassin. The mob has a terrific intelligence system, probably better than most police departments. I don't care where you run to hide, as long as you have to work, the mob is able to find you. They had a connection with someone in the U. S. Social Security office who could check records for them. As soon as the guy used his Social Security card—and you can't work at a legitimate job without one—bang, the word got back to the mob where the guy was working. In a matter of hours the hit man was on his way to case the area and set up the murder.

"They have other ways too. They have doctors. If there is something basically wrong with the guy, like a defect, a scar, a special allergy, or a history of a particular disease that needs special treatment, the mob uses connections it has with various medical associations and doctors to check around the country to find the guy with the problem they know he has. It might take months, even years, but the mob has so many doctors on the hook, putting their money out with the mob on loansharking, that they have a built-in intelligence system.

"Doctors are big with the mob. They have so much buried money, money they don't report to the tax boys. They want that money to work for them, but if they invest it legitimately, the tax men will find out. So they invest it with mob people. In Boston, there were dozens of doctors who provided money to mob guys for loansharking. The doctors got 1 percent per week return on the money they gave the mob, and the mob made another 4 percent a week on his money. There were other doctors that mob guys had set up in compromising situations with broads or queers, and they used that to blackmail them. Still others fronted at nightclubs for mob people or in other business enterprises. Anything to get the under-the-table money that Uncle Sam can't find out about. Doctors are bigger crooks than mob people, at least the ones I've met and know about.

"Beyond the doctors, the mob has the cops. They use crooked cops to check anything out anywhere in the country.

If the FBI is keeping a guy under wraps that the mob wants to hit, they use the cops to try and find out where he's hidden. They'll have a high-ranking cop contact the FBI and say they want to question the guy for suspicion of a robbery or a burglary. The FBI is too cute for them on this. They know better than to deal with local cops when they have an informer stashed. They just tell the local cops that they don't have him under their control any more—that the Justice Department has taken him over. The FBI will never give local cops a flat 'No.'

"They'll just waltz the cops around the yard a few times. But even without information from FBI files, the mob can reach into police files all over the country, even in honest departments, to find out about a guy. All you need is one crooked cop asking for information, and they have hundreds on their payroll.

"What they can't get from cops, they get from crooked probation and parole officers, who keep track of guys freed from jail on parole. These people usually have a good line on where a guy they've once handled has gone. For the right price, there were guys in probation in New England who would finger their mother. The mob knew that and used them.

"Don't ever underestimate the mob. They're smart. They'll run a victim down through insurance company checks. Everybody has insurance, even a guy on the lam. He's got a car, or a house, or life insurance, or boat insurance. Whatever it is, it has information on where he is or what he does in the application for the insurance. When he fills out that application, the mob's guns can nail him. They have hundreds of insurance offices of their own, and they start making checks on a target by saying he owes them back premiums or they have to find him to pay off an award. Whatever the reason, if the sucker bought insurance, he's as good as a dead man.

"The same thing is true of drivers' licenses or car registration. They can check through paid-off people they've got in state license bureaus to find out if a guy took out a new license in a neighboring state, or anywhere in the country, for that matter. And if you think that's bad, think about this. If you've got kids, they have to go to school. Once they do, if they're using the same name, the mob can trace you through transferred school records. That's why an informer has to change his identity completely as well as his appearance if he wants to stay a step ahead of the assassins. Very few make it. Sooner or later they find you."

18

Three Hustlers

In the years during and following the Irish gang wars, three colorful people happened into the life of Vincent Teresa. Two were minor thieves assigned by Henry Tameleo to work under Teresa's wing. They were to become outstanding con men and money movers under Teresa's guidance, helping him reach the heights in free-wheeling swindles that reached from London to Miami and that clipped millions of dollars from unsuspecting victims. The third person was a woman, a go-go dancer who dazzled Teresa when she gyrated in a cage at the Ebbtide nightclub. The two men furthered Teresa's criminal career, but the woman was partly responsible for Teresa's eventual downfall.

The first of this trio was Robert Cardillo, a forty-year-old thief.

"In every kind of business there is, the people you meet can teach you something. I don't care whether they are educated people, ignorant people, morons, or professors: Everyone is another steppingstone in learning. In life on the street, you learn something from everybody you bump into. You learn or you starve. Now, in the rackets, a college degree isn't worth a dime. It's street savvy that counts, and there is more intelligence in an ounce of street savvy than in a thousand pounds of book knowledge. Take Bobby Cardillo. He's typical of what I mean. I told you something about him earlier, about his being a compulsive thief and stealing a bedroom set from a department store in broad daylight. When Bobby uses a phoney name, he uses the name Parker because he can't spell any other name. But you won't meet a shrewder son-of-a-bitch in all your life. This guy has made millions of dollars hustling on the street, and he was worth his weight in diamonds to me.

"Bobby's about six-foot, weighs in at about 260 pounds. He's got a big stomach on him like me. He's a real greaseball. By that I mean, he's not from the old country, but he came from poverty and he shows it. He had to live with fifteen other people in the same room when he was a kid. He's a sloppy dresser, he eats like a pig, but don't match wits with him. Tameleo sent Cardillo to me. Cardillo was hustling merchandise in Revere and he was looking for an outlet to sell big loads of goods to. Teddy Fucillo, one of the old timers of the Boston mob, knew Cardillo and recommended him to Tameleo as a good prospect for the mob. Tameleo called me one night at the Ebbtide and told me: 'You get ahold of this kid, Cardillo, and you take him over.' So I met with Bobby and told him that from that point on—it was in 1963—he was working for me.

"I found Bobby had a lot of guts and a shrewd mind. You couldn't put anything over on him. He was a natural-born moneymaker. Everybody thought he was a dumb kid and they thought I was crazy to take up with him, but he proved himself almost immediately to me. It was in 1964. Things were pretty bad then with all the heat from the gang war. Money was hard to come by, particularly in the amounts I needed. One day Bobby went to a toy warehouse in Everett to see a friend. While he was talking to the guy, he looked at the lock, a big padlock that was on the loading door. He read the numbers on it, memorized them, and went to a key man he knew and had a key made up for the warehouse. We made close to a half million bucks stealing toys from this warehouse, all because Bobby was savvy enough to take the lock numbers and have a key made.

"Cardillo was some character. He had one fault. He was a compulsive thief. You couldn't walk through a department store with him because he was always stealing things. He'd have three grand in cash in his pocket, and he'd go and grab a thirty-nine-buck typewriter for his kid without paying for it. If he saw a new shaving lotion that cost a couple of bucks, he'd stuff it in his pocket. It was stupid, taking a chance on a bust for shoplifting for a few lousy bucks. But that's the way Bobby was. One of his favorite gimmicks was to swipe packages waiting for other customers at Jordan Marsh's, another big discount department store. He'd read the names on the packages that were being held for customers on the ground floor where customers came to pick up their stuff. If he saw one name that was on a bunch of packages, he'd call over some kid, pay him two bucks, and tell him to go pick up the packages for 'Mr. Miller,' the name that was on the packages. He didn't know what was in the packages. He didn't care. It was just something to swipe. When Miller came for his packages, they were gone, in Cardillo's car.

"Bobby had been married twice. He hated his first wife, Adeline, but every two years he'd buy her a new car so his kids would be able to ride around in a new Cadillac. On holidays, he'd call Adeline up and tell her to meet him at Arthur's Farm. When she arrived with the car, he'd load it with turkeys, roast beef, fish, cases of liquor, toys, you name it. At Christmastime he'd almost have to get a trailer to bring all the stuff back for his kids and her. No matter who it was in his family, they got the best of everything, they never wanted for a thing.

"Bobby was also a great practical joker. We used to hang around the Thunderbird in Miami Beach where we did our hustling to pay for the Florida vacations for our families. Now, the Thunderbird was a favorite vacation spot for a lot of top mobs guys. Sam the Plumber—The Count, we called him [Simone DeCavalcante, boss of a New Jersey crime family] —was always there. So was Big Tuna [Anthony] Accardo, one of the bosses of Chicago. There were dozens of top hoods, most of them from Detroit, Chicago, and New Jersey, staying at the Thunderbird during the vacation season. We'd be in there hustling diamonds, or stocks, or crooked card and dice games. We didn't make a helluva lot of money there—a grand or fifteen hundred a night, maybe—but whatever Bobby and I made we'd whack everything up with everybody there, maybe thirty or forty mob guys, because we were all hustling together. They'd do the same for us when they made a score. We'd lead a sucker into the game and whack him out of his loot, and I'd give a piece to Accardo and DeCavalcante, whoever was around at the time. I'd say to Accardo: 'Hey, Tony, here's a couple of hundred.' He'd answer: 'I didn't do anything.' I'd just shake my head and tell him: 'Take it—what's the difference? You were here.' We were all there for a vacation. In times like that you share the wealth. It doesn't hurt, and you make friends that can help you later on.

"When we weren't at the Thunderbird, we were all over the Fountainebleau spending a mint while we watched the floor shows. Lots of bellhops and doormen and waiters that worked at these places were on the take. Like one bell captain at the Thunderbird. We'd order rental cars through him with stolen or counterfeit credit cards. He knew what we were doing. He'd keep an eye on the credit card hot sheets and warn us when to switch cards. Or he'd tell us to unload the car we'd been using because the rental agency was getting nosy. Then he'd get us a new car on another credit card. Every tip he gave us was worth twenty bucks to him, so what the hell did he care? Meanwhile, we had the use of new Cadillacs or Lincolns for nothing for weeks on end. Christ, Bobby and I needed six cars between us just for our families. We had other guys who let us move hot cards at the Fountainebleau and at the Hilton Plaza.

"The mob stole Miami blind. They, all of us, bought clothes with hot cards, they paid for their rooms with the cards and their meals and entertaining—their whole vacation was on hot cards. Not only that, but we'd hustle thousands of bucks a week by working deals with clothing store owners and restaurant managers who would write up phoney bills on the hot cards, collect half the amount for their trouble, and give us the other half.

"Now, at the Thunderbird, there was a bellhop that Cardillo and all the mob guys loved to play practical jokes on. At night the kitchen used to close around 10 P.M., so we'd have the bellhop get a big tray of sandwiches, milk, and coffee for the night. He'd put it somewhere and leave for a minute and Cardillo would hide the tray. When he'd come back, the tray would be gone, and he'd run to Cardillo. 'Where's my tray?' he'd ask. 'What tray?' Bobby would answer. The poor guy would then run to the manager, who'd come upstairs. All the time, the bellhop would be hollering, 'They stole my tray.' The manager would come in, take a look, and there would be the tray. He'd bawl the bellhop out for being careless and then leave. We drove that poor bellhop crazy with pranks like that.

"The worst was reserved for late at night. We'd call the guy over and I'd say: 'Tonight, I want a raspberry lime, but the straw has got to have red stripes.' Everybody in the place would then want straws with red stripes. 'Where am I going to get straws with red stripes?' he'd ask. There would be twenty-five of us in the lobby all wanting red stripes. The poor guy would go over half the city of Miami to find the straws, but he'd come back with the right ones. The next night Accardo would decide he wanted a special hamburger. 'I want a hamburger, but I want it cooked only on one side,' Accardo said. 'Which side?' the bellhop would ask. 'The side that isn't cooked.' Then he'd add: 'But I want it with red relish.' Out would go the bellhop, and sure enough he'd have exactly what we asked for. We all kibitzed a lot with the guy, but he got good tips, maybe forty bucks a night, from everybody there.

"DeCavalcante was a nice guy. He's in jail now on a gambling rap, but he was down-to-earth for a boss. They call him a greaseball in New Jersey because he eats kind of sloppy. He likes the label 'The Count' because he said his parents were royalty. Whether it's true or not, I never gave a damn. The thing that impressed me about him was that he never tried to act like a big shot. I remember he would call his home in New Jersey at 2 A.M. every day to see if his son was home. When the kid wasn't, he'd swear like a pirate at his wife. 'You stupid broad,' he'd say. 'You go find him and don't come back until you do.' I'd ask him why he got so excited over where his son was. 'The kid's going to end up in jail if I don't crack down.' When I'd ask why he didn't simplify the problem by bringing the boy and his wife to Florida, he'd look at me as if I was crazy. 'Vinnie,' he'd say, 'I need a vacation!'

"Florida was fun, but it was trouble for me too. That's where my wife Blanche caught up to a girl I was running around with—a girl that caused me nothing but headaches and money. Her name was Rose, Rose Marie Neves. She was a go-go dancer, but she ended up being damned near a millionaire because of me.

"I met Rosie at the Ebbtide where she was a go-go dancer for one night. I walked in one night and there she was in the cage, moving that body of hers like she was on fire. I took one look and thought to myself: 'Wow—where did she come from?' I called our club manager, Bucky, over, and asked him about her. He said he'd just hired her. She was nineteen years old at the time, about five-foot-five, with one helluva figure. She wasn't any raving beauty, but there was something about her black hair, something about her that I just couldn't get out of my mind.

"Up to that night, I'd never had one particular broad. I fooled around, but nothing serious. Look—I loved my wife, I still do—in fact, I always did. But when you're on the street eighteen to twenty hours a day, working with wiseguys . . . well, everybody's got a girl, whether they're married or not. I didn't. I was the only one who didn't, and I didn't want one. I figured it was a sucker's play. I'd have to give up my wife, my family—for what? If I want to fool around, there's a zillion girls available. But when I bumped into Rosie I was hooked. I took her out of that cage, and she didn't have to dance any more. It was the worst thing that happened to me in my life. It ruined my work: It hurt my family. They went through real torture. The worst time was in Florida when Blanche found out that I hadn't dropped Rosie as I'd promised her I would. Jesus . . . that was terrible.

"I know it's hard to understand, but I was real close to my family even though I barely saw them to talk to them. When you're a thief, a mob guy, you're out every waking moment pushing a buck, looking over your shoulder. I don't know how the hell we had time to even have our own kids. I was young then and I didn't have the consuming bug to make money. It's a miracle the kids turned out as good as they have. That's because of Blanche. She was a terrific mother. She had to be. I wasn't around to do the things a father should do.

"Blanche had found out about Rosie and moved heaven and earth to make me stop seeing her. I'd promised I'd stay away from her, and I intended to keep my promise. Anyhow, I took the whole family to Florida, put them up in a plush rented house near Miami, and I was busy hustling in the Thunderbird. The last thing on my mind was Rosie. Then I heard the loudspeaker: 'Mr. Teresa, will you please pick up the phone?' So I pick up the phone and I hear: 'Hi, hon, how are you?' I almost dropped dead. 'What the hell are you doing?' I asked. 'Christ, you sound nice and clear, like you were across the street.'

"I should have bit my tongue. Rosie giggled. 'It should,' she said. 'I'm in the phone booth in the drugstore across the street.'

"At that moment I wanted to put a gun to my head and blow my brains out. 'You're where?' I screamed.

" 'Across the street with the kids,' she answered. She had two kids by a previous marriage, and she'd brought them with her. Now I really had problems, not the least of which was keeping Blanche in the dark. That wife of mine had a temper like a stick of dynamite when the fuse was lit. Then Rosie added: 'You've got to pick me up. I'll be standing out on the street with a suitcase.'

" 'Don't move,' I said. 'I'll be right there.' I ran outside, jumped in my Caddy, and zoomed across the street. There she was, with the kids, standing on the corner. I stopped the car. She put the kids inside and started to climb in while I was putting her luggage in the trunk. Just as I closed the trunk, who the hell do you think is driving up the block behind me? Blanche, that's who, with my daughter, Cindy, and my youngest son, David. Blanche screeched to a stop, and just as she did, I jumped in the Caddy, made a fast U-turn, and raced off down the highway, Collins Avenue.

"As I go by, my wife whipped her car around and started blowing the horn and chasing me. All I wanted to do was get this broad and her kids to the Holiday Inn and leave them. Blanche was driving like a wild woman. She's blowing the horn, bumping into the rear of my car, smashing into me, trying to run me off the road. She's wild. I figured I'm going to get killed before this trip ended. Finally I pulled over or Blanche forced me over, I don't remember which. Now at this time, behind Blanche, there was a cop trying to follow all of us with his siren wailing and all. By the time he arrives and stops, Blanche is pounding on my car. I had the windows rolled up and the door locked and she's outside screaming at the top of her lungs: 'Open this door . . . you black bastard.' That's what she called Rosie because she was Portuguese and a little dark-skinned.

"Finally, the cop comes up and stops. 'What's the trouble here?' he asks. So I get out of the car, locking the door as I get out. Blanche is still pounding on the door, trying to get at Rosie.

" 'I got to tell you the truth, officer,' I said. 'My wife—the woman pounding on the car—caught me cheating, and now there's a big stink. She's 100 percent right and I'm wrong, but if this girl gets out of the car, my wife will kill her or they'll kill each other.' Oh man, Blanche was furious. She was livid. I'll never forget it. While I'm talking to the cop, she jammed a lighted cigarette in my face, she kicked me in the shins and anywhere else she could move that foot of hers. I looked at that cop as if I wanted to die. 'Please—you got to do me a favor,' I said to him. 'You got to hold my wife here for a few minutes so I can escape and get this broad out of here or there's going to be a lot of trouble.' The cop was very understanding. He kept Blanche at bay while I drove off. Finally, I dumped Rosie in a hotel someplace. Blanche threw me out of the house we were renting for four or five days. My kids talked her into taking me back, but Rosie stayed in Florida for the whole winter and I wound up paying all her bills.

"From the time I met Rosie in 1964 to that time in Florida in 1968, Rosie was nothing but trouble for me and my family. It was a nightmare. It was as if she had a spell over me. I couldn't get her out of my blood. I bought her a house in Marblehead [Massachusetts] for about forty grand, then I spent another thirty grand furnishing it for her. I took her to Europe, to the Caribbean, everywhere I went. I'd leave Blanche home and take this dizzy broad. Who the hell knows what the attraction was. She didn't hold a candle to Blanche in looks. She sure as hell was no raving beauty. She did know how to wear clothes, but that wasn't the difference, because no one knows how to wear clothes or look better in them than Blanche. She was good in bed, but I've had better. You know, when I'd go to London with her, it was like bringing a ham sandwich to a banquet, but I'd still bring her.

"I think it was because she was always ready to go and do what I wanted—whatever it was. If I called her up at midnight and said: 'Pack a bag, we're going to Antigua,' she was right there. There were no complications, no demands. I gave this girl everything under the sun, but she never in all that time—and it lasted four years—asked me for one thin dime. I guess I spent maybe a half million bucks on her in that time, and I think I'm shaving it so as not to look silly. Cash, house, cars, clothes—man, what clothes—jewels, furs. She had more clothes than you could put in a thirty-foot room. I'd take her to New York and on a weekend spend twenty-five grand buying her clothes and showing her the town. It was crazy, insane.

"The strange thing about the way Blanche reacted was that

during this period with Rosie I had a secretary, Joan Harvey, who was a terrific blonde. This girl had everything. Don't ask me why, but Joan was crazy about me. She was dying to go to bed with me—and I'm no prize package. She'd do anything. She didn't even want to get paid working for me in my office. Now, Blanche knew about Joan and how she felt, but it didn't faze her. Joan would even stay with us in Florida occasionally, but Blanche didn't bat an eyelash. Blanche used to say: 'Boys will be boys,' and that's it. But Rosie—that was something else. Rosie was a threat to her family, and for this—hell, Blanche even went after her with a gun one day.

"I was in New York at the time and Blanche was fed up. Rosie had called her a couple of times suggesting that she give me a divorce. I didn't want a divorce. By this time, I just wanted Rosie out of my hair. But I couldn't stay away from her. I had a colored guy, Waldo, working for me at the time. He'd saved my life years before. His name was Walter Winfield. I'd got into a jam in Lynn in a bar one night and belted a guy, knocking him out. As I walked out of the joint, someone, to this day I don't know who, hit me over the head with a full bottle of beer. When I woke up I saw Waldo standing over me, and I started screaming: 'You black son-of-a-bitch!' But he hadn't done it, and he drove me to the hospital. 'You're in bad shape, mister,' he said, 'let me help you.' When I got to the hospital, they said I had a bad concussion. You couldn't see my ear, where I'd been hit. My face, my eyes, my nose were like balloons. Without Waldo I might have died. So I put him to work for me. He was a policy runner, but I put him in charge of a small loanshark racket I had—small loans of a hundred bucks to a grand each. He was in charge of about thirty grand, and a more honest guy you couldn't meet. Just before I went to jail, I gave him the loanshark book and told him everything he collected was his. He was a very faithful guy and a real friend.

"While I was in New York, Blanche went to Waldo and told him to drive her to Rosie's house. Waldo said he didn't know where her house was, but he knew where Rosie's mother lived, so he took her there. Waldo idolized Blanche. He thought she was the greatest woman to walk the face of the earth, and he'd have done anything for her. When they got there, Waldo didn't know what Blanche had on her mind. She had taken a gun from our bedroom and put it in her purse. When she got in the house with Rosie's family, she pulled the gun out. Thank God, Rosie wasn't there. Blanche would have shot her and wound up in jail on a murder rap. Waldo took the gun from her. There was a terrible beef. Blanche told Rosie's mother: 'You keep that tramp daughter of yours away from Vinnie or I'll kill her!' She meant it.

"Life got to be hell for a while after that. Rosie started making demands for the first time. She'd want me at her house all the time. Christ, when I'd get there, the first thing she'd have when I walked in the door was my pajamas, a robe, and slippers. 'Here—put these on and relax,' she'd say. Then she'd put on music, make a meal for me, and bring me a drink. She'd make a big fuss when I said I had to leave to go home, and we'd wind up shouting. I'd slip out of the house at 4 A.M., while she was sleeping, and head for home. One night she came running out of the house stark naked as I drove off. She tried everything in the world to make me break with Blanche. I'd tell her: 'Rosie—I'm not ever going to get divorced—now, forget about it. Go get yourself some guy and keep everything: the house, the jewels, the money. Marry someone. I'll give him a job. Look at me. I'm out of shape. I'm an old man. What do you want with an old man like me?' She'd just smile, give me a sexy look, and be all over me like an octopus.

"The worst part was when she started calling the house and telling Blanche: 'I love your husband. I can't live without him.' Blanche would blow her stack and scream: 'You want him because he gives you money.' Then Rosie would cry. 'Take everything. I don't want anything. I just want Vinnie,' she'd say. It was a bad situation. One day she came to my house, and Blanche answered the door. When Rosie asked to come in, Blanche answered: 'I'm sorry, I don't talk to dirt—I walk on it. Get out of here, you—' She came back a second time, and there was such a big ruckus that I had to slap Rosie in the mouth and throw her out. Then she'd call Blanche and tell her she was on this trip with me and that trip, and then she'd describe obscene things that we were supposed to be doing together but weren't. It drove Blanche wild. Finally, Blanche couldn't take it any more. She called Henry Tamelco. Now, Henry thought the world of Blanche. He used to send all kinds of things to her, not because he was getting fresh, but because he respected her. He'd say: 'Blanche is an angel, Vinnie . . . you're a lucky man.' Every now and then he'd call Blanche up and ask her if anything was wrong, if I was treating her right. 'If Vinnie does anything out of line,' he'd say, 'you let me know. I'll straighten him out.' Finally she let him know. She called him, crying on the phone.

"It couldn't have been an hour later before Tameleo called me in to the Office with Raymond Patriarca. 'You're fooling around with this pig and she's no good,' Tameleo said. 'You're ruining your married life. What are you, crazy?'

"I looked at both of them, these two moralists. 'Listen to you two,' I said. I point to Tameleo. 'You've been running around with Tillie for seventeen years.' Then I turned to Patriarca. 'And I don't know how long you've been with Rita. You're talking about me, and you been worse than me.'

"Tameleo turned gray. So did Raymond. I'd gone too far and I knew it. Tameleo snapped, 'Well, that's our business. We don't hurt our families. Our wives don't know about it. Stay away from her or we're going to whack Rosie out.' They were going to kill this girl over this.

"Things finally came to a head a few months later. I was staying at the North Shore Motel in Revere. I hadn't been home with Blanche. I'd been bouncing around with Rosie again. It was in the afternoon. I don't know how they found out, but someone told them I was there at the swimming pool with Rosie. So who the hell comes walking up to the pool but Lou Grieco and Maxie Baer and Tameleo. I said: 'Hey—what did I do?' This looked like an assassination squad.

"Tameleo called me over. He looked like he was ready to cut my head off right then. 'I warned you about this broad,' he said. 'I had another talk with Blanche. She says you're still up to it. You haven't been coming home at night. I don't want to hurt this broad,' Tameleo continued. 'I'm going to talk to her like a gentleman. If she don't understand English, then she's going to be put to sleep.'

"I didn't know what to do. I pleaded with Tameleo. 'Henry,' I said, 'I'm whacked out over this broad. If anyone hurts her, I'm coming for him myself—I don't care who it is. You might as well kill me too—right now.'

"Henry looked at me as though I'd gone stark, raving mad. 'Are you that serious about her?' he asked.

" 'I'm nutty about this broad, Henry—that's all there is to it,' I said. Then I added: 'Look, Henry—leave her alone. I'll make a deal with you. I won't see her again—just leave her alone.' He agreed. I went back to Blanche. Then we went to Florida and Rosie followed. After the Florida episode, I patched things up with Blanche. My wife knew I was trying to stay away from Rosie. Rosie finally got the message and left us alone.

"But by then I was all screwed up. I'd gotten myself into a bunch of wild deals instead of handling things one at a time. My bills for Rosie and my own home as well as my gambling were out of sight. I moved on deals too quick, tried to turn everything into a pot of gold because I needed money. That's the trouble with playing around. You paint yourself into a corner. Mob guys never learn. Broads are their downfall every time."

While Rosie kept Teresa close company, it was Daniel Mondavano who became Teresa's best friend—and eventually his partner in transactions across the world. Mondavano, like Cardillo, was a street thief, a swindler with a glib tongue and a flair for making money.

"Danny became the most valuable property I had in my stable of hustlers. We worked dozens of deals together, all of them profitable. He helped me operate at casinos, he helped me set up loanshark and gambling suckers, he worked in securities deals with me. He was a professional. He was one of the cleverest operators I ever knew. The funny part about him was he didn't have a bad vice. He didn't smoke or drink, and he never gambled the way I did. He had one girlfriend, but his wife and son were the ones who cleaned him out. She'd buy three-hundred-buck dresses and the boy got 250-buck suits and went to private schools. That's where all his money went—to his family, who spent like they were drunken sailors.

"Danny had an uncanny knack of setting up deals that got him into trouble. One of them involved a big contractor by the name of Steven Benson from Worcester. Benson was a millionaire. He had apartment and medical buildings he owned all over the place. One of them was nine stories high. Danny made a sucker out of him. He convinced him that he could pick up a point a week in interest that he could hide from the tax boys. So Benson gave Danny a hundred grand, and now it was time for Danny to hand him eight grand in interest. Danny said that once he gave Benson the eight grand, he could move him for another 150 grand. There was only one problem. He didn't have the eight grand. He asked me to get him a loan from Tameleo. He promised to give me a twenty-five-grand share for helping him, and Tameleo would get two grand in interest for lending him the money for three days.

"I took Danny down to the Office and explained the deal to Tameleo and Patriarca. Patriarca okayed the loan and Tameleo said: 'I'll have to go to Puppy-dog to get the money.' Now Puppy-dog was a banker, a legitimate banker, that Raymond and Henry had in their pocket and who coughed up ready cash in any amount whenever they needed it. About ten minutes later Tameleo returned with the eight grand and handed it to Raymond. Raymond took the money and gave it to Danny.

"Just before we left, Tameleo pulled me aside. He talked loud enough for Danny to hear what he said. 'You go in the car with him,' he said. 'You make sure he gives this money to Benson. Meet this Benson, find out if he's telling the truth. If he isn't, Vinnie, we're going to break his legs and worse.' Danny heard every word.

"So Danny and I walked to the car and we headed straight for Benson's office. 'Danny,' I said, 'no fooling around now. You got to have this money back on time. They're only charging you two-grand interest. You're telling these people that you'll have their money back by Wednesday. Don't goof or you're a dead man.' When we got to Benson's, I watched as he handed the guy eight grand in interest. Benson's eyes lit up like sparklers. He told Danny to return the next morning to pick up the 150 grand for the other deal.

"The next morning Danny and I get in the car and head for Benson's. We have a car radio on and there's a newscast. I'm not really listening. The announcer said something about 'Benson fell off the roof . . .' Danny turns pale. 'What did he say?' Danny said.

'I don't know,' I answered. 'I wasn't really listening.'

" 'Jesus Christ, Vinnie,' he said. 'It was something about Benson and a roof.'

"Finally we got to the apartment house where Benson was supposed to meet us. There was a big crowd of people. We found out Benson had been on the ninth floor fixing something and had slipped and fell. 'Look at that,' Danny said, pointing to the body in the street covered by a police blanket. 'That's 150 grand lying there.'

" 'What are you going to do, Danny?' I said. 'You gotta have Raymond's money tomorrow. They'll put you underneath Benson if you don't have the loot.'

"Danny didn't panic. 'Don't worry,' he said. 'I'll have it for you by tonight.'

"We drove home. I called Henry and told him what happened. 'I don't want to hear about it,' he said. 'That money's got to be here by tomorrow.'

"I figured I'd better call Danny and remind him of the trouble he faced. When I called, his wife said he wasn't home. 'What do you mean, he's not home?' I said.

" 'I don't know what happened,' she answered. 'He never misses supper, but he didn't come home tonight.'

"It's now 10 P.M. I called again two hours later. He still wasn't home. Now I figured Danny had taken it on the lam because he knew he was in trouble. Finally he called me the next day. He was in New Jersey. I'm sweating him out because I have to meet Tameleo that afternoon. I didn't have any money I could lay my hands on. It was all tied up in shylock loans and other things. I figured I'd wind up going to a loanshark myself because I was responsible for the loan. 'Danny, don't leave me like this,' I said. 'I'll have to go to a loanshark and borrow this money myself if you don't come back.'

" 'Vinnie,' he said, 'I don't know where I'm going to get the money. I've got this one prospect I've been trying to move for about six months, but he's as hard as nails. I might be able to raise half of it in the next hour.'

" 'Okay, Danny,' I said. 'Call me back and let me know what you do right away. To tell you the truth, I'll go borrow it. I'm not going to see you get whacked out for a lousy ten grand.'

"Sure enough, an hour later Danny called back. 'I got it all,' he said. 'The sucker came through.'

" 'Leave your car in Jersey,' I said, 'and grab the first plane for Boston. I'll meet you at the airport.' I didn't want Danny to waste a minute. I wanted him to pay Tameleo and Patriarca himself. If you broke your word with them you were through. He arrived about two hours later, just in time for the meeting with Tameleo. After he handed Tameleo the money, Danny had it made. He could have written his own ticket with Tameleo because he'd kept his word.'

"From that moment on, Danny and I were off and wheeling as partners. He was a friend, the only real friend I had and trusted. I'd have trusted him with my life. I did many times. He never once let me down. I let him handle all our money. We worked together like Mutt and Jeff. And with Cardillo as the other part of the combination, we had a gold mine operating and Tameleo knew it. Now Danny's doing fifteen years in jail for transporting bonds in the New Jersey case, and later I got him another twelve years when I had to testify against him in a securities case that also involved Cardillo. I hated to do it, but I had no choice. I tried to convince Danny to do what I had done—become a government witness. He wouldn't do it. He was a standup guy. He didn't have the same motivation I did. But before he went to jail, Danny did big things with Bobby and me. We could have stolen the world if I hadn't got fouled up with Rosie. Jesus, when I think about it I just get sick."

19

Gambling Junkets

Until 1965, Teresa's criminal enterprises were primarily limited to the New England area, with occasional forays into Florida. His stature within the crime empire of Raymond Patriarca had grown as his moneymaking ability expanded, bringing millions of dollars to the treasuries of the bosses and his confederates. But Teresa, unlike his mob contemporaries, was not content with the largely provincial operations of the Office: localized loansharking, hijacking, check and credit-card fraud, swindles, and gambling. Teresa sought new horizons and, ironically, it was through a rather mundane local criminal sideline that he was to reach a new plateau in the world of crime—one that would lead him to the lavish world of the millionaire hoodlum.

"I had a friend in Las Vegas, a guy I'd known when he lived and worked in Revere as a musician. His name was Ralph Gentile. He'd moved to Las Vegas, got into some trouble gambling and finally straightened himself out to the point where he had opened a used-car lot: Skyview Motors on Boulder Dam Highway. One day, it was in late 1964, I got a bug in my mind to call Gentile and see how he was doing. At the time, an associate of mine, Fred Sarno, who'd worked a check-cashing scheme and bank swindle with me, was heisting cars and unloading them in nearby states. Sarno was making money, but not what I thought could be made in the racket. So I called Gentile and asked him if there was any chance he could handle some hot cars.

" 'I'll take all you can send me,' he said, 'as long as they have papers [car registrations and clear titles].'

" 'Are you shitting me?' I asked. I hadn't really expected him to be interested. Like I said, it was only a hunch that made me call.

" 'Vinnie, so help me . . . I'll not only take all you can supply, but we'll sell them at full price out here,' he said, 'I've got a terrific market for convertibles with air conditioning.'

"I told Gentile he'd start getting shipments of cars in the next few weeks. Then I went to Sarno. Sarno had been clipping cars off the street. He'd pull off the serial identification numbers from the doors and underneath the hood and replace them with new identification numbers he'd get from junked cars. Then he'd obtain registrations and lien clearances [guarantees against debts] through contacts he had in the Motor Vehicle Department. All the registrations were handled through a friend he had who ran an insurance business in the Boston area. It was a good little operation, but that was the trouble: It was small-time.

"I had a talk with Sarno and with his insurance friend. First, I wanted Sarno to concentrate on air-conditioned Cadillacs and Lincolns, particularly convertibles. Instead of using serial numbers from junked cars, he started sending thieves to New York where they would steal the serial-number plates from parked Cadillacs and Lincolns. Then he'd have the new stolen serial-number plates riveted on the cars he'd had stolen. To get good documentation, we used the name of a bankrupt company in Lewiston [Maine] as the seller of the car. Every car we planned to sell would be registered as sold by that company. The papers were then filled out by our insurance friend, who got fifty bucks for each registration and lien he obtained. With those in hand, we sent the lien form and the Massachusetts registration to Carson City [Nevada] and got a clear title back on the car from the state of Nevada. That way Gentile had no trouble selling the car.

"It was a beautiful setup. In eighteen months I moved 172 stolen cars to Gentile. He sold the cars for an average of forty-five hundred bucks each. My overhead was a grand: five hundred bucks for Sarno for the package [the stolen car with paper work] and five hundred for the driver and his expenses when he drove the car to Nevada. That left thirty-five hundred bucks on each car for Gentile and me to split. That was a fast six hundred grand for the two of us, and this was just a sideline with me.

"It was during this time that I was shipping cars to Gentile that I got involved with casinos. I got a call from Gentile one night. He wanted me to get fifty to sixty gamblers together. 'I can fix it so we can run junkets to the Sahara,' he said.

"Now, the Sahara I'd heard about. It was a big Las Vegas casino. But junkets were something new to me. I didn't know the first thing about them, and I told Gentile. The idea, he said, was to fill a plane up with as many as a hundred gamblers with good credit ratings. The gamblers wouldn't have to pay a dime. They would first fill out an application stating how much credit they had, what banks they did business with, and how much money they had invested in stocks and real estate. The casino involved would then make a credit check. Once they had credit approved by the casino, they could board a junket flight from Boston or New York or wherever to Las Vegas, spend four days and four nights there, and the casino would pick up their tab. All food, accommodations, and airline tickets would be paid for by the casino. All they had to pay out was money for expenses for telephone calls and tips to hotel personnel and, of course, whatever they spent gambling.

"For arranging a junket, Gentile said, the Sahara would pay us fifty bucks a head. Now, that's a quick way to pick up five grand—putting a hundred good gamblers on a flight—but at the time I wasn't interested in handling it myself. I had other fish to fry, so I suggested that Gentile work with a young guy who worked with me from time to time: a kid by the name of Joe Napolitano. Joe was from Maine. I knew his father, Mickey, who was a made guy and who had helped me set up the jade theft and some other holdups in the Maine area. Joe had also worked with Rudy Sciarra in moving counterfeit American Express credit cards.

"Gentile agreed, but he wanted me to supervise whatever Joe did. He didn't trust most mob guys, not that I blame him. I called Napolitano, explained the operation to him, and got him started running junkets to the Sahara with Gentile. It wasn't long before the two of them had expanded the junkets to the Dunes Hotel and the Flamingo Hotel.

"For a while I just kept an eye on Napolitano to make sure he gave Gentile a fair shake. I didn't take a cut of the pie because I had a lot of other things, including the hot cars and loanshark rackets, going for me. Then I decided to go on a couple of the junkets to see how things were going. Now, about this time Carlo Mastrototaro started running junkets to London, England, and to some of the Caribbean areas. That looked like it had more potential to me. It was getting hard to make an illegal buck in the Las Vegas area because the feds were swarming all over the place, trying to find out how mob people were skimming money from the big casinos.

"I never really got involved in skimming. Raymond Patriarca and Henry Tameleo were getting a regular piece of the skim, like other mob bosses. They offered me a piece, but I couldn't see putting up fifty grand to buy a point in a place like Caesar's Palace. They told me that for fifty grand, I'd get a guaranteed fifteen hundred bucks a month income in skim money—that's money taken from the profits before it ever gets to the counting room, where the tax agents are around to record the daily take. Patriarca had assigned one of the top gamblers of our area, Elliot Paul Price, to keep an eye on operations at Caesar's Palace so he wouldn't get any short counts. Price used to go back and forth from Miami to Boston to talk with Meyer Lansky and Jimmy Blue Eyes [Gerardo Catena's crime captain, Vincent Alo] and deliver messages from Patriarca, Tameleo, and Joe Lombardo. The idea was okay. It was a nice, steady income, but I didn't like the idea of tying up a hundred or two hundred grand to get income. Besides, the heat that the tax men were putting on Vegas made it look like a poor investment to me.

"It wasn't long before I found out that the really big money was to be made on the foreign junkets. There were no tax men to count up the loot in the casino's back room, there was no heat over points, politicians were bought off, there were just good, solid crooked casinos owned by the mob to deal with.

"One of the places I took a look at was the island of Antigua in the British West Indies. You couldn't have found a more crooked place if you tried. The big casino then was the Mamora Beach Hotel Casino. Now it's part of the Holiday Inn chain and it's straight, but then it was the hottest spot in Antigua. The mob had carte blanche there. The two guys running the show for the mob—this was in early 1966—were Charles [Charlie the Blade] Tourine and Angelo [Chippo] Chieppa. Charlie the Blade is a member of the Genovese family, or what is now called the Gerardo Catena crime family. He was an old-time casino operator, and he worked with Meyer Lansky in Havana when Cuba was a mob playland. Chieppa was a made man, like Tourine, and he used to be the bodyguard for The Boot [Ruggerio] Boiardo, a vicious old Genovese captain who used to burn bodies of mob hits at his estate in Livingston [New Jersey]. Chieppa walked around Antigua like he was king. Taxicab drivers used to call him 'the boss man.' He was built like a billiard ball, with a big stomach and a bald head, but he was always dressed perfect. Tourine couldn't read or write, but don't ever try to outfigure him. He's a genius at figures, at working out percentages and odds. He worked for Boiardo too, but he was closest to Frank Costello, the old crime boss.

"I found out on my first trip there that as long as the government in Antigua got a piece of the action, they didn't give a damn how the casino was run. For the piece the mob gave them, the government made the people of the island cooperate with anyone dealing with the casino. Anywhere you went on the island, the people rolled out the red carpet for you if you were from the mob. As soon as you got off the airplane and headed for customs, the first thing they'd ask was if you were going to the casino. If you were, your baggage was checked right through without anyone looking at it. If you weren't, you spent a lot of time in customs while they checked everything.

"The way things worked on a junket to Antigua was this. There was a fifty-fifty split on the casino winnings taken from the people you brought on the junket. Everything at the casino was in the bag. Card sharks, dice manipulators, all kinds of crooks worked for Charlie the Blade. They had women dealers handling the Twenty-One card games with marked cards; switchmen who moved mercury-loaded dice in and out of the game to control it. There wasn't a game in the place that wasn't rigged, and there wasn't a person they wouldn't take. They rigged a game that a former Vice President of the United States played in. They even took a few bucks in a rigged game from the Premier of the island.

"Because of connections I made at the Antigua Horizon Hotel-Motel, I was able to set up card and dice games in a suite of rooms with a patio overlooking the ocean. It couldn't be beat, what with the ocean, the silver moon, and the hordes of broads around. Now, of course, whatever games we ran were crooked. Danny Mondavano was with me at the time, along with Joe Napolitano. To set up an operation like this requires organization. What I did was change Napolitano's operation from just running junkets into a much more profitable setup, where we got a split from the casino because of mob contacts and then, after we were through at the casino, set up suckers in games in our rooms. That's where the real money was.

"To do this you had to have mechanics who could control the games, broads who would entertain the suckers, and a cool-off man who, after a sucker had been stripped of his money, could calm the sucker down and make him feel like he'd had a good run for his money. That's important. Always leave the sucker smiling and happy if you can. It avoids a lot of hassles, and the sucker can then usually be taken for more later on. The broads were usually hookers we brought from New England or arranged for locally. They weren't pigs, but good-looking prostitutes who got good pay for their entertainment of the suckers, who never knew they were hookers. The mechanics were our own experts. They were provided by Carlo Mastrototaro, who had given me a clearance to run junkets into the area and cleared the way for the casino split with Charlie the Blade.

"The best of the mechanics was Yonkers Joe Salistino. He was a genius with cards. I've never seen anyone like him. He got to be a regular on the casino circuit with me. When we had a sucker to clean in a game, Yonkers Joe would set up two duplicate sets of cards. One set was stacked and kept by Joe. We'd let the sucker shuffle the other deck. Then Joe would cut the shuffle. While the sucker was watching him, Joe would switch the decks, replacing the sucker-shuffled deck with the stacked deck. Then, while the sucker dealt the stacked cards, Joe would give signals. A closed hand meant raise the sucker. Three fingers meant get out. If the sucker bet ten grand, I'd double the pot. We always played pot limit in our games—that is, the size of your bet was limited to the amount in the pot. The sucker never had a chance in a game like that. I don't care how smart you were, Joe could set up a cooler [stacked deck] in front of you and you'd never spot it. I knew he was doing it and I couldn't spot him.

"The cool-off man was a specialist in the art of conning a sucker. I had one of the best in the business with Tony [Robert A.] DiPietro, a real fast-talking, smooth operator who worked for Mastrototaro. Later on he was grabbed for smuggling rigged gambling equipment to Haiti, and he was thrown out of Yugoslavia for running illegal games. Now I hear he's among the missing. But in 1966 he was the best cool-off man from New England. Along with Tony and Yonkers Joe, I had Napolitano, Mondavano, and sometimes Bobby Cardillo. It was a helluva combination.

"Antigua taught me that there was big money to be made running gambling junkets if you handled them the right way. I took trips to casinos around the world and I found the world was a mob oyster. No matter where you went, the mob had its finger in the pie somewhere and usually it was Meyer Lansky's finger. London, England, is a good example of what I mean. There were a half-dozen moving casinos in that city. A number of them had rigged games and Angelo Bruno, the mob boss of Philadelphia, had a piece of a couple of them that I knew about. The trouble was that most of the London casinos were what we called off-beat. They didn't cater to a class crowd. They were bad . . . bad for the kind of business I was in. I was bringing top credit gamblers to casinos, not a bunch of flaky shysters. I didn't want them hustled and stripped. When you take a gambler, you take him subtly, not with a sledgehammer on his head. If you don't use the subtle approach, he won't come on future trips with you or recommend friends, and then you lose a good source of income. He's got to think he's at least got a chance. The worst of these off-beat clubs were the Villa Casino and the Victoria Sporting Club. The Victoria was strictly a Bruno operation. He had his own junket operating to that club. He owned a piece of the club until the English government gave him the heave-ho. They called him an undesirable character. Then he got busted in Philadelphia with Teddy Fucillo, a mob guy from Boston, and Phil Testa, one of Bruno's top men. The cops also grabbed a manager of the sportsman's club.

"When you went to some of these off-beat clubs, you had to watch your eyeteeth. They stacked the odds according to the people in the game. If it was a smalltime game, they played it straight, but if there was a sucker in the game that they could grab for thirty or forty grand, they'd rig the game and cut you out of any split. Joey Napolitano and Richie Castucci were jailed, fined and then thrown out of England because they and some other jokers were caught rigging games at the Villa Casino. Napolitano used to run junkets to a lot of Bruno operations with Raymond's okay. As far as I was concerned, the off-beat clubs were nothing but trouble. The Colony Club was something else. That was the class casino of London. We used to call it George Raft's Club before he got kicked out. I'll explain about that later.

"Everyone in the place wore tuxedos and gowns. You'd see royalty there every night and the world's top entertainers. But for food, I've never found a place in the world that topped it. The menus were fabulous, and they had special favorites of the stars on the menus, like the Frank Sinatra Special and the Dean Martin Special. The waiters were all Italian, and the Maitre d' was a guy named Anthony. He used to prepare a special fettucini dish for me that was absolutely out of this world. He'd cook it right in front of me on a rolling cooking cart with chafing dishes. Once you finished eating, the waiter was right at your side, handing you an expensive Havana cigar, which he'd light for you. And while you ate, there was continuous music provided by a roving string quartet. It was fabulous.

"The Colony was controlled by Meyer Lansky and his top aide, Dino Cellini. All the experts like to tell you that Lansky runs the mob, that he's the high commissioner. That's a lot of baloney. Lansky works hand in hand with the mob, or the Cosa Nostra, or whatever you want to call it. It's a partnership, but he runs nothing and no one. He works with Catena, he works with Patriarca, he works with all the mob bosses. He invests their money, sees they get their cut, but he doesn't tell them what to do. He's the one who set up the point system and the skim operation in Las Vegas. He used the mob's money to take control of the casinos and then gave the mob a piece of the profits. The mob has made millions and millions of dollars with his schemes. When he saw things were getting too hot in Vegas he moved his operations to the Caribbean and into England.

"Until recently, when he went to Israel, Lansky had one guy by his side all the time: Jimmy Blue Eyes [Vincent Alo]. Jimmy Blue Eyes is Jerry Catena's man, and he's got one job in life. He's the mob's watchdog. He watches Lansky to make sure he doesn't short shrift the crime bosses, and he protects Lansky from any mob guy who thinks he can shake Lansky down. Anyone in the mob who had any ideas about muscling Lansky would have Jimmy Blue Eyes on his back in a second. Jimmy Blue Eyes had another role. He would check out people for Lansky to see that they had the okay from their mob to do business with him. I know: I dealt with Lansky and Cellini, and my testimony has resulted in indictments against both of them. The federal government tells me I'm the first one they've been able to find willing to say he paid Lansky money from casino profits.

"Now, Lansky didn't come to me and say: 'Vinnie Teresa, I want you to do this.' It doesn't work that way. He can't give orders to any mob guy unless he has an okay from that guy's boss, and to do that he has to go through Jimmy Blue Eyes. If Lansky wanted me to do something for him, he would go to Jimmy Blue Eyes and Jimmy would get in touch with Patriarca or Tameleo and ask their permission to use me. If he tried to call me direct and bypass them, he would be in a lot of trouble. Lansky's too smart to do that. There's no mob guy in the world with the money that man has, and the money he's earned for the mob is astronomical. You can't even count that high with an adding machine. He's a very valuable friend of the mob—always has been and always will be. But he's no more chairman of the mob than I am. Within the mob, it's very clear-cut what Lansky's duties are, and he does them well. He can sit with the bosses because he makes them so much money. But if he got out of line, if he defied them, they'd wipe him out in a second. That's a fact, and anyone who says anything different just doesn't know what the mob is all about, he's just blowing smoke.

"When you wanted to run junkets into the Colony Club, the man you made arrangements through was either Lansky or his right arm, Dino Cellini. They'd give you the clearance and make sure you got a piece of the profits. If you were a mob representative running a junket to the club, they kicked back 15 percent of all the money lost by the people you brought. That could result in some very serious money being made, because this was a class operation, on a par with some of the best casinos in Las Vegas. The Colony was good for at least three to four million bucks a week in action.

"Unlike most of the casinos around the world, the Colony Club operated honest at the tables. There were no fast mechanics operating behind the tables, no marked cards or loaded dice—none of that. The club odds were seventeen percent —that is, if you bet a grand, the club expected to take no less than 170 bucks of your money, and that was without shading any game. Hell, I lost money in the place myself. There were no special favors for mob guys who got in games. The only area they'd shade for you was in the reporting of your profits. I'd better explain how the junkets collect money and pay the Colony.

"First of all, in order to bring a junket to the Colony, you have to put up a grand for each man you're bringing. If you're bringing thirty people, you put up thirty grand. Out of that grand when you get to the casino, the player gets back 820 bucks in English pound chips—nonnegotiable chips. You must, if you're a player, use those chips. The rest of the money helps pay for your room, your food, and your plane ticket to and from the States. Now, when the customer worked his way through his 820 bucks' worth of chips, he'd go on credit and sign a receipt for more chips. I'd arrange for more chips to be issued to him on credit by the casino. When he got back to the States, I'd collect what he owed the casino, and then Cellini would either come to see me or I'd fly to Florida to pay him. Everything was on paper—the junketeer, a guy like myself, handled all the payoffs to Cellini or Lansky. The playing customer never played with cash if he was on a junket. It was through a credit system like this that we could keep track of what the club took in and what was owed me. Cellini came to my office in Boston at least four times to collect money owed the Colony, and I flew to Florida twice to pay him. Both times Lansky was there. The first time I had over forty grand, and I laid it on the table in front of them. The second time, Lansky sat behind the desk, and I handed him over fifty grand. He put his right hand out, took the money, put it on the desk, and fingered through it. That was the day he and Cellini offered to arrange for me to run junkets to Paradise Island in the Bahamas and the Lucayan Beach casino run by Max Courtney, a Lansky front man. I eventually took a trip to Paradise Island, but I didn't like the setup, even though Eddie Cellini, Dino's brother, was in control of the operation. The Lucayan I used a number of times, and I got a 25 percent kickback on the profits there.

"The one area the Colony Club shaded for mob people was in the area of records. We'd tell the manager running the club, Fred Ayoub: 'Don't put it in your records that we made sixty grand this trip. Put down that we only made twenty-two grand.' That they were glad to do. Not only did we beat the American government on taxes, but they beat the British government on the other end as well. Ayoub was the guy Dino Cellini sent me to see when I first started running to casinos, and he was a guy I dealt with regularly. On paper I never came back with a junket that won over twenty-five grand, but I almost never had a junket that made less than fifty to eighty grand for me, and that doesn't include what we were knocking down from suckers in rigged card parties we held at the Mayfair Hotel. That means the Colony was knocking down six hundred to nine hundred grand on just one of my junkets. You know, you bring thirty to forty good high rollers, people who love to gamble and have money to burn, in a casino like that and they'll lose an average of twenty-five to forty grand apiece in a week. That adds up fast.

"I made the really big money on junkets to London in the hotel. I would rent the Maharaja's Suite at the Mayfair. Hell, I made history in that place. The parties we used to run were the talk of London. You wouldn't believe the people that used to come: the top-name entertainers, the politicians, the judges. The suite had all marble floors, and it had wall-to-wall broads, booze, and food. We'd use the broads, all of them good-looking hustlers, to lay the suckers we wanted to bust out. Then we'd start a card game and ignore the sucker as if he wasn't there. Everybody in the game was a mob guy, a mechanic, a thief, a swindler—what have you. We'd all be betting and winning and losing money like there was no tomorrow. Pretty soon the sucker would want to get into the game. Before the night was out, he'd be cleaned and never know he was in a rigged game. Usually, he figured I'd been taken too, because I'd get out of the game and leave a note for ten grand or more. I remember one guy we knocked out for eighty grand in thirty minutes. He never knew what hit him. By the end of the week of wild parties and crooked card games, if we came out with less than three hundred grand for a week's action, including what we got from the casino, it was a bad week.

"The Colony, at the time I started bringing junkets in, was fronted by George Raft, the actor. I'd known Raft for years. We first met at the Capri [El Casino de Capri], a hotel-casino in Havana, in 1959. Raft was the official host and greeter for the club, which was controlled by Charlie the Blade Tourine, a good friend of Raft's. I was there with a couple of guys from Boston to gamble a little and have some fun. We were having a ball and we didn't pay any attention to reports of fighting in the mountains nearby. We could even hear the gunfire from time to time. Then one morning Fidel Castro and his army took over the city and they told everybody at the casino to stay indoors. We got orders that same day to leave all our clothes, our jewels, and our money in our rooms. A day later, Castro's men hustled us into buses, took us to the airport, and put us on planes bound for the States. I had fifteen hundred bucks in my pocket, but I didn't leave it behind. I put it in my socks and walked on it until I landed in the States.

"At the Colony, Raft fronted for Cellini and Lansky. He was there as an attraction to bring the suckers in. He did his job, and entertainers would flock to the place because they were his friends. In London it became the in place to be. Raft would come down every night, dressed in a tuxedo. He'd meet all the people, sign autographs, dance with the women—he was in the limelight all the time, and he loved every minute of it. I remember I met him later in Miami after he'd been kicked out of London because of his mob connections. They made him the scapegoat, but the cops never cleaned up the hidden ownership of the club. I asked him if he missed the place. 'Vinnie,' he said, 'those were the best days I've had in years. I had a chauffeured Rolls-Royce, beautiful women with me every night, a beautiful penthouse apartment in the Mayfair area, and five hundred dollars a week. Who lived better than I did? What did I care about what was going on in the casino every night or who was involved? I never did anything wrong.' He told me Cellini had put him in the place as a figurehead to draw in people. His movie career was over, and this was a nice way to keep living high off the hog. He was a helluva drawing card, don't ever forget it. That was the best investment Lansky and Cellini made at that club. The English kicked Cellini out of the country and he was the guy that organized a school for the croupiers they needed when they started setting up casinos over there.

"All kinds of entertainers used to show up at the club. There was one night that I nearly wound up in jail on a murder charge because of one of those entertainers. Danny Mondavano and I were there that night. I had Rosie with me and Danny had a hooker named Dawn, a real doll of a girl with a figure that wouldn't quit. At any rate, Danny and Dawn were sitting at a table having a drink. Telly Savalas, the actor, a good friend of mine, was sitting at the table with them. I knew Telly from Boston, where he'd grown up. While they're sitting there, along comes Neville Brand, the actor who played Al Capone in the movies and later was the dumb Texas Ranger in a television series. Anyhow, Brand is half in the bag and he starts edging up against Danny's broad, rubbing his elbow against her tits. Now, Danny's a big boy, strong as an ox and weighs in at about 290. He turned to Telly and said: 'Tell your friend to keep away from Dawn.' Brand isn't listening, and just as I start coming downstairs with Rosie, I see Danny grab Brand by the collar and then, whammo, he hit him a shot that sent him sprawling. Suddenly two or three guys come running over, and it looked like they were going to take Danny apart. So I grabbed a steak knife and started running toward one of them that has a hold on Danny. Just as I got ready to cut this guy up, Freddie Ayoub grabs my arm and shouts in my ear: 'Vinnie, for God's sake, that's a cop there.' I was going to stab a cop, a plainclothesman from Scotland Yard. There was a big stink after that, and they were going to throw Danny and me out of the club until Telly stepped in. He pointed to Brand and told the cop that Brand had started trouble with the girl. A couple of days later, Brand apologized to Danny and me."

20

The Mafia in Haiti

Vincent Teresa walked slowly through the doors of the Presidential Palace. At his side was David Iacovetti, a soldier of the Carlo Gambino crime family, and Joseph (Joe Kirk) Krikorian, the casino gambling representative of Raymond Patriarca. The three men followed a gaudily uniformed officer down endless corridors lined with guards. The floors glistened, reflecting chandeliers. Finally the officer stopped at two huge doors and knocked, then entered, holding a door for the three mob representatives. A vast table covered by a white cloth occupied the center of the room. At the head of the table stood a small black man with white hair and a smartly tailored white military jacket emblazoned with rows of colored ribbons and shiny medals. Thus, in the spring of 1967 did Teresa, hoodlum of Boston, meet François (Papa Doc) Duvalier, President and dictator of the small Caribbean Republic of Haiti.

The meeting had been arranged at the request of Teresa by Iacovetti, a fifty-three-year-old Connecticut mobster and one of New England's most prominent racketeers.

"Dave was very close to Papa Doc. In 1961 and 1962 he had cooked up a scheme to peddle illegal lottery tickets for the Republic of Haiti Welfare Fund Sweepstakes. It was a multimillion-buck scheme. The payoff was to be based on the results of two U.S. horse races, The International, run at Laurel [Maryland], in 1962, and the Kentucky Derby, in 1963. Dave arranged for enough tickets to be printed to pull in six million bucks. I don't know how many of the two-buck tickets they actually sold, but tickets were distributed in Pennsylvania, New York, Connecticut, and other areas to suckers who never knew they were being taken. Each ticket resulted in a kickback to Papa Doc, who made a bundle out of that deal. But that wasn't all Dave did for the old man. When Papa Doc needed guns and the U.S. government wouldn't provide them—in fact, the feds secretly tried to overthrow Papa Doc—Dave arranged to have machine guns and rifles and all kinds of ammunition smuggled to Haiti from his sources in the U.S. Dave made a lot of money on that deal, and Papa Doc was able to turn his army into one of the best-equipped forces in the Caribbean.

"I'd gone to Dave with an idea to run gambling junkets into Haiti. Up to that time, the mob didn't have permission to run junkets into the island. There was a lot of talk about the mob running gambling down there, but there was only a small casino in the city of Port-au-Prince, run by two Jewish guys from New York who were friends of Meyer Lansky and Joe Bonanno. They had a two-bit operation, and it was going nowhere: strictly nickel-and-dime. Dave and Joe Krikorian had approached Papa Doc before about setting up a casino at the El Rancho Hotel, a beautiful little place in the mountains near Port-au-Prince. It really had gorgeous surroundings. Now, Krikorian, Joe Kirk, we called him, worked for Patriarca. He'd been involved in gambling in New England, and he knew a lot about setting up a casino operation. We figured if he controlled the casino and we put in rigged equipment, we'd all make a bundle running junkets into El Rancho.

"Papa Doc sat there listening as Dave and Joe did most of the talking about the casino and I explained the junket operation. While we talked, servants brought in glasses of brandy for us to sip. Dave explained to the old man how much money could be made if he gave his permission for the mob to bring junkets in. Joe Kirk said it was a must, if he was going to make El Rancho a top casino operation, that he bring in his own gambling equipment and his own mechanics to operate the tables.

"Papa Doc just listened. He didn't say much. Once in a while he'd nod or speak soft in that broken French-English of his. You could see he was a very smart guy. He had a good education—you could tell when he talked. He was very short, on the slim side, with tan, not dark black, skin, and he wore glasses. Behind those glasses were piercing brown eyes—eyes that made you feel like he was looking right through you, like he had X-ray eyes. We called them snake eyes. He'd never take those eyes off you.

"Watching him, I thought he'd make a helluva con man. He made all of us think that everything was hunky-dory, but he'd get his point across—he let you know he was Papa Doc, the boss, and don't you ever forget it. He had a will of iron, and he was as hard-hearted as they come. His people were starving, begging in the streets, but he lived in the lap of luxury. All Papa Doc was interested in was how he could make more money. Americans were popular as long as they spent or invested money in his country. But those people he didn't like, those he didn't trust, lived on the edge of a razor blade every minute they were in the country. He thought nothing of putting people up against a wall and shooting them without any trial. He was worse than any crime boss I ever met, and I've met more than a few.

"The meeting lasted for about an hour. Nothing was decided. He thanked us, and we left. A week later, Papa Doc called Joe Kirk and said it would be all right to open the El Rancho casino and bring in mob junkets. There was one hitch. He would approve our bringing in our own gambling equipment, and our own men could work behind the tables, but behind them would be his Tonton Macoutes, his personal goon squad. They would watch the money from the time it hit the table to the time it got to the counting room. And when the money was counted in front of them, they would take out his cut of the pie—every day. His cut was to be 10 percent of all the money bet—not just the profits, but the money bet—and it was to be delivered to him each night by one of his secret policemen.

"That turned out to be a joke. He got a fast count on the money every day. We'd get the Tontons bleary-eyed with a few spiked drinks. They could watch the money all day and never catch the short count. Each of the tables had a cash box, and each box had a false bottom. If you dropped a hundred bucks in cash in the box, all the table man had to do was push a table button and the box bottom opened up, letting the cash drop into a secret compartment. After midnight, everything that went into the box stayed on the top, and Papa Doc got his cut from that portion. But between 8 P.M. and midnight, all the money in all the boxes dropped into the secret compartment. The Tontons would watch as the box was emptied in front of them into a traveling container that went from table to table, and they'd go to the counting room to watch the count. By the end of the week, if his end was fifteen grand in cash, it should have been twenty-five grand. The ten grand had been skimmed off by us. But when it came to credit on junkets, there wasn't much you could chisel him out of. His people watched the books like hawks.

"It wasn't long after the meeting with Papa Doc that I organized and set up the Esquire Sportsman's Club, a corporate front to run junkets all over the world. We located its offices at 10 Emerson Place in a high-rise apartment building in the fancy West End of Boston overlooking the Charles River. Before I set up the operation, I'd gone to Patriarca and Tameleo to explain what I had in mind, and then I went to Carlo Mastrototaro for permission to operate at the casinos where we had contacts. Carlo had the connections with Dino Cellini and Meyer Lansky, and he had an in with other casino operations because he represented Patriarca. It's important to understand why I went to Carlo, even though I knew most of the people at these casinos myself. In the mob you don't just set up any operation you want. You go to the people above you and ask for their permission, and then you cut them in on the profits. You must show them respect. There is a code. We are supposed to be brothers. You don't take bread out of a brother's mouth. I didn't need Mastrototaro, but I had to show him the respect he had coming and cut him in on the profits.

"Now, the way the Esquire Club was to work was that we'd run junkets every month to the Colony, to Haiti, Antigua, Portugal, the Dominican Republic, and the Bahamas. We even ran a junket to Monte Carlo. Each junket was to include no more than thirty big-money gamblers—people with outstanding credit. We had judges, doctors, lawyers, even a lieutenant governor go on our trips. We didn't charter planes, we worked out special excursion deals with the airlines. For every fifteen passengers, we got one ticket free. Thirty people gave us two tickets free. I found the smaller-size junkets were better operations. You got to know the people involved, you mingled with them, and you were able to determine quick who the suckers would be that you could knock out in rigged hotel games. When you have more people than that, you have trouble keeping track of your customers. All my customers were strong gamblers, people with plenty of money. We made sure of each one of them before they left. We had contacts in banks and finance companies who could tell us to the penny how much money a customer had, where it was, and what their principal investments were.

"Under the arrangement I worked out with Mastrototaro, 35 percent of everything that came in belonged to me. Mastrototaro got 65 percent, but out of that he had to pay all the mechanics we used on the junket. Tameleo and Patriarca got a piece of his action. They also got a piece of mine. If I cleared ten grand for myself on a trip, they got two grand, or about 20 percent of my profits.

"Now, because of Mastrototaro, Patriarca, and Tameleo, the Esquire Club got a bigger cut from mob casinos than any of the other junketeers anywhere around the world. At the Colony we got 15 percent of all money bet. We worked out a 25 percent cut in a mob-run club in Portugal. In Antigua, Charlie the Blade and I split fifty-fifty on the profits, and we had the same deal going at a casino he controlled on Madeira Island, off the coast of Portugal. Both of those casinos were as crooked as corkscrews. On rare occasions, I'd run junkets into the Lido Casino in Santo Domingo, which was controlled by Florida crime boss Santo Trafficante. I didn't like that place. It was a real clip joint, and they wanted too big a piece of the pie to make it worthwhile. I made a deal through Cellini and Lansky with Max Courtney to run junkets into the Lucayan Beach Hotel-Casino, and we agreed on a 25 percent piece there. In Curaçao, there were two mob joints, one that gave me a 40 percent cut, the other a 35 percent piece. The whole operation was a gold mine. All I had to do was start the digging.

"By the time I was in operation with the Esquire Club, the El Rancho was really moving in Haiti. Patriarca, Tameleo, and Mastrototaro controlled the entire operation through Joe Kirk. The place was beautiful. It had a kidney-shaped pool in the middle of a beautiful garden, with rooms around it facing the pool. I always had two rooms fronting on the garden and pool. Outside the pool was a huge patio. On one side were more gardens leading to another part of the hotel. It also had an outside bar, and if you walked a little further down, there was a dancing area. Around all of that, under a patio kind of roof, there was the outdoor casino on one side and a large circular bar at the end. Under the roof were two dice tables, five or six blackjack tables, one roulette wheel, and a bunch of slot machines. Everything was rigged. The dice were crooked whenever a player started to get hot. The wheel was controlled, and the cards were marked. You couldn't even get a fair shake on the slot machines.

"With Patriarca as the hidden owner, the mob from all over the country ran its junkets into Haiti. Junket operators controlled by John LaRocca, a mob guy from Pittsburgh who some people say is a boss but he isn't; Angelo Bruno, the boss of Philadelphia; and at least a half dozen from New York controlled by Carlo Gambino, Joe Colombo, and Jerry Catena, moved their junkets in and out. We even had junkets from mob operators in California and Montreal. And for the topping on the cake, the Grace Steamship Line tours were brought in to the El Rancho. But of all the junket guys, I got the best split. The reason was obvious: Patriarca was my boss, and he was getting a slice of my action.

"The Haiti junket setup was like the one in London. Everything was on credit. Every gambler on one of my junkets had to put up five hundred bucks cash in advance. He got his accommodations and his air fare free, and when he arrived he'd get five hundred bucks in nonnegotiable chips to play with. The junkets to Haiti would carry eighty gamblers at a time, because I had more people available to watch the operation. That guaranteed a minimum of forty grand to the casino, and my cut was twenty grand. That was the minimum, but I can't think of a time the suckers on my trips didn't go for at least a grand each, and some went for ten grand or more. Every junket to Haiti was good for between 150 grand and 180 grand to the Esquire Sportsman's Club.

"Now, because I was handling junkets all over the world, I couldn't be on all of them. I might be handling a junket to Monte Carlo when another one was in Haiti. So I took Joe Black [Joseph Lamattina] in as a junior partner. That was the worst mistake I ever made. Tameleo didn't like him and neither did Patriarca. They warned me that I couldn't trust him. I didn't listen to them. If I had, I wouldn't be in the financial trouble I'm in now. I'd have had at least five million bucks to play with, and I wouldn't be telling this story. That may not be true. I think I'd have told the story no matter what happened. I'll tell you why and what Joe Black did to me later. At any rate, I let Joe Black handle most of the junkets into Haiti while I was everywhere else. For a couple of years, he played it straight, never chiseled a dime, and he worked like a dog, hustling the suckers on the trips.

"It wasn't long after I'd run a few junkets into Haiti that I got a call from Papa Doc. He wanted to expand his island casino operations. I don't know why, but he had taken a liking to me. We met again in the Presidential Palace, and I had supper with him. We talked about setting up another casino. At this time there was only the El Rancho and the International Hotel. The International was nickel-and-dime, and none of the good junkets ran in there. They all went to the El Rancho, but Papa Doc figured that another casino would bring in even more action to his city.

"Papa Doc had a string of empty hotels in Port-au-Prince. He had run the owners out and had taken everything over. But his country was starving to death, and he needed more money desperately. 'I'll give you whatever hotel you want,' he told me. 'My minister will show them all to you. You pick the one you like, and we'll give you the money to renovate it in the way you want. You set up and run the casino.' It sounded like a great deal. Then he threw in something extra. 'When you come here,' he said, 'we'll get you a beautiful home up in the mountains, a big estate. You'll live like a king here—we'll make a lot of money together.'

"The old man had other guarantees. There would never be any trouble from Uncle Sam's federal agents. 'You recognize a federal agent—you find any are here,' he said, 'you tell me. I'll have him locked up, and he won't be turned loose until you say so.' Now, I knew he could deliver on what he had said. He used to hide mob guys in Haiti all the time. Dave Iacovetti stayed there for three months while half the federal government looked for him to serve him with a subpoena. Joe Bonanno, the old mob boss, hid in Haiti, stayed at Papa Doc's mountain retreat while half the world's intelligence forces looked for him after he disappeared in 1964. At one time we were going to hide Patriarca there, just before he went on trial in a murder conspiracy, but he wouldn't listen—he thought he'd beat the case. We wanted him to stay in hiding in Haiti until the witnesses against him were eliminated.

"Haiti was Papa Doc's personal preserve. Anybody that went there was known immediately to him. He knew who they were, what they were doing there, and where they went. If he didn't like what he found out, he ran you off the island fast.

"For those of us in the mob who were his friends, wherever we went we were protected by the Tonton Macoutes, his secret police. The Tontons looked more like hoodlums than we did. They always wore dark glasses, expensive sharp civilian clothes, and they all carried guns. They stayed as close to me as mustard plaster wherever I went. They were there as much to protect me as to keep Papa Doc informed on what I was up to. The biggest trouble with them was that they were animals. You'd walk down the street and the people would beg for pennies. They would all be starving. I've never seen poverty like that, and I've been in some pretty rough places. The little kids would ask for gum, pennies, anything. When they got too close, a Tonton would whack a kid across the face or hit him over the head with a blackjack, shouting: 'Get away, get away . . . leave the boss alone . . . leave the boss alone.'

"Even for a mob guy like me who has seen a lot of violence, this was too much. I remember one time that Danny Mondavano, Joe Black, and me and a couple of other guys went shopping in Port-au-Prince. As we were coming out of one of the stores with our packages, a bunch of little kids gathered in front of us, begging for pennies. Danny couldn't resist them. He took a roll of quarters he had from the casino out of his pocket, opened the roll up, and tossed the quarters into the air, shouting: 'All right kids . . . here!' What happened after that made me sick to my stomach. The place exploded. Adults began scrambling on the street, kicking and beating up seven- and eight-year-old kids who were trying to get quarters or keep what they had. They mashed the kids' fingers with their feet, smashed them over the head with anything they could find. It was unbelievable, sickening. I've seen a lot, but I was ready to vomit. There was blood all over the place for a lousy ten-buck roll of quarters. Then the Tontons waded in. They were busting skulls wide open with clubs as we got into a taxicab and drove off. I saw one kid, he couldn't have been more than six years old, hauled into the air by one Tonton and while he was suspended, the Tonton hit the kid's head with a club, squashing it like an egg. You had to see it to believe it. Life is cheap down there.

"I went to Patriarca with Papa Doc's proposal. I could see a golden river flowing into my pockets. It didn't take him long to dry up my hopes. 'Vinnie,' he said, 'it's a helluva idea, but it wouldn't be right. You'd be cutting in on Joe Kirk, and the way you'd operate, you'd knock him out of business.'

"Patriarca was right. Joe Kirk was the first to set the casino operation in motion, and if I did move into my own hotel I would have set up an operation that would have knocked his profits down bad. With Papa Doc's backing and my contacts in the mob, I couldn't miss. The trouble was, Patriarca would have lost face with Joe Kirk and others by letting me operate, even though he'd have made a helluva lot more money. It broke my heart, but I had to call Papa Doc and apologize to him for not being able to take him up on his offer.

"Papa Doc was a gentleman about it. I explained that Joe Kirk was his friend, and if I moved in, I might cut Joe Kirk out. 'My people have informed me that I'd be stepping on his toes and that wouldn't be right,' I explained. 'They're 100 percent right.' Then I came up with a kicker. I wanted to show Papa Doc that I respected him and wanted to keep his friendship. So before I hung up, I asked him if he would like a brand-new Cadillac limousine as a present from me. He was real happy about the idea. 'One thing about the car,' I said. 'It'll be a stolen car.'

"Papa Doc laughed. 'Vincent,' he said, 'don't worry about that. Once it gets to my island, it's safe.'"

21

The Loanshark Swindle

For the money movers of organized crime, gambling junkets provided two important benefits beyond the profits. They enabled mobsters with no other visible means of support to show a legitimate income, thus keeping the tax men at bay. And they provided the mob with a conduit to the upper echelons of society and the business world, where there were huge reservoirs of money to be tapped.

"When mob people operate a junket, we're not interested only in how much money we take at the casino. It may sound like a lot of money when you make sixty grand for a week's work. You have to remember, though, that to operate, you have to pay people, you have to split up those profits with those who provide the okay for a split with the casino. Where you make the real money, where a smart operator makes his killing, is with the suckers you have along on the junket. Your first interest is finding one or two or more suckers on a junket who you can get at your mercy. You wine them, you dine them, you get them into compromising situations. It can pay off in both money and protection for the mob.

"Let's say, for example, you have a judge or a senator along on your junket, and plenty of them went on mine. You arrange for him to be with a hooker, to get a blow job at the suite you've rented. At the same time, the place is set up so that you can get pictures and tape recordings of what is going on. Then, when one of your people gets in trouble with the law, or the mob needs votes on a bill they want passed, a copy of that photograph or the tape recording is sent to him.

"To be frank, I wasn't interested in that part of blackmail. I know junket operators who were and who practiced that. That's one of the reasons, that and money, that the mob has been able to control so many judges and push legislation that helped them. My only interest was in making money, and I used the same technique of wine, women, and song for a different purpose. I made a study of people's characters and weaknesses. I'd sit down with them and start talking about myself—not them. I'd talk about a crap game I went to the night before and watch the sucker's eyes to see if he showed an interest. I'd tell him about places where I found there were all kinds of freewheeling women and watch how he reacted. If the sucker was a fag, I'd talk about a place where the gay people could operate like they pleased while they were on a junket. The idea was to find out what they liked—broads, gambling, fags—and then work on what moved the sucker.

"An example of what I'm talking about was the success I had with two insurance men from a small town in Rhode Island. One we'll call John, the other Bill. Their real names aren't important—they were just a couple of suckers. I had them on a junket to the Colony Club. Both of them tried to impress me. They said they were friends of Raymond Patriarca. A quick check told me that Patriarca had never heard of them. Then I went to work on them. While they were on the trip, I found they wouldn't gamble. Nothing moved them— roulette, dice—nothing. They were starry-eyed at the women they saw moving through the casino. I watched them for a while and listened. All they talked about was the women and the amount of money they saw people throwing around. I had a talk with Danny Mondavano about it. 'I think we can move these two clowns with the right entertainment,' I said. 'You keep an eye on the other suckers while I work on these two. All I can lose is a couple of grand trying.'

"While Danny took care of the card games and parties at the Mayfair, I took these two on a tour of London they'll never forget. I'd already made a check on their credit rating, and I found they were very heavy in the cash department. I took them to plays, nightclubs, parties. I got them a variety of women—all hookers who didn't look or act the role—until their heads were swimming. I'd tell the girls: 'Look, play it like they're great dates. Let them think they're seducing you. Make them believe they're irresistible, but let them know that if it wasn't for Vinnie Teresa, you'd have never gone out with them.' Naturally, I took care of the girls financially. For a week this went on, and by the time we got back to Boston, these two insurance men thought I was King Kong. I'd spent about two grand on them for the week.

"When we landed at Logan Airport outside of Boston, John edged up to me and asked: 'Vinnie—how can you afford to do all this? Don't you file an income tax?'

"I gave him a reassuring smile. 'Of coure I file an income tax.'

" 'But you spend so much,' Bill said. 'I don't understand how you can do it.'

" 'I make most of my money under the table,' I said. 'I got money invested in the loanshark business.' Right away, I could see I'd hit a chord. You can almost smell a man's greed if you're on the street. Then I explained: 'I get a lot of money from doctors, lawyers, insurance men, executives. They put their money with me. Let's say a guy gives me ten grand. I give that guy a point a week in interest and two points a week off the top. Every week he gets three hundred bucks in cash. At the end of fifty weeks, he's got his money back plus a five-grand profit. Of course, I'm making a couple of points a week on his money myself.'

"To two guys from a small town that sounded like a sure-fire scheme. Hidden money they wouldn't have to tell Uncle Sam about—money they could burn on women and parties. Right away both of them wanted to give me some money to invest. I refused. 'I'm sorry,' I said. 'I've got so much money working now and so many people who want to give it to me that I can't take on someone else.' I let it hang there—let them think about it.

"For the next couple of weeks I must have got three calls from them. Finally, I told them to come to Boston. They met me at the Esquire Sporting Club office, and I took them to a nightclub. 'Fellas,' I said, 'I've got a customer who wants to borrow twenty grand. Now, I could probably get the money from a doctor friend I have, but he's been a pain lately—he's been crying on my shoulder, and I don't want to get involved with him again. Do you want in?'

"The two of them jumped at it. They put in ten grand

apiece. For the next couple of weeks I paid them each three hundred bucks, then I tapped them again. In the next six weeks, I took Bill for another sixty-five grand and John for fifty grand. They thought they were in the loanshark business. They thought they'd be rolling in money. I eventually got three hundred grand of their money. Then the bust-out came. They screamed when the interest stopped. I looked at both of them and I laughed. 'Remember the time you mentioned Raymond's name to me?' I said. Their faces colored a little. 'Well, go to Raymond and collect the money from him.' I never heard another word from them. Where could they go? They didn't know Patriarca, and they sure as hell couldn't go to the police and tell them they'd been taken while investing in the loanshark business.

"There were literally hundreds of suckers like that. Some I took for more and some for less, but everyone wanted to be a loanshark, to make money they didn't have to report to Uncle Sam. The funny part about these people is that those with the most money are the easiest to nail. You couldn't imagine the people that are millionaires that wanted to get in on the scheme. They needed money like they needed a hole in the head. But wave that few extra bucks in front of their nose—cash, hidden from the government—and whammo, they jump at the idea. I made scores of so-called millionaires into loansharks. They'd give me their fifty grand and I'd promise them a point a week in interest. That's all they wanted to hear. It was like hitting the winning ticket in the Irish Sweepstakes. They didn't understand. It never dawned on them that if I didn't want to pay them, there was nowhere they could go to complain about it. If they came after me personally, I break their heads. If they go to the cops, they wind up in a trial, their families are embarrassed, they may even lose their business, not to mention their friends. Normally, I'd start a sucker off with ten grand, pay him his point a week for a couple of weeks, then work him up to fifty or a hundred grand or more. When I figured that was all I could take from him, I'd kiss him off. Sometimes there were some hard-headed guys who would try a little muscle. I'd give them a slap in the mouth and send them on their way.

"Some people are harder to sell than others. Take one bright-eyed businessman I ran into from Boston. His first name was Arthur, and he was a swinger. He owned some finance companies. Bobby Cardillo and I bumped into him at the Lucayan Beach Hotel-Casino where we were running junkets. He was a big, lanky guy, about six-foot-three, but he was a real deadhead with women. One of my hustlers, Jimmy the Greek, had tried to move him to a card game, but he wouldn't budge, so I took over. I noticed he was very lonely, very shy when he was around women. He didn't know how to approach them. I talked to a hooker I knew, Betty from New York. She was a beautiful girl, and she knew how to handle herself with high-class people. She had been a model or actress at one time.

" 'Betty,' I said, 'I want to move this guy in a card game. If I make any money, you're in for a little piece. One thing: I don't want you to ask this guy for a dime. I don't want him to know you're a hooker. I want you to fall in love with this guy.'

"I set it up so that she would bump into this guy by accident at the casino bar. Now, I had rented the Governor's Suite at the Lucayan Hotel for the entertainment of my customers. I had my own patio and special service to the suite. I played the role of a millionaire myself, living pretty lavishly. It's important to make an impression like that on the suckers. At any rate, I met Art at the casino bar and bought him a drink. He was alone, and it was obvious he wanted to be with a woman. We sat there for about twenty minutes talking, and in walked Betty. I waved to her and invited her over for a drink. Then I introduced her to Art. She made light conversation with the guy, loosened him up. Then I excused myself to make a long-distance call.

"A few hours later Art came to me. He's like a kid who found new toys under the Christmas tree. Betty had let him seduce her. Then she'd blown his pipes out. He'd never had a woman who'd given him a blow job before, and he was half out of his mind. At that moment I was his friend for life. That night he tried to buy me dinner. He was still with Betty. I was with Rosie, who I'd brought along on the trip. I could never bring my wife along on trips like that. She'd never have understood or approved what was going on, and I'd never subject her to the embarrassment of seeing that sort of stuff. Rosie was different. She was a swinger. She liked the games, the wild parties, the celebrities, the excitement of gambling, the people she met, and she knew the score. She knew men were being set up with hookers and that we were taking them for their shoes, and she couldn't have cared less. In fact, she was amused by it. Blanche always thought I went along on the junkets just to supervise. I never told her Rosie was along or what I was doing.

"After the dinner, I picked up the check and invited him to a little party at my suite later in the evening. 'Bring Betty,' I said. 'You'll be among friends, and you'll have a good time.'

"Sure enough, he and Betty show up. It was a nice party, nothing dirty. There were plenty of women, most of them with their boyfriends and husbands, people I'd met at the casino or brought along on the junket. At about 3 A.M., a few of us decided to set up a card game. On purpose, I didn't ask Art to sit in. Everybody in the game was a mechanic or a shill, and we ignored him as though he wasn't even there. Money piled up around the table. Meanwhile, Betty takes Art into another room and gives him another pipe cleaning. He comes out about twenty minutes later, his face is flushed, and he's got a smile on his face from ear to ear. Now he starts watching the game. The fever gets to him. 'Is there an extra seat?' he asked.

"I looked around the table slow. 'Well . . . there's five of us in here,' I said. I hesitated for a minute. 'Sure, Art. Bring in another chair.' I'd just done him a big favor. Within an hour we've taken thirty-five grand from him, and he decided that was enough.

"'Vinnie,' he said, 'here's my card. My credit's good, I imagine, until we get back to Boston.'

"'Don't worry about it, Art,' I answered. 'Look me up in the morning. We'll have a bite together.'

"He nodded and left with Betty. That morning and for the rest of the day I couldn't find him anywhere. He'd disappeared. Later on I found he'd gone to some other Caribbean casino for some more action and he'd taken Betty with him. But for the moment I thought I might have been suckered myself.

"One morning about a week after I got back to Boston, Blanche rousted me from bed. 'There's some woman on the phone who wants to talk to you,' she said. She was a little irritated. I guess she figured it might be some broad I was going out with. When Blanche mentioned her name, I knew it was Art's wife. I told Blanche it was strictly business. I picked up the phone. 'I'm Art's wife,' the woman said. 'I understand he owes you some money.'

" 'Oh, it's nothing to worry about,' I answered. 'Just a few dollars.' Up to that moment I thought he'd flown the coop.

" 'Art's in the hospital,' she continued. Right then I thought to myself, here comes the bullshit. Then she added: 'But he left a check here for you. Would you mind coming and picking it up tomorrow?'

" 'I'll be down in the morning,' I said. I didn't want to say too much on the telephone because I was a little leary. I didn't know if she was trying to set me up with some cops or federal agents. The less said, the safer, I felt. The next day I picked up the check, and she told me that Art wanted to wish me his best and had said he would look me up when he got out of the hospital. I took the check straight to the bank and cashed it. It was as good as gold. A couple of weeks later, I got another call at the Ebbtide nightclub. It was Art.

" 'How are you feeling, Art?' I asked. 'I hope everything's okay.'

" 'I'm fine, Vinnie,' he answered. 'I'm really in the mood for a little action.'

" 'I'm having a card game tomorrow night,' I said.

" 'How about some women?' he asked. 'Will there be any women around?'

" 'For chrissakes, Art, come on down to the club,' I said. 'It's wall-to-wall women here every night.'

"The next night he came to the Ebbtide, and I'd already set several of the girls up that I wanted to entertain him. They had him off walls in less than an hour. Then he jumped into our card game and dropped another twenty-five grand. Then I made my move.

" 'Art, you know you're an unlucky guy,' I said. 'I feel very bad about this. Why don't you go into business with me? Maybe I can help you get back most of your losses.'

" 'What kind of business?' he asked.

"I said: 'I understand you own some finance companies.' He nodded. 'Why don't you take some of the money out of them and put it on the street with me . . . loansharking? That's where I make my money. I couldn't afford to gamble, running just junkets and this nightclub, you know.' Now, he'd seen me lose a bundle of money in the same game he'd lost in. Naturally, I hadn't really lost a dime, but it impressed him.

"The whole idea appealed to him. He came up with eighty-five grand for loanshark money. All told, I took him for 145 grand just by working on his weakness and shyness with women by using a couple of hookers who I paid a couple of grand to. This guy was a millionaire—a respected businessman in his community. Because of that he was cold turkey. If he beefed to the law, he'd have lost his reputation in the community, in business, and probably his wife as well for playing around. That was an important part of my operation. The people I picked to sucker were people I knew had good financial standing, good reputations in the community, and families. They were people I knew would be afraid to talk because of the publicity and the effect it would have on their families and reputation. They'd have destroyed their business, lost their families, lost everything, if they talked. They figured it was better to take it on the chin than lose everything they'd worked years for. People like that are always easy to take.

"But there are some that you have to approach on a different level. Some, for example, get some sort of thrill out of dealing with people they think are in the Mafia. One insurance man from Providence was like that. I'd had this character on a junket to London. He was short on gambling, but long on the idea of becoming a silent loanshark. He liked the idea of being around wiseguys. He offered to put fifty grand into my loanshark operation. He was convinced I was a Mafioso. I didn't do anything to discourage his ideas. I could see he got a thrill out of secret meetings—a kick out of doing things on the sly. So I arranged one day to meet him at an out-of-the-way bar on Route 1 near Walpole [Massachusetts]. When I arrived, Danny Mondavano was with me, and this character was sitting at the bar, sipping a drink, looking around at people and fingering a long envelope. As I sat down next to him, he looked around to see if anyone was watching, and then he slid the envelope over to me. I took the envelope, motioned to him, and then we walked to a table in a darkened corner where I took a look in the envelope. I started counting the cash that was in it. There was only thirty grand.

" 'What the hell are you pulling?' I growled. 'There's only thirty grand here. I don't want that.' I threw the envelope across the table at him. 'How much was supposed to be in there?' I asked.

" 'There was supposed to be fifty thousand dollars, Vinnie,' he said.

" 'Do you want me to keep up my end of the bargain?' I said. He nodded quickly. 'Then live up to yours. Otherwise, take your money and stick it . . . I don't need your dough.' I started to get a little boisterous, to show the vicious side that a Mafioso is supposed to have, according to the movies. By this time, the guy is shaking like a leaf and stuttering, apologizing. 'You made me come all the way out here for a lousy thirty grand?' I snapped. 'I ought to cut your heart out.'

"Now, my sucker is looking at Danny, hoping for some help. Danny always played the good guy in situations like this. I'd play the tough Mafia boss, and Danny was my understanding aide. 'Take it easy, Vinnie,' Danny said. 'Give the guy a break—maybe he's just a little tight right now.'

"By now my voice had reached a low snarl. I have a gravel voice anyway, but it can get very gruff when I want it to, like you could freeze water with it. 'I don't give a damn,' I snapped. 'If he's that tight, tell him to go put it in a bag and bury it in the ground. I don't need his money.' Then I stormed out of the bar, leaving the little insurance man almost in tears with Danny.

"While I was outside, Danny started to con him. 'Look, Bill, I'm sorry,' he said. 'What can I do? That guy has a quarter of a million bucks on the street. He doesn't need short money like this.'

" 'Can I give you the whole fifty thousand dollars tomorrow?' the insurance guy asked.

" 'I'll talk to Vinnie tonight,' Danny assured him. 'Let me call you later on. Maybe I can convince him. . . .'

"That night Danny called him, and he came right out with the full fifty grand. Two weeks later he came to see me. 'Can you use another fifty thousand dollars?' he asked.

" 'I don't know, Bill,' I said skeptically.

" 'Look . . . I have a total of sixty thousand dollars I can lay my hands on,' he said. 'Take it . . . please, Vinnie, please take it.'

" 'Go ahead, Vinnie,' said Danny. 'Give the guy a break and take his money.' So I took it. The guy never saw a dime. He called a couple of times. Finally, I cut him off. 'You don't want to wind up in a box, you better not call again,' I snapped. 'You're a sucker . . . you been taken. Now shut up.' I never heard or saw him again, but I had 110 grand of his money.

"There were scores of guys like those I've just described whose money we took. Doctors, lawyers, business executives—they all wanted to get in on loansharking. That's how a lot of mob people get their money for their loanshark racket. They keep suckers like that on the hook. They use their money to pull in five points a week, and they pay the so-called honest businessman one or two points a week. I didn't have time to waste like that. I'd take a sucker for all I could, then I'd kiss him off. The trouble was, I spent all I made like there was no tomorrow."

22

The Fall of a Don

Raymond Patriarca's empire was in peril long before he knew it. In 1962 the Federal Bureau of Investigation slipped an illegal electronic bug into his office on Atwells Avenue in Providence. Between 1962 and 1965 the FBI listened daily to Patriarca's conversations with such men as Henry Tameleo and Vincent Teresa. And on October 6, 1966, the mortal blow was struck. It was on that date that Joseph (The Animal) Barboza and three colleagues were arrested by police in the heart of Boston. In Barboza's car, police found a fully loaded Army M-1 rifle and a .45-caliber pistol. The law then began applying a squeeze that was to force Patriarca to make fatal mistakes.

Barboza was a violent, uncontrollable enforcer whom Teresa was using to shake down nightclubs in Massachusetts. After his arrest, Teresa talked with Patriarca about what to do about him.

"Barboza's bail was high—about fifty grand—and Patriarca was thinking about getting Barboza out through some of our bail bondsmen. Then the word came bouncing back. The district attorney, Garry Byrne, had told bail bondsmen that they'd get no breaks from his office, they'd have a hard time with other clients, if they tried to bail Barboza out. He was an untouchable. Byrne wanted Barboza off the streets, and anyone who tried to help Barboza was out of business.

"At first, Patriarca wasn't that upset when he heard it. He never liked Barboza, never really trusted him. 'He's a bum,' he'd tell us. 'He's crazy. Someday we'll have to whack him out.' That someday came sooner than any of us thought.

"It all started with two of Barboza's group of hustlers, Tommy DePrisco and Tashe [Arthur] Bratsos. DePrisco and Bratsos were a couple of enforcers who worked with Barboza. They were well known and tough, and they thought Barboza walked on water. DePrisco's real name was Richard Dipiescia, but he used the name DePrisco. Without Barboza around, they weren't making the money they were used to making in loansharking. They decided the Office had deserted Barboza. They figured if Patriarca wouldn't get Barboza out of jail, they would, so they began shaking down bookies and nightclubs all over Boston to raise the bail Barboza needed. By then the D.A. had raised the bail to a hundred grand.

"The last place these two clowns hit on their shakedown trail was the 416 Lounge—we called it the Nite Lite Cafe. The Nite Lite was a club in Boston's North End owned by Ralphie Chong [Ralph Lamattina]. In the club with Ralphie Chong one day were his brother Joe Black [Joseph Lamattina], Larry Baiona, Phil Waggenheim, one of Baiona's strongarms, and a couple of other people. DePrisco and Bratsos came into the place like 'Gangbusters.' They asked for money to help Barboza out. Baiona just laughed. He said he and his friends wouldn't give a dime. One word led to another, and then DePrisco pulled a gun. 'Empty your pockets,' he said. 'We'll take what we want.' It was a dumb move. Bratsos should have known better. He must have known they'd be hit for holding up made people. A big hassle followed, some shots were fired, and DePrisco and Bratsos were killed in the row that followed. Baiona and the rest of them rifled their pockets. Now, the story that has been going around is that DePrisco and Bratsos had raised seventy grand for Barboza, and that's what the mob took from their pockets. That isn't true. All they had was twelve grand in cash, and that's what was taken.

"Baiona and Ralphie Chong had Waggenheim and some others get rid of the bodies. They put them in Bratsos' car, drove it over to the South End of Boston, and left it near the Division Six police station. DePrisco was in the front seat and Bratsos was in the rear seat. While the bodies were being dumped, Ralphie Chong was busy cleaning up the joint. Some of the bullets had missed Bratsos and DePrisco, and Ralphie Chong had to hang a picture over the bullet holes for a while.

"Now, what Baiona, Waggenheim, and Ralphie Chong didn't know was that there was a police informer in the place, a guy by the name of Joe Lanzi. He was a bartender and part-time owner of the Four Corners bar, and he was in the joint at the time Bratsos and DePrisco came barging in. He ran straight to a cop he worked for, and told what had happened. By then the cops had found the bodies, and they sent a detail straight to the Nite Lite. When they got there, they found Ralphie Chong outside the club trying to clean off a blood-stained rug. They charged him with being an accessory to murder, but they never charged the other people involved. They didn't have enough evidence, I guess.

"Patriarca was furious over the way things were handled. He thought it was a stupid play. What Baiona should have made his men do was bury the two bodies. Without bodies, there would have been no case to worry about. But Ralphie Chong and Baiona were stupid. They thought Barboza was behind the shakedown, and they wanted to let him know what they thought of him for trying to muscle them. So they dumped the bodies, like idiots.

"There was a lot of conferences. Jerry Angiulo told Patriarca that if Ralphie Chong pleaded guilty to the charge, Jerry could fix it with a judge so Ralphie Chong would get a light sentence. Patriarca didn't want a lot of publicity from a trial, and he had a bigger problem with Barboza, who was still in the can and who he was afraid might get ideas about talking because of what happened to Bratsos and DePrisco.

"Patriarca ordered a sitdown, and he sent Henry Tameleo to run the meeting. It was held in the back room at Giro's Restaurant in Boston, a club then owned by Joseph Lombardo, the old mob boss. Lombardo had become the family adviser, the *consigliere*. He was at the meeting with Tameleo, Baiona, Joe Black, Angiulo, Waggenheim, and Ralphie

Chong. There were two mob lawyers also present. They told Ralphie Chong to plead guilty. They said they had a fix arranged in Byrne's office that would guarantee a light sentence. They said the judge would give him a seven-to-fourteen-year stretch, but he'd get sprung in 2½ years. Ralphie Chong didn't like the idea, but he had no choice. Tameleo and Angiulo told him he had to. The orders were from Patriarca, and you don't refuse the boss and live.

"In February 1967, Ralphie Chong went to court and pleaded guilty. But instead of a judge in the bag, he got a judge who was rough. He sentenced Ralphie Chong to two long jail terms. That meant that he was going to spend a long time in jail. There was some wild scrambling, but later they got it straightened out. A smart lawyer figured out that there was something wrong about the way the judge sentenced Ralphie Chong. He won an appeal, and in March 1971, Ralphie Chong was back on the street doing business like always.

"Then on April 18, 1967, they caught up with the informer, Lanzi. Three of Angiulo's enforcers—Benjamin DeChristoforo, Carmine Gagliardi, and Frank Oreto—were driving through Medford at four in the morning. In the front seat of their car was Lanzi, who they'd just shot. They suddenly realized they were being tailed by the police, and they panicked. They tried to shake the tail and couldn't. So they stopped the car on Fifth Street, just a block from where I was renting the second floor of a house on Fourth Street. At the time, I was in Las Vegas on a casino junket. I knew Gagliardi. He was a good street hustler, a real tough kid, but he had a heart as good as gold. He used to play catch with my kids and go out golfing with me from time to time. Anyhow, when they spotted the cops, they made a break for it. Oreto was trapped in the car. He couldn't move the body to get out of the car in time, so the cops grabbed him with the corpse. Gagliardi and DeChristoforo made a dash for it. They ran right through my yard and buried the gun in the ground at a nearby neighbor's.

"The cops tracked their footprints to my property, and they came knocking at my door, waking up Blanche and the kids. They demanded that Blanche let them search our place. She wouldn't. She called me in Las Vegas and told me what happened. They thought Blanche was hiding Gagliardi, and I had to assure them she wasn't. I flew back to town that morning to talk to them. If I'd been home at the time, the cops would have brought me into the case for sure and probably would have charged me. The police didn't catch up with Gagliardi for almost a year. They found him hiding behind a false wall in his mother's house in Medford. DeChristoforo was arrested in New York at about the same time.

"While all this was going on, Barboza was boiling. He'd read about Ralphie Chong getting arrested in the killing of Bratsos and DePrisco, and he started making some wild threats. He passed the word out of jail that when he got out he was going to kill Waggenheim, Baiona, and Angiulo. Then he went too far. He got a message to Chico [Joseph] Amico, who was his closest friend, and gave him orders to whack out Waggenheim. The mob found out, and they hit Chico right outside Alfonso's Broken Hearts Club, where he'd been trying to put an arm on some people to help Barboza. Barboza went wild when he heard what happened. He called Patriarca a fag, and he promised he'd hit everyone in sight for killing Chico. Patriarca and Tameleo heard about it, and then I got a call.

" 'Vinnie,' Tameleo said, 'go see Butch [Frank Miceli of the New Jersey assassination squad] and get a supply of shotguns and rifles. Barboza's got to get hit.'

"So I went to New Jersey and got the guns, and when I got back, Tameleo assigned thirteen of us to various places all over town and along a couple of highways. They were the locations Barboza would go to, and each of us was to lie in wait for him. Tameleo had got the word that Barboza was going to make bail, and he'd set up an elaborate plan to get Joe no matter where he went—whether it was to a nightclub, a restaurant, his house, or the airport. I was assigned, and so was Maxie Baer, Mario Lepore, Tony Blue, Lou Grieco, Benny Zinna, and some other headhunters.

"Now, the way Tameleo planned the hit is typical of the mob's way of doing in its own. The guy that was to set Barboza up when he got out of jail was Guy [Gaetano] Frizzi, a close friend and partner of Barboza who, with his brother, Cono, had got Barboza started as a legbreaker. But then the Frizzis were devoured by their own monster; they ended up working for Barboza rather than giving him orders, and they were scared to death of him. Guy Frizzi was to pick Barboza up when he got out of prison and take him to one of the clubs. He was to follow a particular route, if he could, where they would have an ambush. But Tameleo couldn't be sure that Barboza would let Guy use that route, so he stationed the rest of us in places where he figured Barboza might go to. One of the people who were staked out was Cono Frizzi. Now, what Guy Frizzi and his brother didn't know, and probably still don't, is that Tameleo planned to have Guy hit with Barboza. Tameleo didn't trust Guy, and he figured he'd get rid of two for the price of one. If Cono Frizzi had objected, he'd have been whacked out on the spot too. The whole plan fell through when the district attorney got a tip, went to the judge, and blocked any attempt by Barboza to get out of jail.

"It wasn't long after that that Barboza found out he was going to be killed. I guess [District Attorney] Byrne told him, and two FBI agents who were working on him, Paul Ricco and Dennis Condon, told him. They convinced him that Patriarca had double-crossed him and was going to have him killed. Barboza was frantic. He didn't want to die, and he didn't want to be an informer. He hated informers. They were against everything he believed in. So he wrote a letter to Patriarca. It was on a Sunday in 1967 that I found out about it. Lou Grieco called me and said that Barboza had smuggled a letter out of the jail through a friend. The friend had given the letter to him to give to me because Barboza trusted me and was convinced I would deliver it to Tameleo and Patriarca. I picked the letter up from Grieco and called Tameleo.

" 'Henry,' I said, 'Joe just smuggled out a letter addressed to you and Raymond. I got it. What do you want me to do?'

" 'Bring it here to the house,' he said. 'I want to read it.'

"I drove to Tameleo's house and watched while he read the letter. Then he handed it to me. What it boiled down to—I don't remember all the exact wording—the letter said: 'I wasn't responsible for what Tashe [Bratsos] and DePrisco were trying to do. I didn't tell them to do those things. I'm sorry for shooting my mouth off in here. I'm sorry about Chico. I lost my temper because people were telling me certain things. I didn't mean any harm. All I want to do . . . I'm begging you . . . please . . . let me hit the street. I have a little money left. Let me take my wife and kid and get out. I promise . . . you will never hear from me or see me again. I'll never give you or anyone else trouble. Just let me live.'

"Tameleo looked at me after I'd finished. 'As far as I'm concerned,' he said, 'tell him: "Don't worry about it, Joe. . . ."' and then, when he gets out, we whack him when he least expects it.'

"I didn't like the idea. I'd always liked Joe, as wild as he was, but I didn't see anything else that could be done. 'Well, that's up to you, Henry,' I said.

"Tameleo motioned to me. 'Come on—let's talk to Raymond about it.'

"I drove Henry to Patriarca's house on Lancaster Avenue in Providence. Tameleo tried to talk to Patriarca, but he wasn't listening. He was blowing his top, screaming at the top of his lungs. 'That dirty nigger bastard, I'll kill him. He's gonna get killed in or out of the can. You send the word to him—and that's all there is to it.'

"I shook my head as I looked at Patriarca. 'Raymond—is that the smart thing to do?' I asked. 'You're tipping your hand to this guy.'

"Raymond was wild. He wouldn't listen to reason. 'I want him to know,' he said, 'to spend every night shitting in his pants, this bastard. Who does he think he is? He'll kill this guy and that guy. I'm a fag, he says. I'll get him. He talks that way about me. I'll straighten him out.'

"I tried to calm him down, but all I got was one word out of my mouth. I said: 'Raymond—'

" 'Now, Vinnie, you shut up and do as you're told,' he snapped. 'You go back and you tell Barboza's friend what I said. That's what I want.'

"There was no sense in saying another word. I'd just get in trouble myself. So I told Barboza's friend, a guy named Al. 'Tell Joe this isn't my opinion, this is coming from the top man himself, Uncle Raymond. Tell Joe he's gonna get it whether he's in the can or out. Wherever he is, he's gonna get it. That's all I can tell you. Now you tell Joe.'

"About a week later the FBI agents met with Barboza again, and he began talking. What the hell could the guy do? Patriarca had shoved his back to the wall. It was the dumbest play Patriarca ever made. If he'd done what Tameleo wanted him to do—convinced Barboza everything was forgiven and then, when he got out of jail, whacked him, there wouldn't have been any trouble.

"But when Barboza started talking, there was hell to pay. First Barboza claimed that Patriarca, Tameleo, and Ronnie Cassesso had conspired with him to kill Willie Marfeo. That was true. Patriarca had called him in, and Barboza had worked with Cassesso to try and set up Marfeo. It didn't work; Marfeo was too careful, and he knew Cassesso and

Barboza. As a result of what Barboza testified to, all three were indicted by a federal grand jury for conspiracy to murder. They were all convicted, even though the actual murder was handled by the New Jersey assassination squad.

"Barboza wasn't through talking, though. He accused Tameleo, Cassesso, Roy French [an Angiulo enforcer], Lou Grieco, Pete Limone, and Joe the Horse Salvucci of planning and carrying out the Teddy Deegan murder. I told you before how that was done. They set Deegan up in a bank burglary, and then hit him. I still don't think Tameleo was in on that one. He told me the first he knew about it was when he read about it in the papers. Joe the Horse was just an innocent sucker who Barboza didn't like, but he's doing life because of what Barboza said. He never had anything to do with the hit.

"Barboza also tried to nail Angiulo, Benny Zinna, Vinnie the Pig [Richard] DeVincent, and Mario Lepore for the murder of Rocco DeSiglio. DeSiglio was a tough ex-boxer who thought he could roust the mob. He'd been fingering Angiulo's card games in the Roxbury area, and finally the mob figured out who was behind it. One particular game cost Angiulo's card-game operator sixty grand. Angiulo put out a hit order on him, and Barboza knew about it. He didn't handle the hit. DeSiglio got hit in June 1966. They beat the hell out of him, shot him, and left him in his new Thunderbird in Topsfield [Massachusetts]. Angiulo, Zinna, DeVincent, and Lepore were tried.

"But the jury didn't believe Barboza, and they were acquitted. Patriarca then figured Barboza wouldn't stand up on other trials, either. He figured everyone would beat the cases. That's why he wouldn't listen when we wanted to have him hole up in Haiti—go into hiding until a way was figured to reach Barboza and whack him out. Patriarca said no, he'd beat the case.

"Then other problems came up that caused Patriarca problems. One of Barboza's lawyers was a guy by the name of John Fitzgerald. On January 30, 1968, he got into his car in Everett [Massachusetts], turned on the ignition, and the car blew up. Fitzgerald lost his leg, and he and everyone else blamed Patriarca for it. The truth is, Patriarca had nothing to do with it. It was a jailed member of one of the Irish mobs who had it in for Fitzgerald and arranged for the bombing. It had nothing to do with the Office or Barboza, but Patriarca got the blame anyway.

"When Tameleo got charged, it was the end of the line for him. I don't know what happened to him that last year he was on the street, but it was all downhill. He acted like he was in his second childhood. He started chasing young girls all over the place. He let a clown like Butch [Angelo] Rossi deal with higher-ups from other mobs, like Fat Tony [Anthony] Salerno and Jerry [Gerardo] Catena [both of the old Vito Genovese crime family]. He gave Rossi too much leeway because Rossi kept him supplied with girls. He let Bobby Cardillo do whatever he wanted and pay who he wanted, and when Cardillo chiseled Art Ventola on a split of hot goods, he sided with Cardillo without even listening to Ventola. All of a sudden, Tameleo became a dictator instead of a diplomat, a tyrant instead of a peacemaker, and he began to lose respect in the mob.

"He started doing business himself with every two-bit hustler and punk that came into the Ebbtide instead of going through someone like me or Rossi or Cardillo. Now the punks went direct to him, and he'd give them his home phone number to call him. The next thing you knew, every horse's ass in the city was saying, 'I'm with Henry Tameleo.' It was stupid. Bosses of his stature should never deal with street punks. Before he went off his track, nobody would have dared say they was with Tameleo unless it was somebody like me. If he had, he'd have had him hit in his tracks for throwing his name around. I remember that things got so bad that one day Henry walked into a restaurant and threatened the owner personally because he'd fired a girl that Henry was interested in.

"Finally, when Tameleo was convicted, Patriarca said to me: 'He brought it on himself—he got senile in his old age.' That from Patriarca floored me. Those two guys had been like two peas in a pod. Tameleo gave orders and Patriarca backed them. He never questioned Tameleo's actions in anything. Patriarca felt terrible about what had happened to Tameleo, but to be honest, I think if Tameleo had stayed out of jail and kept acting like he did, sooner or later Patriarca would have had to put him to sleep. He was becoming a drag on the whole organization, and on Patriarca most of all. When Tameleo went to jail for the Deegan murder, Patriarca named Carlo Mastrototaro as second in command, and Patriarca began grooming me. I think that's what he and Tameleo had been doing for years—grooming me to become Patriarca's buffer, the guy who passed the orders of the boss down. If that decision had ever been made by Patriarca, I'd have had to become a made man or they'd have killed me. There was no way you could back out of a situation like that.

"It's funny, but in January 1965, Tameleo had tested me and I'd failed. He wanted me to hit a guy named Barney Villani, a two-bit burglar who Tameleo said was a stool pigeon. I found out later the hit order was recorded on the FBI bugs in Patriarca's office.

"Villani was a little weasel of a guy, about five-foot-three, with a red face that looked like he was born with a veil over it. He had crossed Pete Kattar, that guy that worked for me in Piranha, Inc., and Kattar hated little Barney. He told Don Peppino that Barney was a stoolie, and Peppino told Tameleo. There was no question Barney was a stoolie. But he had three lovely daughters and a wonderful wife, and he was really a harmless little weasel.

"I got soft-hearted. I thought about those three kids and his wife, and I just couldn't do it. I knew all of them. I caught up with Barney and told him: 'Barney, you're in a lot of trouble. You better get out of town fast, otherwise you're going to get whacked out.' Barney took off, and nobody saw him for quite a while.

"Every now and then, Tameleo would ask me what I was doing about Villani. 'I can't find him, Henry,' I'd say. 'The guy's gone. If he comes back, I'll handle him.' That seemed to satisfy him. After Tameleo went to jail, Barney came out of hiding. By then there was a lot of newspaper publicity about the bug in Patriarca's office. One of the stories told how Big Vinnie had orders to kill Villani. Barney presumed it was a new contract, and he came to my rented house in Medford. He was crying, on his hands and knees. 'Please, Vinnie, please . . . I've got a wife and kids . . . please don't kill me.' I looked at the little weasel. I felt like laughing, but I didn't. 'Get the hell off your knees, Barney,' I said. 'I got no reason to kill you now. You go ahead, mind your own business, and stay away from Boston, where there are people who don't like you. They know you're a stoolie, and they'll hit you if they see you.'

"He thanked me and left, but he turned out to be a louse. He left his wife and kids and started fooling around with a broad. That's bad enough, but he didn't take care of his family—he didn't give them a dime. Tameleo was right. I should have whacked him out."

When the FBI and District Attorney Byrne learned of Patriarca's vow to murder Barboza, they knew that there was no prison cell that would be safe. Patriarca's influence reached from police precincts to the offices of state governors and, in fact, into congressional chambers. The FBI came up with a daring plan. Backed by Director J. Edgar Hoover and approved by the U.S. Department of Justice, the plan was to become the forerunner of what is now the most devastating tool the federal government has against organized crime: the witness protection program.

Until 1967, every federal and local agency feared producing its informers as witnesses at trials because they had no way of guaranteeing protection from the mob for the witness and his family after the trials were over. The mob, from one end of the nation to the other, had proved again and again that it was capable of stalking its victim and eliminating him.

To Hoover and prosecutors of the Department of Justice, Barboza represented the best opportunity the government had ever had, up to that time, of breaking through the mob's code of silence to reach the high echelons of the mob. But to provide Barboza and his family with the protection they required —in an area where scores of mob gunmen were itching for an opportunity to catch law enforcement by surprise—strained the manpower, budget, and capabilities of the FBI. What was needed was a combined effort.

Although Barboza was being held in state prison on charges filed against him by Byrne, he was freed in the custody of the FBI to act as a witness against Patriarca. The FBI, unable to handle the job alone, called in an elite, trusted contingent of sixteen deputy U.S. marshals, headed by Deputy Marshal John Partington, an experienced law officer with the highest credentials. For the next sixteen months, the marshals would have the task of living with Barboza and his family, keeping them safe and in a proper frame of mind for the trials that were to come. During those sixteen months, Hoover would often call personally to determine how the Barboza protection detail was progressing and what problems were faced. That it worked so well is a tribute to both the FBI and men like Partington.

The first test of the protection plan came on a fall day in September 1968, and it was Teresa who tested it.

"The feds had taken Barboza to an island off the coast of Gloucester, a place called Thatcher's Island. It was an old lighthouse station that reminded me of a candle sitting in the middle of a basin. It was surrounded by high rocks, and the living area and houses were below those rocks. It was a place where the rats ate bugs, the snakes ate the rats, and the birds ate everything in sight. It was a hell hole, and I can't imagine anyone living there. If it wasn't covered by fog, it was slammed by seas or rain or snow or whatever.

"At the time, I had a 112-grand, forty-three-foot Egg Harbor yacht that I'd bought through the Esquire Sportsman's Club. It was a dream boat that I called the *Living End*. It was fitted out with the best radar, and it had a master stateroom with its own private bathroom. There was another stateroom with double bunks, bureaus, mirrors—the whole works. From the staterooms, you stepped up three steps to the parlor, the living-room area. That was carpeted, with a big couch that opened into a bed. There were plush swivel chairs, a tape stereo that was piped all over the ship, a big dining table in the middle, and beyond that was a large galley with a refrigerator-freezer, a three-burner stove, a stainless-steel sink, and a booth where six people could sit and eat. Below the forward area were bunk areas for the captain and the first mate, and another bathroom. On the upper deck, I had beach chairs and an open bar with a sundeck. The boat even had chrome-plated anchors. It was a gold mine for the Esquire Club. I made 150 grand on it in crooked card games in the first two months I had it. But in September 1968, it had another mission.

"Patriarca had found out through the newspapers that Barboza was being kept on Thatcher's Island. He called me in. 'You take Pro Lerner up there and case the island,' he said. 'See if you can get Barboza.' When we got there we began cruising around the island. We had rifles with 'scopes and shotguns on board. They're legal to have. We looked at the island through binoculars and a telescope. We couldn't get near it. While we looked, we could see men in what looked like coveralls, walking posts and carrying carbines and sidearms. We never could see Barboza. Pro Lerner said that it would be suicide to try to reach Barboza. He had a wetsuit and was a terrific skin diver, but he said the chances of getting close enough to throw a shot at Barboza were a million to one. When we got back we told Patriarca."

What Teresa wasn't aware of was that Partington and other deputies had a tip from the FBI that an attempt might be

made to breach the island security. Forewarned, they had
turned the island into a fortress, and they spotted Teresa's
craft cruising back and forth. That, however, was not the end
of attempts to reach Barboza.

"After a while, the FBI and the marshals moved Barboza
from the island to a big estate in Goucester [the Dolliver's
Neck estate owned by millionaire John Babcock Howard].
The place was surrounded by dense woods. The marshals and
Barboza lived in servants' quarters, a duplex, on the estate,
and they had German shepherd guard dogs with them to spot
and smell out intruders. Patriarca found out where they were
and sent Pro Lerner to see if he could get at Barboza again.
Pro went in alone, on his hands and knees. He lay in the
woods for five or six hours in the rain, looking for an opening, an opportunity to throw in a shot with his 'scoped rifle.
He came back and told Patriarca there was no chance. He
said if he could have got a shot in, he'd have been killed in the
attempt. Pro Lerner was no run-of-the-mill mug. He was a
paid assassin, the best around, and if he couldn't get to Barboza, no one could, and Patriarca knew it.

"Patriarca even had Red Kelley see if he could set up Barboza when he came to the courthouse to testify. He had Kelley case the courthouse, and no one could case a place like
Kelley could. He made notes on every nook and cranny of the
courthouse and on the movements of Barboza by the marshals. He said they changed their routine so many times, that
Barboza was so well covered, that he could never make a plan
that the mob could use to hit Barboza. In fact, Kelley was so
impressed that when he later got busted and indicted by Byrne
on a 524-grand armored-car robbery in December, he agreed
to talk and testify against Patriarca and others only because
the marshals and the FBI had proved they could keep Barboza and his family alive. Kelley's story led to Patriarca's conviction for planning and ordering the Rudy Marfeo and Melei
murders. His testimony also nailed his friend Lerner, Rudy
Sclarra, John Rossi, and Robert Fairbrother, who were in on
the job. The FBI's still looking for a couple of other guys who
disappeared after they were charged in the case.

"All of these things, or at least most of them, would never
have happened if it hadn't been for Patriarca's temper and decision to let Barboza know he was going to whack him out
wherever he was. Joe would never have talked if he thought

Patriarca had forgiven him. He'd have done his time, come out of jail, and then been whacked without ever expecting it. But Patriarca was bull-headed.

"Patriarca forced Barboza to talk. Then Kelley joined him, and the ball was rolling. When the feds showed they could keep both of them alive, others in the mob decided to talk, including me. But that wasn't all that contributed to Patriarca's downfall. The porkiness of Louie the Fox Taglianetti cost Patriarca and everyone in the mob.

"Louie the Fox was one of Patriarca's most trusted aides. He had, when the chips were down, helped whack Mad Dog Nazarian when Patriarca thought his life was in danger. He was also one of Patriarca's big moneymakers, controlling the bookmaking, numbers, and loanshark rackets of the mob in the Providence area and the outlying suburbs.

"Because he was active, the Internal Revenue agents built a case against him for tax evasion. Louie the Fox lived like a king, but he was tight as a crab's ass when it came to paying taxes. If he'd declared a higher income and paid more taxes, the tax boys would have had a tough time nailing him. I always declared a pretty good income, up to fifty grand a year, because I knew it would be very tough for them to prove I spent more. I also had a lot of corporate fronts to hide the movement of my money.

"In 1966, Louie the Fox went on trial for tax evasion. But before he was tried and convicted in April of that year, his lawyers got a tip that the FBI had bugged Patriarca's office. Now, no one in the mob knew what had happened up to that time. Louie the Fox thought it was just a federal gimmick to try and rattle them. He didn't think anyone could have bugged Patriarca's office. His lawyers believed it, though. They told him that he should cop a plea and they'd get him a light sentence. He wouldn't listen. He went to Patriarca and told him what the lawyers said. Patriarca told him to plead guilty, that he'd only do short time. 'Do the bit and forget about it,' Patriarca said. 'If they have tapes like you say, they can destroy us.'

"Louie the Fox wouldn't listen. He insisted that his lawyer make the FBI produce the tapes. They did. That's when the whole world blew up for Patriarca. They only made public a small part of all the transcripts of the bugs, the parts that were supposed to relate to Taglianetti. But the tapes turned the spotlight of publicity on the Office and its operation, they disclosed conversations about murders and robberies and buying politicians. Christ, the newspapers went wild. They wrote millions of words, and everyone who knew Patriarca shunned him like the plague.

"Patriarca was half out of his mind with fury. He wanted to kill Louie the Fox right then and there. He didn't, but Louie the Fox got it when he got out of Lewisburg [federal penitentiary] and came back to Providence after serving his time on the tax case. They whacked him out a few months after he hit the street in November 1969. I'd warned Louie the Fox not to go back to Providence when I met him in Lewisburg. I told him: 'Louie, you're a millionaire. You have a big yacht—take a long cruise. Patriarca has it in for you. There's hard feelings. If you go back, the first thing that will happen is that you end up with a serious headache [a bullet in the head].'

"Louie the Fox didn't want to know. He said he had to go back. He said that a bunch of young punks had taken over bookmaking and loanshark rackets that he'd run all his life. He vowed he was going to wipe them out and put things back in order. He should have listened to me. On February 6, 1970, a couple of gunmen caught him with a girl by the name of Elizabeth McKenna at the Massassoit Apartments in Cranston [Rhode Island]. They killed him and the woman as he left the apartment. I guess the woman got it because they didn't want any witnesses.

"Between the bug, The Animal [Barboza], Kelley, and Patriarca's stupidity, the New England mob empire began to crumble. Patriarca got a five-year term in Atlanta [federal penitentiary], and after he went to jail there was nothing but trouble for those of us who had been his men. The Boston branch of the mob, Anguilo in particular, had always hated me and a few others. He'd hated me in particular because I didn't have to take his orders; in fact, I *gave* orders to him from Tameleo and Patriarca. With Tameleo and Patriarca gone, I was fair game. But it took a while for me to realize what was going to happen. I was too busy making money, thinking up new swindles, to watch my back. That's where I made a big mistake."

23

Stock Swindles

Along the Lynnway in Lynn, Massachusetts, the best-known car agency is the one owned by Boston Red Sox baseball star Carl Yastrzemski. Through this dealership pass hundreds of thousands of dollars' worth of Ford automobiles each year. Its customers and the business community of Lynn recognize the agency as a respectable business run by an outstanding young sports figure. It wasn't always that way. Before Yastrzemski bought up the agency's assets, the dealership was a booming business owned by salesman Al Grillo—and the mob.

Until the mob, represented by Vincent Teresa, dug their claws into him, Al Grillo was one of the business success stories of Lynn. He had come to Lynn from North Carolina, established himself as a salesman, built a respectable business reputation, and set up the Al Grillo Ford Agency. Business boomed, and Grillo became a relatively wealthy man. Then he met Teresa.

"Al Grillo was a little squirt, about five-foot-three, with black curly hair and an Ivy League appearance. But down deep in his heart, he was a thief. I met him through a race-track hustler who had moved him for five-grand booking action at the dogtracks. The hustler told me that Grillo loved to be around wiseguys and had an overwhelming desire to get into the loanshark business. For a grand, the hustler, a kid named Donnie, said he'd turn Grillo over to me. I agreed, and Donnie introduced me to Grillo, telling him I was an important shylock he could do business with.

"Once Grillo and I talked, I knew I had a beautiful sucker on my line. It was just a matter of reeling this fish in. His eyes shined when I offered to give him 1 percent a week on any money he gave me. The first week we met he came up with five grand. He was supposed to turn over ten grand, and when he came up short I blew my top—I let him know he wasn't dealing with some punk from the streets. I threw the money back in his face and started to walk out of his place. When you have a sucker like this, you have to let him know at the start who is the boss. You have to establish in his mind that he is in serious trouble [about to be murdered] if he plays games with you. Grillo got the message right away. He begged me to take his five grand, and he came up with the other five grand to boot.

"For the first few weeks, I paid him his 1 percent. He came up with another ten grand. In a matter of months, I had taken him for 200 grand, including a new forty-five-grand house for my family in North Reading [Massachusetts,] thirty grand to furnish it, money for a new pool, and a couple of cars. By now he wasn't getting the interest money I'd promised him, but he was intrigued by dealing with wiseguys. To give you an example of what I mean, I should tell you about a jewelry deal I suckered him on.

"A couple of thieves I knew had broken into a jewelry store in the Chelsea [Massachusetts] area and taken thirty grand worth of jewels. One of them came to me with the jewels. Now, we—the mob—had a deal with police in Chelsea and Revere that we wouldn't stage holdups or burglaries in their areas. In return, they let us operate like we wanted in gambling and loansharking. I knew it wouldn't be long before the cops passed the word for us to get the jewelry back for them. That was our agreement: If anything was taken in a heist, it was up to the mob to find out who did it and to get the property returned to the cops. Knowing Grillo's weakness for shady deals and wiseguys, I came up with a scheme to milk some extra money from him. I sent Joe Napolitano and Richie Castucci, who ran the Ebbtide for Tameleo and me, to see Grillo with the jewels.

" 'You tell Al I sent you, that I told you if I wasn't around, to go see Al Grillo,' I told them. 'Let him take the jewelry and get it appraised. Then offer to sell it to him for twenty grand. He'll try and reach me, but I'm not going to be around. I'll tell my wife to tell him I'm out of town. That way when the beef comes he won't be able to run to me.'

"Castucci couldn't figure out what I was up to. 'I don't get it, Vinnie. You mean we turn the jewels over to him even when the law is going to want the stuff back?'

"I gave Castucci a kind of impatient look and sort of growled at him. I wasn't really being fair to him because he didn't know what I had in mind, but I had a real bad headache and I was a little quick on the trigger. 'Look,' I snapped, 'the first thing he'll do when he gives you the money—and be sure you handle this at night—is take the jewels and do one of two things. He can't go to the bank with them, and he won't take them home because he's afraid. So he'll either put them in the agency safe, and I don't think he'll even do that because he doesn't want anyone in the company to know what he's up to, or he'll hide them in one of his cars.' I hit it right on the head. They let Grillo look at the jewels in the afternoon so he could get them appraised, and they arranged to collect money from him that night. When they met him that night, they put a guy on the roof, like I instructed them, to watch what Grillo would do through a window. Grillo could come up with only nine grand in cash, telling them he'd get the rest of the money from me when I came back to town. Sure enough, after they left, Grillo headed for a new Thunderbird in the shop, opened the car trunk, and hid the jewels beneath the spare tire. Then he left and my men broke into the joint, pried open the trunk of the car, and took the jewels, which they brought back to me with the nine grand.

"The next day my telephone almost came off the hook with calls from Grillo. Finally, I answered one of the calls. 'Hey, Al, what are you doing?' I asked.

" 'Vinnie, I've got to see you, right away,' he shouted, real excited. 'Can you come over to the agency? Where have you been? I've been trying to reach you.'

" 'Calm down, Al,' I said. 'I been in New York. I'll be down to see you in an hour. Then we can talk.'

"I got to the agency about an hour later, and he tells me the story about buying the jewels and then having them stolen. Then I landed on him. 'You stupid jerk,' I shouted. 'You got a helluva nerve dealing with these people when I'm not around.

What right have you got dealing in something like this when I'm not here?'

" 'Well, they mentioned your name—' he tried to explain.

" 'Mentioned my name?' I roared. 'What if some bum came up to me and mentioned your name and said, "Give me ten grand."? Would I give it to him?' He shook his head. 'Well then, what the hell did you do this for?'

"Grillo was all confused now and scared to death. He'd always been afraid of me, but he liked to think he was with the wiseguys by hanging out with me. I'd taken him around to a few places, let him mingle with some of the wiseguys. It made him feel big, and he began believing he was working for me and the mob.

" 'Well, I had the jewels—' he tried to say.

" 'Had the jewels!' I snapped. 'That's the biggest sucker play of them all. I don't know what I'm going to do for you, Al—I don't know how I'm going to get them back. How much were they worth?'

" 'About thirty thousand dollars,' he answered meekly. 'I had them appraised.'

" 'Give me five grand,' I said. 'Maybe I can look around and buy them back for five grand.' He gave me the five grand. A few days later, the cops put the word out that they wanted the jewels returned, and I arranged for them to be brought back. The papers carried an item about the jewels being recovered. I told Grillo I'd paid the five grand for the jewels and they were being returned to him when the cops grabbed them. So Grillo was out fourteen grand trying to be a thief himself.

"Grillo was important to me for another reason. He was the first sucker I used to move stolen securities. Actually, in his case, the first stocks I moved through him were counterfeits. That was in 1967. What I learned from that deal helped me move millions of bucks' worth of stock later through people I bled dry on casino junkets.

"It was in the fall of 1967. Grillo was in a panic. I'd used him and his money to open up the Esquire Sportsman Club. He'd put up thirty-five grand for the furniture and other equipment I needed on the promise that he'd get a cut of the action. I'd even put his business manager, Jack Hirschfeld, on my payroll as president of the company. I owned Hirschfeld. He was in hock up to his ears to me for shylock loans, and I gave him a chance to work off some of the loans by fronting as the owner of the junket club at a salary of five hundred bucks a week. But Grillo was in hock also. I'd taken him for more than two hundred grand, and he was frantic for money. He came into my office one day to cry on my shoulder.

" 'Vinnie, I'm desperate,' he said. 'I'm going to lose my company. I know I can't raise any money, but what the hell am I going to do?'

"Danny Mondavano was in the office with me at the time. He'd just been arrested for handling some stolen bonds in New Jersey. 'Ask him if he knows anything about the bond business,' Danny said to me.

"Grillo heard him. 'Sure I do,' he said quickly. 'I know a lot about it. My father's been in the stock and bond business for years.'

"I looked at Grillo and thought about what Danny had said. I knew what was on his mind, but I'd never dealt in stocks or bonds before and I didn't know a thing about them. But I figured nothing ventured, nothing gained. Grillo must have read my thoughts.

" 'If you can get some bonds,' he said, 'I have a guy in Boston, a lawyer, who can move them—stolen bonds.'

"I agreed to see what I could do. I called Tameleo and asked him about it. He suggested I go see Jack Mace, the big New York fence. Tameleo gave me the okay to deal with Mace and cleared my credit with him. We met in the jewelry center in Manhattan. Danny was with me. The first guy Mace took us to see was a Brooklyn thug known as Joe Jinks. He was a stocky runt, just a little over five foot, with dark hair and a wide-brimmed hat. He had a whole bunch of bonds— Standard Oil of California and International Telephone and Telegraph—but he wanted 30 percent of their value. That sounded like too much to me, so I said no to the deal. That night Mace took me to a bar in Brooklyn. In the bar were Artie Todd [Arthur Tortorello] and his brother Pete. Artie Todd is one of the biggest dealers in hot securities in New York. He used to work for The Doctor [Carmine Lombardozzi]. Now I hear he's on his own, but works for the Carlo Gambino crime family.

"At the meeting, Mace told Artie Todd that I had an okay from Tameleo to pick up some bonds. We all walked to a back room of the bar, and they handed me an envelope. Inside were some Standard Oil of California bonds. In fact, they were duplicates of the ones shown earlier to me by Joe Jinks.

Now my mind starts clicking. How is it that this guy Todd has the same bonds that Jinks had? What was this, some kind of joke? Then I noticed that they looked brand new. It bothered me. 'These look like queers [counterfeits] to me,' I said to Artie Todd. 'Are you sure they're not queers?'

"Artie Todd looked at me for a moment and then whispered something to Mace and his brother. They stood there in a circle, nodding to each other and whispering. Finally, Artie Todd turned back to me and said: 'Yeah, Vinnie, they're queers.'

"Now I was pissed off, and I let them know it. 'What the hell are you bullshitting me for?' I snapped. 'I'm over here on an okay from Raymond and Henry. Don't give me this shit . . .'

" 'You're right, Vinnie,' Artie Todd said, 'but we didn't think it'd make that much difference to you.'

" 'To me it makes a lot of difference,' I said. 'I got to tell [explain to] a guy I'm doing business with.'

"After a lot of dancing around I finally took about fifty grand worth of the queers and brought them back to Grillo. I agreed to pay them twenty points, about ten grand, for the bundle. When I saw Grillo I told him the bonds were queers. 'Can you still unload them?' I asked. Grillo agreed.

"While Grillo was busy moving the bonds, I called Butch Miceli [of New Jersey]. I figured if these were counterfeits, the best place in the world to get counterfeits was from Miceli's crew. I figured Butch would give me a better deal on them. I was right. Miceli had the same bonds, and he delivered another fifty grand worth of them to me for nine grand.

"Several days later, Grillo handed me an envelope with 19,500 bucks in it. He said that was the first part of the money he would deliver on the fifty grand in bonds. He said he was taking out small loans on the bonds from a bank. A few days later, he turned over another eight grand. Now, out of that 27,500 bucks, nineteen grand had to go to Mace and Miceli, and another four grand went to Tameleo and Patriarca. That left Danny and me with a lousy forty-five hundred bucks, but we had the remaining fifty grand in queer bonds free and clear. Then the roof caved in. Grillo said a teller at the bank had spotted the bonds as phonies and had called in the FBI. 'The money has to be paid back,' he said.

" 'There's nothing I can do about it,' I said. 'The money's all gone. I had to pay some people for the bonds.' When he left, I burned the other fifty grand in bonds. I didn't want any evidence around for the FBI to grab.

"That was the end of my dealing with Grillo. He tried once to have me muscled by one of Angiulo's enforcers, Benny Zinna. I guess he'd run to Zinna, told him a sad tale, and promised him a piece of whatever Zinna could get from me. Benny came to my yacht, the *Living End,* to tell me Grillo now worked for him and that he'd come to collect some money that I owed Grillo. 'You must be out of your mind, Benny,' I growled. 'Do you know who you're talking to? Get the hell out of here before I break you in half and feed you to the fish.' A few years later Benny got shot in his car. It couldn't have happened to a nicer guy. I couldn't stand that little weasel."

Although the Grillo escapade turned out to be a flop financially, it didn't discourage Teresa from the marketing of stocks and bonds. It merely whetted his appetite. He could see there was big money to be made with more careful manipulations. The vehicle he chose to move stocks was the Esquire Sportsman Club junket operation. It provided a natural supply of suckers who, once cleaned out in rigged card games, would be anxious to recoup by handling the stocks. One of his first victims was a man by the name of Ray Neid.

"Ray Neid was a business manager for a big company. He had a ton of money. I don't know where he made it all. He had trotters, a big house, and cash to burn. Then he met me on one of my junkets to the Colony Club in London. I caught up with him and three other suckers in one big game at the Mayfair Hotel suite I had rented. It was a game to remember. It only lasted two hours, but when we were through it turned out to be worth more than a million bucks to me. But in terms of actual cash, it was worth about eighty grand. I had four mechanics and shills working that game for me: a guy I know only as Carmine from Connecticut, Yonkers Joe, Tony De-Pietro from Boston, and Jimmy the Greek [James Pechilis, a Boston gambler]. Ray Neid lost forty grand. A doctor named Lenny Berger from Baltimore dropped twenty grand. We also cleaned a New York lawyer named Martin Fox out of eighty-five hundred bucks, and the balance came from other gamblers who got into the game. Neid and Fox became important to me later for moving stock. I conned Dr. Berger into the loanshark business and then took him for another twenty-five grand that I told him I'd pay interest on. I just pocketed the money.

"The game in London just whetted Neid's interest in games. He started coming to my yacht for games in Boston and we had some wild ones, complete with broads. We turned that boat into a floating casino. He dropped another hundred grand in games on the boat. Like I said before, I paid for that boat in the first two months I had it by taking 150 grand from card players in rigged games. Before the *Living End* burned in an accident and sank, I must have picked up over a million bucks in rigged card and dice games on board.

"It was toward the end of 1967 that I put Neid to work for me. He was in bad shape. He'd lost more than 150 grand to me, and he needed money desperately. I'd gone to Mace again for some securities: two hundred grand worth of U.S. Treasury bonds. Now, Mace had a special niche in the mob. He was sixty-four years old, six-foot-two, with snow-white hair and a rugged build for a man his age. He was the top fence in the country, bar none. He'd buy anything, and he'd come up with the cash right on the spot. He always had a ton of money at his fingertips. He was trusted by the mob, but it wasn't always that way. To avoid going to jail one time, he'd become an informer for a New York police agency; at least, that's what the mob believed. They gave him a terrible beating—put him in the hospital. He claimed he'd been hurt in an automobile accident, but Larry Baiona said the mob had sent a couple of black enforcers after him to give him the beating. They'd really done a job on him. 'Maybe you'd better not deal with him,' Baiona said. 'You know, once an informer—'

"I brushed off Baiona's warning. 'He's got enough on me to put me away for a hundred years if he wants,' I said. 'He hasn't said anything yet about me. I might as well keep dealing with him.' Baiona just shrugged.

"I picked up the two hundred grand—two bonds—from Mace and Artie Todd in early 1968. Both had been stolen from the Wall Street brokerage house of Merrill Lynch, Pierce, Fenner, and Smith. I was to pay them forty-five grand for the bonds once I sold them. The first hundred-grand bond I gave to Neid. I told Neid that if he could move the bonds, he'd get a piece of the action and he could recoup some of his losses. At that point he'd have sold the Empire State Building for me to get back some of what he'd lost.

"Neid had a friend by the name of William McLaughlin who was willing to make a connection with a friend of his in a New York bank. Later on I turned McLaughlin into a loan-shark for me and took him for a bundle of dough. McLaughlin's idea on the stock was to have Neid cash one hundred-grand bond through his New York connection, and McLaughlin'd cash the other hundred-grand bond through a bank in Worcester. The Worcester end worked fine. I got eighty grand, and he and Neid split up the other twenty grand. Then Neid went to New York. I'd given him some phoney identification to use to cash the bond with. Everything was supposed to be fixed. A guy at the bank, for a few thousand bucks, was going to cash the bond. It went like clockwork. The bank took the bond and the contact told him to come to the bank the next day to get his check from the cashier. Then a seventy-five-buck-a-week clerk blew the whole thing sky high. He got suspicious about Neid's goddamned license, called the cops, and they arrested Neid for having false identification. He got a probation out of the deal, but we lost the bond a month later when someone in the bank found it was stolen. They never charged Neid with moving the bond, and I paid for his lawyers. I didn't want the kid to go to the can.

"That was the second transaction that didn't work out too good, but it didn't discourage me. It was obvious to me that there was a lot of money to be made in the stock market, and I was throwing money around like water on parties, on Rosie, on clothes, on high living that you wouldn't believe. I was even dumb enough to drop eighty grand in a casino game in London. That's how stupid I became—betting in a casino, where any wiseguy knows he can't win in the long run. It was about this time that I bumped into Joe Schwartz. He opened up a whole new world for me.

"It was in early 1968 that I first met Schwartz. I had a cocktail party going at the Maharaja Suite of the Mayfair Hotel in London. Schwartz had been at the Colony Club gambling. He hadn't come with my junket, so I didn't know him. Somehow he found out there was a swinging party at my place and decided to drop in.

" 'Mind if I join the party?' he asked.

"I looked at this guy and wondered who the hell he was. He wasn't a bad-looking guy. He was about five-foot-nine, with grayish, wavy hair and a reddish complexion. He spoke with a thick southern drawl, and it was obvious from the way he dressed that he had money. What the hell, I figured, one more couldn't hurt this party. 'Sure, come on in,' I said. 'Have a drink and enjoy yourself.'

"It didn't take long to see that I had a real swinger on my hands. He had more than a few drinks, then he got tied up with some of the women. Before I knew it he was half in the bag, making eyes at everything in skirts. I don't need a building to drop on my head. This was a guy to work on.

"While he was playing with one of the girls, we set up a crap game for a few of the suckers that were at the party. I had a hunch this Schwartz might jump in, but I wasn't sure. There were other suckers to concentrate on anyhow, and I wasn't worried about it. The way the game was to work was to have Butch Rossi come out as the big winner. All the winnings would go to him, and I'd collect the loot from him later on and work out the splits. Suddenly, while the dice are rolling, in jumps Schwartz. In twenty minutes he drops seventeen grand.

"Schwartz didn't have enough cash to cover the loss, but after a little talk with him I guaranteed his credit. Then I decided here was a sucker worth devoting some time to. For the next three or four days in London I got chummy with him. I wined and dined him. We went to see Juliet Prowse perform at a nightclub, and we talked a lot. He was a millionaire, but he was as greedy as hell. It's just like I said earlier: The more money they have, the easier they are to take. This guy was a beauty.

"Just before I left for Boston, Schwartz gave me his business card and told me to call. He said I ran the best junkets in the world. I told him I'd be glad to call. Then I asked him how he'd like to pick up some money in the loanshark business with me. 'Come down to my office in Baltimore,' he said. 'We can talk better there.' So soon after getting back to Boston, Danny Mondavano and I flew to Baltimore to meet Schwartz. I told him I'd take ten grand of his money, and he'd get three hundred bucks a week back in interest.

" 'Vinnie, I'm going to be honest with you,' Schwartz said. 'I'm a millionaire, but it's hard for me to lay my hands on cash. Everything is tied up in investments. Now, I don't want my name linked with you in business. I've brought in someone to protect my interests: Stuart Harrison. He's in the other room.'

"I looked in the other room as Schwartz walked toward it, and all I could see was this skinny little creep skulking around inside. I turned to Mondavano and said, 'If this is supposed to be the local tough guy protecting Schwartz's interest, if this is all we got to go through in this place, we can take the whole damn town over.' Danny grinned from ear to ear.

"We all sat down for a roundtable. Harrison was a nervous-type kid, thin, a smart dresser with black hair. He jumped, bent over, or squatted whenever Schwartz moved his finger. He had to. Harrison was in the insurance business, and every bit of his insurance covered Schwartz's apartment buildings, construction, and whatnot. Schwartz wrote out a check for ten grand and handed it to Harrison. He told him to take it downstairs—it was made out to Harrison's insurance company —cash it, and bring the ten grand back. With that Schwartz and I were in the loanshark business. Now, unlike the others, I fully intended to pay Schwartz every nickel he had coming. I figured he could be the open door to scores of suckers all over Baltimore. It was like investing in Fort Knox to me.

"A short time later I arranged for another meeting with Schwartz and Harrison. We were going to take a trip to Haiti to look over a possible site with Joe Kirk where Schwartz might build a new hotel-casino. Schwartz was convinced he could make a bundle out of it with us managing and operating the casino, skimming funds off the top, while his people ran the hotel. I'd got Patriarca's approval for the idea. I didn't like the idea of cutting Joe Kirk in because I didn't trust him, but Patriarca said I had his personal guarantee that Kirk would play ball. Joe Kirk had screwed us up once on the deal already. He was supposed to meet with Schwartz and me in Boston but didn't show up.

"To make up for Joe Kirk's dumb play, I'd bought first-class round-trip tickets for Schwartz, his fifteen-year-old son, and Harrison for a flight to Haiti with a stopover at the Hilton Plaza Hotel in Miami Beach, where I'd made reservations. I'd taken three suites at the hotel.

"We all met at the Hilton, and I took them on a tour of the nightspots. We spent some time at the Fountainebleau watching Frank Sinatra, and then we headed for a well-known mob hangout, The Bonfire, on Seventy-ninth Street. There we picked up some hookers and headed back to my suite for a party. It turned out to be a helluva blast. Schwartz had put his son to bed before we went out on the town. Once inside the suite, the hookers stripped naked and ran around the place like wild Indians, with Schwartz in pursuit.

"A couple of hours later we started a crap game. Schwartz played for a few minutes and dropped a couple of hundred, but he was more interested in broads than dice. Harrison went the other route. He was convinced the game was rigged. He didn't really know, but he thought it was. 'I'm the most unlucky guy in the world,' he said. 'When I gamble, I always lose. Is it all right if I bet against myself?'

"I just shrugged and gave the high sign to the mechanic I had working in the game with a couple of shills. 'Sure, Stu, anything you want,' I answered. All we had to do was change losing dice to winning dice. We handed the dice to him. He threw seven passes [seven winning combinations] in a row and lost 12,400 bucks betting against himself.

"I could see Harrison was shook, but I didn't have the slightest idea what he had on his mind. I could see Schwartz out of the corner of my eye busy with one of the broads. Harrison started to wobble toward another room. I thought to myself, what the hell is he up to? I followed. The next thing I know he's opening a window and starting to climb out. I grabbed him. 'Whoa,' I said, 'where are you going?'

"'I can't face it,' he cried. 'I'm going to kill myself.'

"I pulled him back inside, sat down with him, and cooled him off. 'It's early,' I said. 'I'll get you even—don't worry about anything like a few grand. Joe said he'd pay whatever you lost anyhow. What are you worried about?'

"We had to call the trip to Haiti off because of news that there was some sort of riot on the island. They were throwing Molotov cocktails around. Schwartz didn't like the idea of investing in a place where there was that kind of trouble. I agreed with him. I headed back to Boston with Danny. When I got back, I ran into Fred Sarno and Bobby Cardillo. They had fifty-three grand worth of Jefferson City school bonds that were stolen. They'd been stolen from the mails at Kennedy Airport in New York by a gang of thieves who specialized in airport thefts and who dealt with members of the Colombo family, and Sarno had got his hands on them. He got to be a major mover of stolen securities for thefts arranged at Kennedy Airport. He and Cardillo wanted eleven grand for the bundle. I figured now's the time to start using Harrison. I gave him a call. 'Stu, this is Vinnie from Boston.'

"'Yeah, Vinnie, how are you?' he answered.

" 'Remember I said I would help you get even?' I asked.

" 'Sure, Vinnie. What have you got in mind?' he said.

" 'Well, I have a friend who is a bookmaker,' I said. 'He just got hit for the number here, and he needs some cash right away. He's got some bonds—Jefferson City school bonds. They are as good as gold, and you won't have a bit of trouble selling them. He wants to cash them, but if he does it himself the tax boys will be on his neck. He's willing to let you make a pretty good score on them if you'll handle them. You'll make part of your twelve grand back on this deal.'

" 'You're kidding!' he said.

" 'No I'm not . . . but you got to move fast on this deal,' I warned.

" 'Can I tell Joe Schwartz?' he asked.

" 'I don't care who you tell—just move on them,' I said. 'I'll send Danny and another friend of mine, Fred Sarno, down with the bonds.' Sure enough, Harrison moves like a flash on them. He walks downstairs from his office to a bank and comes back with an 80 percent loan on the bonds: 47,400 bucks. I gave him eight grand and then paid Sarno his eleven grand. The rest Danny and I split up. A week later I called Harrison and told him to sell the bonds, which he did, and I gave him four grand out of the six grand we got out of the final sale. Now he was even, and happy as a pig. I knew I had a new sucker for moving securities.

"It couldn't have been more than a week after that that I got ahold of Jack Mace. He had 253 grand in U.S. Treasury bonds—all stolen—that could be moved. I made a deal to buy them, and I called Harrison and told him to come to New York with his wife. Now was the time, I figured, to wine and dine him and let him know he's already sold stolen bonds. He didn't know the Jefferson bonds were hot. Now I had him on a hook he couldn't wriggle off.

"He arrived in New York the next day with his wife. What a doll she was. She'd been a chorus girl in Las Vegas. What the hell she saw in him I'll never know. She was ten times as smart as he ever could be. I really put on a show for them, and I wound up buying her a mink coat. It's always nice to have the wife on your side when you're dealing with a sucker. 'Pick out any coat on the rack,' I told her. She did, and a mink hat to go with it. It cost me eighteen hundred bucks for the day—I got a break on the buy through Mace—but it was a worthwhile investment.

"We had a suite of rooms at the Americana Hotel. I pulled Harrison aside after he dropped his wife off with her new mink at the room. 'You have any trouble with the bonds I gave you?' I asked.

"He looked surprised. 'No . . . why should I have had trouble?'

" 'They were stolen,' I answered.

"The blood drained from his face. He started choking, stuttering. 'What do you mean, they were stolen?'

" 'Just what I said,' I snapped. 'Now, don't worry about it. We're going to make a mint together. The stuff I give you from now on will have been taken from vaults. The owners won't even know they're gone for a year or more, and by that time they'll be buried in somebody else's vault.' Then I dropped the bomb on him. 'The reason I'm telling you this is I've got a chance to get my hands on some prime merchandise: three hundred grand worth. Now we can really start making some money.'

"The worried look was replaced by a broad grin. He wanted money so bad he could taste it. He had an expensive wife with high-priced tastes, and he wanted to keep her happy. 'Okay,' he said, 'I'll go for it. I need cash—as long as you tell me there can't be any trouble. . . .'

"I bought the 253 grand worth of Treasury bonds from Mace and Artie Todd for twenty points, about fifty grand, at the Reo Coin Shop on Seventh Avenue, where both of them operated out of from time to time. Harrison went back to Baltimore, and the next day Danny brought the bonds down to him. He took the first hundred-grand bond to his friend in the bank and got a 70 percent loan on it: seventy grand. I let him keep eighteen grand as his end to make him happy. A couple of weeks later Mondavano and Joe Black picked up another hundred-grand bond from Mace for me as well as some smaller bonds. They brought them to Harrison in Baltimore, and he took out another 70 percent loan. This time I let him keep twelve grand. All told, we got about 230 grand out of the deal, and I gave Harrison thirty grand. He was now prime meat for bigger and better deals.

"While I was moving him on stocks, I was also keeping close to Schwartz. I still wanted to set up my own casino, and opportunity came knocking through a friend who introduced me to an old Dutchman by the name of Jeffrey Breitner. Breitner had a lease on 280 acres of land—beachfront—in

Curaçao, and he had a contract with the government. What a package he had. He had feasibility reports, blueprints, permits, everything you could ask for. All he needed was seven million bucks.

"I went to Patriarca with the information. 'Raymond,' I said, 'I think I have a sucker who will move this whole deal: Joe Schwartz from Baltimore. All I'm interested in is the casino. I'll need two million bucks in cash from you to bankroll the casino. I'll get Schwartz to foot the rest.'

"Now, Patriarca doesn't part with money like that quick, but he trusted me all the way. I'd never short-changed him, I'd always given him a cut of whatever I made. He remembered that. 'If you can get that kind of a deal, Vinnie, you got the money . . . don't worry about it. If you got the doors about to open and you need the cash, I'll have it for you, no sweat.' The way I had it planned, Patriarca, Tameleo, Carlo Mastrototaro, and I would be partners in the deal. Patriarca wanted to cut Angiulo in. He was going to make Angiulo come up with the cash I needed.

"I headed back to Boston and called Schwartz, explaining the whole thing to him over the phone. He was wild about the idea, but at that moment I was en route to London with a junket. Schwartz decided to come himself. So I got ahold of Breitner and told him to meet us at the Mayfair Hotel in London and to bring all his reports with him. Naturally, I paid for his fare and accommodations. Schwartz took one look at the reports and fell in love with it. 'It's terrific, Vinnie,' he said. 'We have no problems at all. When you get back, you come to Baltimore and I'll set up an appointment with one of my lawyers who works for the Sheraton chain. We can get 80 percent financing without even going through a bank with them.'

"All of a sudden I'm getting into this thing for nothing. The only thing I have to come up with is the cash for the casino, and that's all set. My only problem was getting my people into the casino. I knew the government screened people to keep hoodlums out of the casino operation, but I also knew that one of the casinos down there was in the bag—a real mob setup. I decided the best thing to do was go to Curaçao and look the whole deal over before I made any more moves.

"Now, I hate to take trips without making money on them, so I brought along some of my best shills and mechanics— Mondavano, Jimmy the Greek, and Tony DePietro, and Ray

Neid, along with a couple of suckers Neid knew. We cleaned the suckers out of eighty grand at a card game at a casino. Then I had another brainstorm. Why not take a bite out of one of the so-called legitimate casinos they had in the area? The one I chose was the Flamboyant. It was owned by two Jewish guys who had no mob connections that I knew about. Once we got to the casino, I conned them into giving me unlimited credit. They checked other casinos where I had good mob connections in Las Vegas and London, and they found I had unlimited credit there. So they agreed to let me play on credit.

"The plan I had was simple. I'd get into a dice game at the casino. Jimmy, Danny, and Carmine from Connecticut would get into the game also. I'd play like a sucker: betting against the house. They'd bet a like amount with the house and against me. Tony DiPietro played with me as a partner, and we played like two jerks from Coney Island. Between us, we dropped sixty grand. At the other end of the table, my shills won more than sixty grand in cash. We acted as if we didn't know each other, and they walked out as I began having a talk with the manager. He wanted a check right then. I told him he'd have to wait until I got to Boston. There was a small hassle, but finally they agreed to come to Boston to pick up the money.

"We stayed around Curaçao a couple of days, checking out the site. It looked terrific. We even got in a playful mood at the Flamboyant. We fed mickies to the band they had in the dining room one night. They all got sick as dogs. The night we left Curaçao, only one of the band had showed up for work. One guy almost died. I found out later the band didn't play at the hotel for three days.

"When I got back to Boston, I took the sixty grand to Mastrototaro to hold. He was the one guy in the mob that I trusted. He'd never short-change you a nickel, you could go to sleep on that. I wanted him to hold it for thirty days. If in that time we got no kickbacks from anyone in any of the mobs for screwing the casino, we'd all split it up. The only guy that showed was some clown of a lawyer from New York representing the casino.

" 'I hear you got hit pretty bad at the casino,' he said. 'The casino has asked me to pick it up.'

" 'I'm a little short now,' I told him. 'Give me a week or two.' By the time the clown came back, something terrible had happened.

"I'd gotten three hundred grand worth of stolen U.S. Treasury notes from Mace for sixty grand. Mastrototaro had put up twenty-five grand of that amount, in return for my guarantee that he'd get thirty-five grand back. Mondavano picked up the notes from Mace and brought them down to Schwartz. Schwartz went to Las Vegas, but instead of unloading them through a bank, as we'd planned, he got plastered and tried to push them on a casino cashier. When the cashier wouldn't accept them, there was a beef, and Schwartz was arrested by local sheriff's deputies. The FBI jumped in the case because they were stolen U.S. securities, and Schwartz blew the whistle on me. I had to pay off what I owed Mastrototaro with the proceeds from another stock deal. Anyhow, a federal grand jury in Baltimore indicted me on multiple counts of transporting 880 grand in stolen securities and conspiracy.

"That's how much I'd moved through just those two clowns. Out of all that money, I cleared 350 grand for myself. Most of that I blew on wild living. It's hard to believe, I know, but it isn't when you're spending it. It was cabareting all over the world. It was nothing to run up a three-grand tab at the Copacabana in New York, and I was spending a fortune on Rosie, not to mention what I had to spend at home. My own house expenses alone were running over five grand a month. Then I liked to dress well. I remember one week I went for eighty-five hundred bucks alone at a New York tailor that Artie Todd used. My shirts cost thirty-eight bucks apiece, my suits five hundred bucks each. I paid 120 bucks for shoes, and I'd buy them by the half dozen, and slacks never cost me less than a hundred bucks.

"So when this clown came around for his money for the casino, I wasn't about to give him a dime. I'd had no complaints from the mob about hustling the casino. All I had to worry about was a lawyer.

" 'You've got to pay this,' he said.

" 'Look, don't bother me any more,' I snapped. 'If you're connected with someone, you'd better have them call me.' Then I got a little nasty. 'I'm going to the can. I got twenty years staring me in the face. You think I'm going to worry about your sixty grand?'

" 'But who's going to pay it?' he yelled.

" 'Jesus, it ain't going to be me,' I roared back. 'Now get the hell out of here before I split your head open for you.' I never heard a word from him or the casino after that. We had their sixty grand, and there wasn't a thing they could do about it."

24

The Fall of Vincent Teresa

The main problem that Teresa faced as the result of his indictment was the need for additional money to pay the costs of bail and attorney's fees (eventually to top more than two hundred thousand dollars). And so within a month after his indictment, Teresa was back trafficking in stolen securities, business as usual.

"Blanche didn't bother me about the indictment. She was upset by it—so were the kids—but they knew better than to interfere in my business affairs. That was a firm rule in my house. Blanche took care of the house and kids, and I took care of making money. Whenever she asked too many questions about what I was doing, I'd just tell her to mind her own business. 'I'll take care of making the money,' I'd tell her. 'You keep your mind on the kids and the house.' It was as simple as that. Blanche never really understood what I was involved in. She knew I had crooks for friends, but she didn't question my right to associate with them. She knew better.

She knew I was involved in the junket business and she knew I was a gambler, but beyond that she knew very little except what she read, and she didn't give me static. I'd been indicted before and beaten the rap or got suspended sentences, and she just accepted that that was my way of life. She didn't like it, but she had married me for better or worse, and that was that. I wish the hell things had been different for her. She's a wonderful woman, a fine mother and wife, but that was my way of life and I couldn't have changed.

"My indictment was toughest on my kids. David, Cindy, and Wayne went through hell when I was arrested. The papers made a big splash, and the kids in the schools went to town on it. Kids are cruel to each other, crueler than adults can ever be. The kids of North Reading were no exception. They needled Wayne about his hoodlum father, and he got into a fight and beat the hell out of some of his hecklers. They told David I was a lousy gangster, a racketeer, that I belonged in jail. So David got into fights. I don't know how many times Blanche was called to the principal's office about my sons getting into fights. He told her he didn't blame them—they were just defending their father. But the fights had to stop, he said, or they'd have to be suspended. Blanche never said a word to me about it. I didn't find out about it until long after I went to jail. The cruelest thing happened to Cindy. She was just eleven years old at the time, and she had come to a social studies class. All of the kids had been instructed to bring in a current-events item of importance that week. Cindy brought in something about the war in Vietnam, but two of her classmates brought in a headline story about my arrest. Cindy ran from the class crying her heart out. She cried for days after that. Blanche kept it from me, but she went to the principal and filed a complaint. He called the parents of the two kids who were involved into his office. It's lucky I didn't know who they were while I was still on the street. I'd have beaten the hell out of the parents for letting their kids hurt a classmate like that. I mean what I did, I did, my kids didn't—why should anyone take it out on them? They're innocent, and so was Blanche. Just because I wasn't a respectable citizen, why should they suffer? If the truth were known, most of those so-called respectable citizens were worse than I ever could be. It was the 'honest' citizen who I always wound up dealing with in stolen securities or in turning into loansharks because they were so greedy. They make me sick.

"The indictment by Uncle Sam didn't slow me down. I was mad as hell at Schwartz, but I had no way of laying my hands on him, and I didn't want to do anything that might foul up my operation. It couldn't have been more than a couple of weeks before I was out on a junket to London. Martin Fox, a New York attorney who I'd taken for eighty-five hundred bucks in a crooked game, was along. I sat down with him and talked about stocks. He had some good ideas about moving stolen securities. The best idea was to open up a numbered account in a Swiss bank and work through a friend he had in Canada. His Canadian contact would bring the stocks to Switzerland, have them sold, and deposit the money in the numbered account. That way there would be no names for the federal government to track down. Fox wanted a thousand bucks to open the account, and I gave it to him. The next day he left London, flew to Switzerland, and opened our account.

"We flew back to the States, and several weeks later I called Fox at his office in New York. Nothing was moving on the Canadian-Swiss operation, and I was getting edgy. When I talked to Fox, he had a new idea with more immediate potential. A client of his, a Charles L. Lewis of Atlanta, owned an independent airline, Nationwide Air Service, and wanted to borrow a quarter of a million bucks. Fox said that if we could come up with some good securities, Lewis had a contact at a southern bank where he could put the securities in for a large loan if we would let him borrow some of the money.

"Fox threw in one ringer. 'This guy won't deal with the stocks if he knows they're stolen,' he said. 'He wants to borrow legitimate money. He'll sign papers for it and put up shares in his company, but I think we can pull it off and give him stolen securities if the stuff you can get is as good as you say they are.' Then he added: 'I can send someone down under a phoney name with the stock. I'll tell Lewis that the guy is all right, and I'll cosign on the papers. Now, can you get a million dollars' worth?'

"It sounded like a good idea. I called up Jack Mace and told him exactly what I had in mind. 'I want some street stock that will bring an 80 percent loan in a bank,' I said. 'It's got to be reliable stuff.' Mace said he'd look around. A week or so later he called me.

" 'Vinnie, I've got just the stuff you're looking for,' he said. 'I've got nine hundred shares of IBM—street-named stock.'

Now, street-name stock is stock assigned to a particular brokerage house. The name of the broker, not the actual owner, is printed on the stock. That makes it negotiable because the stock has an authorized signature on it. It's like having cash in your hand. You can sell it anywhere in the world.

"I flew to New York with Mondavano, and we met with Mace and Artie Todd. The stock, they said, was ice cold. It had been heisted from the vaults of the E. F. Hutton brokerage house in New York, and they didn't know it was missing. The trouble was, Mace said, that all they could lay their hands on were nine hundred shares—about 285 grand worth. They wanted twenty points as their end, or fifty-seven grand. I agreed, took the stock, and turned it over to Fox.

"Now, Fox had picked the name of Henry Sturgeon for the go-between to deal with Lewis. To pose as Sturgeon, Joe Black came up with a hustler he knew named Howard Finklestein of New York. The way the deal finally worked, Lewis was to get a hundred-grand loan, and we were to get the balance. The stock was transported to Lewis, who had a friend named Walter A. Jernigan. Jernigan was a friend of Bobby Baker [the former U.S. Senate aide to Lyndon Johnson], who wound up in jail, and both of them were buddies of Bebe Rebozo, who's the president of the Key Biscayne Bank in Florida and a guy who is a close friend of President Nixon.

"Now, I didn't know about Rebozo or Jernigan, and I couldn't have cared less. All I was concerned about was the money. The loan was arranged for 195 grand. Lewis got eighty grand and gave us ten thousand shares of his airline stock, and we got 115 grand. Later on, I understand, Lewis had Rebozo sell the stock at face value. I don't know who got the remaining ninety grand. It sure as hell wasn't me.

"The only reason I mention this case is that it shows how the mob can involve some big people in a stock swindle. They might not even know they're involved in dealing in hot stock. All they're interested in is making money. That's the way the world is. Money is its god.

"All I wound up with out of that whole lousy deal was about thirty grand. I had to pay Mace his money—fifty-seven grand—and there were other people I had to pay. One of them was a guy named Murray Feinberg, a millionaire businessman who owned the Beacon Valve Company of Waltham [Massachusetts.] When the IBM stock was sold, Rebozo's bank issued two cashier's checks: one for twenty-five grand, the other for ninety grand. I went to a friend of mine, Gerald Meyers, who owned the Boston Boat Sales Company. I'd bought my yacht, the *Living End*, from him. At the time, he had five grand in payments on the yacht coming. I asked him to cash the two checks I had. When I mentioned the amounts, he just whistled. He agreed to try and cash the twenty-five-grand check first at the New England Merchants Bank in Boston, where he knew a bank officer. I went with him. The teller agreed to cash the check, and, he said, he'd overlook a requirement that they report to the Internal Revenue Service the cashing of any check over ten grand. I paid Meyers the five grand I owed him, plus twenty-five hundred bucks for cashing the check for me. Now I had the ninety-grand check to get rid of. Meyers didn't want to handle it because of the Internal Revenue Service. He referred me to his uncle, this millionaire Murray Feinberg of Waltham, who could cash large checks through his company without raising questions.

"I met Feinberg at a restaurant with Joe Black and my secretary, Joan Harvey. I told him I had a check to cash from the sale of stolen IBM stock. He wanted 5 percent for cashing any large checks. I agreed. Five days later, Joan picked up about eighty-five grand in cash from him. He took out the balance as his fee. So now out of the original 115 grand, I had paid out 12,500 bucks to Meyers and his uncle for cashing checks, and another fifty-seven grand to Mace. The irony of paying Mace that much is that he made more on the deal than I did. He'd bought the stock for twenty-one grand from Gus [Cosmo] Cangiano, a made guy from the Joe Colombo mob in Brooklyn who I later had several deals with. Mace and Artie Todd's profit was more than thirty-six grand. All I had left was 44,500 bucks, and out of that I gave Ray Neid five grand for helping me, Finkelstein got five grand, Joan got a couple of grand, and so did Phil Waggenheim, who I used to keep an eye on Feinberg. That left thirty grand for Joe Black and me to split up. Fox had the stock from the airline to hold for both of us, and he probably got a kickback from Lewis for arranging the loan. Later on, Fox got two and a half years in federal prison for being in the deal, after I testified against him. Murray Feinberg was indicted but not convicted—he's currently under medical treatment.

"That gives you an idea of what can happen in some of these big stock swindles. The guy that wheels them has a lot of people to pay off along the way. Sometimes he winds up with peanuts on the deal. The important thing out of this deal to me was the contact I'd made with Feinberg. Now I had a guy who could cash big checks for me without any problem, and he was a legitimate businessman out to make a fast buck for himself. In fact, he put money out on the street with me at 1 percent a week and became a behind-the-scenes loanshark just to get his hands on more money."

Teresa didn't let any grass grow under his feet. Stock manipulations looked like an easy way to make fast money, despite his indictment. By now his victims at casino junket card games were falling all over themselves to come up with deals for Teresa that would enable them to make money, to recoup their losses to him. Neid was the fastest mover of all, and he was something of a sharp operator. He'd been put on the payroll of the Esquire Sportsman Club after Teresa had taken 150,000 dollars from him in rigged card games. He had also lost his job as manager of an industrial firm, and now he worked full-time on swindles for Teresa, swindles he was convinced would help him recover his losses. Almost overnight, Neid had turned from respectable businessman to accomplished thief and swindler under Teresa's careful guidance and firm hand. Neid, in fact, became so adept at the art of chiseling, Teresa found, that he swindled his teacher out of twenty thousand dollars in one transaction alone.

"As I testified at the trial, it was in late July or early August of 1968, while we were still working on the IBM deal, that Neid came to me with a new opportunity. He had a connection at the stock firm of Dempsey-Tegeler who was willing to move hot securities if we followed certain procedures. I listened. Neid said his connection was a guy named William Durkin, who was later found innocent when he was tried in the case.

"Neid said that we would have to establish an address under the name of Robert Daly. The broker wanted us to use that name because Daly was a customer of his firm and often moved stocks in and out of sales; I agreed to the idea, and I contacted Richie Castucci, who agreed to let us use his father's address at 126 Centennial Avenue, Revere. As a test we moved about 120 grand in miscellaneous stolen stocks through the system. There were no kickbacks. I gave Feinberg five points to cash a 120-grand check. Then I decided it was time to make a big move. I called Jack Mace.

"Mace had half a million bucks' worth of debenture bonds of the Mountain State Telephone Company of West Virginia. They had been stolen from the vaults of Hayden Stone stockbrokers of New York, and he said they weren't hot. Mace wanted forty grand out front before turning over the stock because he had other people to pay. I agreed. The trouble was, I didn't have that much cash available. I was pouring money into lawyers as well as the Esquire club to pay off some bills.

"Now, in earlier days, I'd have just called Henry Tameleo and that would be that. I couldn't now. He was in jail. I couldn't even get to Patriarca. He didn't want anyone near him from the Boston mob because the FBI was watching him like a hawk, waiting for him to make a mistake. We wanted to give them no excuse for a bust while he had the murder case hanging over his head. My other alternatives were Jerry Angiulo, who I hated, and Larry Baiona, who I could live with. I don't know why, but I didn't call Carlo Mastrototaro. He was either out of town or tied up, but I didn't call him. So I called Baiona.

"To deal with a guy like Baiona you have to sweeten the pot to get his money. He's a helluva loanshark, but he's tighter than a crab's ass when it comes to parting with loot. If he hadn't been convicted on a jewelry theft case recently and sent to jail, he'd probably have replaced Patriarca as interim boss of the Office. He was one of Patriarca's favorites then. Now he's in a whole lot of trouble with Patriarca. I wouldn't give a plug nickel for his life when and if he gets out of jail if Patriarca walks free. In fact, he almost got killed in jail in May 1972 by a street-hustler friend of mine, Joe Navarro. I better tell you about that before I continue about the stock swindle. It's important because it shows you the type of person Baiona is, the way he thinks.

"Navarro I've known for years. He's a tough apple, a good hustler, and he takes no crap from any of the wiseguys. After I went to jail he started hanging around with my former secretary, Joan Harvey. They got to be pretty close, and I guess, in his way, he was in love with Joan. Anyhow, Joe heard word on the street that Baiona had put out a contract to kill Joan because he was afraid she was going to join me as a witness and open up to federal authorities. Joe had also had a bitter argument with Phil Waggenheim over me. He had said that I was right to turn them in because they had swindled me out of millions. As a result, Phil Waggenheim had Joe shot in the head in Boston. They made one mistake. They didn't kill Joe. One shot hit him in the hand and a second shot bounced off his skull. He went to the hospital—he actually drove himself after being shot.

"That started an open feud between him, Waggenheim, Baiona, and Joe Russo, then one of Baiona's and Angiulo's musclemen. It became a question of who was going to get killed first, until Joe Navarro went to jail for a hijacking in Pittsfield. He got a five-to-seven-year term. He got into Walpole [prison] on a Wednesday. At the time, Baiona was in the same prison, and they'd had some bad words. The next day he was sitting in his cell and he saw Vinnie the Butcher [Vincent Flemmi], Ronnie Cassesso, and a third guy walking toward him, and they looked as if they were carrying shivs. He figured it would be stupid to be caught in the cell by himself, so he busted out of the open cell and started walking down the corridor toward the prison control center, where he figured there would be some guards.

"As Navarro walked down the corridor, Baiona came walking down the corridor talking to a guard. Navarro went wild and he jumped Baiona and began beating the hell out of him. As he did that Flemmi and Cassesso jumped him from behind and Flemmi stuck a six-inch shiv in his side, just missing his kidney. Baiona got up from the floor and started after Navarro, but Navarro grabbed a nearby wheelbarrow and knocked Baiona down again. That has put the kiss of death on Navarro. You can't whack a guy like Baiona and walk away from it.

"Now Navarro is willing to talk. While I was in Florida in May 1972, I called Joan Harvey. She told me about an attempt by one of Baiona's men to try and kill her when she was in New York. Then she said Navarro was willing to talk if he could get protection and work a deal with the federal government. I sent her to FBI agent Bob Sheehan. Maybe Navarro can sink a few more of these double-dealing wiseguys in Boston.

"Anyway, when I approached Baiona for the money for the bonds, he wanted sixty grand for the forty grand I wanted to get from him. It was a stiff deal, but I had nowhere else to turn, so I agreed. When I got the money, I called Mace, and he flew in to Boston with the securities. I gave the bonds to Neid, who said he gave them to Durkin. A short time later a check for 480 grand was mailed to our address in Revere by the brokerage firm, Dempsey-Tegler. I gave the check to Joan Harvey to bring to Feinberg, who deposited it in his company account. Feinberg then gave me about 256 grand in cash, after taking out twenty-four grand for cashing the check. The balance he gave me in four cashier's checks for fifty grand each. That presented a few problems.

"The first person I paid off was Baiona. I gave Joe Black sixty grand to take to him. Then I gave Neid twenty grand as his end of the deal. He was to give another hundred grand to Durkin for moving the stuff for us. Later on, when I talked to a guy who said he was Durkin on the phone, I found out Neid had only given him eighty grand. The sneaky little bastard had pocketed twenty grand more for himself. Then I headed for New York with the checks. I had Martin Fox, the lawyer, cash one check in return for five grand that I owed him. The day he cashed the check I called Artie Todd. He said he couldn't come up with that much money right away, but he was going out to supper with Carmine Lombardozzi that night. 'Why don't you come along, Vinnie?' Artie Todd said. 'Maybe Carmine can handle it for you.'

"We all met at a Sicilian restaurant in Brooklyn. I forget the name, but the food was great. Joe Black was with me. We joined Lombardozzi and Artie Todd, who were at a table with their girlfriends. Now, Lombardozzi was one of the biggest stock movers in the Carlo Gambino mob. He'd been involved in security swindles for years. He'd also got in some trouble with Gambino by getting the daughter of a Gambino soldier pregnant. There was a big sitdown over it. Lombardozzi was demoted from a crime captain to a regular made guy. He was still a big money mover, though, still very important to Gambino, and Artie Todd buzzed around him like a bee does with honey.

"I showed Lombardozzi one of the checks and told him where it was from and what the deal was. He gave me a big smile. 'No problem, Vinnie,' he said. He made a phone call, and ten minutes later a guy came over and picked up the check. An hour later the guy returned with cash, including sixteen one-grand bills. Those thousand-buck bills didn't bother me. On a junket, they were easy to unload. In the States it was another matter. If you took a thousand-buck bill to a bank, they'd take your identification because the Internal Revenue Service makes them report anyone who cashes thousand-buck bills.

" 'You don't mind thousand-buck bills?' asked Lombardozzi.

" 'Not a bit,' I answered.

" 'How would you like to buy them—like, a hundred of them for ninety grand?' he said.

" 'I'll take all you got,' I said. 'I'll take three hundred grand worth right now.' I had three hundred grand in cash in my pockets at that moment.

"Artie Todd didn't like the way things were moving. He was a little jealous—a little shook that Lombardozzi was willing to deal with me and let me make money that he normally would make. He piped up: 'No, we can't do it, Carmine—I got a deal to move them tomorrow.'

"I didn't push it. There was no sense making enemies. But that was typical of Artie Todd. He was a little weasel. He bowed and scraped to Lombardozzi, and I know he was double-dealing him on the side. Todd was about five-foot-eight and built rugged, with light hair. He was a real mover, a good hustler, don't get me wrong. I just didn't like the way he scurried around everybody.

"With all the traveling back and forth, I eventually cashed all the checks. Feinberg cashed two of the checks. It was the most profitable deal I'd had since the 880 grand in stocks I moved through Schwartz and Harrison in Baltimore. The trouble with it was that a large hunk of what I was making was going to lawyers, who were charging me a fortune for defending me in the Baltimore case.

"In April 1969, I went on trial in Baltimore. I knew I was in trouble from the start. Both Schwartz and Harrison were witnesses for the federal government. They'd made their deals with the feds to keep their own skirts clean. I decided my only way out after they testified was to take the stand myself. Maybe, I thought, I could con the jury. It was a dumb play. They not only didn't believe me, but they didn't waste any time finding me guilty. The judge freed me on a hundred grand bail, and my lawyer filed an appeal of the conviction. But now the panic was on. I faced twenty years in jail, and I had two other cases hanging over my head in state courts, not to mention lawyers demanding more money to handle the appeal. I took a good look at everything, and I realized I was in a real jam. I didn't have any money, to speak of, salted away for the family. There was about three hundred grand in cash in a safety deposit box that was in both my name and that of Joe Black, but I wanted a helluva lot more so that my family could live in comfort while I did my time.

"Before the conviction, Bobby Cardillo and I had begun dealing with Gus Cangiano. Gus was a happy-go-lucky guy, a good businessman for a young guy. He had a brother, Frank, who was pretty lazy, but Gus was all action—always moving, hustling. He barred nothing. He handled counterfeit money, counterfeit postage stamps, stocks, pornographic books and films, as well as crooked playing cards and dice. You name it, he had it, whether it was typewriters or cars, whatever came off the streets of New York and Brooklyn. He even took his own pornographic stag films himself. He had his own photo lab, and he was pretty clever in the way he could put a film together. One of his biggest sources of income was from stolen securities, most of which he bought from the gang of young thieves who operated at Kennedy Airport in New York, O'Hare in Chicago, and at a lot of other airports throughout the country. These thieves stole at least one hundred million dollars in securities alone, and they fenced a large part of the loot with Gus Cangiano.

"Gus was a nice guy, one of the few really nice guys I met in Brooklyn. He'd give you anything on the arm. I know a lot of guys who would go in to see him without money that needed stuff to hustle at Christmastime. One of his hottest items around the holiday season was fake perfume—Chanel No. 5—in a phoney bottle. It cost sixty cents a bottle for him to produce, and the real stuff sold for about thirty bucks in the stores. He could produce, with chemists he had working for him, any kind of top perfume. He'd let the street hustlers take the gaff [phoney perfume] on the arm and pay him when they sold it. There is only one way you can tell a gaff of Chanel from the real thing. The phoney, for some unknown reason, has a little edge at one corner of the bottle top. They can't seem to get the top as smooth as the Chanel bottle.

"Gus even handled phoney shaving lotion. There wasn't anything he wasn't involved in. The strange thing about Gus was that his boss, Joe Colombo, was always screwing him. I remember Gus used to say about Colombo: 'You can't trust the guy. He tells you you have protection here, and you don't have it. He tells you this is going to happen, and it don't. In the meantime, he's taking my money every week. I got to do business with this guy. I got no choice.' At the time Gus was averaging more than four grand a day in business.

"Cardillo and I went to Gus because we had a big deal on the fire. Cardillo had a lawyer friend by the name of Bernard Berman. He'd cooked up a scheme to use stolen stock to take over the assets of a couple of insurance companies. The idea was to take them over and bust them out, sell off their assets. To handle the deals he had in mind we needed twelve million bucks' worth of stock.

"The deal sounded terrific to me, and I went to see Gus. He sent Frank with me to an apartment house where they had a closet filled with stolen stocks. I spent five hours looking them over. There wasn't anything they didn't have, from American Telephone & Telegraph to United Smelting and the Purex Company. Bobby arranged to get the stock from Gus and turned them over to Berman. Berman later used it to take over a London and an Alaskan insurance company. They put the stock up as collateral for control of the companies, then they milked them dry. I never saw a dime of the money. I don't even know if Cardillo paid Gus Cangiano for the stocks. By that time I was in jail, and Cardillo had screwed me out of my end. Now he's doing eighteen years on two stock cases because of my testimony. It wasn't a matter of being vindictive, either. I testified against him and others because I had no choice. But I'll explain that later on. Berman got three years, and is appealing his conviction.

"While I was on trial in Baltimore, I worked another stock swindle with Cardillo, Dave Iacovetti, and a member of the Chicago mob named Tony DeRosa. DeRosa was close to Big Tuna Accardo and Momo Giancana, the bosses of Chicago, who I knew. It was a minor swindle that netted five of us just forty-three grand. But by that time I was desperate for money, and we had other deals planned.

"Then the world started to crumble. In April 1969 the jury found me guilty of the Baltimore stock swindles and a federal judge sentenced me to twenty years. I don't mind admitting that I was really shook by the conviction. I felt sure I'd beat the case. My attorney was convinced I'd won it. What a kick in the head.

"My lawyer appealed right away, and on June 13 the judge freed me on a hundred grand bail. I figured I had at least six months to make a bundle for the family before I might have

to go to jail. Like I told you, all through my life, I wasn't one
to save money. I spent like a drunken sailor on a binge. I had
the best, my family had the best, so did my friends. Money
meant nothing. There was always tomorrow, and when tomorrow came I'd make and spend another bundle. I just
never thought about salting money away for a rainy day. It
never occurred to me. Even the three hundred grand in the
safety deposit box wasn't for security; it was run money in
case I ever needed loot in a hurry to get out of the area. I
knew damn well that three hundred wasn't going to take care
of my family for twenty years.

"Just before the conviction was announced, I had arranged
a deal with a Boston businessman I knew. He was big in
apartment buildings, air conditioners, and refrigerators. His
father was a mob guy in the old days, but this guy was pretty
much on the edge of the mob. He was as skinny as a pickle,
about five-foot-three, and he wore thick glasses. His name was
Bernie. I remember one night we were in my apartment at a
Miami hotel and Bernie was busy laying some hooker he'd
picked up. After he cooled off, he came into the main room
and sat down on the floor, crosslegged. He was stiff drunk and
stark naked except for this sheet he had wrapped around him.
He looked like the reincarnation of Mahandus Gandhi, the little religious leader of India. But Bernie was anything but religious.

"When Bernie sobered up, we began talking stocks. It was
his first venture into hot securities, but he came up with a
beaut of an idea. He had a friend in Venezuela who might be
able to arrange something. A few days after we talked, he
brought his friend to my suite. I still can't remember the guy's
full name, but his first name was Antonio. We met, and Bernie said Antonio was a sharp thief. He and Antonio said if I
could come up with five million bucks' worth of hot stocks,
Antonio was willing to exchange the stocks for four million
bucks in coffee futures. Now, the futures might be worth only
four million that year, but the next year they might jump to
five million or more. I told him it was a deal.

"I made a quick trip to Brooklyn and saw Gus Cangiano.
He wanted a half a point, 250 grand, for five million bucks'
worth of Gulf & Western stock that had been heisted from
the mail at Kennedy. The stock was hot, but that didn't matter to Antonio. I agreed to the deal with Gus, who gave me
the stuff on the arm. Then I turned the stock over to Bernie

and Antonio. Before I could collect my end, about three million bucks in coffee futures, I went to jail. I never heard a word from Bernie or his friend. They waltzed off with everything. Bernie didn't pay Gus either. He didn't even know him.

"All told, between the insurance deal with Cardillo, the coffee futures with Bernie, a hundred grand I had on the street in loanshark money, and the cash in the safety deposit box, there was at least seven million bucks due me. But that wasn't all I had going. Joe Black and I had worked out another scheme with a guy by the name of Marvin Karger. He was the nephew of Lou Fox, the old Jewish mob boss of Revere. When Fox died, Karger came racing back from Maryland, and instead of going to his uncle's funeral, he went straight to a car where Lou Fox had a bundle of money hidden in the trunk of a car in a tire. It was a couple of hundred thousand bucks.

"At any rate, Joe Black and I worked out a deal with Karger, who had a good business front, to buy almost two million bucks' worth of securities from Jack Mace for about twenty points. Now, I'd set up the deal and made arrangements with Mace for them to pick up the stock. Again, it was when I was in jail that the deal was actually made. While I was behind bars, they moved the stock. Joe Black was supposed to protect my end, 750 grand. Naturally, he didn't.

"Black was also supposed to protect my interests in the Esquire club and in some land that he, Ray Neid, and I invested in in 1968. The land, about twenty acres all zoned residential, was in a very exclusive area of Weston [Massachusetts]. We bought it from a guy that Neid knew who was desperate for money. It was worth well over three hundred grand when he sold it to us, but we bought it for 120 grand in cash. Now, in that section of Weston, the least you can build a house for was sixty grand, and by the time I went to jail each acre was worthy thirty grand. That meant the land was worth at least six hundred grand. A third was to go to each of us. I never saw a dime of it.

"Now, Joe Black was a guy I had trusted like he was my brother. In fact, I treated him like a brother, taking him into my operation against the advice of Tameleo and Patriarca, giving him a split on deals he should never have got, moving him in mob circles he could never have reached without me. The trouble with me was I was always with the underdog, and Joe Black was an underdog in the New England mob. Nobody liked him except me. Even Blanche hated him. He was a worker, though. He'd follow my instructions to the letter, he respected my decisions, and I had no reason to mistrust him —not until May 1969, when I had an auto accident and wound up in a hospital. Then I found out from Feinberg that Joe hadn't paid interest to him on a thirty-grand loanshark loan that Feinberg had invested with us. Feinberg was upset, and I was mad as hell at Black. Feinberg was like gold to me in cashing checks on stock deals. And you don't kill the golden goose.

"Then I found out other things about Joe Black, and it was at this point I knew Joe Black had to go. I'd have to whack him out."

25

The Arrest

At 8 A.M. on June 30, 1969, Vincent Charles Teresa pushed himself up slowly from his bed and forced his hulking frame to a sitting position, gasping for breath from the effort. He was exhausted from his desperate scramble for money. His health was bad, largely due to his obesity and an ailing heart. He was still recovering from injuries received when he fell asleep behind the wheel of his car, demolishing it, and it was agony for him to lift his 325 pounds from bed.

"I remember I just wanted to lie there in bed that morning and forget the whole damned thing. It was a beautiful day. I felt like just sitting by the pool and relaxing. But I couldn't afford that luxury. I had to make money, a whole lot of money."

Teresa, in fact, had big money waiting for him that very day, the result of a plan to rifle the bank account of the United Fruit Company of Boston.

"Two of my street men, both of them real good hustlers, had come to my office at the Esquire Sportsman's Club a while earlier. They had pages of blank checks from the United Fruit Company and one check with the proper authorized signature on it. I'd had Joan Harvey trace the signature on half a dozen checks made out to phoney names. The amounts we made out the checks for were then registered in club files as expenses for junkets, gambling trips. In other words, if someone came to us from the company about the checks, we'd just show them our books with the phoney entries that showed the people the checks were made out to had lost this money on gambling trips.

"I tested the whole deal out right away. I cashed one check for seventy-five hundred bucks at the State Street Bank and Trust Company in Boston without a problem. In the books the guy who the check was made out to was credited with getting back three grand in cash, with the other forty-five hundred bucks paying off a gambling debt. We cashed two others in other banks. No problem. All told, we had taken United Fruit for twenty grand. We had checked with the bank United Fruit did business with in New York. It was a revolving account with millions of dollars in it. If you had a check for a million you could have cashed it. Money from all over the world poured into this account."

The ease with which Teresa and his men had cashed checks for twenty thousand dollars convinced him that a big fleecing was in the offing. His eventual goal was a million dollars.

"I figured I'd cash one big check and see how it went, and then get down to business if everything worked out. So that day in June, I had a ninety-five-grand check sitting in Boston with Jerry Meyers, the owner of Boston Boat Sales. He'd promised to have the cash ready for me. And if that went through without a problem, I was set for a really big score on United Fruit. I mean, what the hell, I was going to jail for twenty years. How much more time were they going to give me for forging checks?"

Teresa gulped down a quick breakfast. Blanche left with his son Wayne for a dental appointment. Cindy had left earlier to go out with friends. Only David, Teresa's sensitive fourteen-year-old, had remained.

"David wanted me to take him to the riding academy. It was on my way to Boston, so I told him to get ready while I dressed. I put on my gray silk suit and a tailored shirt. The suit cost me five hundred bucks. I had a Manhattan tailor named Cye Martin make it. A lot of mob guys like his clothes. The shirt cost me fifty bucks—the collar had to be specially cut to fit my bull neck. Even the tie cost a fortune. It had to be cut a special length so it would fit over my stomach."

Teresa met his son at the door, and together they walked to the car, a gleaming, new seven-thousand-dollar Buick that Teresa had leased to replace his smashed Lincoln. Teresa walked around the rear of the car to the driver's side, but before he climbed in, he looked nervously around the neighborhood. He didn't know why he should be nervous. Still, that sixth sense of his was working—that strange, tingling feeling that warned him when danger was near.

"As I backed the car slowly out of the driveway, I noticed a car parked down below on Hickory Street with three heads in it. I thought to myself: 'Hey, there's something funny going on here.' Then I saw another car at the top of the street with three more men. I knew there was going to be trouble. I knew it wasn't a hit. The mob don't waste six men just to kill one guy."

Teresa slipped the car into gear and drove slowly toward Chestnut Street, three hundred yards away. Suddenly there was a squeal of tires and a screech of brakes. One car stopped behind him. A second crossed in front and stopped. A third came up close on the left, blocking off any escape from the driver's seat. As Teresa's gaze spun from car to car, men with guns leaped from the still-rocking automobiles.

" 'Hands up, Teresa—this is the FBI!' this agent yells. Whoa, I figured, this is dirty pool. I was boiling mad. Here I've got my kid in the car and these guys are making like 'Gangbusters.' I looked at David, and the poor kid was white as a sheet and trembling. He didn't know what the hell to think.

"I stepped from the car with my hands raised. 'You sons-of-bitches,' I screamed. 'Couldn't you wait till I let my kid out of the car? What are you, animals?' They didn't say nothing. They just pushed me against the car, made me put out my hands and spread my feet, and they searched me. All the while David's just looking. He was scared to death, and his eyes were glistening. He was fighting back the tears. He wanted to cry, but he wasn't going to let me see it. Then this other agent helped him from the car.

" 'We have a warrant for your arrest,' one of the agents said. 'Your bail has been revoked. You'll have to come with us.' "

The words stunned Teresa. Bail revoked. Time had run out. It wasn't supposed to run out. He was supposed to have at least three months. What had gone wrong now? He looked at David and patted him on the shoulder.

"I told David to go straight home and tell his mother what happened. I told him to have her call the lawyer. 'Don't worry, David,' I said, 'I'll be okay—I'll be home by tonight.' I didn't believe it and I don't think he did, but he did exactly like I said."

As David turned and started walking slowly toward his home, an FBI agent got into Teresa's car. He drove it back to the driveway and left the keys dangling in the ignition. Underneath the dash, less than a foot from where the agent had turned the key to stop the engine, was Teresa's hidden revolver.

* * *

Teresa was taken first to the FBI headquarters in Boston, where he ate several hamburgers, and then to the county jail in Worcester. The FBI told him nothing, and it was three days before Blanche was allowed to see him. He learned that his lawyer had tried to get his hundred-thousand-dollar bail reinstated but that the Boston commissioner of police, Edmund L. McNamara, had prevented it.

"The commissioner had written to the federal judge that sentenced me and asked that my bail be revoked. He said I was a menace to society, that if I stayed on the street, I would further crime and corruption in Boston and that there could be some murders. He didn't know how right he was. He'd stopped me cold on maybe twenty million bucks in deals. Not only that; he saved the life of Joe Black. Now I wouldn't be able to whack him out."

Nor could Teresa, as he'd hoped, kill a man named Ken

Smith. Smith was an official of the Lynn Bank and Trust Company of Lynn, Massachusetts. He had conspired with Teresa to approve loans of up to four thousand dollars each on a variety of names that ranged from known mob figures to names selected from tombstones. Teresa had paid Smith a percentage on each loan given him and, in turn, used the bank's money to finance loanshark activities that brought in 6 percent interest a week. He was careful, however, to make payments on the bank loans on time. Unbeknownst to Teresa, however, Smith had other swindles going, including a fraudulent real-estate transaction that utilized bank funds. The real-estate maneuvers had attracted the attention of federal and then state auditors of the attorney general's office of Massachusetts.

"Smith had panicked. He kept calling me about the auditors, and then I found out the attorney general's men were checking into loans. Christ, I knew when they spotted the known mob names those loans were made out to, they'd put a squeeze on this guy and he'd fold. I was convinced I'd have to whack him out. I had a plan to take him on a trip to Haiti, where I had friends, and plant him under the ground. No one would ever find him there. No cop or federal agent would be allowed in Haiti to investigate me. If I let him testify, he'd bury me and a lot of friends. I had to put him to sleep. But now I was yanked off the street and couldn't get at Smith."

Behind the bars of the Worcester prison, Teresa was like a caged animal. He hated the jail. For him, it was a new experience. In twenty-eight years of crime, he had been arrested thirty-two times, yet never spent more than a few days behind bars. Now he was stuck in Worcester.

"What a hell hole that place was. They had no toilet facilities, no water. You were supposed to shit in a bucket. There were broken, dirty, rotten beds to sleep in, and if you wanted to shave, you had to get the razor from the hack. They allowed you two shaves a week and a shower every three days. When you wanted water to drink, you put your cup outside the cell and a guy would come along three times a day with water and fill it up. The food wasn't too bad in the mess hall. I've had worse. But the place—it was a hell hole. I felt for the guys that had to stay there for any time. At least I was getting out, even if it was to go to another prison.

"Once the feds sent me to Lewisburg [penitentiary], Joe Black made his move. He sold the property we had together, he sold the Esquire Sportsman Club, he collected my end on the stock deal with Karger, he took the hundred grand in street loanshark money I had, and he cleaned out the safety deposit box. He walked away with better than four million bucks of money I had coming to me, money I had planned to stash for Blanche and the kids. With the money, he took off Sicily, where I hear he's supposed to be in hiding with all that loot. He's wanted for trial in at least six federal cases, and I'm a witness in every one of them. For some reason, they've never found him to bring him back for trial. If he ever goes to trial, that's one guy I'll look forward to testifying against. He'll wind up with two hundred years in jail terms. The chances are, though, that he'll never be tried. He'll be lucky to stay alive. There are a lot of people in the New England mob who are just dying to whack out Joe Black.

"The irony of this is that if Patriarca hadn't been sent to jail and if Tameleo hadn't been thrown in the can, Joe Black and Bobby Cardillo would have never got away with my money. One of Patriarca's hard-and-fast rules was that the money his men made and had invested was protected no matter how long they were away behind bars. And he made sure that their families were fully taken care of. Blanche and the kids would have wanted for nothing. I'd never have talked, never said a word, if Patriarca and Tameleo had been out on the street protecting my interests. But they weren't, and Jerry Angiulo and Larry Baiona didn't do a thing to help me out, or my family. I think that's why I still have a sort of loyalty to Patriarca and Tameleo. They always treated me right. That's why I refused to testify against either one of them—and I could have buried them both. What for? They treated me right. Patriarca has beaten the state murder case in Rhode Island against him because Red Kelley folded like an accordion in the retrial of the case. Good luck to him as long as he leaves me and my family alone. If he don't, I'll nail him to a wall.

"The fact is that if Mondavano hadn't been sent to jail on the New Jersey stock deal, my money would have been protected, just like I protected his interests while I was on the street. Like Patriarca, my rule was to protect the families of those who worked for me. If they went to jail, and there were more than a few that did, I made sure that envelopes went out to their families every week. At Christmastime or at Thanksgiving, I'd go around to the families of my people and bring them toys for the kids and a bonus so they'd all have a good holiday. Like when Al Judd, the guy I used to deal with in bank robberies, went to jail. At Christmas, I went to his house and gave his wife, Lillian, five hundred bucks, and I made sure she got toys for the kids. Sometimes the toys were heisted stuff, but the kids had whatever they needed.

"There was another guy who'd done some work for me, Frank Ambruglia. He didn't really work very often for me, but he was jailed and he had five kids, and I liked the guy. I'd call his wife and see how she was doing. If she needed a hundred or five hundred bucks, she got it. I'd tell her, 'Don't be embarrassed to call when you need something.' There were many times she called, and she never walked away with less than two hundred bucks.

"When Danny went away, his wife got 250 bucks a week from me, every week until the day I went to jail. His son used to pick it up from me, and once or twice a month I'd slip the kid a hundred bucks for himself. He was eighteen, and a kid needs pocket money at that age. I made sure he had it. Just a couple of weeks before I went to jail, Danny's wife bought me a beautiful silk smoking jacket. It must have cost her eighty bucks. It was just her way of showing that she appreciated what I'd done for her and the family. When I went to jail, I left instructions with Joe Black to make sure Danny's family continued to get a couple of hundred every week out of my money. The bastard never gave them a dime. No one helped them after that. I supported Danny's family for eleven months before I went to jail. In fact, the day Danny went to jail, he had collected twenty grand for me on a stock deal. He never had a chance to give it to me because they wouldn't let him out on bail after he'd been sentenced. He told me that he'd left the money in a bureau drawer in the bedroom of his house. I went to see his wife and told her. She said she knew, that she was on her way over to my house with the money when I dropped in. Then she handed me the money. I counted out ten grand and handed it back to her. 'Here, this is in case you have any odds and ends to take care of,' I said. 'From now on, until Danny gets out, you get 250 bucks a week.'

"That's the way things had been in the New England mob with Tameleo and Patriarca. There was a feeling of loyalty and responsibility to each other. Nobody in that mob failed to make money; that's why there was almost never any real trouble internally. If Patriarca's men went to jail on a rap, no matter how long they were away for, it was the responsibility of the mob to take care of them. Even when Joe Barboza was in jail, before he made the mistake of threatening Patriarca, he got his nine hundred bucks every week. The money was delivered to his wife, just as though she was drawing a pension. Barboza never wanted to be an informer. He got backed to a wall, like I told you. One thing about Barboza. If he'd been on the street when I was in jail and I'd sent him word that Joe Black was chiseling the money that Blanche and the kids had coming, he would have found Joe Black, no matter where he was on the face of the earth, and squeezed that money out of him. Then he'd have whacked him out.

"The screwing that Joe Black and Bobby Cardillo gave me turned me sour on the mob. But that wasn't the reason that I became an informer myself. There were the other things that happened, the things that involved my family. My family comes first. Their safety was the most important thing in life to me. It still is."

26

On Mafia Row

"At Lewisburg, the protection that Mafia Row gives to incoming prisoners is helpful in ways that go beyond getting you a good haircut and better clothes. Jobs, for example. Each man coming in has to be assigned to a job. If you have friends inside, you're advised in advance where the best places are to work. Most of the jobs given to new prisoners are in the kitchen—cleaning tables, pots and pans, sweeping or mopping floors—dirty jobs. I didn't want any of that kind of crap. My friends of Mafia Row told me to put in for a job in the yard, because they had a hack supervising those jobs that would approve of taking me. To make sure that everything went okay for me, Louie the Fox, who was serving time for tax evasion, went with me to see the yard hack. I walked over to the hack and spoke to him. 'My name is Vinnie Teresa.'

"The hack looked like he was bored just being alive. 'Yeah, I know,' he said. 'Okay, get a lawn mower.'

"I looked at him like he'd lost his marbles. 'Whoa,' I said, 'get a lawn mower?'

" 'That's what I said,' the hack answered. There was a little edge of annoyance to his voice that I didn't like, but I thought it was best to be friendly, sort of con the guy a little.

" 'I can't push one of those things,' I said. 'I have high blood pressure—heart trouble. Forget about the lawn mower business.' What I said was true enough. I'd had a couple of minor heart attacks, and I've always had high blood pressure because of my weight—325 pounds—my work and the hours I kept. They call it hypertension. It was on my prison record, so I wasn't giving him a line.

" 'Okay,' he said, 'what do you want to do?'

" 'What Louie the Fox does,' I said. 'I want one of those sticks with the needle on the end. I want to go around and pick up the papers.'

"He just smiled a little, and nodded, handing me one of the sticks. Then he led me to a piece of land about twenty by ten feet. 'That's your piece of property to keep clean,' he said. 'You stay there and pick up the papers each day.'

"That's what I did, and I enjoyed it. I'd go there at eight in the morning, and by 8:15 A.M. my job was done. From there I'd go to the ballpark nearby and meet Danny Mondavano. Danny started work early in the morning. He worked in the bakery shop as a baker, and he loved it. When he got through at eight, he'd come out and run five miles at a clip around the track. When Danny was out of prison, he was fat, weighed about 290 pounds. But while he was in prison he was as trim as an athlete. He was down to 183 when I left.

"We'd stand there and talk and pretty soon Louie the Fox, Henry Stanford, and Buddy Powers, two bank robbers from Massachusetts, would join us. There was a Chinaman we used to call Tommy Shu, and the kid nephew of Vito Genovese, and a lot of other people I knew from Boston who'd stand around and gab. We'd play a little *boccie* ball or just shoot the breeze and kill the morning that way. There were no guards, just the yard boss. Most of the prisoners were working lawn mowers, working hard. I just cleaned that little square, and I was through for the day.

"I told you about Lillo, the boss of Mafia Row. After the first few card games, Lillo and I began hanging around together. He'd come by and wake me up in the morning. He was always up at the crack of dawn. 'Come on, Fats,' he'd shout. 'Let's get going for breakfast.' I never used to eat breakfast before, but I started going there with him, and I have to admit the food was good. They had eggs and cereal, bacon every day, fruit juices, delicious fresh melon from the farm, coffee, milk, tea if you wanted it, and toast. A couple of times a week they had pancakes and ham or sausage. Lillo and I got to be very close. When it would come time to go to the movies—they had movies twice a week—he'd go with me or alone. He'd shout: 'Come on, Fats, let's go to the movies—I got the candy.' He'd never bother with anyone else.

"Now, the men that worked in the yard didn't like me, most of all because I was from Boston, and the Boston mob was hated. But because I was close to Lillo, they treated me with respect. They were all scared to death of him. He bullied everybody up there. Vincent Rao [consiglieri in the family of Thomas Luchese] was petrified by Lillo. He'd literally shake in his pants. Lillo would look at Rao and roar: 'You big fake, you stupid bastard, what are you doing in the can? You're not supposed to be here with all your damned money.' Rao was a multimillionaire many times over, and Lillo and everybody knew it. Lillo would be kidding when he said it, but Rao was scared stiff.

"I remember there were two guys who used to work for Lillo who were in the can with us. They'd been arrested with Lillo on the narcotics conspiracy case that he was convicted on. Lillo claimed he'd been set up in the case by the stupidity of one of these guys, a big, stumbling jerk by the name of Big John. He used to work with Lillo and the other clown who were at Lewisburg with us. Lillo told me he was picked up because of their stupidity in handling junk. He said he'd had a cop and a boy fly in from Florida to testify that he was in Florida when the conspiracy took place, but the jury didn't believe him because of the way these clowns had operated and used his name. He was bitter about it, and when he saw these clowns in a prison corridor he was livid. If he got near them, he'd spit at the floor at their feet. *'Scifosa . . . grinudo,'* he'd snarl at them in Sicilian. Think of the lowest form of anything, the slimiest objects that come from the ground, that's what he was calling them. There's no English word to equal the contempt meant by those Sicilian words.

"Lillo had a special job. He worked in the prison hothouse raising plants. He loved to work with plants. When I was through with my work in the yard and tired of passing the time of day with some of the people, I'd walk over to the hothouse to be with Lillo. There was a special attraction: Lillo would cook for a few—a select few—of us in the hothouse. He had a small grill in the place—a homemade one that he'd built with a small barrel that was cut in half. Near that was a small refrigerator. I never found out how he got that. He kept cream and butter and milk and meat in that. The grill he'd fill with chopped up wood. Over the top he'd put a little screen. Occasionally, he would also have some charcoal for the fire. There he'd be, humming to himself, making some peppers and eggs or steak and eggs. The eggs he got from Danny Mondavano. Every morning, Danny would steal eggs from the bakery and wrap a couple of dozen of them around his legs, underneath his pants. He'd bring them out and give them to me. I had a huge pocket made inside my prison jacket, and I'd put the eggs in there and bring them to Lillo. The steaks came from the butchers, all prisoners, who he'd pay so much a month for them. The money would be sent to their bank accounts at home. There was one butcher named Max. Every month, Lillo's wife would send fifty bucks to Max's account. For that Max supplied us with tenderloin steaks, those are the best steaks money can buy. Sometimes we'd get steaks twice a day. Lillo got olive oil, vinegar, macaroni, peanut butter, salt, and pepper from the prison officer's mess that was supplied by a relative of Buffalo crime boss Stefano Magaddino. As for the vegetables, he grew peppers and tomatoes in the hothouse, and there was all we wanted for those of us who were his friends.

"Now, only a few were privileged to eat these snacks with Lillo. Jimmy Hoffa would come down now and then after he finished his work in the mattress shop. Mondavano was allowed to eat with us and, on occasion, Louie the Fox. But even though only a few were allowed to eat with him, everybody supplied him with whatever he wanted. To give you an example of how he ruled, I have to tell you the story about Lillo's cats. In prison, no one is allowed to have pets—no one. But Lillo had three cats, and they ate better than most of the prisoners. Every morning they had pure cream for their breakfast with an egg beaten up in it. The cats were sort of a symbol of freedom to Lillo. He used to say: 'At least they can get outside—they go outside the wall.'

"The hacks almost never came to the hothouse, and when they did, it was just to be sociable. None dared tread on Lillo. I remember one problem came up with a hack because of Lillo's cats. It was a Friday, and we were having fish in the prison dining room. Lillo sidled up to me and said: 'You're not eating your fish, are you, Fats?'

"I shook my head. 'I wouldn't eat that crap.'

" 'Well, I want to take it for the cats,' he said. He walked up the row to one of the hacks and announced: 'I'm taking Vinnie's fish.' Then he put it in a plastic bag with his own fish. The hack didn't seem to mind, so Lillo sort of added insult to injury. 'Those cats are pretty hungry. I'll take two pieces.'

"The hack was standing behind the row where the prisoners went through the food line to eat at the tables. 'Hey,' he shouted at Lillo, 'you can't take two—only one piece to a man.'

"Lillo turned around. He gave him a look that froze him in his tracks. 'Hey, I said I'm taking two or three pieces for my cat.' His voice was low and soft, but he had ice on the end of his tongue.

"The hack stared back at him. 'I said you can't take them,' he snapped.

"Lillo's eyes narrowed, and that sneer of his looked worse than ever. His voice was soft, but it was menacing. It made my blood run cold the way his words came out. 'You got kids at home?' he asked.

"The hack looked startled. 'What?'

" 'I said, you got any kids at home?' Lillo said again. 'You want to see them?' He sort of paused for effect, letting the words sink in. The hack seemed to nod. 'Good . . . then shut your mouth.' Then Lillo took five pieces of fish slowly, one by one while the hack looked, and he put them in his plastic bag. What he said he meant. He wouldn't have hurt the kids, but the hack would have had an accident one day in prison. He wouldn't have lived to see his kids—just because of a couple of lousy cats. But that was Lillo. No one defied him.

"There wasn't anything Lillo couldn't take care of in prison, but being close to him at times caused me problems. I'd been in G Block for about two months when the first of my problems came up. It was football season, and in prison that is the biggest time for gambling. Now, to the average guy, football season means eyes glued to the television set or a trip to the local stadium. To Danny Mondavano, it meant a sure-fire way to make some money—bookmaking.

"In prison, money was always a problem. The kids in prison could make up to twenty-five cents an hour in the prison industry. If they really hustled, they could make seventy to eighty bucks a month. Since they could only spend twenty bucks in prison—the maximum allowed—that meant they had fifty or sixty bucks to send home to their families, enough to pay the rent for some of them. Danny was in a worse fix. At the bakery, he could only make ten bucks a month, not enough for him to live on let alone help his family. He knew his wife and kid were in a rough way, so he started operating a football pool in the prison.

" 'What the hell are you getting involved in all this crap for?' I asked him.

"Danny shrugged. 'I need the money.'

"Then one weekend the roof caved in on him. He blew 254 cartons of cigarettes to bettors. He didn't have the money to pay for a carton, let alone 254 of them. In prison you can be in serious trouble if you don't pay off. The niggers there would put a shank in your back for a pack, let alone a carton, and cigarettes are money in the prison. He came to me, and I sent word out to Blanche—I had Jimmy Hoffa get a call to her at home. I told Hoffa: 'When your lawyer comes to see you, have him call my wife and tell her the next time she comes to bring me two hundred-buck bills in her pocketbook.' He agreed. Now, Blanche visited me every two weeks. She'd get there at 8 A.M. and stay till 3 P.M. She was only technically allowed three hours a month for visiting, but we had a good hack at the visiting room. If it wasn't busy, he'd allow Blanche to stay seven hours on each visit. He did the same for Lillo and some others. There were really some nice hacks in that prison, and they didn't ask for a quarter. They did us favors because we kept G Block clean—we had law and order in our own area, and that made less work for them. That they appreciated.

"When Blanche arrived, she gave me the two hundred-buck bills, and I slipped them to Danny, who bought off his creditors with cash, which is at a premium in prison. A carton cost about two bucks and thirty cents, but cash money was more valuable. That, I thought, ended the incident. Then one day, while I was sitting in my cell by myself, the hack in charge of the block came to see me. We called him Mr. B., a real nice guy who never bothered anyone.

" 'Vinnie—can I talk to you a minute?' he asked.

" 'Sure, come on in,' I answered.

"He sat down on the cot and closed the cell door. 'I understand,' he said, 'that you were a pretty big man on the outside.'

" 'I got by,' I said.

" 'You were spending a lot of money—bookmaking,' he continued.

"I thought to myself, what is this guy looking for, a touch? 'I got by,' I said again. 'I made a living. What are you trying to say?'

" 'Look, Vinnie, I'm here to give you a little warning,' he said, very sober. 'The warden gave orders to everybody in this area—all the hacks—to keep their eye on you. He said that since you came in here, you've taken over the prison, that you're the new leader of the prison.'

"I couldn't believe what I was hearing. 'Are you kidding?' I asked. 'I'm not leading anybody. I mind my own business.'

" 'Vinnie, I'm telling you—friend to friend,' he continued. 'You've been all right with us—you and Lillo—and we know you're all right. But that's the story. They're watching you. They figure you're taking over all the bookmaking action in the prison; all the stakes are coming through you. You're the new boss of the prison.'

"That could mean serious trouble, and I knew it. Some prison fink had found out I helped Danny and had run to the warden with the tip. 'Mr. B.,' I said, 'you tell the warden, all I want to do in this place is my time and mind my own business. I'm not taking any football action. I don't know who is, and I don't want to know anybody who is. You're a nice guy, Mr. B., and I'm not stepping out of line in your block.'

"He looked at me for a long minute or two. 'Since you're telling me that,' he said, 'I'll take you at your word.'

"I hadn't been there two months and suddenly the heat was on me. Every hack in the prison was afraid to come near me. I almost got transferred to Atlanta, the hell hole of the federal prison system, because of it. Another hack told me about that. He said I'd been marked by the warden as a troublemaker. To this day I don't know how the word got around about me, but I had to talk to Lillo to straighten it out. Of course, I have to admit things must have looked funny to the warden. I came straight out of receiving and hit the yard with an easy job. I had the best of clothes and I ate steaks and there would be a crowd of guys hanging around me, talking in the yard areas.

"When I told Lillo he just smiled. 'Don't worry about it, Fats,' he said. 'I'll talk to somebody.' He did. I don't know who it was, but they laid off of me after that.

"It was wintertime by this time, too cold for me to go around picking up papers with a needle. I told Lillo I couldn't take the cold. I never could.

" 'Get ahold of Tony Pro [Provenzano],' he said. 'I think they have an opening in the radio room. One of the guys is getting paroled next week. There's a long line ahead of you waiting for the job, but don't worry about it. It's yours.'

"So I saw Tony Pro and told him Lillo told me to apply for the radio room job. I didn't have any idea what it was. When I found out, it was easy to see why everybody in the prison wanted it. Tony Pro explained: 'Every morning, before breakfast, you go to the radio room and you press a button,' he said. 'When you do that, you're through for the day.'

"I couldn't believe what I was hearing, but that was the truth. The button you pressed turned on the radios in the cells throughout the prison. Every cell has a set of earphones, and the prisoner just plugs them into the wall. There are two stations: two holes. One station plays tape music, the other, the radio. The daytime man just plays the radio all day. At night, another crew comes on to play tapes that run for an hour and a half at a clip before they are changed.

"I got the job. It was beautiful. Just before breakfast, I'd go in and push the button at 6:45 A.M. After eating, I'd come back and write a couple of letters. I had my own office in the radio room, with chairs and a lamp. But it was a dull job—there wasn't enough for me to do, and I got a little lonely. After a while I started walking outside to see the yard gang and talk. Then one morning I saw a yard hack arguing with one of the prisoners, a guy named Ed Stanton. They were arguing about the garbage detail. I walked over and poked my nose in. 'What's the trouble?' I asked.

" 'I can't get anyone on this goddamned garbage detail,' the hack said.

"Now I don't volunteer for things normally, but this hack was a nice guy and I had nothing better to do anyhow. 'Look,' I said, 'why don't you let me handle it? Tell you what I'll do. Give me a list of who you have available. I'll organize the whole outfit for you. I guarantee whatever work you got will be done before the day is out. You can go sit in your office all day.'

"I never saw a hack look so surprised in his life. 'Really?' he said.

" 'Positively.' I answered.

"He handed me the list, and I went to work. I talked to each of the prisoners on the list. I set up a schedule. Instead of a guy working five days a week, he worked no more than three days. Suddenly there were no beefs, and all the work was getting done. Everybody was happy. That's when I decided if you have to have schedules and things, you should have an office. An empty room, where they stored old rubber boots, rakes, and other junk, struck my eye. It was located next to the hack's office. 'Can I use this room?' I asked.

" 'What are you going to do with it?' he asked. 'There's nothing in there but a bench.'

" 'If I get a desk and chairs in there, can I use it and make it a little hangout?'

"He looked at me as if I were crazy. 'Sure, go ahead,' he said. Then he scratched his head and looked at me a second time. 'Where the hell are you going to get a desk and chairs?'

"I just smiled at him. 'Leave that to me.'

"So I got ahold of a couple of guys from the New York mob. We took one of the four-wheeled garbage carts and went to a prison area where the case workers were. I noticed that prisoners were painting one case worker's office and they had put his desk outside in the hallway. We picked the desk up, put it on the four-wheeler, and hauled it away. While my friends were pushing the desk, I was walking behind them, pushing a swivel chair. We brought it to the hack's building and put it in the new office room I had set up. The yard hack was so pleased at the way things were going on the garbage detail that he had a stinger made for us—an electric metal coil that you can put in water to heat it up, boil eggs, or make coffee with. One of the prisoners added to our comfort. He made us a frying pan out of a stainless-steel ashtray and fixed it up with a detachable handle. When we wanted extra breakfast or a snack, we made fire bombs out of the toilet paper and cooked over the burning, balled-up paper.

"There was a little Mexican fag I'd gotten out of some trouble, and I had him come in and make curtains for the windows. He swept the place out regularly and cleaned up after us. That's where we spent the day. We'd play cards, yap a lot, and generally enjoy ourselves. We even had Hoffa draw us up a union agreement from the Teamsters. We called the office Club Lewisburg, Local 865. I was listed as president on the charter. To become a member, a prisoner was charged one pack of cigarettes. Weekly dues consisted of a few cigarettes a week. If you didn't have cigarettes, you could bring eggs, donuts, coffee, cream, whatever.

"Hoffa was a pretty decent guy, really. He was treated good at the prison because of Lillo, but he didn't get or ask for special privileges. He was in maximum security because he wanted to be. He was afraid of the blacks. He didn't want to get involved with them. He stayed in a cell right across the hall from me. He was well protected, and you couldn't have got him out of there with dynamite. He worked in the mattress shop, turning out one mattress a day. He'd go to work at 8 A.M., take an hour for lunch, and be finished by 2 P.M. I'll say this for Jimmy. He helped many a guy who was ready to be paroled. They wouldn't have made it but for him. He'd send word out to union officials he knew, and they'd provide a job for the guy, put him to work on a truck or a loading platform. Jimmy was pretty well liked by all of us. He offered me a job one time. 'You come to work for me, Vinnie,' he said. 'I'll make you public-relations director. With your gift of gab, you'll be terrific.' The job he offered paid thirty grand a year with a new car, and he promised another five grand a year after the first year on the job.

"Jimmy was convinced I wouldn't be at Lewisburg long. He'd read the transcript of my case, and he said I'd win an appeal. He couldn't understand how I'd been convicted with all the trial mistakes he saw. In prison, everyone is a jailhouse lawyer, but Jimmy had been through enough cases to honestly know something about it. Then he asked me if I had any money stashed.

"Now, at this time I didn't know Joe Black had stolen everything I had. I wasn't even aware that Blanche wasn't getting weekly support money from the mob. Every time I'd ask her how things were, she'd say fine—that she got money every week. So I told Hoffa I had a few bucks put aside and I had prospects of getting more. 'But what good is it?' I said. 'I can't spend it—they'll watch me like a hawk and grab it.'

"Hoffa shook his head and asked me if I'd ever heard of a guy named Lou Poller. Poller worked for the Miami National Bank, and his specialty was taking money that had been gotten illegally and 'washing' it—cleaning it up and legitimizing it. Whatever money you'd put with Poller, he'd take 10 percent. It might take him a year or two, but if you gave him ten million or one million, that money would be invested for you in something legitimate. You'd be able to pay taxes on it. No one knew how he did it—he had his own ways—but he was a master at it. Hoffa offered to write me a letter of introduction to Poller.

"Poller, I found out later, was one of Meyer Lansky's men, and he washed the mob's money through the bank. It came out in the form of real estate, apartment buildings, and business ownership, like motels or hotels or mobile-home companies. The government could trace all day and never find anything illegal. He did the same thing for some other mob people that Phil Simon did for Jerry Angiulo, Patriarca, and Tameleo. Simon was hooked up with Lansky and worked at the same bank as Poller did. That bank was used to wash millions and millions of dollars for the mob. I never got a chance to use the letter or Poller, who took off for Israel with Lansky. Joe Black and Bobby Cardillo took off with all the millions I had coming.

"Once Hoffa drew up the agreement for us, the Club Lewisburg really hummed. Lillo thought we were all crazy. He'd come by in the morning on the way to the hothouse. 'Hey Fats,' he'd shout, 'are you still working in there?' I'd wave to him and smile. He'd just shake his head and walk slow toward the greenhouse while I'd go over the daily work list, asking those on that day's detail how they felt. If anyone said he was tired, or sick, I'd move someone else onto the detail. Everyone was happy. Instead of working till 3 P.M., everyone was through at 9 or 10 A.M. The garbage was picked up, the streets were all swept, the grass was cut, and the yard was spotless. The yard hack was as happy as a pig.

"Now, the cigarettes I'd get as union dues, I'd use to buy hot chocolate or coffee or tea, that is, I'd trade them off at the commissary. Then everyone would sit around the club—they all brought their own cups—and drink what they wanted to and play casino, rummy, whisk, whatever interested them. It was a lot better than walking around in that cold yard all day, trying to hide from the hacks and keep warm. Finally, it all came to an end because of one of the few bad hacks we had at the prison, a drunk we called FBI Smith. He raided the Club Lewisburg.

"There had been a big item on the bulletin board for weeks. 'Whoever stole the desk, return it . . . no questions asked.' When it didn't turn up there was a big beef. We even had one of the prison filing cabinets in the club, and pictures from *Playboy* magazine decorated the walls. Then one of the more friendly hacks tipped us that FBI Smith was going to raid our clubhouse. Rather than let him find a thing, we threw the desk and chair and filing cabinet on the garbage truck. When Smith arrived demanding the table, it was on the way out the gate to the dumps. He never found a thing.

"All things concerned, Lewisburg wasn't half bad during the time I was there. Christmas was the best time, even for guys who were lonely. The corridors were all decorated gaily. At the prison church they had a big tree that we decorated with lights and Santa Clauses that moved. It was really beautiful. It was at this time of the year that they had a band playing Christmas carols as you came out of the mess hall. The prisoners got in the spirit of the holiday. They pledged two or three bucks a man out of their prison accounts for the orphans. Some even gave ten or fifteen bucks. Every year the prison came up with three grand for the orphaned kids, sometimes more. I thought that was kind of nice.

"Christmas dinner was terrific there. They allowed my family—Blanche, the kids, and some other relatives—to come to dinner there Christmas day, and it was really something . . . soup to nuts. They had real turkey, delicious dressing, raisin, mince and pumpkin pie, fruits and nuts—just like you'd eat at home—for forty cents a person. And you could never find a better fruit cake than what Danny used to bake. If the recipe called for fifty pounds of fruit, he'd put in a hundred. It was terrific. The guards used to take them home; they weren't supposed to, but they did. Each cake weighed ten pounds. He'd start making them before Thanksgiving, and by

Christmas you could hardly find any. Everybody would be scooping them up. Lillo had two or three in his cell at a time.

"Most of the hacks, as I said, were really decent people. There were a few miserable ones, like FBI Smith. He was a lieutenant, a real mean bastard. He hated everybody, including himself. He would come to check your cell with a surgical mirror, put it beneath your linings, your locker. He'd check every cell bar. Most of the hacks would just bang them, not Smith. He'd bang them, shake them, push them to make sure they hadn't been tampered with. If he saw three guys talking, he'd try to hide around the corner to hear what they were saying. Someday, somebody is going to kill him. I might have, to tell the truth, if I'd stayed there much longer. I had some trouble with him. He was always pushing, not just with words, but with actions. You had all you could do not to take a swing at him once in a while.

"There were others who were a pain, like a lieutenant I got to know. He was okay when he was sober, but he'd come in drunk a lot of times and hassle prisoners, pick an argument, and then get guys sent to the hole for nothing. And then there was a German lieutenant who I had a real bad beef with. I'd caught a disease on my feet and it was painful, and I had to walk with a cane I got from the hospital. Now, the chow line was a mile long at suppertime, and I couldn't stand on the line with my feet. So I would come with a friend and he'd stand in line, holding a place for me while I sat down. When it came close to the serving area, he'd motion to me and I'd take my place. Most of the hacks understood. Not this lieutenant. One night I hobbled over to Mondavano and got into line.

" 'Where are you going?' snapped this lieutenant.

" 'I'm coming in here . . . I got this bum foot,' I explained.

"He looked at me with a smirk. 'End of the line.'

" 'What do you mean, end of the line?' I said. 'I do this every night. I got a bum foot. That's why I got this cane.'

" 'I don't care,' he said. 'End of the line unless you have a medical pass.'

" 'I don't need a medical pass and you know it,' I shouted. I was getting very hot under the collar by this time. 'I came in with these men.'

" 'Don't argue with me,' he screams, 'end of the line or in the control bench.' Now, before you're sent to the hole, to solitary, they send you to what they call the control bench, where they let you argue your case before sending you to the hole. It's a formality. You can't win.

"At this point, I no longer gave a shit. I was mad as hell. 'I'm not going to the end of the line and I'm not going to the bench, and you can do whatever you think you could do,' I shouted.

"Then he put his hands on me. That was a mistake. No man does that. I whipped the cane into the air. 'Don't make me split your head open here,' I screamed. 'Get the hell away from me and get your hands off me.'

"That's when he called the goon squad, four or five hacks over. I looked at them, 'Don't put your hands on me,' I said. 'Just tell me where you want me to go.' I followed the lieutenant outside the mess hall.

" 'You shouldn't talk to me like that in front of everybody,' he said.

" 'Well, you shouldn't push me around like you did,' I answered.

" 'I'm a lieutenant,' he said.

" 'And I'm a human being,' I said. 'I don't care what you are. If I had done something wrong, I'd be the first one to go to the back of the line, but I didn't do anything wrong.'

" 'All right,' he said, 'but do me a favor. Go to the other mess hall and eat there tonight so I won't be embarrassed and we'll forget about the whole thing.'

"That's what I did, and it was the last time we had trouble. We became the best of friends after that. Whenever he saw me after that, he'd wave and shout: 'Hi, tiger, how are you tonight?' If I'd have let him back me down in front of everybody, I'd have lost respect. He had the same problem.

• • • •

"The biggest problem at Lewisburg was the division of blacks and whites. There were far more blacks than whites, and the blacks thought they were being stepped on by the hacks. But Mafia Row and the blacks had a very good relationship. The blacks knew that the Italian population of the prison stuck together and was strong and was ruled by Lillo. They respected Lillo. They never called him Lillo, they called him Mr. Galente. When we'd walk upstairs to play cards and some blacks were sitting at our regular table, they'd get up, clean it off, and sit at another table before we reached it. They knew what area we sat at in the movies, and it was never touched. A lot of them were shoemakers. Whenever we walked in for shoes, they gave us the best treatment possible. In turn we treated them with respect. Even the Black Muslims, who didn't want anything to do with white people, treated Lillo and Mafia Row members like they was gods.

"But even so, you could feel the racial tension bubbling in there. The Southerners and the blacks were always at each other's throats, insulting each other, calling each other dirty names. Not the Italian population. We showed them all the respect they deserved as long as they didn't get out of line.

"Once in a while there was some real trouble, but it was rare. The most serious problem involved Lillo. A new black had come to our block from Philadelphia. He was put in charge of sweeping floors, and he used to hand out the newspapers. One afternoon, the paper didn't come until 4:30 P.M. Lillo yelled out the door, 'Hey, where's my newspaper?'

"The new black didn't pay any attention. He was bullshitting with another black at the end of the cellblock. He was standing there with the newspapers under his arm. Lillo yelled again. 'Hey, bring my newspaper down here.'

"The black yelled back, 'For Christ sake, shut up.' He didn't know who Lillo was. Lillo's cell door was next to mine, and I saw it open like it was jet-propelled. I opened mine quick and followed because I knew what was going to happen. Lillo jumped the black, grabbed him by the throat.

" 'You black son-of-a-bitch,' he screamed. 'Who are you telling to shut up?'

"The black shook Lillo loose and shouted back at him. 'Who the hell are you, you old bastard?' Then he shoved Lillo. I tried to step between them, hold the black guy back, but by this time Lillo doesn't want to know anything. Now there are a couple of us trying to pull Lillo away. The hack is watching, but he won't even come down into the cellblock. He figured if he came down it would be curtains for him too. Finally, we pulled Lillo away and I told him I'd talk to the black guy.

" 'Talk to him,' he screamed. 'Don't talk to him—he's a dead man.'

" 'Nah, Lillo, don't do that,' I said. 'That'll just cause a lot of trouble.'

"Finally we got Lillo calmed down and I went back to talk to the black man. 'I don't know who you think you're goofing around with,' I said, 'but let me warn you now: This is a dangerous man you're fooling with. Unless you apologize now you won't make it till morning if he puts the X on you.'

"By this time the black had figured out who and what he'd stepped on and he was scared to death. 'Look—I just came here,' he said, 'I didn't know.'

" 'You shouldn't shoot your mouth off in here,' I said.

"The black guy did the only thing he could. He walked up to Lillo and said: 'Mr. Galente . . . I didn't know . . . I'm sorry.'

"Lillo sneered at him as though he was dead already. 'Don't say you're sorry,' he snarled. 'Just shut your mouth. From now on, don't talk unless you're spoken to.' I don't think Lillo ever spoke to him again and the black never said a word, but the papers were delivered on time after that.

"Lillo ran the prison even when he was moved to the prison farm. Every Sunday, he'd come back to church to hold counsel—talk to everyone and find out what the problems were. Before church, we'd all assemble at the control center—a big open space about forty by forty yards, all cobblestone. We'd stand there and wait for Lillo. He'd come and he'd talk to Hoffa, to Rao, to me, to a few others. If there was anything important that couldn't wait for the Sunday counsel, we'd send a message out to the farm through a prisoner to tell Lillo to come to the prison hospital the next morning for a talk. He'd make an appointment to go to the hospital, give some excuse about not feeling good, and we'd meet in the physical therapy room where a Boston guy we called Big Sid was in charge. We'd take a whirlpool bath, get a rubdown, a sunlamp, have coffee or cocoa, and discuss our business. They had a helluva hack in there who had lost an ear to an inmate. The inmate had cut it off in a fight. The hack would see us come in and say: 'Hey, here comes the whole Mafia.' I'd walk up to him and ask: 'Would you excuse us? We'd like to talk.' He'd nod, smile, and walk outside without another word.

"That's the way things were at Lewisburg. I'd have taken my full time standing on my head there if I hadn't turned informer and left."

27

The Death of Joe Valachi

"I began my career as an informer in December 1969, right there in the Townsend County Jail in Maryland—I'd been sent to Maryland from Lewisburg, to talk with the FBI. I told the agents the story of my stock operations, I laid it all out for them—who was involved and what was happening. It took hours."

Teresa, however, was reluctant to open up completely, to tell everything he knew. Despite the urgings of the FBI agents, he held back. And so the FBI and state law-enforcement officials began to work a squeeze play on Teresa. He was flown to Boston and allowed to be put on trial by the state of Massachusetts for his role in the swindle of the Lynn Bank and Trust Company he had performed with Ken Smith. The FBI was sympathetic but said that, under the circumstances, there was nothing it could do to help its new informer escape the trial because it was a state affair, not a federal proceeding. But Teresa thought he caught a hint that if he ever should decide to tell all—well, then it was just possible that something might be done.

"I didn't know until they got me to Boston that I was going to be tried for my involvement in the Ken Smith bank swindle. That was a shock. This swindle was the operation where I'd arranged for loans—tombstone loans—and used the

312

bank's money for loansharking on the street. The Massachusetts attorney general's office had broken the case wide open. I didn't know it then, but a state trooper assigned to that office by the name of Richard Schneiderhan and his boss, Dennis Crowley, had done a number on one of my suckers, Jack Hirschfeld [former partner of Al Grillo and a loanshark victim of Teresa], and Hirschfeld had been talking. So had Ken Smith. All I did know was that they had put together a tough case against me and that I was walking into a stacked deck for the trial.

"While I was waiting for the trial, Blanche saw Hirschfeld in a corridor and spoke to him. 'Gee, Jack, we're sorry . . . it looks like you have a tough case to face,' she said.

"Hirschfeld shook his head. 'If you think I have a headache, wait till your husband gets here.'

" 'What do you mean?' asked Blanche.

" 'I'm taking the stand against him,' he said matter-of-factly. 'I'm going to bury him.'

" 'I wouldn't do that if I were you,' Blanche said angrily. 'I don't think Carlo [Mastrototaro] and some other people would like what you're saying. In fact, I'm going to call Carlo when I get home.'

"Hirschfeld waved his hand at her. 'I wouldn't do that, Blanche,' he warned. 'Carlo is the one that told me to testify . . . he and Joe Black. They told me to come here and bury Vinnie.'

"Blanche was shocked, but it was nothing compared to how I felt when she told me. I knew I had to make a move, fast. I whispered to Blanche. 'Here's what I'm going to do,' I said. 'I'm going to cross them up: I'm going to plead guilty and ask for a postponement of sentencing. While I'm doing that, you call this agent—Jack Kehoe—on the phone and tell him to ship me to Pittsfield [state prison]. You tell him I want to talk to him. Tell him now I'll talk to him—in spades.'

"When I went to court, I pleaded guilty and asked for and got a thirty-day postponement. Then the FBI had me shipped to Pittsfield, where I began telling Kehoe and agent Bill Welby the whole story, a lot that I'd held back before in our Baltimore discussions. In return for my testimony, the Justice Department made and kept certain promises. They agreed to provide protection and subsistence for my family. They agreed to get a reduction in my jail time, from fifteen years to five years, which made me eligible for parole in 1971. And they agreed to do what they could in getting sentences suspended that I had pending in state cases provided I cooperated with state authorities.

"I not only cooperated, but before I was through—and I may still be testifying against some other people when this book comes out—I'd been responsible for twenty-seven convictions involving twenty-one mob people and there were other indictments pending against twenty-seven other mob people. I also later agreed to cooperate with Senator John McClellan and his Senate Permanent Subcommittee on Investigations, and I testified publicly for them. As far as I'm concerned, that subcommittee and their key investigator Philip Manuel are the finest group of people I've ever dealt with in my life. They've helped me and lived up to the letter of their promises, and then some. They've shown an honest concern for my welfare and that of my family, and I couldn't do enough for them, no matter what they ask. They're doing a job on the mob, and if the public is smart it had better start to listen to what they're saying at their public hearings.

"At any rate, after we agreed to a deal and I started talking, the Justice Department arranged to have me transferred to La Tuna [federal penitentiary] near El Paso [Texas] to finish my jail time under special guard. That's where I met Joe Valachi.

"Joe Valachi was the first made guy to publicly testify about the inner secrets of the mob. Joe wasn't an educated guy, he wasn't even a big-time operator, but he knew a lot of the mob people and he opened the eyes of the public about the mob. He's the one who coined the name Cosa Nostra to describe the mob. In New York and New Jersey, some of the bosses informally called it that. In New England like I said, we just called it the Office, or the mob.

"La Tuna isn't a Lewisburg, let me set you straight on that. It's hot, it's dry, and it's miserable. Instead of a cellblock with men I could talk to, I was put in an isolated area near the prison hospital in what they called a strip cell. It was a cell where they normally kept nuts. It's called a strip cell because that's what it is—stripped. There was nothing inside to begin with. The prison itself is relatively small. The prisoners were mostly Mexican and Indian, and the guards were almost all Mexicans. Frankly, you couldn't have met a nicer bunch of hacks. In the beginning, I was leary about them all. They all came from poverty. All I could think of was that somebody would wave a big chunk of dough in front of one of them and that would be the end of me. I was wrong. They couldn't do enough for me. They tried their best to make me comfortable.

"La Tuna is about twenty-one miles from El Paso. When you approach it, it looks like a Spanish adobe church. Day or night, you can see for miles around from the prison windows. Miles and miles of Jalopeño peppers and corn and grass rippling in the breeze. Once in a while, you could see the roadrunners, those lightning-fast little birds that run across the desert on their feet, or the giant jackrabbits skipping across the ground. But beyond that, it was the dullest landscape I've ever seen in my life.

"I arrived on May 8, 1970. Blanche and the kids had arrived in El Paso days before. When I had agreed to talk, the FBI had scooped Blanche and the kids up from our home in North Reading, packed our furniture and belongings, and quartered the family in a motel in Cape Cod across from the state police barracks, where I was temporarily kept under close guard. She stayed there three weeks. I was sent from there to Baltimore to testify before a grand jury, and it was while I was in Baltimore that she drove down with the kids, my sister, and a nephew to Texas. The government had picked out a small, four-room apartment for her and the kids to live in. It wasn't large enough for all of them. For almost four weeks, Blanche stayed at a Howard Johnson motel searching for a home large enough that she could afford to rent. It was miserable for them. The kids had no family, no friends around. The schools were strange. They couldn't use the telephones or write letters—they couldn't even write my family or Blanche's family for fear the mob would rifle the mail and get a hint of where I had been taken.

"Through it all, and I spent fourteen months in La Tuna, Blanche never complained. The government provided her with seven hundred bucks a month. The monthly rent for the house she found was two hundred bucks and, after paying electric, water, and gas bills, she was lucky if she had 350 bucks to buy food and clothes and pay medical bills. It was tough on her, but there were some nice FBI agents there. There was one agent who checked her daily to see that she was all right. When he found she was short of money, he'd take a hundred or two hundred bucks from his own pocket and lend it to her until the subsistence check came in. But the guy who was the greatest through all of it was Jack Kehoe.

He stuck by me and the family. He's a good conman, a tough guy, and he knows the criminal mind. Moreover, he's not the snobbish type of cop that looks down the end of his nose at a mob guy. Jack worried about me, about Blanche, about the kids, and there were many times that he helped Blanche out.

"My first day inside La Tuna wasn't what I'd call my best. I was taken to the hole, a cellar room, to be isolated from other prisoners. Prison officials were afraid of other prisoners getting to me. After a couple of days of that, at my urging, they let me move into the split cell with another witness, a kid named Rinky who had testified against Joe Bonanno. Rinky, I never did learn his true name, was a smart-ass. I had some trouble with him one day over food. The hacks used to bring us our food at mealtime since we couldn't eat in a mess hall with other prisoners. The plates always had a portion of Mexican beans, which I couldn't stand. So I asked the hack to just bring me meat and potatoes and forget the vegetables. To be nice, the hack always made sure I had a little extra portion of potatoes and meat. Rinky didn't like it, and one day he made a fuss with the hack, threatened to report him to the warden. After the hack left, I took Rinky inside the room, whacked him in the mouth, and knocked him out. After that we had no more trouble.

"My room had a television set, a desk and a chair, and a small toilet that only the guards could flush. Now, down the corridor from my room, about twenty steps away, was the room of Joe Valachi. He had a big room right off the hospital, complete with its own bathroom, a rug on the floor, a nice view of the road approaches to La Tuna, a television set, and a little stove. And all around his room were electric heaters. Joe was forever cold.

"Four times a week—Monday, Tuesday, Wednesday, and Thursday—they'd let Valachi and me go out for an hour in a small patio where trustys were normally allowed. The first couple of times we went out, Joe wouldn't even come near me or talk to me. He was scared stiff. He had heard of me and he was convinced I was there to kill him. So one day I walked over to him and said: 'Joe, let's have an understanding between you and me. I'm in here for the same reason you are—I'm an informer. I'm not about to whack you out, and don't get any silly ideas about whacking me out, because then you will get hurt. I'm going to be here for quite a while. We're all going to be here for quite a while. While we are, why don't we become friends? Let's trust each other.' After that, Valachi and I got along.

"Valachi was a nice, quiet old man. He was bitter about Vito Genovese, Frank Costello, and Johnny Dio [John Dioguardi, a soldier in the Thomas Luchese crime family who was party to a conspiracy by Genovese to murder Valachi in Atlanta federal penitentiary]. He hated them and he talked constantly about their treachery, about their attempt to kill him and how he had killed an innocent inmate who he thought was one of the killers sent to whack him out.

"Now, Joe had been an opportunist on the street. He was the type of guy who would knock Genovese when he was with, say, Gambino, and then knock Gambino when he was with Genovese. It was part of his makeup—he couldn't help himself. He didn't have the mentality to make it on his own in the mob. The most money he ever made was sixty grand on counterfeit gasoline ration stamps during the war. He was strictly a small-timer: a B&E guy, an occasional hit man, a go-fer—the guy who would go for this or go for that when anyone of importance told him to. To the mob, Joe was a *facci due*—two-faced in Italian. No one trusted him in the mob long before he talked.

"But in the months we were together, I really got to like that old man. In the summertime—he was very old and getting weak in 1970—I took a pair of white pants and cut the legs off, made shorts for him so he could sit out in the Texas sun on the patio. At La Tuna, it got to be 110 degrees in the shade, if you could find the shade. He'd sit out there in his shorts and I'd made him feel good by taking a hose and squirting him with water to cool him off. It was one of his delights, one of the pleasures he had that hour a day we had together in the patio. But he was nutty about the mob trying to hit him. I remember a couple of times while we were out sunning ourselves, a small plane passed overhead, circling the patio. Joe was convinced that that plane carried a hit man who was going to shoot us. The FBI checked it out, and as a precautionary measure they kept us out of the patio for a while and instructed the guards to fire some shots at the plane if it came too low. It never came back after that.

"Joe loved to cook Italian food on his little two-burner stove. Blanche would bring up food twice a week to the prison, and he'd make macaroni with sauce ingredients my wife would bring up. He was great at making sauces and soups.

That's what we both survived on at La Tuna because we couldn't eat the crap they served us from the prison mess. Every day, he'd talk about Italian food and how it should be made. I still have a letter he wrote to Blanche, telling her how to make spaghetti sauce. He always used to call her 'Mommie,' and the letter began: 'Dear Mommie: To make raw tomatoes sauce just put some oil in a pot or frying pan, a little powder garlic. This recipe is for two, then you judge if for 4. Say about 6 tomatoes—squeeze them with your hand and put them in the pot. Then you put say, 3, cups of water—let them boil with cover on for half hour to get the substance out of the tomatoes. Then take cover off and simmer it down to become sauce. By the way, I forgot, after you put tomatoes in the pot, put a large spoon of black pepper in the sauce also a pinch of oregano. Let cover off until sauce is made, of course, you taste sauce to your liking. Good luck to you, all my mob, a good mob. Joe. P.S. I'm having a feast with the bullions [bouillon cubes] tonight—Sun. I'm starved. I had beef soup with hard bread. I feel fine thank you. If you think about it, we are out of oregano. O.K.'

"It was a typical Valachi recipe. He sent others to us. I wish I'd saved them. Some of his recipes were great.

"Other than talk about food, Joe liked to reminisce a lot. Every day, four days a week we'd talk and, to be honest, most of the time I couldn't understand what he was talking about because he talked in riddles. He'd talk all the time about hits —murders—always about hitting this guy and hitting that guy.

" 'Joe,' I'd say, 'talk about making money.'

"His face would kind of wrinkle up. 'How can I talk about making money, Vinnie?' he'd answer. 'I never made any.'

"He never stopped talking about Genovese and how he was given the kiss of death. 'Vito kissed me on one cheek,' he said, pointing to the right side of his face, 'and I turned around and kissed Vito's other cheek. "Here—how do you like it?" I told Vito.' Valachi'd talk about Joe Beck [Joe DiPalermo, a Genovese family narcotics dealer], another of the guys at Atlanta who tried to kill him, and how Beck gave him a steak sandwich that was poisoned. 'I wouldn't eat for three days one time because I was scared to death,' he said. Then he told how he killed an innocent prisoner who he thought was Beck coming to kill him. 'I thought I'd killed Joe Beck—I killed the wrong guy. They showed me the picture, and he looked like Joe Beck. I killed the poor guy for nothing, and Joe Beck is walking around free.' It was like a record he had to replay in his mind day in, day out, to justify what he'd done. But I listened.

"Valachi was bitter about other things. He believed he'd been given the business by the government. He kept saying over and over that Bobby Kennedy [the late Senator Robert F. Kennedy, then U.S. Attorney General] had promised him he would get out of jail, but it was all a snow job. Let's face it: Valachi did blow the country wide open when he talked, but he really didn't harm any of the mob. What he did do was sell a lot of newspapers, and the publicity gave the Justice Department help in building an army against the mob. But they couldn't let him out of jail—not after killing an inmate.

"Joe was very, very sick when I was with him. He had cancer, high blood pressure, gall bladder trouble, and prostate gland trouble. He was in pain all the time with arthritis, and he was always cold. It could be 110 degrees outside, but inside his room it would be 130 because he had all the electric heaters turned on, going all the time. My wife used to bring him wool stockings, heavy woolen sweaters, a hat for his head, and mittens. It would be 130 degrees in that room and he'd be sitting there, all huddled up, shivering with heavy woolen clothes on and the heaters going full blast.

"The last Christmas he was alive, December 1970, I knew he was dying. Warden [William] Zachem knew it, and he tried to do everything to make it easier for Joe. One day, just before Christmas, I asked Warden Zachem for a favor 'Joe is so lonely, warden. At least I got some company twice a week.' Zachem nodded. 'On Christmas afternoon, my wife is coming to the prison. She's bringing me a box of Italian food. When she leaves, could I go to Joe's room? Could we spend a couple of hours together and bullshit back and forth? At least it will seem like Christmas to the poor old man.'

"Warden Zachem thought about it for a minute, then he smiled. 'Sure, go ahead, Vinnie.' He cleared it with the hacks and they let me into Joe's room, which was always locked.

"We spent three hours together that afternoon. We ate. Oh, Joe was as happy as he'd ever been. We had stuffed artichokes my wife made, lasagna, sausages, meat balls, fruits, nuts, and some delicious turkey with all the trimmings. He was like a kid. He laughed and joked, and he was genuinely happy when I told him: 'Don't worry, Joe, we're both going to get out of here soon.'

" 'Really, Vinnie? Will we really?' he asked. It was pathetic, but it was like a shot of adrenalin for him.

" 'Here's what you got to do, Joe,' I said. 'You got to get hold of a lawyer. We'll tell him that you were temporarily insane when you killed that inmate by mistake. We'll get your case reopened.'

"He grinned from ear to ear as I talked. 'Then, with all the time you've done in the can, with all you've done for the government, the federal judge will say: This guy's done a helluva lot of years already, and he'll let you free with the government's backing.'

"He was like a kid at the thought of something like that happening. He looked eagerly at me, and he said: 'And where am I gonna go when I get out, Vinnie?'

"I put my arm around his shoulders and gave him a gentle bearhug. 'You're going to come and live with me and Blanche and the kids,' I said. 'I should be out in a year or so, and you'll come and live with me.'

" 'Really, Vinnie?' he said. 'You're not just kidding me, are you? I can come and live with you and Mommie?' He never called Blanche by her name, always Mommie. He'd watch for her twice a week as she'd come walking up the prison path, and he'd wave to her. He looked forward to seeing her, probably because she was always bringing him goodies, Italian delicacies, like sausages, cheese, salami, tomato paste, and olive oil. When he'd see her through the bars, he'd shout: 'Hi, Mommie, how are you?' And at Christmastime or on one of the kids' birthdays, he'd always send a card. He was such a pathetic figure then. I really felt so bad for that man.

"It was in February 1971 that I got a call from Jack Kehoe. He said that Senator McClellan's committee was putting together a hearing on the mob's infiltration of the stock and bond business. 'They want to talk to you, Vinnie,' he said, 'but you don't have to talk to them. I think if you do, it might help you with your parole.' Then he told me they were square shooters and that the best of them was Phil Manuel. He also pointed out one other thing. If I didn't talk, they could subpoena me, slap me with contempt. That would have hurt my chances for parole. I didn't need the warning. I was ready to talk to them anyhow. I found they were on the up. After I testified, Senator McClellan wrote the parole board and recommended my immediate parole because I'd been a big help to the committee. Up to then, I'd been turned down three times for parole. Later, it was through Phil Manuel that I was able to have my wife with me in Florida while I testified. Later he arranged for her and the family to stay with me in Michigan in a rented cottage on a lake while I was under federal protection. It made the ordeal of testifying a lot easier, and for the first time in years I got to go out and fish with my kids.

"What impressed me most about that committee and its investigators was that they talked straight to you—not off the top of their heads. They said they couldn't promise a thing, but they also said they would see what they could do. All they wanted from me was my story of life in the mob. To me it didn't seem that important then, but to them it was. They said it would blow the lid off things in the stock business. I didn't believe them. They were right and I was wrong. I made headlines from London to Tokyo.

"During that period I was to testify I helped them get another witness, James Schaefer, one of the Kennedy Airport mail thieves, to loosen up and talk. Schaefer was very shaky. He'd made a promise to testify, and he was getting cold feet. He thought the committee was handing him a line, and he was ready to back out of his agreement. So Phil Manuel asked me if I'd talk to him. Schaefer and I, at the time, were staying in the same motel under the protection of the U.S. Marshals Service.

" 'Call the kid over and talk to him,' Manuel said. 'Let him hear your side of the story. Don't snow him. Tell the truth.'

"That's exactly what I did. I talked to him like a Dutch uncle, and I meant every word I said. 'Kid, these people can help you,' I said, 'They'll help you get your parole. They'll help protect your family and get some subsistence for them. Maybe you won't even have to go back to the can and maybe you will, I don't know. I can't promise you anything. But I'll tell you one thing: You're dealing with a real man when you deal with Manuel. He's a guy you can trust—he'll do all in his power to help you. But understand one thing: Don't lie. Tell the truth. It won't be a bed of roses, but it'll be better than you had it before.' We talked for more than two hours. Right after that he testified about the mail thefts for the mob at Kennedy Airport and how the stocks were turned over to the Joe Colombo mob in Brooklyn.

"Early one morning at La Tuna I was sitting around waiting for a visit from the McClellan investigators when I heard some commotion from Joe's room. I yelled: 'What's the matter, Joe?'

" 'I'm sick . . . I'm sick,' he answered, very weak.

"I couldn't see him, but I could just about hear him. So I started banging on my door: 'Guard . . . guard,' I shouted at the top of my lungs.

"The guard came running. 'What's the matter?' he said.

" 'Get a doctor over here, fast,' I said. 'Joe's sick.'

"It was on a Saturday [April 3, 1971], and the guard said that the doctor wasn't at the prison on Saturdays.

" 'Well, get somebody around here,' I said. 'The old guy is really sick—he needs help.'

"They sent a guy, I guess some sort of medic, to see Joe, then a lieutenant of the hacks came to my room. "Joe's asking for you,' he said. 'He's in bad shape. You want to go see him?'

" 'Of course I do,' I answered and started out my cell door toward Joe's room.

"The lieutenant was very squeamish. Joe had the shits and was throwing up. Here I am—I never did anything like this in my life. I didn't think I could ever do it, but I thought this much of the man. There I was, cleaning him up, wiping the dirt off him, washing him, putting clean pajamas on him. Then he'd do it all over again and I'd change him again as well as the sheets to his bed. I had to run to the bathroom myself and throw my guts up. The corpsman or medic was helping me. All the while, Joe would whimper: 'Please Vinnie . . . please don't leave me. You're the only one I got . . . don't leave me. I'm dying.'

"I tried to comfort him the best way I could with the street talk he'd known all his life. You didn't baby Joe Valachi. That's the worst thing you could do. 'Joe,' I growled, 'don't give me any of that dying shit.' It made him feel like a tough guy if you yelled at him a little. 'Now you stop that talk or I'll whack you in the head.' He smiled weakly at me. 'You're not dying, Joe . . . don't worry about it. Tomorrow we'll go out and get the sun . . . you've just got a little gas in your gall bladder.' He was throwing up something awful: bile—green, smelly bile.

" 'Vinnie, please,' he said softly, 'let me hold on to your arm so I can feel you.'

" 'Joe, stop that,' I snapped. 'I'm telling you, you're not dying.'

"He sort of laughed a little. 'What a friend you are,' he said. 'You won't even let me die when it's my time. You know I'm dying, I know I'm dying.'

"I couldn't take much more. 'Joe, don't talk like that,' I said as sincerely as I could make myself say it. 'I got to go outside, but I'll be right back.' As I walked outside, a doctor was coming in. He wasn't the regular prison doctor. He'd been brought in as an emergency measure. He examined Joe and said he was having a gall bladder attack. He said he'd give him something to rest. I came back into the room for a minute. Joe looked around the room for me and spotted me. 'Vinnie . . . don't leave me,' he pleaded, 'please don't leave me.'

"I shook my head from side to side. 'Don't worry, Joe . . . I'm sitting right here.'

"The doctor gave him a shot of morphine and something else, and he started going to sleep. Meanwhile, the investigators from the McClellan committee, Bill Gibney and Gene Anguilla, had arrived at the visitors' room to see me. While Joe was dozing, I slipped out of his room, cleaned myself up, and went down to see them. Before I left, I said softly to Joe: 'Go to sleep, Joe . . . I'll be back in a couple of hours to see you.' I don't know if he heard me or not.

"I was in the visitors' room talking to the investigators when there was a knock on the door. It was my caseworker, John Glendennan, a real decent, understanding guy who tried his best to help the prisoners he dealt with. I looked up. 'Hey, John, what are you doing here on a Saturday?' I asked.

"He looked a little strange. 'Oh, nothing . . . really . . . something came up and I had to talk to one of your friends.' Then he motioned to Anguilla and said: 'Can I talk to you for a minute, Gene?' I didn't know what the hell was going on, but I left the room. I found out later that John had just told Gene that Valachi was dead. They were afraid to break it to me because they knew Joe and I were close and they were afraid I might take a flop with my heart trouble.

"Gene came back in the room. 'Tell you what, Vinnie,' he

said. 'I think we'd better break it up now. I'm a little tired. I'll see you in Washington in a couple of weeks.' I nodded and walked back upstairs toward my room with one of the hacks.

" 'How's Joe?' I asked the hack.

" 'Joe? Didn't you know?' he said. 'Joe died right after you left the room.'

" 'What?' I shouted. 'That's two hours ago. Why couldn't someone let me know?'

"The guard was startled. 'Well, we figured you—'

"Just as he was talking, I could feel my heart pounding and my mind going blank. They had to send a doctor for me to give me a shot. I felt weak. As I walked back toward my room, I could see Joe's room—I could see the bed, with the blanket pulled up over his head. They left him in that room until late that night—eight or nine o'clock.

"Joe's death hit me hard. We'd become good friends. When they held a service for him at the chapel, I didn't go. I wasn't and I'm still not a religious man. But I got ahold of the priest, Father Hoolihan. He was a nice guy who used to bring Joe and me books to read and some food. He didn't preach a lot, just talked straight talk with you. 'Father,' I said, 'could you hold a mass for Joe in his room for us?' I motioned toward a new cellmate I had, a guy we all called Gonzales. He had been with the Mexican secret police, a general of some kind, and got involved in dealing in heroin with some French smuggling ring. He'd been caught and to protect his girlfriend and a superior, he took the rap. Later his girl was found with her throat cut in a ditch in Mexico City. Gonzales tried suicide once in a San Antonio [Texas] prison, and later he made it after I left La Tuna. He cut his throat.

"Father Hoolihan agreed, and he held a high mass in the room. He did the mass in three languages: Spanish, for Gonzales, English for me, and Latin. I thought that was damned decent of the man.

"After Joe died, I thought his family—his wife or son—would claim his body. I'd been shipped out on the following Monday to Florida, but I called El Paso. 'What's the story?' I asked Blanche. She didn't know, but she said she would call the warden.

" 'Mr. Zachem,' she said, 'we don't want Joe buried in any potter's field, like a charity case. You just give me the body and I'll put him in a nice Catholic cemetery where he'll have a nice headstone.'

" 'Please don't worry, Mrs. Teresa,' he said. 'Someone is going to claim the body.' Then he called me and told me: 'Now, Vinnie, don't get mad about it, but that woman from Buffalo that Joe used to write is claiming the body. We're giving her the body and the money and whatever he had.'

"Joe had left everything to the Buffalo woman in a will, but I was still a little upset. She knew Joe through letters she wrote him after he testified before the McClellan committee in 1963. They'd been writing each other for years, but that's as far as it went—letters to each other. That's all I knew about her. 'I don't care about the money. Is she going to give the guy a decent burial?'

"Zachem assured me she was. 'She promised she would, and we're going to make sure she does.'

"So they shipped Joe's body out. She got the money and his papers. She buried him, and I found out later that they put him in the ground at a cemetery in Niagara Falls. He didn't have a headstone because she was afraid the mob would try to desecrate his grave. Maybe she was right. Now there are days that I miss old Joe and the talks we had. Blanche misses him sometimes too. In his own way, he was very gentle, even though he was a killer. I think what bothers me most is that he suffered so much those last few months in prison. It was terrible to watch."

28

Witness Against the Mob

Vincent Teresa's appearance before the McClellan rackets committee radically changed his life. Overnight his gravel voice, his huge frame, and his heavily jowled face became familiar to many of the millions of Americans who watched him on television. Thousands of newspapers all over the world featured stories about his activities, particularly Piranha, Inc., and printed his photograph.

It was instant heat. No longer could Teresa sit by a motel swimming pool with his federal protectors without being recognized. Elevators in hotels and federal buildings exposed him to a celebrity-conscious public, and passengers aboard commercial airliners recognized him and at times even asked for his autograph. His family, too, was suddenly put in jeopardy. One Boston newspaper article, for example, revealed that Teresa's wife was living with her children under her maiden name of Blanche Bosselman, a valuable cue for the mobs' assassins.

Yet in one way the publicity was also a blessing. Texas was no longer safe for the Teresas. Federal prisons where mob figures and their associates were quartered could no longer be considered havens for a man of Teresa's importance.

"It was the McClellan committee that saved the day for me and my family. The game plan had been to keep me at La

Tuna for several more months, but the government couldn't play by those rules now. So Phil Manuel and Senator McClellan recommended that my family and I live together under the protection of the U.S. Marshals Service for as long as I had to testify in future trials. That outfit, the marshals, had become responsible for the protection of all federal and state witnesses against organized crime.

"In the beginning, it was tough. I was being run in and out of courtrooms and grand juries like a Yo-Yo. None of us had a permanent place to stay. While the marshals tried to find a place that was safe for us to live, Blanche, the kids, and myself had to live in motels. It was terrible. We're not small people. There were five of us in two rooms, and we had to eat and sleep and talk in those rooms every day, day in, day out. We couldn't go outside those rooms for fear of being recognized. On either side of us were rooms full of marshals. There was no privacy. We all grated on each other's nerves. Frankly, I don't know how we survived that.

"But the marshals did a terrific job providing protection for us. Once in a while they'd manage to sneak us out to a restaurant they had checked out thoroughly, but it was a bitch of a way to live, especially for the kids. What the hell could they *do?* They could watch television, read a book, play some games, but that was it. For more than a month, that's all they had. Those kids were great. They hardly complained, they did their level best to please me, and all I could think of was what I had failed to do for them. There were days I hated myself for bringing this on them, but they were always reassuring me that what I had done was right, best for all of us in the long run.

"To be honest, I still don't know if I did the right thing for them. It's right from the standpoint of straight society, but for them—that's another story. They've been through hell these last three years, and all they have to look forward to with me is a lifetime on the run. I tell you, a man can feel awful proud, ten stories high, when he's got a wife and kids who stand by him like mine have.

"The threat of the mob, from the time I started talking to the FBI, was always with me, wherever I went. I could cope with it. But for Blanche and the kids it was hell. When she lived in El Paso while I was at La Tuna, she had to send the kids out to school and worry every minute of the day whether someone would spot them. Whenever she or the kids saw a

Massachusetts license plate on a car, they shook like leaves. Blanche was smart enough to know that the mob had sly people—she had lived long enough with me to learn that. So she was careful, and in being careful, her nerves became razor sharp. The same happened to the kids.

"It isn't normal for the mob to go after the family. The old Mafioso would never have done that. They'd just track you down, and that would be that. But in Boston, there was a different breed in charge—animals like Jerry Angiulo and Larry Baiona—who threw the rule books out a window years ago. They'd already tried to get Cindy and Blanche. My family understood what could happen and their guard was up, but it took its toll. My youngest son, David, gained fifty pounds. Cindy, my only daughter, got as big as a house. They ate because of their nerves—because they lived on the edge of a volcano twenty-four hours a day. They couldn't live like normal teen-age kids. They went to school under Blanche's maiden name, but they couldn't mingle and go out with other kids like most kids do. When school ended they had to head straight back to the house. They couldn't leave the yard of the house. They couldn't ride something as simple as a bike or go to the corner luncheonette for a soda. They couldn't see a movie or go to a school dance or football game. All they had was confinement to a small house in a strange town with strange people all around. It was worse than being in solitary for the kids. They knew that their mother would be sitting in the house, timing them from the moment school let out at 3:30 P.M. untill the time it would normally take to get home. If they were a couple of minutes late, Blanche would be out in the car, looking for them. Wayne, my oldest son, would go hunting in the desert. He threw caution to the winds, and he gave Blanche some gray hairs in the process. But he was a big boy and he figured he could take care of himself, despite her warnings and mine.

"One thing everyone knew—Blanche, the kids, the FBI, the prosecutors—all of them: If the mob captured one of them, I'd have shut up tighter than a clam. There's no doubt about that. I'd have had to agree to keep quiet until they released whoever they kidnapped, and I'd have had to keep quiet even after that because I'd have been afraid they'd grab one of them again. If that had ever happened, I'd have told the federal government: 'You let the mob nail my kid. You were supposed to protect them. That means I have no more deal with you.'

"Thank God, that hasn't happened. The federal marshals have done a great job in protecting all of us, particularly in those early, hectic months when the whole world knew who I was and what I was doing. Without that kind of protection, it would be impossible for a mob guy to turn and talk. You have to have that sense of security that they provide, not just for yourself, but for your family. No state agency could do what the federal government has done. The marshals I've met in the last few years with only a few exceptions are the most dedicated group of men I've met in my life. They've been willing to lay their life on the line for me. Whenever I went to court, the marshals were standing in front of me and at my sides. If someone had started opening up, they would have been the first to be gunned down, but I never saw one of them hesitate or complain about what they were doing for me.

"Almost right after I testified before the committee, they had their first test. I was sent to Boston, to the Superior Court building, for a grand jury session and for interviews by police agencies from the six New England states. In one day, I had to answer questions in fifty two interviews because they were all upset over what I'd said before the committee, and they were trying their damndest to punch holes in what I said instead of cleaning their dirty linen. They didn't succeed, but while they were trying, the mob was busy on the street below.

"It would have been comical if it wasn't so serious. There were two men looking over cars at the street level of the building. One was a giant of a guy, about six-foot-five with a leg in a cast and walking on crutches. The other guy was a little weasel of a man with a red face. One of the marshals spotted them and asked me about them. At the same time a detective went downstairs to see if he could make [identify] them. The description of the little guy, I told them, fit Barney Villani, the little punk whose life I'd saved by not carrying out a hit contract for Henry Tameleo. The bigger man sounded like Tommy Rossi, a bank robber and sometime hit man for the mob. The detective came back and said that was who they were. I told the agents that Rossi always used the broken-leg gimmick to case banks. 'Check his cast,' I said. 'I'll give odds he doesn't have a broken leg.' They did. Sure enough, it was a phoney.

"The FBI detained them for questioning but had to release them. They hadn't committed a crime by taking license plate numbers. Of course, what they were trying to do was get a line on where I might be stashed, through the license numbers, or they might have been getting ready to relay the license numbers to waiting assassination squads who would have looked for the numbers and hit us on the highway as we left the area. John Partington, the security specialist in charge of marshal protection details for witnesses in the New England area, immediately changed all the license numbers on all the cars that we were using, and they hustled me out of the area with an army surrounding me.

"It was during that same period that the feds found out that the mob, according to informers, had put a five hundred grand price tag on my head. That sounded like a lot of money to me, but the figure was probably accurate. The only thing is, anyone who tried to collect it would have been a dead man. Dead men can't be witnesses. That's the trouble with these big-figure contracts you read about the mob putting out. It's propaganda for street punks. That way they have every two-bit gunsel on the street looking to make a score, a name for himself. The more guns you have working for you, the better the chance of getting the target. But once the target is dead and the gunslinger tries to collect for his work, that's when the mob will show its true colors. They'll eliminate the guy that did the job and that way there are no problems to worry about later, not to mention the fact that they save five hundred grand.

"Court appearances are the most dangerous event in the life of a guy like myself. Under this system we call justice, the defense has an advantage. The mob's lawyers can find out exactly who is testifying against their client and when he's going to testify, and they alert the mob. That means the federal government or the state has to be as tricky as possible in bringing a witness to a courthouse, because you can go to sleep on the fact that the mob will use that appearance to try to set you up.

"When I was scheduled for a court appearance, the marshals would move me from wherever I was holed up with my family to a safe-house somewhere in New England. I'm not going to give the location because they have to use the place to protect other witnesses. But its name is no joke: safe-house.

The one I stayed at was like a fortress. It was built by a recluse millionaire. It was a large house with dormitory-like bedrooms upstairs, a large kitchen, reading room, and control center downstairs. The control room was filled with all kinds of electronic gear. They controlled a closed-circuit televison that surveyed the outside grounds as well as all entrances to the house, including a roof skylight. It also controlled electronic sensors that they had in the yard and in all the windows that would trigger alarms when anyone approached who shouldn't. In an emergency, it had an underground bomb shelter with walls of concrete a couple of feet thick.

"They would fly me there by commercial airliner. Sometimes I'd land in Connecticut, other times in Rhode Island. Then I'd be taken to a prearranged location by helicopter, where they'd transfer me to cars and move me to the safehouse a couple of days before my court appearance. Sometimes, I'm afraid, I gave the marshals heart failure on my flights. Because I'm so big, they fly me under the seat-and-a-half program: two seats for the price of one and a half. Naturally, there would be a couple of marshals seated behind and in front of me. The trouble was that people were always recognizing me or thinking they recognized me, like the time a woman walked up to my seat on one flight.

" 'I know you,' she said. I looked at the marshals. They were pale. All of us felt like taking a parachute out the door right then and there. 'You're—you're Minnesota Fats—the pool player.'

"I smiled, played it straight, and nodded.

" 'Could I have your autograph?' she asked.

" 'Sure,' I said, and while the marshals looked like their teeth were going to fall out, I put my John Hancock on a slip of paper: 'Best regards, Minnesota Fats.' Then the crew of the aircraft wanted signatures, so I obliged them, but when they asked if I could give a demonstration in their recreation room, I had to beg out, telling them I had to make an appearance at a local stadium that night.

"Flying commercial jets has its drawbacks. The government does it because they have problems with the Defense Department when they use military planes. All the bureaucrats fight over who has jurisdiction over what and who should be budgeted for what. It's ridiculous. The result is that they use commercial jets, and sometimes you bump into the strangest people. Like the time I had to testify in Boston against Bobby Cardillo in January 1972. That was a nutcracker from the moment it started.

"Cardillo was already in jail with eighteen years in prison facing him as a result of testimony I'd given. But there was another case hanging fire on a securities transaction we'd worked together. Just as I was getting ready to leave, Cardillo's attorneys subpoenaed Blanche and Wayne. I blew my top and refused to go. I got a call from Ted Harrington, the strike force director in New England. Harrington has been very fair to me. He's a helluva prosecutor, and he's done a real job on the mob in New England with his strike force. He said he was willing to let the case go by default if that's the way I felt, but he warned that if Blanche and Wayne didn't show, that Larry Baiona would try the same thing in another trial that was still pending in the Massachusetts state courts. At any rate, he convinced me to honor the subpoena, and he promised that Blanche and the kids would have no problems. He should have told Blanche that. For a week she was a nervous wreck.

"We all boarded a commercial jet and flew to Providence from Washington. When we landed, Partington and his army of deputies were there waiting with a helicopter. The chopper flew us to the Massachusetts state police headquarters in Framingham, where I saw Jack Kehoe. He'd just been named boss of the Massachusetts state police. Kehoe arranged to take Cindy and David to a home, where the troopers would stay with them throughout the day. Blanche, Wayne, and me were taken in a paddy wagon in a convoy of cars filled with armed troopers and marshals to the Federal Building in Boston.

"Before we got into the tunnel leading underneath the Federal Building, the first in a series of disasters struck. The driver of the paddy wagon suddenly had to stop short. I wasn't expecting it, and I flew out of my seat head-first into the metal wall of the wagon. It nearly knocked me for a loop. There was blood streaming down my face and a big lump on my skull. I felt dizzy most of the day. Harrington wanted me to go to a hospital for X-rays, but I wasn't having any of that. With what I knew about doctors on the mob payroll in Boston, I wouldn't have gone near a Boston hospital if I was on my deathbed.

"Finally, in the afternoon, they put me on the stand, and I testified. I found out that Cardillo had called the judge a bum during the trial and had stormed out, only to be restrained by deputy marshals, who hauled him back in. Testifying in that case was Al Grillo, the sucker Ford dealer I'd used to buy my house. Grillo had made a deal to testify to avoid jail, but he played games with defense attorneys and they made a monkey out of him. His testimony was filled with inaccuracies, and the jury didn't believe him.

"After I testified, Cardillo's attorney asked to see me. I didn't have to talk to him, but I was interested in knowing why Cardillo had subpoenaed Blanche and Wayne. He didn't know, but I guessed it was Henry Tameleo who was behind it. He'd been in jail with Cardillo for a while, and he was the one who knew most how upset I'd be if they subpoenaed my family. Cardillo's attorney agreed that Blanche and Wayne had nothing to do with the case and refused to call them to the stand. Cardillo blew his top and tried to fire his lawyers. The judge wouldn't allow it. Don't ask me how or why, but the jury acquitted Cardillo. They didn't believe Grillo. I don't know, maybe they didn't believe me. But I'd told the truth, and all I was interested in doing at that point was to get the hell out of Boston and back to our home.

"When we arrived back in Providence, we had to take a plane to Hartford. There were two marshals with us. We landed in Hartford without incident, but we had a two-hour lay-over there. The marshals made one mistake: They kept us all in the lobby at the terminal. While we were sitting there, talking, I looked up and almost froze in my seat. Standing thirty feet away from me, big as life, was Frankie Skiball [Francesco Scibelli of Springfield, Massachusetts]. Skiball is an old-time made man, about sixty years old and as tough as they come. He's short, about five-foot-two, and kind of chubby, with a scar on the upper left side of his nose. But he's a dangerous man. He'd kill you as soon as look at you if he thought you were a danger to him.

"I took a long, long look at him and stood up. I figured if I was going to get it, it was going to be standing up, away from my family. As I stood up, my sons David and Wayne recognized Skiball before the deputies did. They both jumped right in front of me. 'Sit down, Pa,' David said. I felt flushed all over. It was the proudest moment of my life. My two boys—they thought enough of their father to jump in front of him, to get in the line of fire and protect him. They were ready to do battle for me.

"I think Skiball was more frightened than I was. The deputies found out he was booked on the same flight to Washington that we were, but he never boarded the plane. You can bet your life on one thing, though: he made a fast call to Larry Baiona to let him know where I was headed. That put all of us in a very tight situation when we arrived at Washington National Airport. We had to get special transportation from the plane to the police security area at the airport and then wait while the deputies checked the area for any possible hoods. Then we had to sneak out of the airport area for the home that the federal government had rented for my family outside of Washington. I won't say where we had the house— a nice four-bedroom, Colonial-style home located in the heart of a big development. The marshals may want to use that house someday for somebody else. But it was the most comfortable place my family and I had had to stay since we'd left North Reading. Months later we all had to move from the area because things got too hot. I nearly got caught in a mob trap right in the heart of Washington.

"I'm supposed to be smart in the ways of the mob. I'm supposed to be wary of any setup. Well, in March 1972, I wasn't smart, I was stupid, and it could have cost me my life.

"For more than a year the Boston *Herald Traveler*, a big daily newspaper, had been fighting a million-buck libel suit filed against them by George Kattar, the millionaire real estate financier who had been my partner in Piranha, Inc., and some other deals. They'd written a story about him, but they didn't, at that time, know he was my partner. They linked him with the mob and he sued, and they were having a hard time proving their theory. So they came to me, hoping I would connect Kattar to the mob. I hoped they might help me financially if I would give them a sworn affidavit and answer questions by both their attorneys and Kattar's attorneys in a pretrial examination. I was in need of money real bad, and Jack Kehoe advised me to go ahead. So I agreed, and a meeting was arranged at the U.S. Marshals' headquarters in Washington, D.C.

"My first mistake was agreeing to give them a couple of weeks to set up the meeting and give them a date and time that I would appear at the marshals' office. I should have known better, and to be honest, everyone involved in the meeting from the federal government should have known better. But none of us were thinking. A kind of a mental lapse, I'd guess you'd say. After all, we were dealing with a newspaper, not the mob. What I and everyone else had forgotten was that Kattar would know in advance the time and place of the meeting through his attorney.

"The night before the session, I didn't sleep all night. For some reason, I just couldn't get to sleep, so I stayed at a friend's business establishment and answered his switchboard just to keep active. When daylight came, I was too tired to drive. Now, I'd made another mistake before this. I'd got into a bad habit of driving by myself from my home to the marshals' office and parking across the street in a public parking garage. Anyone who knows anything about me knows I don't like to walk far, so they'd look for the closest garage. I was following a routine, and for anyone who has been on the street as long as I have, you don't follow routines and survive. Because I was tired, I decided not to drive. Instead I asked one of the deputies, Jimmy Colasanto, if he'd take me in with him. He was glad to, and he came over to pick me up at 8:00 A.M. with another deputy, William Marshall, a helluva nice guy who'd been on many protection details with me in the past, as well as visit my home with his wife and kids.

"We all drove into Washington, but instead of arriving at 10:00 A.M. like we were scheduled to, we arrived at 8:45 A.M. They parked the car in a federal lot, and we walked slowly up Twelfth Street, Northwest, to the marshals' office. As we almost reached the door, I looked across the street at the garage where I normally parked. Standing at the edge of the entrance were three men. One was well-dressed, in a dark, expensive suit with black hair and a hat. He was recognizable to me, but I couldn't put the face to a name. Next to him were two men dressed in construction clothes. Now, there was a lot of construction going on in the area, but most of those on the jobs were black men. Both these men were white. Their hair was well combed, their work clothes were spotless, their shoes polished. The three of them stood there, eyes fixed on the entrance to the marshals' headquarters. I was still groggy, half asleep, and my mind wasn't clicking. I sensed danger, yet I didn't react the way I normally would.

"We walked slowly into the building while the three men watched, and took an elevator to the second floor. I walked into the office of Reis Kash, the chief deputy in charge of protection of witnesses and courthouses throughout the United States. Kash had become more than a protector, he was a friend and he knew his business. He was straight-arrow and trying to do the best job possible. He had even had me lecture at a training session of his deputies on organized crime. They were in for training in witness security, and I talked to them on what to look for when trying to spot a mob assassin. They gave me a standing ovation at the end of the session.

"At any rate, I sat in Kash's office and sipped some coffee he'd had brought to me while we talked. Then he called a deputy in and told him to prepare the conference room on the third floor.

" 'Conference room?' I asked. 'What do we need a conference room for? There's just three of us attending this meeting.'

"Kash shook his head. 'We've got twelve people here for this meeting, with closed-circuit television.'

" 'Twelve people?' I said. 'Who the hell are they?'

"Kash pulled out a list. Then he read them, and when he reached the name of George Kattar, it hit me like a thunderbolt. I'd been suckered. Kattar himself was going to be there, to set me up. 'Reis, get me the hell out of here,' I said. 'This is a setup.'

"Quickly, I briefed him on who Kattar was and what his role with the mob was. Then I described the three men across the street. Now I knew what it was about them that made the hairs on the back of my neck crawl. They were an assassination team waiting to spot me as I drove into the garage and either hit me as I walked from the garage to the marshals' office or take my license number, trace it, and then hit me at their convenience when I walked out of the house I was living at. They might have even planned to rig my car with a bomb —which could have cost someone in my family their life, since I rarely drove myself; I usually had Wayne drive me around.

"Now we had a problem about getting out of the building. Kash immediately called off the scheduled meeting with the attorneys and Kattar and he ordered them all from the building. Before they decided to move me, deputies were sent throughout the building to check it out. They found two men at the bottom of a rear stairway where they might have planned to take me out. When they asked the two men what they were doing there, they told the marshals they got claustrophobia riding in elevators and preferred to walk down the stairs. They were hustled out of the building under escort.

Once they were gone, a team of marshals moved me out the stairway and into one of two waiting cars. The second car was a backup to prevent any attempt to follow us. Then we raced out of the city at seventy miles an hour and took a series of different routes that carried us across a couple of states before we reached my home. Kattar they tailed from the International Safeway Supermarket, which is next to the marshals' office, around the block. He walked here, he walked there, apparently waiting to see them take me out. Finally, he got into a cab and went to the airport. Everyone else in the group of twelve scattered. It was a close call, but it wasn't the only close call I had.

•   •   •

"In the three years that I've been under the protection of the marshals, the man I grew to have the most confidence in was Partington. He's not a bureaucrat or a politician who got his job because he knew somebody. He's an ex-cop, a guy with better than fifteen years' experience on the street. He cuts red tape and sometimes he gets in trouble for doing it, but he's a man who thinks of the people he's protecting first and the politicians who order him around last.

"Partington was the man in charge of 95 percent of all the protection details the deputies moved me on, whether it was to New England or Florida, New York or Washington. He's what they call a security specialist, and there are only ten like him in the country. He headed the detail that protected Joe Barboza long before the federal government ever came up with the Witness Protection Program. He lived for sixteen months with Barboza, day and night. To this day I don't know how he stood it. It had to be one of the most nervewracking jobs in the world. Partington has one thing in his favor. He's the closest thing the federal government has to a thug on the right side of the law. He knows everybody who is anybody in the mob and he knows their habits, where they are, what they do, and how they think. He's always thinking, figuring out new schemes to keep the mob off balance while he moves a witness. He's protected every top mob witness from Barboza to Red Kelley to me and Bobby Daddieco as well as scores of others. Most important, he's kept all of us alive because he has good informers and close contact with every federal agency you can imagine. He had a partner by the name of Bud

Warren who is almost as good as he is, and I met a deputy in Detroit, Ken Renzi, who has a lot of moxie and brains. But Partington is the best, bar none.

"Partington isn't afraid to talk over a plan with the guy he's protecting. He'll go into the details of the move and, if you have a suggestion, he'll listen. He may do it his way anyhow, but he'll listen. He treated all witnesses like men, not like animals. There are some deputies who think mob witnesses are animals and shouldn't be given any special treatment. They're the ones who've never been on the street, who got their jobs because they had connections with politicians or some group with influence. John gave us respect and we gave it back to him.

"To move me in and out of courtrooms, John used every trick in the book and a lot that weren't. On one occasion, when he suspected the mob had some assassins in the area, he found a narcotics agent that resembled me and put him in a car backed by escorts. It was 8:00 A.M. and I was scheduled to testify at 10:00 A.M. in a case against Larry Baiona. He sent the narco into the court area with an escort and sirens blaring. Newspapermen, television, court officials, everybody, particularly the mob, thought I was already in that courthouse. At ten minutes of ten, I came riding quietly into the courthouse complex in a mail truck with Deputy Marshal James Gardiner. I laid down in the back of the mail truck while they drove into the tunnel beneath the courthouse. No one paid the slightest bit of attention to the mail truck. I came up through the rear entrance and left the same way I had come.

"It was on one of those details that Partington got a tip about another mob plot to kill me. An informer of his had overheard conversations between two street punks who used to work for me, Pete Martinelli and Tony Chiula. Both of them were working for Larry Baiona at the time. They were talking about alternate plans to hit me. The first plan called for a hit in Baltimore when I was testifying against Carlo Mastrototaro and some others. They were going to hire some hippie radicals, like the Weathermen, to throw a bomb in the courthouse to scare me. It never came off because Partington put on such a show of force that no one would have dared come near the courthouse. Then they decided to hit me and take some marshals along to boot when I was to appear for a trial of Baiona. Their plot was simple enough. I was going to testify in a state courthouse in Boston. They were going to have men stationed to watch which elevator I took. When they saw me go in, they were going to signal some friends on an upper floor. Those on the upper floor were to drop a bomb down on the elevator as it rose to the floor where I was to testify. That plan went up in smoke because Partington threw a security blanket around the courthouse that no one could have broken through.

"I have to admit I had a nervous time at that Baiona trial. I can still see Baiona jumping from his chair as I testified, shouting: 'You're a lying pig!' It was when I was describing how I'd borrowed forty grand from him to pay for some stolen securities. What bothered me was some of the things that had happened before I testified as well as what happened inside the courtroom. Every day I appeared in court, I could see a half dozen of Baiona's assassins in the audience. They tried to stare me down, catch my eye, make gestures to make sure I knew I was a dead man. I just looked back at them. Sometimes I'd smile. One of those in the audience was Roy Thomas, a close friend of Baiona's and Phil Waggenheim's. He's a hit man and has been for years and years. He was brought in from Florida just for this trial to try and whack me out. He never got the opportunity, thanks to Partington.

"Every day, Partington and his deputies brought me into the courthouse a different way. One day we'd use a car, another day a paddy wagon. He'd send in decoys with sirens blaring and then we'd wander in quietly after they arrived. The last night we left in a blaze of glory, with four marshal cars, three state police cars, and forty armed guards. Baiona beat the case, but it wasn't because I didn't tell the truth. There were some problems in evidence and with other witnesses. It was only one of three cases that have been lost where I testified, and I've testified about eighteen times already.

"The ordeal isn't over for me or for my family. As I tell my story now, I still have to appear to testify against Meyer Lansky and Dino Cellini in a tax-evasion case based on the money I paid them for casinos and junket operations. And I have to testify against fourteen others in Massachusetts who were involved with me in race track fixes. The federal government tells me that no other witness in history has testified in so many organized crime cases and put so many mob people in jail. I guess that's so, but it means I've also got more enemies in the mob than anybody else, and that isn't an easy thing to live with.

"I know that my future is pretty uncertain. I have to live each day as if tomorrow will never come. I know that no matter where I am, what name I live under, what work I finally do, mob assassins will be hunting me. They never give up. I also know that once I'm finished testifying, that is the end of my federal protection. I'll be on my own. As it is now, I'm pretty much on my own. I have a new home—I can't tell you where, for obvious reasons. I have a new identity and so does my whole family. It's as if my whole past was wiped out—as if Vincent Teresa didn't exist. And I'm going to have to adjust to a new way of life. It won't be easy. I'll be getting government subsistence as long as I testify in cases. That's because I can't take any job or go into any business while I still have to appear in courtrooms and live a life that bounces me from one state to another for a court or grand jury appearance.

"The thing that bothers me about it is the effect it has on the kids. They can no longer use or be proud of the name Teresa. They have to live with Social Security cards, drivers' licenses, insurance policies, bank accounts, and school records that bear a strange name that has no meaning to them. It's hard to accept that Vincent Teresa stopped existing a couple of years ago.

"My hope is that I can find a normal life for myself and my family some day. I've got to scale down my weight, both for appearance's sake as well as my health. We've got to find a new location somewhere in or out of this country where we can settle down to a new way of life. For at least another year, I'll still be on parole. After that, the string to my past life of crime will have been cut. There's no way I'll go back. I couldn't if I wanted to. I'd be a dead man if I tried. All I want is to find a nice, normal job where I can work eight, ten hours a day and earn a living. I don't want to be rich, just provide enough for my family to enjoy the kind of life most people take for granted.

"You can hope and pray for a lot, but a guy like myself has to face up to the fact that for as long as I live, the mob will hunt me. They won't forget. They can't. They have to prove to others that one guy can't get away with what I did and still live. Maybe they're right. I hope not. Others have made it. They didn't testify against as many as I have, but they've made it just the same. One stock swindler I know of turned straight and became not only a respected member of his new community, but a millionaire legitimately. I'm not thinking that big. Whatever comes from this book, it goes to my kids for their future.

"I do know that every day of my life will be a test of my knowledge of the street, my ability to spot bad situations before they can happen. I can't go to restaurants like other men without a disguise of some kind. I can never get involved in government or local politics without tipping my hand. I have to be more careful than other citizens about obeying the law, so as to prevent arrest and a fingerprint check, which could result in breaking my identity cover. Whatever I have to do I'll do because I want more than anything to give my family what they never got from me in the past: hope for the future and a father who is home to care and help.

"But whatever I do, wherever I go, whatever name I live under, I intend to keep fighting the mob in any way I can. I'll help my law-enforcement friends whenever they need me, short of testifying in many more trials. I've had enough of them. The strain is too much, and each time you appear you lower your odds for survival. The mob is a cancer on this land. Don't think for a moment it isn't. It's worming its way into every legitimate business you can imagine. It's a house guest when you sit down to eat because a lot of the food is manufactured or distributed by mob-controlled firms. It reaches into your pocketbook when you go to a racetrack, buy a dirty book, sit down at a swanky restaurant, sleep in a motel or hotel, or deal with some banks. It costs you money when your food or lumber or television sets are transported in mob-run trucks or when a truckload of cigarettes or liquor is hijacked because that's tax money that should have eased your burden. I can tell you to stop buying cheap cigarettes or cars that have ridiculous price tags, but you probably won't because everybody looks for a bargain, everybody has some larceny in his soul. But when you do that, you're just helping the mob rape your bank account, because the manufacturer makes up for his loss by raising prices.

"When you come right down to it, there isn't anything the mob doesn't touch. They reach congressmen just as quickly as they reach state houses and police precincts. They corrupt businessmen and unions, you name it. And unless the public smartens up, unless the news media keep pounding away at the threat the people face from the mob, one day it's going to reach its greedy hand into the White House. Anyone who thinks that can't happen is a damned fool. There isn't a state in the union where the mob doesn't have influence. They have stolen so many billions in securities that you can't dream that high, let alone count. And just because some of the top mob guys have been thrown in jail doesn't mean things have slowed down. I can't give you an easy answer about how the mob can be wiped out. I'll tell you one thing, though: Eliminate their profits from bookmaking and numbers and you have them on the ropes. I don't mean just legalize gambling. That's part of it. But you have to make laws and make the courts enforce them that puts the street bookie in jail. If the big guy loses that army of bookies he has, he's out of business, and no bookie is going to risk going to jail if he knows that's what happens when he gets busted.

"Anyhow, that's really your problem. My problem is to stay alive."

A Mafia Miscellany

After he completed his autobiography, Vincent Teresa was asked to reflect generally upon the Mafia and life within it. What follows are some of those reflections.

"Sometimes life in the mob is fun. Take me, a guy with an eighth-grade education. I've beat big businessmen, bankers, legitimate millionaires, guys with all kinds of education. It's a nice thrill.

"We're not Robin Hoods, but none of us like to take advantage of a guy that can't afford to be taken advantage of. You get a twinge of bad conscience. You say to yourself, 'Jesus, with all the good suckers in this city, why did I have to nail this poor sucker?' But when you hit a high-faluting guy, a guy who can afford it, there's enjoyment in that.

"Sometimes in the mob you have to do things you don't like. Sometimes people that were real close to you have to be put to sleep. It has to be done, because the orders come down, and it's either you or them. But you feel bad about these things. I went to so many goddam funerals of guys who were like brothers to me that I can't count them. You say to yourself, 'Why did this have to happen?' But the old guys just stand there at the funeral with stone faces on, and they go over and kiss the widow and say 'Gee . . . it's rough . . . I'm sorry' when it was *them* that put the husband away. When Romeo Martin got it, who the hell do you think were the pallbearers? The two guys that killed him.

"Here's what life in the mob is like. You wake up every morning with the first thought in your mind: 'Don't trust anyone except maybe your immediate family.' Not even your best friends. Take Frankie Imbruglio; if Frankie was a threat to me, I would have to put him to sleep, and if I could do it to Frankie, Frankie could do it to me. Or take Henry Tameleo. He was like my godfather, but you could never tell when someone might have whispered something in his ear about you. So there again you had to be careful. You got to be suspicious of everyone, and it's kind of a lousy feeling. You walk out of your house in the morning and you don't know if anyone's going to take a shot at you from the house across the street. That's one of the reasons a lot of mob guys have a girlfriend; they don't want to bring heat to their house, so instead of going home, they go with a broad. It's a lonely life, a life you got to learn to lead outside your family, completely by yourself."

"If you gotta go out and kill a guy, you gotta make yourself believe it was him or you. You justify it to yourself, but you never confess it to the priest. There are certain priests who are on call to mob guys, they won't snub a mob guy, they'll comfort his relatives. These priests, they say that mob guys are Catholics and we're entitled to the same religious comfort like anybody else. If you want to tell the priest the truth, that's fine with him and if you don't, it's on your conscience. You can lie to the priest but you can't lie to the Guy Upstairs.

"Church-going is dying out in the mob. But the old guys still go to church, they light candles, they pray to the Virgin Mary and so forth. It's from the old country. A lot of the old guys have their own chapels in their house. And the women, they still go. They aren't supposed to know what their husbands are doing, they're told to sit in the corner and mind their own business. But they aren't so stupid; they know. And so they go to church and light the candles and pray for their husbands and sons not to be killed.

"There's a lot to be said for going to church when you're in the mob. It's all you have to cling to. It helps you face the job."

"Normally a mob wife is very quiet and serene. She does nothing but stay home and have babies, do the shopping, entertain her husband's friends and keep her mouth shut. It's a man's world, and that's the way it's supposed to be.

"But once in a while there's a strong woman, if the man is

fool enough to let her get away with it. Years ago, there was Butsey Morelli's wife. She was a very, very smart woman, and she helped advise Butsey in the early part of his career as he took over the mob in Rhode Island and the New England area. She was well thought of by all the old Mustache Petes and she had plenty of power. Once, later on in years, Butsey was running around with a girl named Tina. Tina feared for her life, because she knew that if Butsey's wife ever found out about it, with one phone call she could have Tina put to sleep.

"Vito Genovese's wife was another one. She was a lot of trouble for the mob. Genovese was mean to her, and so she opened up and told everything she knew about him in a divorce case.

"I remember there was a guy named Rusty—he's big today with the Bonanno mob—who had a wife called Connie. She was a real tough broad. Before she married Rusty she was a bookmaker and a shylock. Guys would borrow money from her and figure that because she was just a broad they could make a mark out of her. But Connie fooled the hell out of them. She'd have their legs broken, or she'd go down and shoot them herself.

"She stayed in business after she married Rusty. Once Rusty shot two guys and one of them survived, and he fingered Rusty to be killed. Rusty went on the lam, but Connie decided to get the guy for fingering her husband. She had him set up and gunned down in a cemetery.

"Later she found out that Rusty was playing around with another broad. She waited for Rusty outside of the courthouse where he was appearing, and she shot him on the courthouse steps. He finally had to have her put to sleep. She was cut down by a shotgun.

"Broads like that, though, are rare."

"Any mob guy who thinks his kids don't know what he's doing is a damned fool. Maybe when they're young they don't know. But when they get to be teen-agers, it's kind of difficult to hide. They don't know everything you're doing, but they know you don't go to work every day and take a lunch basket with you or clean out sewers or anything like that. They know that you keep odd hours, that when you feel like staying home, you stay home. They know that there's no money problems. The kid can see the kind of company you keep, when the guys come to visit you in your home, you know, or when he hears your conversations over the phone. Sometimes it can't be avoided. As for the killing, they imagine it, but they don't want to know it about you personally, about their own fathers. But they read things in the papers, and they hear things from other kids in the street, and they figure it out.

"Most of the kids are proud of their fathers, the way a normal kid is. Sometimes they aren't. Now Butsey Morelli's son, he never knew for years. Butsey kept him in the shadows. But then when there was that thing in the Boston papers about Butsey being involved in the Sacco-Vanzetti murder, the son was very disillusioned. I knew the son, and when this happened he came up to visit me at my house on Cape Cod. He was very hurt and so forth, very ashamed, I think because his old man kept it a secret. Today he's a pharmacist.

"I never actually sat down with my kids and told them I done anything, but I never really tried to hide anything from them either. I am what I am, and that's the way it is.

"But I tell you, if my sons had ever wanted to go into the mob, I would have broken both their legs. I want my kids to go to school, and I think everybody else does in the mob too. You don't want the mob kind of life for your sons, the danger, the police invading your home and pulling you out of there in front of all your neighbors, your family. You don't want this for your sons. I'd just as soon say to them, 'Here, I made a lot of money the hard way. You take it and go into something legitimate.' Let's face it, we're just like anybody else. You don't want to see your kids hurt, and I don't want to see mine hurt either.

"Most of the bosses keep their sons out, positively. That's why, nine out of ten times, you won't see a mob guy's kid going to college in the same area where he lives. They'll send him out to Notre Dame, if they live in New York, or Texas U or someplace like that. Get him out, get him away from everything so he can't see what's going on. We're not basically ashamed of what we do, we just don't want our families to do it too."

"If you're on a plane sitting next to a mob guy, you'll probably never know. Nine times out of ten, when a mob guy is traveling alone, he'll sleep or just lay there with his eyes closed, because he don't want to bother with anybody. If he should happen to talk with you, he'll talk about everything but the mob. He'll say he's in the food produce business. Unless he's a clown, he'll dress very conservatively, dark clothes, white shirt, hair well trimmed, like a businessman out of Wall Street except maybe his features might be a little tougher looking. His nails will be nice and manicured and polished.

"The one way you can tell a mob guy is that his clothes will always match. His shoes will always match his socks, and his socks will always match his suit, and his tie and his hat will always match the outfit he's got on. In fact, the overcoat will probably be made from the same material the suit is made of. They dress very, very well. It's not that they're flashy; it's just that everything they're wearing is money.

"There are a couple of mob peculiarities I've still got myself. Number One is big tipping. And Number Two is that you always want the best of everything. It's hard to break the habit. Like I always wanted the best seats in the house, and I'm just now getting to where I ask for a seat in the back—so I won't be spotted."

"Mob nicknames usually have a purpose. A lot of the time it's like a code name, for protection. Like when you talked with Henry Tameleo over the phone, you call him Skinny Man—that was his code name. No one ever called Patriarca Raymond over the phone; they called him George. A lot of times a guy is given a nickname for the way he looks, a peculiar habit he has. They gave Lamattina the name Ralphie Chong because he had slanted eyes and looked like a Chinaman. Old man Joe Palladino, they called him Joe Beans because he'd go into the same restaurant every day and order a big plate of beans. When he had a son, they called him Little Beans. I used to call Butch Rossi Bruce because he reminded me of a fairy. He hated that. Rossi used to run to Tameleo and ask him to please stop calling him Bruce, and Henry would say, 'You know, you do look like a Bruce.'

"There was a guy named Eddie. They'd say, 'Where's that guy Eddie—the little short guy Eddie—you know, the guy that's always in Miami?' 'Oh,' they'd say, 'yeah, Eddie, Eddie Miami.' That's how a nickname starts.

"They used to call Joe Barboza 'The Animal.' Of course, there was an obvious reason for that. He was an animal."

"Except for Barboza, the assassins I've known personally are all very cool-headed individuals and live a very straight life. They very seldom even drink; they go to the gymnasium and work out. All the killing isn't done by just walking up and blowing a guy's brains out. Sometimes the hit man might have to scale a wall or lay on his belly two or three hours waiting for someone—it isn't all that easy. They've got to be in good physical shape, cool of mind and most of all they've got to have will power. Sometimes they might be setting up a guy and all of a sudden a cop's car comes by; they've got to make sure they got enough guts and *coglioni* between their legs to stay there and make out like nothing's happening—even though they've got a sawed-off shotgun bulging inside their coat."

"I liked *The Godfather*. The mob guys went to see it, but not the old-timers. They wouldn't even get near it, they wouldn't be in the same building with it. It offends them, it makes them look bad, it makes their families look bad, it's like a sacrilege. Brando ought to get an Academy Award. I've known quite a few dons in my time, and he played it just right —nice and quiet and slow, never raised his voice, a good sense of ideas about principles—just the way the old Mustache Pete men are. They're not loudmouth, they're home people. When they get finished with their business, bang, the old-timers go home and have their plate of spaghetti.

"I'll tell you the truth, the book was a helluva lot better than the movie. In the movie, they started when the don was already on the top of the pile. But in the book, they showed how he started in the slums. He came over to this country to be an honest man, but he couldn't be honest because they wouldn't let him. Now, that's the truth, that's the way it was. You don't think all these Mustache Petes, these old-timers, came over here purposely to take over the country? They came over here to work, and they worked their asses off until they couldn't get any more work, until people began pushing them around because they seemed ignorant, and they couldn't talk the language. When that happened, they went back to the way they were in the old country, they became animals again.

"The audiences cheering the killers in *The Godfather*—that just shows you how bloodthirsty this country is getting. They don't realize that it wasn't good guys getting the bad guys, it was bad guys wiping out bad guys. For me, the real feeling of the picture was that, regardless of who won, the mob was still there."

"The old-time bosses can't understand people like me. They

went for robbing banks, hijacking, the rough stuff. When I went to the don and told him I'd figured out a stock swindle where I could make half a million, he'd look at me like I was crazy. He'd say, 'You talk about half a million dollars like it was chopped liver.' He'd say, 'Do you know how many banks you have to rob to get half a million dollars?' I'd say, 'That's a sucker's game now, Raymond, robbing banks.' You rob a bank, you get twenty-five or thirty grand, and you do it with a gun. But today your mob men are real intelligent people. They may look like thugs, but believe me, those wheels are always turning, always figuring out schemes, and only one out of ten needs to work. If you use your wits you can rob a million in thirty days. And with pen and paper, no guns."

"The New York mobs are in trouble now. A lot of the respect, the discipline is gone. It's like Henry Tameleo used to say; they're a bunch of drugstore gangsters. He was right as rain. Most of the bosses they got now are second-liners. Carmine Tramunti was a nobody, a bum, but now he's the head of what used to be Three-Finger Brown's [Thomas Luchese] outfit. Natale Evola's an old-timer, but he's no Joe Bonanno. He can't even fit into old Joe's socks, let alone his shoes. He hasn't got the guts that's needed. He's like Tramunti . . . he'll do what the old don, Carlo Gambino, wants done. He won't stand up. He hasn't the backbone. You'll see what I mean when Lillo [Carmine Galente] gets out of the can. Lillo will eat Evola alive, and he'll wipe out Gambino unless Gambino gets to him when he's walking out the gates of Lewisburg. Lillo's the man to watch. If he lives long enough, he's going to be the first real Boss of Bosses since Lucky Luciano ran the show.

"The way I see it in New York is that all the killings in 1972 were just a primer of things to come. That's why they're bringing in the aliens. Lillo's brought in an army of men because he wants guys he can depend on when he makes his move. These aliens are made guys from Sicily, real old-country Mafioso, mostly young. They've got papers of recognition so they get the same respect in this country that an American made guy has, but they aren't members of the mob in this country. They're well trained, well disciplined. Lillo and Joe Burns [Anselmo, a Boston captain], Steve Magaddino [Buffalo crime boss], Gambino and even Tramunti are bringing them in across the Mexican and Canadian borders. The old

Mustache Petes and a few of the smart bosses are recruiting them for just one thing: to bring back respect and honor in the Honored Society.

"These Sicilian Mafiosi will run through a wall, put their head in a bucket of acid for you if they're told to, not because they're hungry but because they're disciplined. They've been brought up from birth over there to show respect and honor, and that's what these punks over here don't have. Once they're told to get someone, that person hasn't a chance. They'll get him if they have to bust into his house in the middle of the night, shoot him, bite him, eat him, suck the blood out of his throat. They'll get him because they were told to do it.

"These aliens aren't trouble until they get the word. When they do, look out: it'll be another Night of the Sicilian Vespers, when they wiped out a couple of hundred guys across the country in one day during the gang wars of the Thirties. That's what's going to happen in New York. They're going to use the aliens to get rid of those who don't do as they're told, don't show the respect they're supposed to.

"At the same time, the bosses are going to reorganize things. Maybe the five mobs in New York will become one big mob. They're practically that now, because Don Carlo tells all the other New York bosses what to do.

"The one kicker could be Lillo. He hates Gambino. He swore to me he was going to make Gambino kiss his ass, make him beg for his life when he got out of jail. He used to blow his cork to me about the stupid things going on in New York, and he swore he was going to straighten them out when he got out. Visitors from the outside were coming to see Lillo twice a week at Lewisburg, and they just had to be talking with him about New York and getting things ready.

"Lillo never said why he hated Gambino so much. Maybe it was because he was so close to Joe Bonanno and felt Gambino engineered a raw deal for Joe. Maybe it's something else. But I know this. If Gambino doesn't get to Lillo first or make a deal, Lillo will get Gambino, and there will be the biggest gang war you ever heard of."

"Crime families can vary in size. In New York, Gambino had maybe a thousand made men; in our family in New England we had a hundred and fifty. Between New Jersey and New York you might have two thousand five hundred people.

In the whole country, there is probably six thousand five hundred. But these are just the made men, remember. There are another two hundred to three hundred thousand other mob guys working for the made guys. Nothing gives the mob a bigger laugh than when some expert says the mob is nothing to worry about because there are only six thousand members. Hell, behind those six thousand you've got a whole army, not counting all the people who aren't Italian but who work with the mob.

"It's amazing how much the families vary around the country. Take Detroit. The Detroit mob is a very solid, close group of people and very dedicated to old man Joe Zerilli. They stay to themselves, they don't tend to do business with the rest of the country. Not that they're separated; don't misunderstand me. A phone call will put them in service to any other family. But if they can avoid outside contact, they will. They don't need it, they've got everything going for them. They've got the union business, they're strong in most of the unions. But the big thing isn't dues, it's the vast fortunes of the union that's available to them for legitimate businesses. There's terrific money there. Do you realize that nine out of ten hotels in Las Vegas were built with union money? Any kind of union fund, the mob goes after. The Detroit mob is the specialist in this.

"Chicago is an eat-'em-up-alive outfit. Everybody is for themselves. I knew Sam Giancana before he took it on the lam. I used to hang around with Tony Accardo down in Florida, and Anthony DeRosa went to the can on my testimony. The one bad thing about that outfit is that they're snow dealers—they deal in junk, heroin, hand over fist. They're like that outfit in New York in Harlem, the Luchese family, who are the snow dealers. In Chicago, everyone is struggling to get on top, and they don't give a damn who gets it in the back.

"I dealt with Lou Greco in Montreal. It's a big gambling operation there, and it spreads right down into this country. They're big in smuggling in aliens too. Joe Burns [Anselmo] has been bringing guys in through Canada since I was a kid; I think he brought in nine tenths of all the Chinamen in Boston and New York, through Greco. Joe Burns made them pay through the nose, and he's a very, very wealthy man because of it.

"In Atlanta, it's a funny thing. I was sent to Atlanta to try to take over that town. I met with the two biggest bookmakers in the city, sat them down in the Americana Hotel there and told them who I was and what I was there for. One of them said, 'Well, okay, we'll set up another meeting for tomorrow and we'll discuss it.' At five-thirty that morning the police came banging on my hotel door. 'Come on,' they said, 'get your clothes and pack, you're leaving town.' What happened was, the bookmakers were too cute. They had the X with the law, and they put the finger on me. The cops told me, 'Don't come back or we'll make sure you find some problems here.' That's how it was then. I don't know how the town is now.

"In New Orleans, that's a good group down there. Or it used to be. It was very tight. They're all in deathly fear of Carlos Marcello because he's got the law, all the politicians in the state, right in his hip pocket. You just can't go against him.

"The smartest mob in the country? I'll tell you, I think our mob in New England was. We made more money in that little New England area per man than they did anywhere in the country."

"Let me tell you something: I'm the proudest guy in the world to be an American. Before I went to jail I had plenty of chances to take off and go live in a villa on the Italian coast, but I wouldn't leave this country. I'd rather spend twenty years in the can in America than twenty years free in Italy. The reason is, I love this country, and that's the way it is with most mob guys. The mob will not stand for anything against this country. They'll rob from government arsenals and rob government stock and sell it; but if they could discover that anyone's trying to overthrow the country or anything like that, they'll fight him.

"Most mob guys that I know of vote. We vote whatever is the best way to make money. If it's going to be one of these guys who is going to be on the reform kick all the time, we'll all band together and vote against him. I'm a registered Democrat but I voted for Nixon in 1968, and I bet the mob really turned out for Nixon in 1972."

"The only thing that I miss about the mob is the money. I've never been happier in my life than I am now, even though I live in fear and so does my family. But there was more fear before. I don't have to worry any more about the phone ringing at two in the morning and hearing, 'We're having a special meeting . . .', which meant that someone was going to get hit, and, God knows, it could be you. I don't have to worry about the police kicking in the doors and dragging me out of the house in front of my family. I never had much time with my kids, but now I'm getting to know them. Now I see that I wasted the best years of my life. You never retire from the Mafia; you either die or hide. But until they find me, I'm going to enjoy my life with my family."

A Glossary of Mob Terminology

The Arm: Buffalo crime family of Cosa Nostra

B&E: robbery accomplished by breaking and entering

Bag man: a conveyor of money

Banana race: a fixed horse race

Biscuit: a gun

Boosters: smalltime street thieves

Bust out: to bankrupt

Case: to check out, to size up

Clean: not carrying a gun

Clip: to take money from

The Commission: the ruling body of the Cosa Nostra, consisting of from nine to twelve bosses of crime families

Consigliere: an adviser

Contract: an assignment to murder

Cooler: a stacked deck of cards

Cool-off Man: accomplice in a crooked gambling game who calms down a heavy loser

Cop: to steal

Cosa Nostra: close-knit criminal society whose members are of Italian-Sicilian ethnic origin only; sometimes called the Mafia, which was its Sicilian antecedent

Crime family: a unit of Cosa Nostra operating in a specific territory, composed of men tied together by loyalty to their crime boss and sometimes by actual blood relationship

Don: a ranking boss of crime family, usually applied to men born in Sicily

Enforcer: a hoodlum who beats or kills for his superior

Envelope: a cash payment

Fence: one who specializes in handling stolen merchandise

Finger: to mark for murder; to inform on

Gaff: a phoney

Greaseball: an old-country Italian or Sicilian; someone of Italian origin who looks or acts slovenly

Hack: prison guard

Half-assed wiseguy: one who aspires to Cosa Nostra membership

Headcrusher: an enforcer, a strongarm man

Headhunter: an assassin

Heat: unwanted attention from the law or the press

Hit: a murder assignment, or a murder; to murder

Hit the mattress: to go into hiding

The Honored Society: the Mafia of Sicily

Hot items: stolen goods

Juice: loanshark interest

Juiced horse: a doped horse

Legbreaker: a hoodlum who beats people for his superior

Made guy: an indoctrinated member of the Cosa Nostra

Mafioso: strictly speaking, an elder statesman and former member of the original Mafia of Sicily and the United States

Make: to identify; also, to induct as a member of the Mafia

Man of respect: a ranking, senior member of a crime family

Mechanics: card and dice manipulators who rig games

The meets: a conference of criminals

The mob: a crime family; the entire Cosa Nostra; often loosely interpreted to mean a confederation of criminal organizations with members of varying ethnic backgrounds

Mustache Pete: an elder statesman and former member of the original Mafia; in the early 1900s, they were famed for their long mustaches

The Office: New England crime family of Cosa Nostra

On the arm: on credit

On the pad: paying regular bribes

The Outfit: Chicago crime family of Cosa Nostra

Pigeon: an informer

Put the X on: to designate for murder

Put to sleep: to murder

Queer: counterfeit

Right arm: underboss

Score: money made from a criminal enterprise; to make money criminally

Serious headache: a bullet in the head

Serious trouble: about to be murdered

Shills: hirelings who play in rigged games in order to draw in victims; they are often "mechanics"

Shiv: knife

Sitdown: a criminal meeting; a mob peace conference

Spit box: the urine sample in a horse or dog race

Stone killer: a particularly cold-hearted professional murderer

Stoolie: an informer

Straight: a noncriminal

Uncle Sugar: the FBI

Whack out: to murder; also to astound or overwhelm

Wiseguy: same as made guy; an indoctrinated member of the Cosa Nostra

A Directory of Mob Members and Associates

AND THEIR PRESENT STATUS, IN THE CASE OF THE MORE IMPORTANT FIGURES

(Listed alphabetically by true last name or by first part of nickname)

A

Frank (Frankie Shots) Abbatemarco—New York racketeer ordered killed by Profaci family and executed by Gallo family

Anthony (Big Tuna) Accardo—a Chicago crime boss; a bodyguard of Al Capone; lives in River Forest, Illinois and Florida

George W. (Billy Aggie Agostino) Agistoteleis—murdered head of a group of armed bandits in Boston; masterminded the Plymouth Mail Robbery

Al Judd (see Albert Georgio)

Vincent (Jimmy Blue Eyes) Alo—crime captain to Gerardo Catena; in jail

Albert (The Executioner) Anastasia—chief of Murder, Inc., and once boss of what is now known as the Carlo Gambino crime family; murdered in 1957

Gennaro (Jerry) Angiulo—Boston crime boss and a top man in Patriarca's mob; lives in Massachusetts

The Animal (see Joseph Barboza)

Joseph (Joe Burns) Anselmo—Patriarca family member and Mustache Pete living in Massachusetts

Artie Todd (see Arthur Tortorello)

Fred Ayoub—former manager of the Colony Club in London

B

Joseph (The Animal) Barboza—New England mob's enforcer now in California State Prison for murder

Frank (The Bear) Basto—member of the Carlo Gambino family's assassination squad; lives in New Jersey

The Bear (see Frank Basto)

Joe Beck (see Joseph DiPalermo)

Edward (Whimpy) Bennett—murdered by Patriarca family

Walter Bennett—brother of Whimpy; eventually killed by the mob

William (Billy) Bennett—murdered by Patriarca family

Nicholas Bianco—a former Patriarca mobster; now a Colombo family crime captain

John (Futto) Biello—captain in the Genovese mob; murdered in Miami

Big-Nose Sam (see Salvatore Cufari)

Big Tuna (see Anthony Accardo)

Billy Aggie Agostino (see George Agistoteleis)

Bingy—cousin of Bobby Daddieco; died in arson attempt

The Blind Pig (see Alfredo Rossi)

Blondy (see Joe Simonelli)

Ruggerio (The Boot) Boiardo—old Genovese captain; lives in New Jersey

Joseph Bonanno—deposed Brooklyn boss who lives in retirement in both Arizona and California

Salvatore (Bill) Bonanno—son of Joseph Bonanno

The Boot (see Ruggerio Boiardo)

Arthur (Tashe) Bratsos—partner of Joseph Barboza; murdered by mob

Philip (Buccola) Bruccola—retired New England crime boss, now hiding in Sicily

Angelo Bruno—crime boss of Philadelphia, now in jail for contempt

Buccola (see Philip Bruccola)

The Butcher (see Vincent Flemmi)

Butsey (see Frank Morelli)

C

Cosmo (Gus) Cangiano—Colombo family soldier, fence, and securities swindler; appealing federal conviction

Robert Cardillo—Patriarca family associate now in federal prison for securities swindle

Ronald (Ronnie the Pig) Cassesso—made man in the Boston mob; now in jail for murder

Richard Castucci—ran the Ebbtide nightclub for Teresa and Tameleo

Anthony (Maxie Baer) Cataldo—a New England mob soldier and enforcer; lives in Massachusetts

Gerardo (Jerry) Catena—New Jersey mob boss; currently in New Jersey state prison for contempt

Dino Cellini—Lansky aide now living in Italy to avoid federal prosecution in tax cases

Salvatore Cesario—enforcer, loanshark, and sometimes bodyguard for New England underboss Gennaro Angiulo

Ralph Champy—late uncle of Teresa

Charlie the Blade (see Charles Tourine)

The Cheese Man (see Frank Cucchiara)

Chickie Spar (see Anthony Dellarusso)

Angelo (Chippo) Chieppa—a made man and former bodyguard for Ruggerio Boiardo

Chippo (see Angelo Chieppa)

Paul Colicci—ex-boxer and onetime friend of Patriarca's; murdered by mob

Joseph Colombo—ex-Brooklyn crime boss, permanently disabled in an attempted assassination in June 1971

Michael (Trigger Mike) Coppolo—bodyguard to Albert Anastasia

Joseph (Little Bozo) Cortese—strong-arm man for Michael Rocco

Frank Costello—(see Francesco Saveria)

The Count (see Simone DeCavalcante)

Max Courtney—front man for the Lansky gambling operation

James Coyne—small-time hood dealing on the fringes of the mob

Crazy Joey (see Joseph Gallo)

Frank (The Cheese Man) Cucchiara—semi-retired member, attended Apalachin crime meeting in 1957

Salvatore (Big-Nose Sam) Cufari—boss of Springfield, Massachusetts, mob; an elder statesman; lives in Springfield

D

Robert Daddieco—Patriarca family associate and holdup expert; now a federal witness against the mob

Anthony (Tony Blue) D'Agostino—enforcer for James McLean

Waddy David—Boston numbers operator who worked for Ilario Zannino; murdered by mob

Salvatore (Flungo) DeAngelis—bag man for Lou Fox

Simone (The Count; Sam the Plumber) DeCavalcante—boss of a New Jersey crime family; now in federal prison

Benjamin DeChristoforo—an Angiulo enforcer; in jail

Aniello Dellacroce—Gambino underboss and New York's second most powerful mobster; now in jail in New York City; faces trial for tax evasion

Anthony (Chickie Spar) Dellarusso—ex-owner of The Frolics nightclub in Revere, Massachusetts

Angelo DeMarco—hoodlum killed by Patriarca for calling him a "fag"

Thomas Deprisco (Richard Dipiescia)—partner of Joseph Barboza; murdered by mob

Anthony DeRosa—member of the Chicago mob; involved in stock swindle with Teresa; now in federal prison

John (Johnny Dio) Dioguardi—a soldier in the Thomas Luchese crime family; now in federal prison

Joseph (Joe Beck) DiPalermo—a Genovese family narcotics dealer

Robert A. (Tony) DiPietro—operator who worked for Mastrototaro on the gambling junkets; Teresa's "cool-off" man, now missing

The Doctor (see Carmine Lombardozzi)

Don Peppino (see Joseph Modica)

E

Thomas (Tommy Ryan) Eboli—close aide to and later murderer of Anthony Strollo; murdered in Brooklyn in July 1972

Natale Evola—current boss of the old Joseph Bonanno crime family; lives in Queens, New York

The Executioner (see Albert Anastasia)

F

Fat Al (see Al Samenza)

The Fat Man (see Vincent Teresa; also Joseph Magliocco)

Fat Tony (see Anthony Salerno)

Frank Ferrara—operated wire service for the mob

Peter (Skinny Pete) Fiumara—crime family associate; owner of nightclub in suburban Boston

Steve (The Rifleman) Flemmi—New England mob hit man; brother of Vincent Flemmi; now in hiding, on the lam

Vincent (The Butcher) Flemmi—New England mob hit man; brother of Steve Flemmi; now in jail

Flungo (see Salvatore DeAngelis)

Lou Fox (not to be confused with Louie the Fox Taglianetti)—financial wizard for Massachusetts mob; now dead

Joseph Francione—New England mob figure killed in personal dispute with Joseph Barboza

Frankie Shots (see Frank Abbatemarco)

Frankie Skiball (see Francesco Scibelli)

John (Sonny) Franzese—Colombo family captain, now serving fifty-year sentence in Leavenworth federal prison for bank robbery and conspiracy

Roy French—an Angiulo enforcer; in jail

Cono (Connie) and Gaetano (Guy) Frizzi—brothers; close friends and partners of Joseph Barboza

Teddy Fucillo—an elder statesman of the Boston mob

Futto (see John Biello)

G

Carmine Gagliardi—an Angiulo enforcer

Carmine (Lillo) Galente—Joseph Bonanno's original underboss, now in Lewisburg federal prison on a narcotics conspiracy charge

Joseph (Crazy Joey) Gallo—Brooklyn crime figure, assassinated in April 1972 in New York's Little Italy, apparently for arranging attempt on Joseph Colombo. Brothers: Albert (Kid Blast), lives in Brooklyn; Lawrence, died of cancer in 1968

Philip Gallo—a crooked cop in Revere, Massachusetts, who protected the mob in return for his payoff; no relation to the Gallos of Brooklyn

Carlo Gambino—New York crime boss, most powerful in the nation; sits as chairman of the Cosa Nostra Commission, the ruling body

Vito Genovese—New Jersey crime boss; died in prison in 1969

Albert (Al Judd) Georgio—compulsive gambler, premier burglar and bank robber; a partner of Teresa's; now in jail

Sam (Momo) Giancana—Chicago crime boss; now in hiding in Mexico to avoid federal prosecution

The Gimp—see Lou Grieco

Joseph (Joe Jelly) Giorelli—premier assassin of the Gallo gang; believed murdered

Nicola Giso—Boston bookmaker; one of Lombardo's top gambling operators and loansharks

Johnny Grasso—bookmaker and owner of several race horses; now dead

Lou Greco—Montreal Mafia boss; a leading trafficker in narcotics

Lou (The Gimp) Grieco—New Hampshire Mafioso now in jail. Called "The Gimp" because he limps

Al Grillo—Lynn, Massachusetts, businessman swindled by Teresa; in hiding

H

Joan Harvey—secretary to Vincent Teresa

Steve Hughes—Irish assassin who made attempt on Teresa's life

I

David Iacovetti—Gambino family soldier now in federal prison for securities fraud

J

Jimmy Blue Eyes (see Vincent Alo)

Jimmy the Greek (see James Pechilis)

Joe Beck (see Joseph DePalermo)

Joe Black (see Joseph Lamattina)

Joe Burns (see Joseph Anselmo)

Joe Jelly (see Joseph Giorelli)

Joe Kirk (see Joseph Krikorian)

Joe Putsy (see Joseph Puzzangara)

Joe the Horse (see Joseph Salvucci)

Johnny Dio (see John Dioguardi)

K

George Kattar—financier, Patriarca mob associate; under indictment for tax evasion

Peter Kattar—mob associate, brother to George; lives in Massachusetts

John (Red) Kelley—armed-robbery expert and former Patriarca family associate who became a federal witness

Joseph (Joe Kirk) Krikorian—casino gambling representative of Raymond Patriarca; lives in Rhode Island

L

Joseph (Joe Black) Lamattina—New England mobster, now a fugitive from federal warrants for securities theft; in hiding in Sicily

Ralph (Ralphie Chong) Lamattina—a Patriarca family soldier

Meyer Lansky—Jewish mob boss and Cosa Nostra's financial adviser; faces trial on federal indictments based on author's testimony

John LaRocca—Pittsburgh mobster

Larry Baiona (see Ilario Zannino)

Maurice (Pro) Lerner—a Patriarca family assassin; now in federal prison for murder conspiracy

Lillo (see Carmine Galente)

Peter Limone—the right arm of Gennaro Angiulo; in jail

Joseph Linsey—philanthropist, financier, ex-bootlegger; associate of Mike Rocco and Patriarca; lives in Massachusetts

Little Beans (see Joseph Palladino)

Little Bozo (see Joseph Cortese)

Joseph Lombardo—Massachusetts crime boss; died in 1969 of natural causes

Carmine (The Doctor) Lombardozzi—ostracized Gambino family captain, now living in Brooklyn; major securities swindler

Louie the Fox (see Louis Taglianetti)

Thomas (Three-Finger Brown) Luchese—former crime boss; died in 1967 of natural causes

Salvatore (Charlie Lucky Luciano) Luciana—the former boss of bosses; died in 1962

M

Jack Mace—top New York fence for the mob; now in federal prison for securities swindle

Mad Dog (see Jackie Nazarian)

Stefano Magaddino—crime boss of Buffalo; lives in Buffalo

Joseph (The Fat Man) Magliocco—underboss and brother-in-law of Joseph Profaci; died of natural causes

Carlos (The Little Man) Marcello—Louisiana crime boss, now living in Jefferson Parish outside New Orleans

Rudy Marfeo—killed by Patriarca's squad for threatening Patriarca

Willie Marfeo—brother of Rudy; killed by Patriarca's squad for running independent dice games and for slapping Tameleo

Romeo Martin—small-time thief and enforcer for Barboza; later murdered

Peter Martinelli—a pimp and loanshark partner of Teresa

Carlo Mastrototaro—New England underboss; replaced Henry Tameleo; now in federal prison for interstate securities swindle

Maxie Baer (see Anthony Cataldo)

Bernard McLaughlin—murdered head of one of the most powerful factions of Boston's "Irish Mafia"

Edward (Punchy) McLaughlin—murdered in Irish gang war

George McLaughlin—now in Massachusetts state prison for murder

Frank (Butch) Miceli—Carlo Gambino crime family soldier, ran the New Jersey assassination squad; now in federal prison

Mike the Wiseguy (see Michael Rocco)

Joseph (Don Peppino) Modica—retired New England don now living in Massachusetts

Momo (see Sam Giancana)

Daniel Mondavano—Patriarca family associate; now in Lewisburg federal prison for securities swindle

Frank (Butsey) Morelli—the first crime boss of Rhode Island; now dead

Munge (see Angelo Rossetti)

Salvatore (Sally the Sheik) Mussachio—a Profaci captain; lives in Wantagh, Long Island, New York

Chris Mustone—low-echelon thief and armed bandit; a partner of Teresa; lives in Revere

N

Joseph Napolitano—hoodlum from Maine who worked with Teresa on gambling junkets

Michael (Mickey) Napolitano—one of Tameleo's tipsters; from Portland, Maine

Jackie (Mad Dog) Nazarian—Patriarca mob assassin; murdered by Patriarca enforcers

Nene (see Nazzarene Turrusso)

Rose Marie (Rosie) Neves—go-go dancer and former mistress of author

O

The Old Man (see Joseph Profaci)

Frank Oreto—an Angiulo enforcer

P

Joseph (Little Beans) Palladino, Jr.—son of a well-known Boston bookmaker and partner of Teresa; lives in Massachusetts

Joseph (Joe Beans) Palladino, Sr.—Boston bookmaker; still alive

Rocco Palladino—brother to Joseph Palladino, Sr.; died in 1971

Joseph Palombo—the former rackets boss of Gloucester, Massachusetts

Joseph Paterno—Gambino family captain, now living in New Jersey; boss of family assassination squad

Raymond Salvatore Loredo Patriarca—New England crime boss, now in Atlanta federal prison for conspiracy to murder

James (Jimmy the Greek) Pechilis—a Boston gambler

James (Jimmy Doyle) Plumeri—Carmine Tramunti family captain murdered in September 1971

Pro (see Maurice Lerner)

Joseph (The Old Man) Profaci—the olive oil king; head of New York crime family; died of natural causes in 1962

Anthony (Tony Pro) Provenzano—a Genovese crime family captain and former top executive of the International Brotherhood of Teamsters

Punchy (see Ed McLaughlin)

Joseph (Joe Putsy) Puzzangara—small-time hood who dealt on the fringe of the mob

R

Ralphie Chong (see Ralph Lamattina)

Vincent Rao—the *consigliere* of the old Thomas Luchese family (now known as the Carmine Tramunti crime family)

The Referee (see Enrico Tameleo)

The Rifleman (see Steve Flemmi)

Michael (Mike the Wiseguy) Rocco—powerful Boston mobster; worked for Joe Lombardo; now dead of natural causes

Ronnie the Pig (see Ronald Cassesso)

Rosie (see Rose Marie Neves)

Angelo (Munge) Rossetti—operated wire service for New England mob

Alfredo (The Blind Pig) Rossi—fence man for stolen goods in the Providence area for Patriarca's mob; died of natural causes

Angelo (Butch) Rossi—member of Patriarca mob

John Rossi—Patriarca enforcer

Tommy Rossi—bank robber and enforcer for Patriarca's mob

Joseph Russo—an enforcer for Angiulo

S

Nicola Sacco—a shoemaker and Italian-born anarchist who, along with Bartolomeo Vanzetti, was accused of killing two men in a robbery and was executed in 1927

Americo Sacramone—associate of James McLean

Danny St. Angelo—holdup man for the New England mob

Frank Salemmi—enforcer for Patriarca; in hiding

Anthony (Fat Tony) Salerno—numbers racket king of Harlem

Joseph (Yonkers Joe) Salistino—mechanic for the mob in the Antigua gambling junkets

Sally the Sheik (see Salvatore Mussachio)

Joseph (Joe the Horse) Salvucci—small-time mobster jailed in a frame-up involving Tameleo and Barboza

Al (Fat Al) Samenza—expert horse race fixer at Suffolk Downs, Massachusetts

Sam the Plumber (see Simone DeCavalcante)

Sandy (see Dominick Teresa)

Abe Sarkis—fringe mobster, bookmaker, and owner of the Four Corners nightclub

Fred Sarno—hustler for the Revere mob operations, in jail for arson

Francesco (Frank Costello) Saveria—former New York boss; retired in 1957 after attempted assassination

Scarface (see Dominick Teresa)

Rudolph Sciarra—assassin and credit-card counterfeiter for the New England mob; in jail for murder

Francesco (Frankie Skiball) Scibelli—old-time made man from Springfield, Massachusetts

John Scimone—bodyguard of Joseph Profaci

Joe (Blondy) Simonelli—biggest race fixer in the New England mob

Skinny Pete (see Peter Fiumara)

Anthony (Tony Bender) Strollo—underboss to Vito Genovese; murdered in April 1962 by Eboli, body never found

T

Louis (Louie the Fox) Taglianetti—assassin for Patriarca and his gambling boss in Rhode Island; murdered by mob

Tony Talia—small-time Boston hoodlum

Enrico Henry (The Referee) Tameleo—New England underboss, Patriarca crime family, now in death row in Massachusetts State Prison for murder

Tashe (see Arthur Bratsos)

Cosmo Teresa—Teresa's father, who was not a mob member

Dominick (Sandy; Scarface) Teresa—former Lombardo family member living in semiretirement in Massachusetts; uncle of Teresa

Giuseppe (Mickey) Teresa—an uncle of Teresa; now dead

Vincent Charles (The Fat Man) Teresa—the author; No. 3 man in New England mob; formerly aide to Patriarca and Tameleo; groomed for underboss role

Vincenti Teresa—Teresa's grandfather, a Sicilian Mafioso who became a Boston crime boss

Three-Finger Brown (see Thomas Luchese)

Pilgrim (Billy) Tomasino—arsonist for the Boston mob

Tommy Ryan (see Thomas Eboli)

Tony Bender (see Anthony Strollo)

Tony Blue (see Anthony D'Agostino)

Tony Pro (see Anthony Provenzano)

Arthur (Artie Todd) Tortorello—Gambino family associate and securities thief; now appealing five-year conviction for securities swindle

Charles (Charlie the Blade) Tourine—a Vito Genovese crime family soldier and casino expert

Santo Trafficante—Florida crime boss

Carmine Tramunti—New York crime family boss who replaced Thomas Luchese as boss; lives in the Bronx, New York

Trigger Mike (see Michael Coppolo)
Nazzarene (Nene) Turrussa—cousin of Don Peppino and member of New England mob advisory council; died of natural causes

V

Joseph Valachi—Vito Genovese soldier who turned informer; died in La Tuna Federal Prison in 1971
Bartolomeo Vanzetti (see Nicola Sacco)
Arthur Ventola—owned and operated, with his brother Nicholas (Junior), Arthur's Farm, center for mob conferences and clearinghouse for stolen goods; lives in Massachusetts
Barney Villani—small-time burglar said by Tameleo to be a stool pigeon
Robert Visconti—a gambler; loanshark friend of Teresa's; lives in Massachusetts

W

Phil Waggenheim—a strong-arm man for Ilario Zannino; now in prison
Whimpy Bennett (see Edward Bennett)

Y

Yonkers Joe (see Joseph Salistino)

Z

Ilario (Larry Baiona) Zannino—No. 2 man in Boston mob; now in Massachusetts State Prison on a jewel-theft conviction
Anthony Zerilli—son of crime boss; owner of Hazel Park racetrack in Detroit
Joseph Zerilli—Detroit crime boss; lives in Florida and Michigan
Benny Zinna—an Angiulo enforcer; murdered by mob

3
BIG BOOKS
ABOUT ORGANIZED CRIME

THE GODFATHER
by Mario Puzo   Crest   A1708 $1.65

The most revealing novel ever written about the criminal underworld of the Mafia. "What makes this such a nonstop page turner is its utter believability."—*Los Angeles Times*. Illustrated with photographs from the movie.

HONOR THY FATHER
by Gay Talese   Crest   X1743 $1.75

In this monumental work, packed with fascinating details and intimate reporting, and written in the style of a novel, the author portrays the secret society known as the Mafia—the most discussed and the least understood subject in America. "A blockbuster."—*Publishers Weekly*. Illustrated with photographs.

CAPONE
by John Kobler   Crest   Q1704 $1.50

Never-before-published facts in this matchless biography of Public Enemy Number One. "*Capone* is more than an absorbing biography. It is a powerful, masterfully written social document about one of the most bizarre, frightening periods in American history."—*National Observer*. Illustrated with photographs.

FAWCETT

Wherever Paperbacks Are Sold

FAWCETT CREST
BESTSELLERS